رؤية والسيطرة

SEE & CONTROL

على الشياطين   DEMONS

&

و

الآلام   PAINS

From My Eyes, Senses and Theories

من خلال ملاحظتي وأحاسيسي ونظرياتي

By

تأليف:

Rizwan Qureshi

رضوان قريشي

100% true information and incidents about

Demons & Pains

معلومات صحيحة 100% وحوادث تتعلق بالشياطين والآلام

A TEXTBOOK ON DEMONS

كتاب يتحدث عن الشياطين

Description of Invisible World In the same way the visible world is comprised of human beings, animals, reptiles, insects, etc., the invisible world is comprised of different kinds of creatures.

1) Parallel to human beings are demons.
2) Parallel to wild animals, reptiles, and poisonous insects are different kinds of diseases, sicknesses, infections, pains, etc.

So, the invisible world is not composed of only *demons*.

The Difference between Demons and Pain/Diseases

Demons are more sensible, like humans. It's easy to communicate with them. And they listen most of the time.

You can stop a man by just asking if he is doing anything bad. For example, if a man is killing a deer illegally, you can ask him to not kill the deer. If that man does not listen to you, you can threaten him with a call to the police, and that may stop him from illegally killing any animal. So, demons are close to humans but are not exactly like humans. Just imagine making a boy or girl invisible and giving him or her the powers of *demons*, and then imagine how many problems this "person" could create for someone.

Pains, sicknesses, and diseases are close to wild animals, wild reptiles, or poisonous insects. For example, if a lion is ready to pounce and hunt a deer, it will never listen to you if you request that it not hunt the deer.

You cannot threaten a lion with the police to prevent his hunting of the deer. The only way you have to stop wild animals or poisonous insects is killing them or shooting them. But all kinds of pains, diseases, and sicknesses are invisible to us, and they cannot be killed by a regular kind of weapon or gun.

تعد طريقة وصف العالم الخفي هي الطريقة نفسها عندما نقوم بوصف العالم المرئي والذي يحتوي على الكائنات الحية والحيوانات والزواحف والحشرات، الخ... حيث يتكون العالم الخفي من أنواع مختلفة من المخلوقات.

1) بالتوازي مع البشر هناك الشياطين.
2) موازاةً أيضاً مع الحيوانات البرية والزواحف والحشرات السامة يوجد هناك أنواع مختلفة من الأمراض والسقم والعدوى والآلام، الخ...

نستنتج من ذلك أن العالم الخفي لا يتكون فقط من الشياطين فقط.

الاختلاف بين الشياطين الآلام/الأمراض

تعتبر الشياطين أكثر عقلانية مثلهم كمثل البشر. حيث أنه من السهل الاتصال بهم. وهم أيضاً يستمعون الينا معظم الوقت.

بإمكانك منع شخص من عمل شيء سيء. على سبيل المثال، إذا قام شخص بقتل ظبي بشكل غير قانوني، بإمكانك منعه من فعل ذلك. وإذا لم يستمع ذاك الشخص اليك، بإمكانك تهديده بالاتصال بالشرطة وبذلك بإمكانك ايقافه من قتل الحيوان بشكل غير قانوني. لذلك، فإن الشياطين (الجن) تكون قريب من البشر ولكنها ليس بالضبط شبيهة بالبشر. فقط تخيل وجود صبي وبنت بشكل خفي وتم منحهما نفس القوة التي يمتلكها الجن، ومن ثم تخيل كم من المشاكل التي قد يسببها ذلك "الشخص" لشخص آخر.

وأيضا، فإن الآلام والسقم والأمراض تكون قريب من الحيوانات البرية والزواحف أو الحشرات السامة. على سبيل المثال، إذا جهز أسد ما نفسه للانقضاض واصطياد ظبية، فإنه لن يستمع إليك أبداً إذا طلبت منه أن لا يقوم بقتل تلك الظبية.

فليس باستطاعتك تهديد الأسد عن طريق الاتصال بالشرطة لمنعه من اصطياد الظبية. حيث أن الطريقة الوحيدة لمنع الحيوانات البرية أو الحشرات الضارة من قتل بضعها هي قتلهم. ولكن جميع أنواع الآلام والأمراض غير مرئية بالنسبة لنا، ولا يمكننا قتلهم باستخدام السلاح.

Demons/pains/diseases: What do they look like?

All these things in the invisible world, including demons, pains, and sicknesses/diseases, are flying objects. When they are flying in air, they are small objects that look like black smoke. Most of them look like small smoke bubbles or small pieces of thread. Some are similar to small flying spiders. They do not look the way we see them in movies or pictures/photographs—big, dangerous teeth; long legs and hands; black skin; twenty feet tall; and red eyes. They are nothing like that.

There are few diseases and pains that you can immediately feel when you receive them from another body. But there are a few diseases that you manifest pains after a certain time. Why after a certain time? Because those diseases take a few days to damage the organs or make a wound anywhere in body. Once they inflict damage on or wound the body, the body gets sore, and people start feeling pain. Those invisible insects (diseases) do not care how much we get hurt. They just act like leeches and keep eating the organ or part of the body affected until they damage that part completely. For example, if you leave uncovered food in an open atmosphere, what will happen? Flies and other small insects will come and will start eating that uncovered food. If initially four insects are there and eating that uncovered food, if you kill those four insects, four more new insects will come and will start eating that uncovered food. Regardless of how many insects you kill, new insects will keep coming until you cover that food. In the same way, I can remove any sickness, disease, or pain from anyone, but if they do not fix their symptoms, new diseases will come to them and keep hurting them.

Even if someone keeps taking medication, that doesn't mean he or she is cured. The reason is that there are so many diseases to hurt or damage that organ or part of the body. But what can I do? I can remove those insects from their bodies by using my powers. And that sickness or pain will not come back easily, if someone is taking care

الجن/ الآلام/ الأمراض: ماذا تبدو؟

تمتاز جميع هذه الأشياء في العالم الخفي من ضمنها الجن والآلام والأمراض/ السقم بأنها أجسام طائرة. حيث أنها عندما تطير في الهواء تبدو كأنها أجسام صغيرة وتظهر كأنها دخان أسود. حيث تبدو معظمها وكأنها فقاعات دخان أسود أو قطع صغيرة من الخيوط. ويشبه بعضها العناكب الطائرة الصغيرة. وأن تلك الأشياء لا تبدو لنا كما نراها في الأفلام أو الصور - كالتي لها أسنان كبيرة وخطيرة وأرجل وأيدي طويلة وبشرة سوداء أو يبلغ طولها عشرون قدماً وعيون حمراء اللون. ولكن في الحقيقة إن تلك الأشياء لا تشبه كل ذلك مما وصف في الأفلام.

هناك القليل من الأمراض والآلام التي تشعر بها مباشرة عند التعرض للعدوى من جسم آخر. ولكن هناك أمراض أقل تشعر بآلامها بشك واضح بعد وقت معين. ولكن لماذا بعد وقت معين؟ إن السبب وراء ذلك هو أن تلك الأمراض تأخذ بضعة أيام لتدمر الأعضاء أو احدث جروح في أي مكان من الجسم. حيث عندما تلحق الضرر أو الجروح في الجسم، يتعرض الجسم للقرحة أو الالتهاب ومن ثم يشعر الناس بالآلام. ولا تهتم تلك الحشرات (الأمراض) حول كمية الضرر الذي يلحق بأجسامنا. حيث تقوم تلك الحشرات فقط بعلق الجسم وتبقى تأكل العضو أو جزء من الجسم المعرض للعدوى حتى تقوم بتدمير ذلك الجزء بشكل كامل. على سبيل المثال، في حال تركك لطعام مكشوف في جو مفتوح، ما الذي سيحدث؟ سيقوم الذباب والحشرات الصغيرة الأخرى بأكل الطعام المكشوف. وفي حال كان هناك أربع حشرات في البداية تقوم بأكل الطعام المكشوف وقمت بقتلها، ستأتي أربع حشرات أخرى لتقوم بأكل الطعام المكشوف مجدداً. بغض النظر عن عدد الحشرات التي تقوم بقتلها، ستأتي حشرات جديدة الى الطعام المكشوف حتى تقوم بتغطيته. وبنفس الطريقة، بإمكاني ازالة أي مرض أو ألم من اي شخص، ولكن إذا لم يقم الشخص بعلاج أعراضها، ستأتي أمراض جديدة وستؤذي جسمه.

وحتى في حال استمرار الشخص في أخذ الأدوية، فإن ذلك لا يعني بأنه/ها قد شفي تماماً. وإن السبب وراء ذلك هو أن هناك العديد من الأمراض تقوم بالحاق الضرر لذلك العضو أو الجزء من الجسم. ولكن ما الذي بإمكاني فعله؟ بإمكاني ازالة تلك الحشرات من أجسامهم باستخدام قوتي الخاصة بي. ولن يعود ذلك المرض أو الألم الى الجسم بسهولة في استمرار الشخص

of symptom or damages created by invisible insects/disease. Once invisible disease or insect attack to any part or organ of the body, they do not leave that organ ever. Regardless, someone keep taking medication to heal that internal damage or wound, but, still that disease/insect will not give up eating or damaging more and more that organ. So, at that point when, usually at initial level, when damages/ wound is not bad and someone is taking proper medication, at that point, I can request/insist that disease/insect to leave that organ. So, no further damage and healing medication can heal quickly.

Whenever I go inside anyone's body, means, when I communicate telepathically with that demons/pain and request or insist them to quit and leave. I have no clue what I will find out inside his or her body. For example, if someone calls or comes to me with a migraine or backbone pain or sore tooth, I don't have any clue at that moment if that person has any kind of cancer or a virus or liver damage or high blood pressure or any other kind of dangerous disease. Once I start treating people, I have to deal with all the problems they have with their body. Cures depend on how much of the body and its organs are already damaged. *Most of the time*, all new pains and diseases come straight into my body from that sick body. If that sickness is meeting with me for the second or third time, it does not come to me. Sometimes sicknesses leave that sick body really fast, and sometimes they leave that body even before I start my treatment.

Anyone can get sick. It is just bad luck, regardless of whether a creature is human or animal. But modern science and medication are very effective. To treat people, I usually add my magic to certain medications. I only perform this magic when I cannot fix any sickness or pain without medication. Most of the time, there is no need for any medication during treatment, but I always suggest people use medication to fix the symptoms. Once I treat someone, I am usually able to move/remove all sickness, regardless of whether it is just a head pain or cancer or HIV or

بأخذ الأدوية للعلاج من الأعراض والضرر التي تسببه تلك الأمراض/الحشرات الخفية. وعندما تهاجم الحشرات أو الأمراض الخفية أي جزء أو عضو من الجسم، لا تترك ذلك العضو أبداً. بغض النظر عن قيام شخص ما بأخذ الأدوية للشفاء من الجروح، إلا أن المرض/الحشرة لن تستسلم في أكل أو تدمير بشكل أكبر في ذلك العضو. لذلك، وفي تلك الحالة في المستوى الأول وعندما تكون الجروح/الأضرار لست بتلك السوء وقيام الشخص بأخذ الأدوية الصحيحة. فبإمكاني في تلك الحالة طلب/الإصرار بأن يقوم ذلك المرض/الحشرة بترك العضو. وبالتالي لن يكون هناك مزيد من الأضرار وبإمكان الأدوية علاج العضو بشكل أسرع.

وقتما أدخل جسم شخص ما، أو عندما أقوم بالاتصال بشكل تخاطري مع تلك الشياطين/الألم والطلب منهم مغادرة الجسم. ليس لدي أدنى فكرة عن الذي سأجده داخل الجسم. على سبيل المثال، عندما يأتي أو يتصل بي شخص يعاني من صداع نصفي أو ألم في عظام الظهر أو التهاب الأسنان، لا يكون لدي أدنى فكرة في تلك اللحظة اذا ما كان ذلك الشخص يعاني من السرطان أو فيروس أو تلف في الكبد أو ارتفاع ضغط الدم أو أي نوع من الأمراض الخطيرة. عندما أبدأ بعلاج الأشخاص، علي أن أتعامل مع جميع المشاكل التي تعاني منها أجسامهم. حيث يعتمد العلاج على مدى التلف أو الضرر الذي تعرض له الجسم وأعضاؤه. وفي معظم الأوقات، تنتقل جميع الآلام والأمراض من جسم المريض الى جسمي بشكل مباشر. في حال مواجهتي لذلك المرض للمرة الثانية أو الثالثة، فلا ينتقل الى جسمي. وأحياناً ما يغادر المرض جسم المريض بشكل سريع، وأحياناً أخرى يغادر حتى قبل أن أبدأ بمعالجة جسم المريض.

يتعرض أي شخص للمرض. حيث إنه لحظاً سيئاً التعرض للمرض بغض النظر حول ما اذا كان بشر أو حيوانات. ولكن العلم الحديث والأدوية عادة ما تكون فعالة جداً. لمعالجة الناس، أقوم عادة بإضافة سحري الى بعض الأدوية. أقوم باستخدام هذا السحر فقط عندما لا أستطيع معالجة أي مرض أو ألم بدون الأدوية. وفي معظم الأوقات، لا يوجد هناك حاجة لأي نوع من الأدوية أثناء المعالجة، ولكن دائماً ما أقترح على المرضى أن يقوموا باستخدام الأدوية لعلاج أعراض المرض. عندما أقوم بمعالجة شخص ما، عادة ما أكون قادر على نقل/إزالة جميع الأمراض بغض النظر حول ما إذا كان ألم الرأس أو سرطان أو مرض نقص المناعة المكتسبة الإيدز أو

anything. After I cure him or her, it depends how someone takes care of fixing the sources and symptoms of his or her diseases.

Twin, Angel, or Hamzad

Twin angel, or hamzad, is not part of our bodies or spirits. It is a demon who has been around us since we were born. Usually, one demon really controls us completely—our emotions, dreams, thoughts, and other matters in our life. Usually, that demon stays around us to keep our bodies possessed all our life until a stronger demon decides to possess our bodies. Most of us are unaware of the control these demons have over us. Usually, the twin angel demon, or hamzad demon, thinks he/she is the owners of us. This is only one-way traffic. These demons know everything about us. They operate us however they want. On other hand, most of us are totally unaware of them, their actions, and their control on us. But a few people have faith and believe that hamzad is a shadow of their bodies or spirits. Some of them hold to some practices to control the hamzad. Most of the time, demons are more interested in controlling us instead of us controlling them. If a human is more powerful, he or she can control these demons after some practice, but if he or she fails, that hamzad will kill the person—or at least screw up his or her mind, which means those demons will have complete control of that person's mind. Usually, those kinds of people are considered mentally ill or sick. Nobody can control his or her demons or another's demons until someone is strong enough mentally and can control his or her mind. Otherwise, demons are pretty much invincible lions, and they do not give their control to someone else easily. This is part of their negative nature. You need to be somebody extremely strong mentally to play or mess with them.

Evil Eye: Causes, Reasons, and Effects

Around us, inside our house, around our house or work place, and everywhere, we have millions of different kind of demons around us. Demons exhibit pretty much the same kinds of qualities, habits, and

أي مرض. بعد قيامي بمعالجة المريض أو المريضة، يعتمد على مدى قيام المريض بالاهتمام بعلاج مصادر وأعراض المرض الذي تعرض له.

التوأم، الملاك، الملاك التوأم

لا يعتبر الملاك التوأم جزء من أجسامنا أو أرواحنا. فهو عبارة عن شيطان يكون حولنا منذ ولادتنا. في الغالب، يقوم شيطان واحد بالتحكم بنا بشكل كامل — حيث يقوم بالتحكم بعواطفنا وأحلامنا وأفكارنا ومسائل أخرى من جوانب حياتنا. وعادة من يبقى ذلك الشيطان حولنا من أجل إبقاء أجسامنا مملوكة من قبله حتى يقرر شيطان أقوى بالسيطرة على أجسامنا. ويكون معظمنا غير مدرك لسيطرة هذه الشياطين علينا. وأيضا عادة ما يعتقد شيطان الملاك التوأم بأنه مالكنا. فهذا هي السير باتجاه واحد. حيث تعلم هذه الشياطين كل شيء عنا، ويقومون بتسييرنا كيفما شاءوا. وبطريقة أخرى، يكون معظمنا غير مدرك تماماً بوجودهم وأفعالهم وسيطرتهم علينا. ولكن القليل من البشر المؤمنون ويؤمنون أيضاً بأن الملاك التوأم هو ظل لأجسامنا أو أرواحنا. حيث يقوم بعضهم بعمل بعض الأفعال للتحكم بشيطان الملاك التوأم. وفي أغلب الأحيان، تكون الشياطين أكثر اهتماماً في السيطرة علينا بدلاً من أن نقوم نحن بالسيطرة عليهم. وفي حال كان الإنسان أكثر قوة، يقوم بالسيطرة على هذه الشياطين بعد القيام ببعض الأفعال. ولكن في حال فشل الشخص في السيطرة عليهم، يقوم شيطان الملاك التوأم بقتل ذلك الشخص — أو على الأقل ما يجعله يفقد عقله وصوابه، وهذا يعني أنه سيكون لتلك الشياطين سيطرة كاملة على عقل ذلك الشخص. وعادة ما يكون هؤلاء الناس مختلين عقلياً. حيث لا يستطيع أي شخص أو شيطان آخر السيطرة على الشياطين التي سيطرت عليه حتى قيام شخص ما يمتلك القوة العقلية الكافية للتحكم بعقل ذلك الشخص. وبصورة أخرى، إن الشياطين أكثر من مجرد أسود لا تقهر، ولا يسلمون سيطرتهم لأحد بتلك السهولة. وهذه هو الجانب السلبي من طبيعتهم. عليك أن تكون شخص تمتلك القوة العقلية الكافية للعب أو العبث معهم.

عين الشيطان: القضية، الأسباب والآثار

هناك الملايين من الشياطين حولنا وداخل بوتنا وحول منازلنا أو في العمل وفي أي مكان. تمتلك الشياطين أنواع متساوية بشكل كبير من الخواص والعادات

temperingaments that humans do—for example, good, bad, very bad, naughty, evil, extremist, harmless, harmful, jealous, angry, obedient, disobedient, etc. Usually noticeable effects of "Evil Eyes" are the following: loss of health, loss of beauty, sickness, loss of business, bad luck, a lot of obstacles in the way of success, bad relationships with spouses, etc.

There are two ways of getting affected by "Evil Eyes":

1. Automatically Evil Eye
2. Guided Evil Eye

1.   Automatically Evil Eye

As I described several times, demons—or a group or tribe of demons—operate together and use their extraordinary language power of hypnotism, or they possess a body and invite different kinds of invisible insects to create different kinds of pains or to damage different body organs. It doesn't matter if someone is very healthy or beautiful, is a successful business owner, or is very wealthy; this demon—or group or tribe of demons—can choose any person very easily.

Very quickly, those demons can make that healthy person extremely sick; they can destroy someone's beauty in few days. These groups of demons can make a very wealthy person extremely poor by creating all kinds of problems in someone's business. These demons, by using hypnotism, can bring hate between a loving husband and wife, or any couple.

Why do demons do these kinds of things? The answer is this: by nature, they like negative activities, or sometimes we make them unhappy due to our actions or acts. I am 100 percent sure that most of the time they go against us and try to destroy our life or health or family or business because, maybe most of the time unintentionally, we make them unhappy or angry. Sometimes, if we feel too much

والمزاجات التي يمتلكها البشر. فعلى سبيل المثال، تمتلك الشياطين مزاجات جيدة وسيئة للغاية وشريرة والشر والتشدد والبراءة والأذى والغيرة والغضب والطاعة والعصيان، الخ... وعادة ما تكون الآثار الواضحة "لعيون الشيطان" كالآتي: فقدان الصحة، فقدان الجمال، المرض، فقدان العمل، الحظ السيء والكثير من العوائق في طريق النجاح والعلاقات السيئة بين الأزواج، الخ...

هناك طريقتين للإصابة بـ "عيون الشيطان"

1- عين الشيطان التلقائية.
2- عين الشيطان المسيرة.

1.   عين الشيطان التلقائية

كما قم بوصفها مرات عديدة من قبل، تعمل الشياطين – أو مجموعة أو قبيلة من الشياطين- معاً وتستخدم القوة الاستثنائية للتنويم المغناطيسي، أو يقومون بالسيطرة على الجسم وتدعو أنواع أخرى من الحشرات لخلق أنواع مختلفة من الآلام أو لتدمير أعضاء مختلفة من الجسم. ولا يهم إذا كان شخص ما صحي للغاية أو جميلة أو رجل أعمال ناجح أو غني جداً، فبإمكان هذا الشيطان – أو قبيلة الشياطين – اختيار أي شخص بكل سهولة.

وبسرعة كبيرة، تستطيع تلك الشياطين جعل شخص صحيح الجسم مريض، وتستطيع أيضاً بتدمير جمال شخص ما خلال بضعة أيام. وتستطيع هذا المجموعات من الشياطين جعل شخص غني جداً فقير بخلق كافة أنواع المشاكل في عمل ذلك الشخص. وتستطيع هذه الشياطين، باستخدام التنويم المغناطيسي، زرع الكراهية بين الأزواج المتحابين.

لماذا تقوم الشياطين بفعل تلك الأشياء؟ والجواب هو: أنها بطبيعتها، لديها الأعمال السلبية أو في أحيان أخرى نحن نجعلها غاضبة بسبب أفعالنا. وأنا على كامل الثقة بأنه في أغلب الأحيان بأن تلك الشياطين تكون ضدنا وتحاول تدمير حياتنا أو صحتنا أو العائلة أو العمل لأننا في معظم الاحيان وبشكل غير مقصود نجعلهم غير سعيدين وغاضبين. وفي أحيانٍ أخرى نشعر

pride or are proud about our health/beauty/wealth/business, these demons just go against us without any reason. Maybe they just do not like our arrogance. Demons are just like air. And who can fight completely with air everywhere? It is more difficult to fight with them because most of us are not even aware of their presence and activities.

2. Guided Evil Eye

Guided Evil Eyes can be divided in two parts: a.) Controlled Guided
Evil Eye and
b.) Uncontrolled Guided Evil Eye.

a.) The Controlled Guided Evil Eye comes from any demon's doctor or any person who knows how to use or misuse demons under his control. That demon's doctor very easily can assign an assignment for a demon or for a group of demons to destroy the health or beauty or wealth of any person. This thing works for sure; sometimes it takes days or months or years, but it works.

b.) The second kind, the Uncontrolled Guided Evil Eye, comes from people around us—people who are jealous of us or are angry with us for any reason. Any demon or group of demons around them can just decide to destroy the health/beauty or wealth of one person because another person is feeling very jealous or is very unhappy with that person for some
reason. That jealous or angry person is even unaware about the activities of those demons and definitely has no control over those demons. This is nothing, just bad luck.

How demons or invisible insects transfer from one body to another
electronically:

1. Cell phones or regular land phones provide a very easy path or medium for demons/pains to travel from one body to another. Chances are reduced if people, instead of holding the phone

بالفخر حيال صحتنا/جمالنا/ أعمالنا، تعمل هذه الشياطين أعمالاً ضدنا بدون وجود أي سبب. ومن المرجح أن تلك الشياطين لا تروق لها كبرياءنا. والشياطين تشبه الى حد كبير الهواء. ومن يستطيع مواجهة الهواء؟ إنه لمن الصعب مواجهتهم لأن معظمنا لا يدرك وجودهم وأفعالهم.

2. عين الشيطان المسيرة

تقسم عيون الشيطان المسيرة الى قسمين. أ) عين الشيطان المسيرة المتحكم بها. و ب) عين الشيطان المسيرة الغير متحكم بها.
أ)   تأتي عين الشيطان المسيرة المتحكم بها من طبيب الجن أو أي شخص يعرف كيف يستخدم أو يسيء استخدام الجن تحت إمرته. يستطيع طبيب الجن بكل سهولة تعيين مهمة للجن أو مجموعة من الجن لتدمير صحة أو جمال أو ثروة أي شخص. وهذا الشيء يأتي بثماره بكل تأكيد، وأحياناً يستغرق أياماً أو شهوراً أو سنين ولكن ينجح بالفعل.
ب) أما النوع الآخر وهو عين الشيطان المسيرة الغير متحكم بها يأتي من البشر من حولنا – أناس من يشعرون بالغير تجاهنا أو غاضبين منا لأي سبب كان. فبإمكان جن أو مجموعة من الجن تدمير صحة أو جمال أو ثروة شخص ما لأن شخص آخر يشعر بالغيرة تجاهه أو أنه غير سعيد معه لأي سبب كان. حتى أن الشخص الغيور والغير سعيد يكون غير مدرك حيال الأشياء التي تقوم بها تلك المجموعة من الشياطين ولا يستطيع التحكم والسيطرة عليهم. وهذا ما يعرف بالحظ السيء.

كيفية انتقال الجن أو الحشرات الخفية من جسم الى آخر بشكل الكتروني:

1.   تعتبر الأجهزة الخلوية أو الهواتف الأرضية طريق سهل أو وسط ناقل للجن/الآلام للتنتقل من جسم الى آخر. ويتم تقليص فرص انتقال الجن في حال قيام الناس، بدلاً من

up to their ear, use the speaker of the phone and keep the phone away from their ear.

2. Live TV, live shows, live talk shows, live video conferencing, or live Internet conversation can very easily transfer demons/
pains electromagnetically from one body to another.

3.Usually demons/pains use rules of heat travel from one point to a second point—like travel from hot to cold. In the same way, demons/pains travel from a sick body to a healthy body, or travel from a more sick body to a less sick body, electromagnetically.

4.Demons/pains very easily travel from an insecure or scared body to a very secure and bold/brave body. But it does not mean they will never go back to the old body. They may, or they may not.

5. I am not sure if demons like it or if it is their traveling path, but when you stay in front of a weather heater too much, they will be inside your body, especially above the chest. I have not had any experiences of getting demons in my body when staying in front of an air conditioner.

6. We can very easily absorb demons or pains from very short-tempered or extreme behavior people, sick people, scared or drunk or angry people, or animals or trees. But this absorption is usually not permanent. The demons may or may not go back to those bodies.

Almost everybody is possessed by demons.
When do they come out from a body?

Demons are not walking creatures like us. They are not that big in shape or size. They do not look like what we see in movies or pictures with dark black color, big bodies, red eyes, long and sharp teeth, hairy skin, and big ears. No, they do not look like that. They are small, flying creatures with extraordinary, penetrating, expending, and hypnotizing powers. I can see millions of demons flying in the

قيامهم بوضع السماعة على أذنهم، استخدام السماعة الخارجية وإبقاء الهاتف بعيداً عن آذانهم.

2. تعتبر مشاهدة التلفاز وبرامج البث المباشر والمؤتمرات أو محادثات الانترنت وسط ناقل للجن/الآلام بشكل الكتر ومغناطيسي من جسم الى آخر.

3. عادةً ما يستخدم الجن/الآلام أسس الحرارة في التنقل من نقطة الى أخرى – كالانتقال من الحرارة الى البرودة. وبنفس الطريقة، تنتقل الآلام/الجن من جسم المريض الى الجسم الصحيح، أو تنتقل من جسم مريض بشكل كبير الى جسم مريض بشكل أقل حدة بشكل الكتر ومغناطيسي.

4. تنتقل الآلام/الجن بشكل سلس من جسم غير آمن أو خائف الى جسم آمن وشجاع. ولكن لا يعني ذلك أن الآلام لن تعود أبداً الى الجسم القديم الذي انتقلت منه. من المرجح أن تعود ومن المرجح أن لا تعود.

5. ليست متأكداً حيال رغبة الشيطان بفعل ذلك أ, هي طريقها للتنقل، ولكن عند بقائك أمام المدفأة لوقت كبير، ستدخل الآلام إلى جسمك وخاصة في المنطقة العليا من الصدر. لم يكن لدي أي خبرة حيال التعرض للشياطين في جسمي عند الجلوس بالقرب من المكيف الهوائي.

6. نستطيع بكل سهولة ملاحظة الجن أو الآلام داخل أجسام أناس سريعي الغضب أو أناس ذي التصرف الغريب أو المرضى أو الخائفين أو الثمالى أو الحيوانات أو الأشجار. ولكن عادة ما تكون هذه الملاحظة غير دائمة. ومن المرجح عودة أو عدم عودة الجن الى تلك الأجسام.

معظم الأشخاص مملوكين من قبل الجن. متى تخرج الشياطين من الجسم؟

الجن مخلوقات لا تمشي مثلنا نحن البشر. وليسوا بذلك الكبر في الشكل والحجم. ولا يبدون كما نراهم في الافلام أ, الصور باللون الأسود القاتم والأجسام الضخمة والعيون الحمراء والأسنان الطويلة الحادة والجلد الذي ينبت عليه الشعر او الأذنين الكبيرتين. لا، فالجن لا يبدوا كذلك. فالجن في الحقيقة مخلوقات طائرة صغيرة يمتلكون قوى التنويم المغناطيسي. وأستطيع أن أرى الملايين من الشياطين الطائرة في

air everywhere. Demons live on trees. They live inside our bodies. They live inside the bodies they possess.

1) If someone dies, the demon will come out of that body. Only invisible insects or diseases will stay inside that body to eat it, that organ or body completely. This means, demons do not like to live in dead bodies

2) If they don't feel secure that the body in which they are residing is going to be get hurt or damaged or die for example. Demons are different than insects. Demons do not stay inside or around an insecure body. Once they figure out someone is ready to hurt or kill that body, in which demons are living, demons will come out from that body real quickly, even before, that person, animal, will get hurt or killed. You can say, demons are coward or extra careful. No doubt, demons get upset and take revenge when someone especially killed that body, whatever they possessed or living.

Whenever a *rat* passes by me or gets scared and runs away from me, demons immediately come out from that rat and jump into my body. It is so bad when you can sense very clearly a demon penetrating your body. I never feel like this. Several years ago, I may have felt this way when I was a normal person. But now I cannot relax until I convince/ insist demons leave my body. Usually, demons that come out of rats have some kind of bad smell. Even if I just say *hish* to cats, I can see a bunch of demons leave the cat's body and jump inside my body within seconds. During any of these penetrations by demons, I never felt hurt and never felt any kind of pain. Usually, they listen to me and find someone else within a few minutes. After I learned all this about myself, I decided not to kill things with demons anymore, not even a cockroach or any other insect sitting or walking in front of me, because I do not want an extra problem for no reason. I always suggest my sincere friends use someone else to kill insects inside the house. And I suggest that they stay away from home during that process.

الهواء في كل مكان. وتعيش الشياطين على الأشجار وداخل أجسامنا وداخل الأجسام التي تسيطر عليها.

1) في حال وفاة شخص ما، سيخرج الجن من جسم ذلك الشخص الميت. ولكن تبقى الأمراض والحشرات الخفية داخل ذلك الجسم الميت لأكله بشكل كامل. وهذا يعني أن الشياطين لا تعيش داخل الأجسام الميتة.

2) في حال عدم شعور الشياطين بالأمان في جسم ما فإن ذلك الجسم سيتأذى أو يموت. وتختلف الشياطين عن الحشرات. ففي حال شعورهم بأن شخصاً ما سيقوم بقتل أو إيذاء الشخص الذي يسكنون فيه، ستخرج تلك الشياطين بسرعة حتى قبل أن يتأذى ذلك الشخص، أو الحيوان. بإمكانك القول بأن الجن يصبحون غاضبين وينتقمون عندما يقوم شخص ما بقتل الجسم الذي يسكن فيه الجن.

عندما يمر فأر بقربي أو يشعر بالخوف مني، فإن الشياطين تخرج منه بشكل فوري من جسم الفأر وتدخل الى جسمي. وإنه لشيء سيء عندما تشعر أن شيطاناً ما يخترق جسمك. فلم أشعر أبداً بذلك. وقبل سنين عديدة، من المحتمل أنني شعرت بذلك عندما كنت شخصاً عادياً. ولكنني الآن لا أستطيع الاسترخاء حتى أقنع/أو أصرّ على مغادرة الجن لجسمي. وفي أغلب الأحيان، هناك رائحة سيئة للشياطيين التي تخرج من الفئران. وحتى عندما أقول للقط "هش" أستطيع أن أرى الكثير من الجن التي تغادر جسم القط وتقفز الى داخل جسمي خلال ثوان معدودة. وفي أثناء تغلغل الجن الى داخل جسمي، لم أشعر قط بالأذى أو أي نوع من الآلام. وعادة ما يستمعون الى ويبحثون عن شخص آخر غيري خلال بضع دقائق. بعد أن تعلمت كل ذلك عن نفسي، قررت أن لا أقتل أشياء يسكنها الجن ولا حتى الصرصور أو أي نوع من الحشرات التي تجلس أو تمشي أمامي لأنني لا أريد المزيد من المتاعب بدون سبب ما. ودائماً ما أقترح على أصدقائي المقربين ان يستخدموا شخصاً آخر لقتل الحشرات داخل المنزل. وأقترح بأن يبقوا بعيديين عن المنزل أثناء عملية قتل الحشرات داخله.

Demons that come out from human bodies are more powerful and more aggressive. They are more controlling and have different kinds of problems. For example, once they are inside my body/mind, I can't sleep, or my legs and body have a mysterious kind of pain. My ears turn red, and my eyes burn. My neck will hurt and burn, and I can develop either low or high blood pressure. It is not always very easy to convince demons to come out from my body. In the end, I have to go through a procedure, and in few seconds, they leave my body!

Are demons scared of something?

I can describe a few more incidents: One time, I ordered some fake animals and birds, but they looked so real. They included a cat, dog, horse, hen, eagle, rabbit, owl, and pigeon, among others. At that time, I had one real demon friend. He was living in my house. That night, when I came back home, I started opening those fake animal bones. It was a big order. Animals and birds were everywhere in the living room. Several times, I felt that demon continuously on my back. I asked several times that it come out of me, but it was not listening to me. Finally, I figured out that it had some problem with those animals and birds. I cleaned one side of the room and asked it to come out of me. It listened to me at that time. When I opened more boxes, I put those animals and birds again on the other side of the room. As soon as I put them on that side of room, the demon jumped on me again. I tried to convince it that these were not real animals, but it was not listening to me. Finally, I asked my wife if she could take all those boxes to our store. She flatly refused to do so. She just refused, and that demon immediately jumped on her. And she started yelling because of an extremely bad headache she had developed. I asked that demon to leave her alone immediately. It listened to me and came back to my body. After that, my wife was ready to take all the boxes to the store immediately. That happened at 2:00 a.m. in the morning. But the whole time, she was fussing about that demon. That was first time I learned that the demon had some problem with those animals.

إن الشياطين التي تخرج من أجسام البشر أكثر قوة وعدوانية. وهم أيضاً أكثر تحكماً ويسببون المشاكل المختلفة. على سبيل المثال، عندما تدخل الشياطين الى جسمي أو عقلي، فلا أستطيع النوم أو تصبحي رجلي وجسمي يتألمون. ويتحول لون أذني الى الأحمر ويتسببون في حرقة في عيني ورقبتي ومن المحتمل تعرضي لارتفاع أو انخفاض ضغط الدم. وليس دائماً من السهل إقناع الشياطين بالخروج من أي جسم. وفي النهاية، علي اتباع إجراء معين وتخرج الشياطين من جسمي خلال ثوانٍ معدودة.

هل تخاف الشياطين من شيء ما؟

سأقوم بوصف المزيد من الأحداث: في يوم من الأيام، طلبت بعض الحيوانات والطيور المزيفة ولكنها بدأت حقيقية. ومن ضمنها قط وكلب وحصان ودجاجة ونسر وأرنب وبومة وحمامة وغيرها الكثير. في ذلك الوقت، كان لدي صديق حقيقي من الجن وكان يعيش داخل منزلي. وفي تلك الليلة عدت الى المنزل وبدأت بفتح عظام تلك الحيوانات المزيفة. لقد كان طلب ضخم. وكانت الحيوانات والطيور في كل مكان في غرفة معيشتي. وشعرت عدة مرات بأن ذلك الجن وراء ظهري. وسألته مرات عديدة بالخروج من جسمي ولكنه لم يستمع الي. وفي النهاية عرفت أن لديه مشاكل مع تلك الحيوانات والطيور. فقمت بتنظيف جزء من غرفتي وسألته بالخروج من جسمي. وقد استمع إلي في حينه. وعندما قمت بفتح المزيد من الصناديق، قمت بوضع تلك الحيوانات والطيور في الجانب الآخر من الغرفة. وحينما قمت بوضعها في ذلك الجانب من الغرفة، قفز الجن مرة أخرى على ظهري. وحاولت إقناعه بأن تلك الحيوانات مزيفة ولكنه لم يكن يستمع إلي. وفي النهاية، طلبت من زوجتي أخذ تلك الصناديق الى مخزن البيت. وقد رفضت ذلك بشكل قاطع. فقفز الجن على ظهرها مباشرة. وبدأت بالصراخ بسبب صداع حاد. وطلبت من ذك الجن الخروج من جسمها مباشرة. وقد استمع إلي ودخل الى جسمي. وبعد ذلك، كانت زوجتي مستعدة لأخذ تلك الصناديق الى المخزن بشكل فوري. وقعت تلك الحادثة في الساعة الثانية صباحاً. لكنها بقيت طوال الوقت قلقة بشأن ذلك الجن. وكانت تلك هي الحادثة الأولى التي علمت بها بأن الجن يشعر بالمتاعب من تلك الحيوانات.

Another time, I was watching a horror movie. At that time, I had a few demons around me, as usual. That time, I couldn't even count the demons, because I was dealing with so many. That demon was far away from me, and that was why I was not sensing it. But every time that horror movie had any scary scene or loud noise, that demon jumped on me. When this happened several times, I asked it, "What is your problem?"

It seemed to say, "I am getting scared from the ghost in the movie. That's why I am jumping."

I asked it, "Why are you scared of that ghost in the movie?"

It just happened today when I was coming back to home from work. I saw that someone had left the fence door open. I walked that way and tried to close that door, but one green lizard jumped from wall toward that gate. Because of the reptile, I jumped backward. But within a second, the demon from that lizard came out and jump inside my body. It might have been okay if I didn't feel anything, but I feel or sense them so clearly—like someone is hugging me. I hope you can imagine my situation. Something came out from that lizard, and now that demon penetrated my body. I cannot explain my feelings, but I started arguing with the demon to come out from my body and go back to that lizard. I think it took me minutes, and he left my body and went back to that lizard. So, I learned that they leave any body immediately when they figure out someone can hit or kill the insect or animal they're possessing.

Do demons move from body to body or place to place frequently?

No, demons do not move easily. Some of them just live in our houses or business places or trees. Some of them permanently live inside our bodies. They live more comfortably in those areas like the house or workplace, areas that are not in use or mostly dark. I sometimes see

وفي وقت آخر، كنت أشاهد فلم رعب. وكان هناك بعض الشياطين حولي كالعادة. ولم يكن بإمكاني عدها في حينها لأنني كنت أتعامل مع العديد منها. وكان هناك جن بعيد عني قليلاً لذلك لما أكن أشعر به. ولكن كلما كان هناك مقطع مخيف في ذلك الفلم أو صوت عالي، كان ذلك الجن يقفز علي. وعندما حدث ذلك لبضع مرات سألته: "ما هي مشكلتك؟"

وقد بدا لي أنه قال: "إنني اخاف من الشبح الموجود في الفلم. لذلك السبب أنا أقفز عليك."

وسألته، "ما سبب خوفك من ذلك الشبح؟"

وقد حدث ذلك أثناء عودتي الى المنزل من العمل. وقد رأيت أن شخصاً ما قد شعر بأن باب السياج قد فتح. وقد هممت بالمشي باتجاهه وحاولت أن أغلق ذلك الباب ولكن قفزت سحلية خضراء اللون عن الحائط باتجاه البوابة. وقد قفزت للخلف بسبب تلك الزاحف. وكلن بعد ثوانٍ معدودة، خرج الجن الموجود داخل تلك السحلية ودخل الى جسمي. وقد كاد أن يبدوا لي طبيعياً لو أنني لم أشعر بشيء. ولكنني أشعر وأحس بهم بوضوح – كأن شخصاً ما يحضنني. أتمنى أنكم تتخيلون وضعي. شيء ما خرج من تلك السحلية والآن تغلغل شيطانٌ داخل جسمي. لا أستطيع التعبير عن مشاعري ولكنني بدأت بالحوار مع الجن للخروج من جسمي والعودة الى السحلية. أعتقد بأن الحوار أخذ بضع دقائق حتى غادر جسمي وعادي الي جسم السحلية. لذلك، تعلمت في حينها بأن الشياطين تغادر أي جسم بشكل فوري عند معرفتها بأن شخصاً ما يود ضرب أو قتل الحشرة أو الحيوان الذي يسكنه الجن.

هل يتنقل الجن من جسم إلى آخر أو من مكان إلى آخر بشكل متكرر؟

لا، إن الشياطين لا تتحرك بسهولة. حيث أن بعضها فقط يعيش في منازلنا أو في أماكن العمل أو على الأشجار. وبعضها الآخر يعيش بشكل دائم في أجسامنا. فهم يعيشون بشكل أكثر أريحية في تلك المناطق أمثال البيوت وأماكن العمل والمناطق القليلة الاستعمال أو المهجورة وفي الظلام. وفي أحيانٍ أخرى أراها

them flying in one room in my house. I see them stuck on ceilings or walls. I rarely use that room. I go there twice a day only to put my shoes on. I saw a lot of them in the big restroom, too. Usually, I don't go there. I don't see any demons in the restroom I use or any of the other rooms in the house. It is funny, but several times, I saw a bunch flying around me, and when I walked, they moved as well. But they maintain a certain distance from me. I am always thankful for their care and sincerity. Sometimes they show me by doing stuff like that.

Anyway, demons do not move from that house they are living in, regardless of who lives in that house. They don't allow other demons to come to their place. If demons are living inside the body of a person—I am not talking about diseases but about demons—then they move and go everywhere with that body. Those demons are parts of our personalities. Basically, demons, regardless of how many there are, are at least sincere with us. Basically, they are negative energy. They like negative stuff. When you are doing something bad and you are conflicted, your mind or your spirit or your positive energy will try to stop you, but these demons insist that we do something negative all the time. Usually, what actually happens depends on who has more control. If the demons have more control over us, we listen to them and follow them. But if we are in control of our mind and spirit, we do not do bad or wrong stuff easily. Demons get nothing from this. This is just their hobby.

Usually, demons inside our bodies will stay forever unless someone like me removes them from someone else's body, and in that case, the person's body will be neutral for a while. Then another demon will come and start living in that body. They may start helping the person sometimes, but most of the time, they will create problems. I can tell you about myself. I had few habits, I just wanted some things. I'll leave everything. I won't finish that work. But because I have control over myself, I am a different person. I'm not too active. I'm very slow, and I think a lot before I do something. I'm not dying to do crazy stuff. I'm a little bit more mature and more sensible nowadays. I have

تطير في غرفة واحدة في منزلي. وأراها أيضاً عالقة في السقوف أو الجدران. ونادراً ما أستخدم تلك الغرفة حيث أنني أذهب الى تلك الغرفة مرتين في اليوم لارتداء الحذاء. وأرى الكثير منها في غرفة النوم الكبيرة أيضاً. ولا أذهب عادة الى تلك الغرفة. ولا أرى أي من الشياطيين داخل غرفة النوم التي أستخدمها أو أي غرفة أخرى استخدمها في المنزل. إنه لمن المضحك، ولكن العديد من الأوقات أرى الكثير منها طائرة حولي ولكن عندما أمشي هم يتحركون أيضاً. ولكن يحافظون على مسافة معينة مني. ودائماً ما أكون شاكراً لعنايتهم واخلاصهم. فأحيانا ما يستعرضون حولي بعمل مثل تلك الأشياء.

على أي حال، لا تتحرك الشياطين من المنزل الذي يعشن فيه بغض النظر عن من يعيش بداخله. ولا يسمحون لشياطين أخرى بالسكن معهم في نفس المنزل. إذا كان الجن يعيش في داخل جسم شخص ما- ولا أتكلم هنا عن الأمراض ولكن أتكلم عن الجن- فإن تلك الشياطين تتحرك وتذهب الى كل مكان مع الجسم الذي تسكن فيه. وتعتبر تلك الشياطين جزء من شخصيتنا. وبشكل أساسي وبغض النظر عن عددها، إلا أنها مخلصة لنا. وهم الطاقة السلبية أو مثلهم مثل الأشياء السلبية عندما تفعل أشياء سيئة وتصارع نفسك أو عقلك أو روحك أو طاقتك الايجابية ستقوم بايقافك، وكلن تلك الشياطين ترغمنا على عمل أشياء سلبية في كل الأوقات. والذي يحدث عادة يعتمد على الذي لدي تحكم أكبر. في حال أن الجن لدي تحكم أكبر تجاهنا، فإننا نستمع اليهم وتبعهم. ولكن في حال أننا نحن من لدينا السيطرة الكبرى عليهم والسيطرة على عقولنا وأرواحنا، فلن نقوم بعمل أشياء سيئة بتلك السهولة. ولا تحصل الشياطين على شيء منا. فإنها تلك هي هوايتها.

وفي أغلب الأحيان، تبقى الشياطيين داخل أجسامنا للأبد عدا قيام أحد ما مثلي بإزالتها من جسم شخص آخر، وفي تلك الحالة سيبقى ذلك الشخص جسم معتدل لفترة. ومن ثم يأتي شيطان آخر ويعيش في جسم ذلك الشخص. وفي أحيان أخرى من المحتمل أن تقوم تلك الشياطيين بمساعدة ذلك الشخص ولكن معظم الأوقات يخلقون المشاكل له. وأود أن أكلمكم عن نفسي. كان لدي بضع عادات وكنت أود عمل بعض الأشياء. سأترك كل شيء. ولن أنهي ذلك العمل ولكن لدي السيطرة على نفسي وأنا شخص مختلف الآن. لست فعالاً لدرجة كبيرة. فأنا بطيء جداً وأفكر ملياً قبل القيام بأي عمل. ولا أتوق لعمل أشياء مجنونة. فأنا ناضجاً قليلاً وحساس في هذه الأيام. ولدي

a group of people (friends and family). I clean their bodies every day, and their temperaments change as well. None of them act extremist anymore. But normal people are under the influence of the same negative energies and demons from their childhood, so their habits and temperaments are the same.

Shortcut demons like to live in the same place or same body. They do not move easily. If they are too much negative and human is mentally weak then you can see a lot of example of those people talk to themselves all the time and we consider those kinds of people crazy or mentally sick. Demons always try to control human mind 100 percent if someone has a positive personality, I am sure, that person will reject, most of the time, whatever wishes or ideas he will get from demons around him. But a negative minded person will love to adopt negative ideas and wishes/desires from demons. Same way, a weak minded person will give total control of his mind in the hand of a demon. Unconsciously, normal people argue with demons during the thinking. But a weak mind person will start talking to invisible demon, as we talk to other people. So, when that person will start talking to himself, we for sure consider that person, a mentally sick person. And we call those people crazy or mentally ill. I can move those demons from the head of those people, but those people are so weak mentally, so after few days, they will be influenced by other demons and keep bad habits.

I can change your temperament.

If you are a very short-tempered person, if you have anxiety attacks all the time, if you suffer from depression all the time, if you are thinking of committing suicide all the time, if you want to kill anyone, if you are unhappy all the time, if you feel jealous of anyone, or if you have any other negative habits, I can remove those demons from you, but it will not help until you decide to help yourself. How you can change your temperament? Whenever you become angry, depressed, or unhappy, try to convince yourself that your feelings are due to

مجموعة من الأشخاص (الأصدقاء والعائلة). وأقوم بتنظيف أجسامهم كل يوم، ويتغير مزاجهم كل يوم أيضاً. ولم يعد أحد منهم يتصرف بشكل متطرف بعد الآن. ولكن الأشخاص العاديون هم تحت تأثير نفس الطاقات السلبية والشياطين منذ طفولتهم ولذلك فإن عاداتهم ومزاجهم كذلك.

ترغب الشياطين بالعيش في نفس المكان أو نفس الجسم. ولا يتحركون بسهولة. في حال كانت الشياطين سيئة للغاية والبشر ضعيفين عقلياً فإنك سترى الكثير من هؤلاء الأشخاص يتحدثون لأنفسهم في جميع الأوقات ونحن نعتبر هذا النوع من الأشخاص مجانين أو مختلين عقلياً. ودائماً ما تحاول الشياطين السيطرة على عقل الشخص بنسبة مئة بالمئة في حال امتلاك ذلك الشخص شخصية ايجابية، وأنا متأكد بأن ذلك الشخص سيرفض، في معظم الأوقات، مهما كانت الأمنيات والأفكار التي تعرض عليه من قبل الشياطين من حوله. ولكن الشخص ذو العقل السيء ستروق له فكرة التكيف مع الأفكار السيئة والرغبات التي تعرضها الشياطين. وبالطريقة نفسها، سيستسلم الشخص الضعيف العقل لسيطرة الجن. وبشكل غير واعي، يتحاور الأشخاص العاديون مع الشياطين أثناء التفكير. ولكن الشخص ذو العقل الضعيف سيبدأ بالتحدث مع الجن الخفي كما نحن نتحدث مع بعضنا البعض كبشر. لذلك، عندما يتحدث ذلك الشخص مع نفسه، نكون متأكدين بأن ذلك الشخص هو شخص مريض عقلياً. ونسمي هؤلاء الأشخاص بالمختلين عقلياً. وأستطيع أن أخرج الشياطين من عقول هؤلاء الأشخاص ولكن هؤلاء الأشخاص ضعيفون عقلياً وبعد بضعة أيام سيتأثرون مرة أخرى بشياطين أخرى ويبقون على عاداتهم السيئة.

أستطيع تغيير مزاجك

إذا كنت شخص سريع الغضب، وإذا كان لديك هجمات غضب في جميع الأحيان، وإذا كنت تعاني من الاكتئاب وإذا كنت تفكر بالانتحار في جميع الأوقات وإذا كنت تريد قتل أي شخص أو كنت غير سعيد أو تشعر بالغير تجاه شخص ما أو لديك عادات سيئة، فبإمكاني إزالة تلك الشياطين من داخلك ولكن ذلك لن يساعد حتى تقرر أنت بمساعدة نفسك. كيف بإمكانك تغيير مزاجك؟ حينما تكون غاضباً مكتئب، غير سعيد، حاول أن تقنع نفسك بأنك تشعر كذلك بسبب

demons around you. Why are these demons doing this? This is their hobby—that's why. They have nothing else to do. You are their toy. So, when you get angry about small things, do not let the demons boost or amplify your anger. Start thinking, *This is not a big deal.* You need to defeat that demon. If you get more and more angry, you give your control to that demon. But even if I don't help you, you can help yourself by keeping in mind that the demon is playing with your mind and boosting or amplifying your anger more and more. If you decide that you will not let the demon influence your temperament, you will see that the demon will be very disappointed with you, because it will not be able to play with you. If you keep doing this practice for a few days, that demon will give up on you and will find someone else to play.

The same goes for unhappy feelings and depression. I can move those demons from your body very easily, but before that, you need to practice a little bit to gain more control of your mind. That means you need to convince yourself that these unhappy, negative feelings are coming from that demon around you. You need to practice continuously to beat that depression and the unhappy feelings and consequently defeat that demon. This is not that easy because those demons hypnotize and control our minds, but if you have any intention of kicking that problem, I can take out that demon's force from your body; however, after that, it's your job if you want to keep the control over your life. Demons are pretty much like kids. They do not want to leave their toys.

Can anyone control demons?
Can demons become friends?

For both questions, the answer is yes and no. Anyone can control demons, but no human can control demons. If any human has control of demons, it is not because humans have powers. The only reason demons become friends with any human is just because of a relationship of friendship and sincerity. No human can put pressure

وجود الشياطين من حولك. ولماذا تقوم الشياطين بتلك الأفعال؟ إنها هواية عند تلك الشياطين-هذا هو السبب؟ ولا يوجد شيء آخر فعله. فنحن البشر نعتبر لعبة بين أيدي الجن. لذلك، عندما تغضب حيال أشياء بسيطة، لا تجعل الشياطين تعزز أو تقوم بتضخيم غضبك. ابدا بالتفكير، فإنه ليس بالشيء الصعب. بإمكانك هزيمتها. في حال اشتداد غضبك أكثر وأكثر، فإنك تسمح للجن بالسيطرة عليك. ولكن حتى لو لم أساعدك، فبإمكانك مساعدة نفسك بالأخذ بعين الاعتبار بأن الشيطان يلعب بعقلك ويقوم بزيادة غضبك أكثر وأكثر. في حال قررت بعدم السماح للجن بالتأثير على مزاجك، سترى بأن الجن سيكون محبط جداً لأنه لم يكن باستطاعته اللعب معك. وفي حال بقائك فعل ذلك لعدة أيام، فإن ذلك الجن سيستسلم وسيقوم بالبحث عن شخص غيرك للعب معه.

ويحدث الشيء ذاته مع أصحاب الشعور الحزين والمكبوتين. فبإمكاني إخراج الجن من جسمك ولكن قبل أن أفعل ذلك، فإنك بحاجة الى القليل من الممارسة للحصول على المزيد من السيطرة على نفسك وعقلك. وهذا يعني أنك بحاجة الى إقناع نفسك بأن الشعور الحزين والسلبي سببها هو الجن. لذلك عليك الممارسة بشكل مستمر للتغلب على الاكتئاب والشعور والحزين وبذلك فإنك ستقوم بهزيمة ذلك الجن. وهذا ليس بالشيء السهل لأن الشياطين تقوم بتنويم والسيطرة على عقلك، ولكن إذا كان لديك رغبة في التغلب على تلك المشكلة، فبإمكاني إخراج ذلك الجن من جسمك. علاوة على ذلك، عليك أن تحافظ على السيطرة على حياتك. حيث أن الشياطين تشبه الى حد كبير الأطفال. فهم لا يتركون لعبهم بتلك السهولة.

هل يستطيع أي شخص السيطرة على الجن؟
هل بإمكاننا تكوين علاقة صداقة مع الشياطين؟

إن الجواب لكلا السؤالين هو نعم ولا. حيث أنه بإمكان أي شخص السيطرة على الجن ولكن في نفس الوقت لا يستطيع أحد السيطرة عليهم. في حال أن شخص ما يمتلك سيطرة على الجن فإن ذلك ليس لأن البشر لديهم قوى خارقة. بل إن السبب الوحيد وراء ذلك أن الجن يصبحون أصدقاء مع البشر وذلك يعزى الى اخلاصهم وصداقتهم. فليس باستطاعة أي شخص الضغط على

on demons. Demons only stay around a human because of some extraordinary qualities or powers in that human being. Demons are as old as six hundred to a thousand years. Demons live in a group or tribe. Usually, one tribe or group has one leader demon, and all the demons follow instructions of that leader. Just like human beings, some demons are good, and some are bad. Some are religious and follow only the right path, and some are extremely evil and follow the path of the devil. Similarly, there are several ways to communicate with demons. But demons use only hypnotism to communicate with humans and other animals or insects. Usually, very good and extremely religious humans or extremely evil and dirty humans can communicate with demons by just talking or hypnotism.

A tribe of demons, or group of demons, does not have a mixed category. They are either a tribe of good and religious demons or a tribe of evil and dirty demons. As you know, evil and dirty powers are more powerful and dangerous. This is not like this that one person just do some work and have a group of demons under control or I will say achieve their sincerity and demons start following their commands. This is not easy for a common person to just practice few things and achieve incredible powers to have control on demons. People, they spend their whole lives in practicing and learning these kind of super natural powers. Sometimes, they achieve power; sometimes they lost the control of their mind. But, usually friendship or control on demons comes from struggle and effects of generations. These kinds of powers are transferable from one to another person. Demons usually listen to their master. And when old master died, as per instruction of old master, they start obeying new master. Usually, if someone has control of a group of demons, it is like a chain. For example, a thousand years ago, someone started communication with the leader of the demons, regardless of them being good or evil. When that person was dying, he transferred his relationship with demons to one of his students. This communication or sincerity comes from thousands of years, and humans keep dying and keep transferring the command of the leader of the demons to the next generation. Usually, leader demons handle and receive commands with humans.

الشياطين لتصبح أصدقاء مع البشر. وتبقى الشياطين فقط حول شخص ما بسبب بعض القوة الخارقة لذلك الشخص. حيث أن أعمار الشياطين تبلغ من ست مئة الى ألف سنة. وتعيش الشياطين مع بعضها في مجموعات أو قبائل. وفي العادة، يكون لكل مجموعة أو قبيلة قائد من الجن ويخضع جميع الشياطين في المجموعة لتعليمات ذلك القائد. فهم كالبشر تمام، فعناك الشياطين الصالحة وأيضاً هناك الشياطين السيئة. وهناك بعضها المتدين ويتبعون السراط المستقيم وهناك البعض ممن هم شريرين للغاية ويتبعون طريق الشيطان. وبالمثل، فإن هناك العديد من الطرق للاتصال بالجن. ولكن الشياطين فقط تستخدم طريقة التنويم المغناطيسي للاتصال بالبشر والحيوانات الأخرى والحشرات. وفي أغلب الأحيان فإن الأشخاص المتدينين للغاية أو الأشخاص الشريرين للغاية هم من يقومون بالاتصال بالجن عن طريق التحدث إليهم أو عن طريق التنويم المغناطيسي.

ولا تحتوي قبيلة أو مجموعة من الشياطيين على أصناف مختلفة. فهم إما قبيلة من الشياطيين الصالحين والمتدينين، أو قبيلة من الشياطيين الشيئيين والشريرين. وكما تعلم، فإن القوى السيئة والشريرة أكثر قوة وخطورة من القوة الصالحة. وذلك لا يعني بأن شخص ما، يتحكم بمجموعة من الشياطيين ويقوم بعمل بعض الأفعال، يخضع لمطالبهم. حيث أن بعض الأشخاص يقضون حياتهم في سبيل تعلم وممارسة تلك الأنواع من القوى الخارقة. وأحياناً، يحصلون على تلك القوة وفي أحيان أخرى يفقدونها ويفقدون السيطرة على عقولهم. ولكن عادةً ما تأتي علاقة الصداقة أو السيطرة على الجن بعد صراع وتأثير الأجيال. حيث أن تلك القوى الخارقة لدى البشر تنتقل عبر الأجيال ومن شخص لآخر. وعادة مات تستمع الجن الى أسيادها. وعندما يموت السيد الأكبر، وطبقاً لتعليمات ذلك السيد العجوز، يقوم الجن بالخضوع لطاعة سيد جديد. وإذا كان شخص ما يمتلك السيطرة على مجموعة من الجن فهي عبارة عن سلسلة. فعلى سبيل المثال، قبل ألف سنة قام شخص بالاتصال بالجن الصالح منها والسيء التصرف. وعندما كان ذلك الشخص يحتضر، قام بنقل علاقته مع الجن الى أحد طلابه. ويأتي هذا الإخلاص عبر آلاف السنين وعندما يموت الإنسان يقوم بنقل طلب قائد مجموعة الجن الى الجيل القادم. ويستقبل قائد الجن طلبات البشر ويتعامل معهم.

Regular demons that have at least some wisdom are almost equal to a ten-years-old human boy. Now there are people who have good relationships with groups of demons, but there is no one who can say that he or she has control of any demon in any part of the world.

Given my research, I cannot find anyone who is really able to see demons or able to describe how demons look. I have never found anyone who could sense or feel demons. But I can. As much as I read, saw, and heard, most of those humans, regardless good or evil, are using their demon groups to help people achieve success in business or love, or if they are evil powers, then they may be hurting someone in some negative way. Usually, good and religious people bind good demons with holy books. Whenever humans want to use those demons, those humans pray those holy words, and good demons follow their commands. In the same way, evil humans do some evil work, and those evil demons follow those evil commands.

As I said, good and religious demons follow holy books. In the same way, evil demons follow evil tricks; for example, an evil human may make fine knots in a rope, bury that rope in a cemetery, and command five evil demons to do something evil. And then those five evil demons and their coming generations will keep following those evil commands. Evil commands can compel them to destroy someone's business or family or health. It could be anything bad.

Remember, out of 100 percent, 90 percent of people are fake. They have no command or control. They have no power, but they just make people fools. But 1 percent of people are good or bad with a proficient control of demons. I spoke to a few people in this field, but they have powers because their teachers transferred those powers to them, and their teachers taught them how to use the good and evil powers of demons. I have never found any people who could really say that they could feel or sense the touch of demons or they could really see demons. Even they have thousands or millions of demons around them, but they still do not have those senses or eyes that can sense or see demons.

إن الشياطين المنتظمة والتي تتحلى ببعض الحكمة مناسبين لشخص في العاشرة من عمره. والآن هناك أناس لديهم علاقات جيدة من جماعات من الجن ولكن لا يوجد أحد يستطيع بأنه يسيطر أو يتحكم بأي من هؤلاء من الجن في العالم أجمع.

ونظراً لبحثي، لم أستطيع ايجاد أي شخص قادر على رؤية الجن أو قادر على وصف ملامحهم. ولم أجد في حياتي باستطاعته الإحساس أو الشعور بوجود الجن. ولكنني أنا أستطيع فعل ذلك، بقدر قراءتي وما شاهدت وما سمعت عن هؤلاء الأشخاص وبغض النظر سواءً كانوا صالحون أو شريرون ، يستخدمون جماعاتهم من الجن لمساعدة الناس في تحقيق النجاح في العمل أو العمل . وفي حال كانوا يملكون قوى شريرة، فانهم اذن قادرون على إلحاق الأذى بأي شخص بطريقة سلبية. وفي العادة يقوم الأناس الصالحون أو المتدينون بربط الشياطين بالكتب المقدسة، حيث يقوم هؤلاء الأشخاص بالصلاة باستخدام الكلمات المقدسة ويقوم الجن الصالح باتباع أوامر البشر. وبنفس الطريقة، يقوم الأشخاص الأشرار بعمل أشياء شريرة ويقوم الجن الشرير باتباع أوامرهم.

وكما أسلفت الذكر ، تقوم الشياطين الصالحة والمتدينة باتباع الكتب المقدسة. وبنفس الطريقة تقوم الشياطين الشريرة باتباع الخدع الشريرة؛ فعلى سبيل المثال، يقوم شخص شرير بعمل خمس عقد في حبل ويقوم بدفنه في مقبره، ويأمر خمسة شياطين الشريرة بعمل شيء شرير . وبذلك، فإن هؤلاء الشياطين الخمسة تبقى فعل تلك الأعماء الشريرة وينقلون تلك الأوامر الى أجيال قادمة لتدمير عمل شخص ما أو عائلة أو صحة. وقد يكون أي عمل شرير .

وتذكر ، بنسبة مئة بالمئة، أن تسعون بالمئة من هؤلاء البشر خداعون. حيث أنه لا يوجد لديهم أي سيطرة أو تحكم على الجن. ولا يوجد لديهم أي قوة، ولكنهم يجعلون الناس كالحمقى. ولكن هناك واحد بالمئة من هؤلاء الناس سواء صالحون أو أشرار لديهم قوة سيطرة خارقة. وقد تحدثت الى البعض منهم في هذا المجال، حيث أن لديهم تلك القوة الخارقة لأن أساتذتهم قاموا بنقل تلك القوى اليهم وقاموا بتعليمهم كيفية استخدام قوة الشر والخير للشياطين. ولم أجد قط أي من هؤلاء الأشخاص الذين بإمكانهم القول بأنهم يشعرون بالجن أو يرونهم. حتى لو كانوا يسيطرون على الألاف أو الملايين من الجن من حولهم، ولكنهم يبقون لا يملكون تلك الأحاسيس والعيون للشعور أو رؤية الشياطين.

I talked to several people who claimed that demons visit them and communicate with them in the shape of humans. I just asked them if this was really true and if the demons could reverse the process and change themselves from human to demon again. But nothing happened like that. Until today, when I am able to sense, feel, and see demons, I never saw any demon come to me in the shape of a human or communicate like a human. I deal with so many demons every day, some extremely nice, others extremely dangerous, but they are always in their real shape, namely small flying objects similar to flying insects. I communicate with demons twenty-four hours all seven days a week. I demand that anyone show me if these demons can change themselves in the shapes of any human or animal, but it never happens. As a result, I strongly feel that all those stories about demons wandering in the shape of humans are just stories. If there is any change in my knowledge or experience, I will notify you in my next book.

Demons are by nature very naughty and negative. Even if they are very sincere with any human being, they will still show nightmares to that human frequently. Regardless of how much they are sincere with a particular human, that human is still just a toy for them. Demons are not less dangerous than lions, and they have way more power than lions. They can penetrate the bodies, and they have hypnotizing powers that they can use to control minds, temperaments, and feelings.

In my case, I was able to make demons my friend because whenever I was sensing or feeling them, I surprised them by communicating with them and informing their actions. After the initial steps, demons test me again and again by coming from different direction toward my body, and every time, I inform them about their actions. When I was able to see them, I started pointing my fingers to them. Initially, they flew away from me, but slow and steady, they came in front of me and stayed for a while.

وقد تحدثت الى العديد من الأشخاص الذين يدعون بأن الشياطين تقوم بزيارتهم والاتصال بهم على شكل إنسان. وقد سألتهم حول ما إذا كان ذلك حقيقاً والتحول من هيئة إنسان الى هيئة شيطان. ولكن لم يحدث شيئاً من ذلك. وحتى هذه اللحظة عندما كنت أشعر وأحس وأرى الشيطانيين، فلم أرى أي شيطان يأتي إلي على هيئة إنسان أو يقوم بالاتصال بي على هيئة إنسان. وأتعامل مع العديد من الشياطين كل يوم حيث أن بعضهم رائع للغاية وبعضهم الآخر خطير للغاية، ولكنهم يبقون دائماً بشكلهم الحقيقي على شكل أجسام طائرة صغيرة تشبه الحشرات الطائرة. وأقوم بالاتصال معهم على مدار الساعة. أطالب أي شخص، ممن يدعى بأن الجن يتحول على هيئة إنسان أو حيوان، بأن يريني ذلك ولكنه لم يحدث في الحقيقة. وكنتيجة لذلك، أشعر بقوة أن كل تلك القصص حول تجول الشياطين على هيئة إنسان هي مجرد شائعات. وفي حال كان هناك أي تغير في معرفتي أو خبرتي، سأتطرق إليه في كتابي القادم.

إن الشياطين هي بطبيعتها سخيفة وسيئة. حتى أنهم لو كانوا مخلصين جداً مع الإنسان، فهم يبقون يظهرون في الكوابيس لذلك الإنسان بشكل متكرر. وبغض النظر حول مدى إخلاصهم مع إنسان معين، فلا يزال ذلك الإنسان مجرد دمية بالنسبة لهم. فخطورة الشياطين ليس أقل من خطورة الأسد وهم حتى أقوى من الأسود، حيث أنه بإمكانهم التغلغل الى أجسام البشر ويمتلكون قوى التنويم المغناطيسي والتي يستخدمونها للتحكم في العقول والمزاجات والشعور.

وفي حالتي، كنت قادراً على جعل الشيطان كصديق لي لأنه حينما كنت أشعر بهم، كنت أفاجأهم بالاتصال بهم وابلاغهم بأعمالهم. وبعد تلك الخطوات الأولية، تقوم الشياطين بامتحاني مرات ومرات بالقدوم في مسارات مختلفة باتجاه جسمي وكل مرة أقوم بإبلاغهم عن أعمالهم. وعندما كنت قادراً على رؤيتهم، كنت أقوم بتوجيه اصابعي باتجاههم. وفي البداية، هموا بالهروب بعيداً عني ولكن بثبات وصبر جاؤوا إلي ومكثوا بجانبي لفترة.

Third and last and a very important thing is that I do not ask demons to help me when I have to fix any sickness or pain in any human being. God gifted me with some powers, and they come from my mind. Most of the time, I communicate straight to pain and sickness in the body of a human being, regardless of where that human being is in the world. I prefer at least telephone communication to get an update on the reduction of pain or sickness.

If anyone says anything about demons that are magic and can fulfill three wishes or can make us rich, my friends, they are just telling you stories. Real demons are very powerful but mostly use their negative powers. If I ever find a demon with qualities of the magical demon in stories, I will share my knowledge and experience with everyone. I wish they existed so that I could say, "Yes, try to make demons your friend." The best thing is to stay away from them. It is not easy but not impossible. Fighting with demons means fighting with air.

Can demons hear us?

Yes, all demons can hear us, and they take full interest in our lives and discuss us with other demons. They know our family histories because of their age.

How do diseases travel?

Anyone can contract diseases, even though a telephone line connected to a sick person. We can even receive sicknesses if we are watching live TV. We can easily get any sickness from any sick animal or human being. The nature of these diseases is electromagnetic. They can travel with the speed to light from one body to another. The same thing is true for demons.

وإن الشي الثالث والأخير والأكثر أهمية هو أنني لا أقوم بسؤالهم لمساعدتي عندما أقوم بعلاج مرض ما أو أي ألم في جسم شخص. فقد منحني الله ببعض القوى، وتأتي تلك القوى من خاطري. وفي معظم الأوقات، أقوم بالاتصال بشكل مباشر بالألم والمرض في جسم الإنسان بغض النظر عن مكان ذلك الإنسان في العالم. وأفضل بالاتصال هاتفياً للحصول الى معلومات حول تخفيف الألم والمرض.

وفي حال قيام شخص ما بالادعاء بأن الجن يقومون بعمل السحر وتحقيق ثلاث أمنيات أو بإمكانها جعلنا أغنياء، ولكن أصدقائي فهؤلاء الأشخاص فقط يرون لكم الشائعات. إن الشياطيين الحقيقة قوية للغاية ولكن معظمهم ما يستخدم القوى السلبية. وفي حال تعرفي على شيطان بإمكانيات الشيطان السحري كما في الشائعات، سأقوم بمشاركة معرفتي وخبرتي مع شخص. أتمنى وجودها حتى أتمكن من القول "أن أفضل شيء هو البقاء بعيداً أمكان تواجدهم" فليس من السهل فعل ذلك ولكنه غير مستحيل. حيث أن القتال مع الشياطيين كالقتال مع الهواء."

هل بإمكان الجن سماعنا؟

نعم، بإمكان جميع الشياطيين سماعنا وبإمكانهم الاهتمام بجوانب مختلفة من حياتنا ومناقشتها مع شياطيين آخرين. فهم على علم ودراية بتاريخ عائلاتنا بسبب عمرهم الطويل.

كيفية انتقال الأمراض؟

يتعرض أي شخص لعدوى الأمراض على الرغم من اتصال خط الهاتف مع الشخص المريض. ونتعرض لعدوى الأمراض عندما نكون نشاهد التلفاز. ونتعرض لأي مرض بكل سهولة من قبل أي حيوان مريض أو إنسان مريض. فإن طبيعة تلك الأمراض هي الكتر ومغناطيسية. فبإمكانها التنقل بسرعة الضوء من شخص الى آخر وهذا الشيء نفسه الذي يحدث مع الجن.

There is a judgment day for all living creature or not? So, demons/pain, does God has a judgment day for them?

This is very a complicated problem. Every day, I think about it, and every day, new sickness and disease appear all around the world. I believe that sickness and disease are all physical but invisible insects with extraordinary, damaging powers. Sometimes, I think about how God manages these diseases and sickness. They are rapidly increasing, and their population is spreading more and more disease inside humans all around the world. Sometimes, I think about what the logic of Almighty God is in case of disease and sickness.

Given my conception of diseases, God has given us some directions and instructions. He has told us clearly what is good and what is bad. God has given us the concept of heaven and hell. As humans, we are pretty free to choose right and wrong paths. If we choose right path, we will make God happy, and we will get reward from God. And if we choose the wrong and bad path, then God will be unhappy, and we will be punished for that. This ethical paradigm is for human beings. So, I always think, *What is God's management for these diseases and sicknesses? Is there any punishment for these diseases and sicknesses?* After all, they are just free to damage anyone, regardless of human or animal, and they will have no judgment day? Has God also given them two paths? Will these demons get punished if they choose the bad path?

I am surprised these physical diseases, pains, and sicknesses do so much damage and give so much pain to humans or animals or trees. What will be their fate? I don't know what you think, but because I communicate with them and because they listen to me most of the time, I can manage them and insist that they leave a body. That means they have sense and wisdom. It means they know good and bad. With that said, what is God's management for them?

هناك يوم الحساب لجميع المخلوقات الحية؟ فهل سيقوم يوم حساب للجن من قبل الله؟

إنها لمشكلة معقدة جداً في كل يوم، أفكر في ذلك الأمر وكل يوم يظهر هناك مرض جديد في أنحاء العالم. وأعتقد أن كل تلك الأمراض هي جسدية ولكنها عبارة عن حشرات خارقة مدمرة للقوى البشرية. وأحياناً ما أفكر حول طريقة الله في كيفية التحكم هذه الأمراض. فهي في ارتفاع سريع وأعدادها تنتشر أكثر وأكثر داخل جسم الإنسان في العالم. وفي أحيانٍ أخرى أفكر حول منطق الخالق العظيم بخصوص الأمراض.

ونظراً لمفهومي للأمراض، فقد منحنا الله بعض الطرق والتعليمات. وقال لنا بكل وضوح ما هو الخير من الشر. ومنحنا أيضاً مفهوم الجنة والنار. ونحن كبشر أحرارٌ في اختيار الطريق الصواب من الخطأ. وفي حال قمنا باختيار الطريق الصواب، سيكون الإله سعيداً بذلك وسيكرمنا وسنحصل على جائزة من الله. وفي حال قمنا باختيار الطريق الخطأ، فإن الله لن يكون سعيداً بذلك وسيعاقبنا على فعل ذلك أيضاً. حيث أن هذا المثال الأخلاقي هو للإنسان. لذلك، دائماً ما أفكر ما هي كيفية تحكم الله بتلك الأمراض؟ وهل هنالك أي عقوبة لتلك الأمراض؟ بعد كل ذلك، فهي حرة في الطريق التي تتحكم فيها بأي شخص بغض النظر عن الإنسان أو الحيوان ولن يكون لديها يوم حساب. وهل منحها الله طريقان مختلفان؟ وهل سيعاقب الله الجن في حال اختاروا الطريق الخطأ.

إنني متفاجئ جداً من مدى قدرة تلك الأمراض والآلام التحكم والتسبب لنا بالآلام سواءً كنا بشر أو حيوانات أو أشجار. وما سيكون مصيرها؟ لا أعلم بماذا تفكر أنت، ولكن لأنني أتصل مع الجن ولأنني أستمع اليهم معظم الوقت، فبإمكاني التحكم بهم والضغط عليهم للخروج من جسم شخص ما. ويعني هذا أنهم يعلمون الصواب من الخطأ. وبعد قول كل ذلك، ما هي طريقة الله في التحكم بهم؟

Can anyone kill demons, and how?

I don't know if killing is right term to use in regards to management. A few people are capable of doing this, but not me. The people who are capable of killing demons suffer from the revenge of demons, and the next generation inherits this feud as well. These people have control of several extremely powerful demons. First, those demons make a circle around a certain area. For a few hours or days, any demon can come inside that circle, but no demon can go outside that circle. Then these people use their demons to compel regular demons to go inside bottles. Because of these powerful demons, regular demons go inside those bottles of water, and those regular demons are confined in those bottles of water for several hours. During that time, those people throw the bottles of water filled up with regular demons in any river or ocean. Once these bottles of water are filled up with hundreds of demons and are thrown the river or ocean, those demons are confined there until someone takes those bottles out of water and opens them. This is the only way to confine or kill demons. But be careful, because this is a very dangerous way of management. And demons always take their revenge on these kinds of people and their future generations.

Can demons make us suspicious?

In a house or tree or workplace, there are uncountable demons. When they are flying in the air like regular insects, their actual size is very small. As I have said, they have extraordinary powers to expand themselves according to the available room in any human or animal body. I see them flying everywhere all the time. They cannot hypnotize us when they are outside of our bodies. To show us dreams or feed something into our minds, they have to go inside our bodies, and then they can feed our minds anything.

هل بإمكان أي شخص قتل الجن؟ وكيف؟

لا أعلم إذا ما كان مصطلح القتل هو المصطلح الصحيح لاستخدامه هنا فيما يخص السيطرة. فهنالك القليل من الأشخاص القادرين على فعل ذلك ولكن لست أنا. إن الأشخاص القادرين على قتل الجن يعانون من انتقام الجن ويقوم الجيل القادم بتوريث هذه الضغينة أيضاً. فهؤلاء الأشخاص لديهم القدرة على التحكم بالعديد من الشياطين ذي القوى الخارقة. أولاً، تقوم تلك الشياطين بعمل دائرة حول منطقة معينة لعدة ساعات أو أيام. ويستطيع أي شيطان الدخول الى تلك الدائرة ولكن لا يستطيع أحدٌ منهم مغادرتها. ومن ثم يقوم هؤلاء الأشخاص باستخدام شياطينهم لإجبار الشياطين ذي القوى العادية بالدخول الى قناني. وبسبب القوة الخارقة لهؤلاء الشياطين، فإن الشياطين العادية تدخل الى قناني من الماء ويتم حبسها فيها لعدة ساعات. وفي تلك الأثناء، يقوم هؤلاء الأشخاص برمي تلك القناني المليئة بالشياطين العادية في أي نهر أو محيط. وعند امتلاء تلك القناني بالمئات من الشياطين ويتم رميها في النهر أو المحيط، فإن تلك الشياطين المحجوزة في تلك القناني تبقى فيها حتى يقوم شخص آخر بإخراجها وفتح تلك القناني. فهذه هي الطريقة الوحيدة لسجن أو قتل الجن. ولكن كن حذراً لأن هذه الطريقة خطرة جداً للسيطرة عليهم. ودائماً ما تنتقم تلك الشياطين من هؤلاء الأشخاص في الأجيال القادمة منها.

هل بإمكان تلك الشياطيين جعلنا شكاكين؟

هناك عدد لا يمكن احصاءه من الجن في المنزل وعلى الأشجار وفي مكان العمل. عندما يطير الجن في الهواء كالحشرات، فهم يملكون قوة خارقة لتمديد أنفسهم حسب المكان المتوفر في جسم الإنسان أو الحيوان. وأرى تلك الشياطيين طائرة في كل مكان. فليس بإمكان الجن تنويمنا مغناطيسياً عندما يكونون خارج أجسامنا. ومن أجل ظهور الأحلام أو تغذيتنا بشكل في عقولنا، عليها أولاً أن تدخل إلى أجسامنا ومن ثم بإمكانها تغذية عقولنا.

Everyday examples include the following: forgetting about something like wearing a watch or putting purses in our pockets or calling someone and much more. And then when we are not thinking about the lost items, suddenly they come to our mind. This is done by the demon that is around or inside us. That demon will hypnotize us and will feed this kind of information into our mind all the time. Again, demons are different from diseases and sicknesses the same way humans are different from lions or snakes.

Demons feed different thoughts into our minds all the time by hypnotizing us and making us aware of something and then making us suspicious so that we do not trust anyone. Consider the times when someone is trying to tell us something but our minds are not ready to accept what is being said and we show mistrust in some form as a result. Behind all those activities are demons.

Three wishes Demon/Jin or lamp Demon There is no demon who can do a magic to fulfill even on wish through a magic. These are just stories. There is nothing like a Lamp demon

In the past several years, I have never seen any demons changing themselves to other shapes. The only quality they have is that they are able to expand themselves whenever they penetrate anyone's body. Whenever they penetrate the body, I can feel my whole body fill up with them within seconds. Demons are different than diseases. Their effect usually is not a sickness or pain. Whenever I would kill any insect or meet with someone possessed by demons or say *hish* to a cat or dog, demons from their bodies would immediately penetrate my body. I never felt any sickness or pain whenever demons from the air or another body decided to possess my body. I always felt their effects in my mind. They are extremely powerful when it comes to controlling any mind. I sometimes feel slow or sleepy when they try to control my mind. A few times, I had to deal with some extremely powerful demons, but whenever I started communicating with

هناك الكثير من الأمثلة اليومية على ذلك منها ما يلي: نسيان شيء ما كلبس ساعة اليد أو وضع محفظة النقود في جيوبنا أو نسيان الاتصال بشخص ما والكثير. وعندما لا نكون نفكر بتلك الأشياء المنسية، تخطر على بالنا فجأة. ويحدث هذا من قبل شيطان يكون متواجد حولنا أو داخلنا. يقوم ذلك الجن بتنويمنا مغناطيسياً ويقوم بتغذيتنا بهذا النوع من المعلومات في عقولنا في جميع الأوقات. مجدداً، إن الشياطيين تختلف عن الأمراض بنفس الطريقة التي يختلف فيها الإنسان عن الأسود أو الأفاعي.

وتقوم الشياطيين بتغذية أفكار مختلفة في عقولنا في جميع الأوقات عن طريق تنويمنا مغناطيسياً وجعلنا مدركين لشيء ما ومن ثم جعلنا نشك في أن لا نثق في أحد. خذ بعين الاعتبار عندما يحاول شخص ما بإبلاغنا بشيء ولكن عقولنا ليست جاهزة لقبول ما يقوله ونظهر عدم الثقة كنتيجة لذلك. حيث أن وراء كل تلك الأشياء شياطيين.

ثلاث أمنيات الجن/أو مصباح الجن ولا يوجد هناك أي شيطان بإمكانه عمل سحر لتحقيق شيء ما حتى لو كانت أمنية من خلال سحر؟ فكل تلك عبارة عن شائعات. ولا يوجد شيء يسمى مصباح الجن.

في السنوات القليلة الماضية، لم أرى قط أي من الشياطيين التي تقوم بتحويل نفسها الى أشكال أخرى. حيث أن الميزة الوحيد التي يمتلكها الجن هي تمديد أنفسهم حينما يتغلغلون الى جسم شخص ما. عندما يتغلغلون في الجسم، أستطيع أن أشعر بها في جميع أنحاء جسمي خلال ثوان معدودة. وتختلف الشياطيين عن الأمراض. حيث أن تأثيرها لا يظهر من خلال المرض أو الألم. عندما أود قتل أي حشرة أو مقابلة شخص ما مسيطر عليه من قبل الجن أو قول "هش" للقط أو الكلب، تخرج الشياطيين من أجسامهم مباشرة وتتغلغل في جسمي. فلم أشعر قط بالمرض أو الألم عندما تقرر الشياطيين الدخول الى جسمي. ودائماً ما كنت أشعر بتأثيرها على عقلي. فهي قوية للغاية عندما تود السيطرة على عقلي. وأحياناً ما أشعر بالبطء أو النعاس عندما تحاول السيطرة على عقلي. وفي بعض الأحيان، كان يتوجب علي التعامل مع بعض الشياطيين ذي القوى الخارقة ولكن عندما أبدأ الاتصال بهم

them and told them about their actions or point toward other flying demons, they change their behavior immediately. In the beginning, it was difficult. Usually, it would take two to three days to convince a demon to leave my body, but nowadays, I can make any demon my friend very easily and very quickly. Once they figure out that I sense them or see them no one, they start to behave. Simple Demons can do whatever they can do by using their powers of hypnotism or by using their powers of possessing anybody. But by using magic powers, they cannot bring bunch of money for us or they cannot build palace or a home for us. Or they cannot do any of magical tricks, whatever we see in movies or read in story books associated to demons.

A year ago, I selected eight demons. I asked them to wake me up at a certain time in the morning. And at exactly the same time, they would come and wake me up. Most of the time, I was not willing to wake up immediately, so I usually told them that I needed to sleep for thirty more minutes, and they would come back after thirty minutes and wake me up again. Usually, I told them which part of the body they needed to touch to wake me up. I could easily feel their touch when they tried to wake me up.

Once they become aware of me or once they become my friends, they do not come inside my body. Everyone has some special signals to inform me that they are around or want to communicate with me. Only new demons penetrate my body, but once I ask them to come out, they do not stay inside me for more than a few minutes. When I am friendly with all kinds of demons from different parts of the world, I always ask them a few questions. I ask if they can convert themselves into human shape or any animal shape or if they can change themselves into bigger demons when they are in the air or if they can move anything physically. I never find out anything about this from them.

In my opinion, given the data I have collected, the lamp demon that supposedly grants three wishes is just a story, nothing real. Demons cannot change themselves to look more evil like the ones we see in

وإخبارهم عن أفعالهم أو الإشارة الى الشياطيين الطائرة في الجو، يقومون بتغيير تصرفاتهم فوراً. في البداية، كل من الصعب فعل ذلك، وفي العادة قد يستغرق الأمر يومان أو ثلاثة أيام لإقناع شيطانٍ ما في الخروج من جسمي ولكن في هذه الأيام باستطاعتي أن أكون صديقاً مع الجن بكل سهولة وبسرعة. وعندما يشعر الجن بأنني أستطيع الشعور بهم ورؤيتهم، يبدؤون بالتصرف. وتعمل الشياطيين البسيطة ما تشاء باستخدام قوى التنويم المغناطيسي أو استخدام قواها في السيطرة على شخص ما. ولكن باستخدام القوى الساحرة، فهم لا يجلبون الكثير من النقود لنا ولا يستطيعون بناء قصر أو منزل لنا. ولا يستطيعون فعل أي من تلك الخدع السحرية، بغض النظر عن ما نراه في الأفلام أو نقرأه في الكتب متصل بالجن.

وقيل حوالي سنة، قم باختيار ثمانية شياطيين. وطلبت منهم ايقاظي في وقت معين من الصباح؟ وفي نفس الوقت بالضبط، كانت تأتي وتوقظني؟ وفي أغلب الأحيان، لم يكن لدي أي نية في الاستيقاظ فوراً لذلك كنت أقول لهم بأنني أود النوم لمدة ثلاثين دقيقة وكانوا يأتون لإيقاظي بعد ثلاثين دقيقة؟ وعادة ما كنت أبلغهم أي جزء من جسمي عليهم لمسه لإيقاظي. وكنت أشعر بسهولة بلمستهم عند محاولتهم ايقاظي.

وعندما يشعر الجن بي ونصبح أصدقاء، لا يدخلون الى جسمي. حيث أن كل شخص له إشارات خاصة لإبلاغي بأنهم حوالي أو أنهم يريدون الاتصال بي. فقط الشياطيين الجديدة هي التي تتغلغل في جسمي ولكن عندما أطلب منهم الخروج، لا يبقون داخل جسمي لأكثر من بضع دقائق. وعندما أكون صديق لهم، أقوم بسؤالهم عدة أسئلة. أسألهم حول امكانية تحويل أنفسهم إلى هيئة إنسان أو حيوان أو تحويل أنفسهم الى شياطيين أكبر حجماً عند تواجدهم في الهواء وحول امكانيتهم من تحريك شيء ما. ولم أرى شيئاً من ذلك من قبلهم.

وفي رأيي الشخصي، وطبقاً للبيانات التي قمت بجمعها، فإن مصباح الشيطان، والذي من المفترض أن يمنحك ثلاث أمنيات، هو عبارة عن قصة فقط لا غير. حيث أن الشياطيين لا تستطيع التغيير من شكلها للظهور أكثر شراً كالتي نراها في

pictures and movies. They do not look like big or ugly ghosts. They don't have big teeth or red eyes or big nails or long arms, and they are not twenty or thirty feet tall. They are just small, flying object with extraordinary powers.

Can I take any demon out of someone's body?

Yes, very easily, even if they are not around me or in front of me. Regardless of which part of the world people are in, I can move demons if I have seen them or have at least seen their picture. Otherwise, if I have never seen them, then I can do it over the telephone very easily. But I prefer at least to see a photo of people before I help them. The rest is very easy. The same process can be applied to different kind of pains. I can take out any pain from anybody very easily. Though I can help through the telephone, seeing them in person or at least seeing their photos will help a lot. I will fix their pains, but these pains, sicknesses, and diseases always leave some damages or symptoms inside the body. Consequently, those people need to take some medication to fix symptoms if they do not want to suffer from that pain again and again.

When you are talking to yourself? How we talk to demons around/inside us?

Some people move their lips and actually talk aloud to themselves. Most people just talk to themselves without moving their lips. This is normal when we are arguing or fighting or trying to discuss something with ourselves. In all those cases, we are actually communicating with our demons. Demons feed a number of ideas and impressions into our minds, but most of the time, we do not agree with these. For example, consider the times when you are angry while driving. How many times do you think about running your car into a wall or pole or another car but suddenly control yourself and your mind? These kinds of feelings come out from demons through hypnotism. Weak-

الصور والأفلام. ولا يشبهون الأشباح الكبيرة والقبيحة الشكل. وليس لديهم أسنان كبيرة أو أعين حمراء اللون أو أظافر كبيرة أو أذرع طويلة ولا يبلغ طولهم من عشرين الى ثلاثين قدماً. بل إنها فقط أجسام صغيرة وطائرة وتمتلك قوى خارقة.

هل باستطاعتي إخراج الشيطان من جسم شخص ما؟

نعم، وبكل سهولة، حتى لو لم يكونوا حولي أو أمامي. وبغض النظر عن أي جزء من العالم وفيه أشخاص، فبإمكاني تحريك الشياطين في حال شعرت بهم أو على الأقل رأيت صورهم. وفي حال عدم رؤيتي لهم، فإنني أستطيع أن أفعل ذلك عن طريق الهاتف بسهولة. ولكن أفضل على الأقل رأيت صورة لهؤلاء الناس قبل أن أساعدهم. وأما الباقي فهو سهل للغاية. حيث يتم تطبيق نفس العملية الى الأنواع الأخرى من الآلام. فبإمكاني تخليص أي شخص من الآلام بكل سهولة. وعلى الرغم من قدرتي على مساعدة الأشخاص عن طريق الهاتف، إلا أنه على الأقل رؤية صور هؤلاء الأشخاص سيساعد أكثر. حيث أنني أقوم بعلاج آلامهم ولكن عادة لا تترك تلك الآلام والامراض بعض الضرر داخل جسم المريض. وبالتالي، يحتاج هؤلاء الأشخاص لأخذ بعض الأدوية لعلاج أعراض تلك الأمراض في حال أرادوا التخلص من معاناة ذلك الألم مرات ومرات.

متى تتحدث مع نفسك؟ وكيف نتحدث مع الشياطين الموجودون داخلنا؟

يقوم بعض الأشخاص بتحريك شفاههم وفي الحقيقة يتكلمون بصوت عالٍ مع أنفسهم. ويتحدث معظم الأشخاص إلى أنفسهم دون الحاجة إلى تحريك شفاههم. وهذا شيء طبيعي عندما نتجادل أو نتصارع أو نحاول مناقشة شيء ما مع أنفسنا. وفي تلك الحالات، نقوم فعلا بالاتصال مع الشياطين الموجود داخلنا. وتقوم تلك الشياطين بتغذية عقولنا ببعض الأفكار وانطباعات ولكن معظم الأوقات لا نتفق معهم. فعلى سبيل المثال، خذ في الاعتبار الأوقات التي نكون غاضبين أثناء القيادة. كم من المرات التي تفكر فيها حيال اصطدام سيارتك بالحائط أو عمود أو سيارة أخرى ولكن فجأة نتحكم بأنفسها وعقولنا؟ وتخرج تلك الأنواع المختلفة من الأحاسيس من الشياطين عن طريق التنويم المغناطيسي. ويصبح

minded people give more control of their minds to demons, so they have no control of their lips during communication with demons.

Wild wishes, bad wishes in our mind. Demons generate/ feed wild and crazy desires/wishes in our mind all the time.

Demons are free creatures with a lot of time on their hands. They have nothing to do if they are not fighting with each other. If they are around us all the time, they will feed wild and bad wishes into our minds by hypnotizing us. They will keep insisting that someone commit suicide, or they will create sexual desires or jealousy or hatred or other kinds of negative and bad wishes. These always come from demons around us. Sometimes they insist you slap someone or punch someone for no reason. They can easily amplify or boost our anger. They can easily make us sadder. They can keep us depressed for no reason. If you feel more negative qualities in yourself, then you need to start rejecting all those negative thoughts and wishes to reduce their control of your mind. If we follow them, they will enjoy more and will keep us in trouble all the time. Demons are responsible of feeding us all the crazy thoughts and wishes within our mind.

Fortune or Past or Present tellers
Past tellers usually has at least one demon for their Purpose

How come few people are able to tell us about our past, present, or future affairs? Usually, those fortune-tellers have a few or one very sincere demon around them, and they can easily communicate with their demons. As I have said several times, there are always a few demons in every house or office and/or around any human or animal. Those demons are around us for generations. They know everything about us and our family affairs and our family problems. When someone goes to fortune-tellers of any kind, those fortune-

الأشخاص الضعفاء عقلياً أكثر تحكماً بعقولهم عن طريق الشياطيين. لذلك هم لا يتحكمون بشفاههم أثناء التواصل مع الجن.

الأمنيات السيئة في عقولنا. تقوم الشياطيين بتغذية عقولنا بالأمنيات المجنونة والسيئة في عقولنا طوال الوقت.

إن الشياطيين مخلوقات حرة وتمتلك الكثير من الوقت. ولا يوجد لديهم أي شيء لفعله في حال عدم القتال مع بعضهم. وفي حال تواجدهم حولنا جميع الأوقات، سيقومون بتغذيتنا بالأمنيات السيئة عن طريق التنويم المغناطيسي. ويصرون أن يقوم شخص ما بالانتحار أو يقومون بخلق رغبات جنسية أو الغيرة أو الكراهية أو أي نوع من الامنيات السيئة والسلبية. وفي أحيانٍ أخرى، يقوم الجن بإقناعك بصفع أو ضرب شخص آخر بدونٍ أي سبب يذكر. وحيث يستطيع الجن تعزيز غضبنا بكل سهولة. وبإمكانهم جعلنا أكثر حزناً أو جعلنا مكتئبين بدون أي سبب. وعند شعورك بأشياء سلبية في نفسك، فإنك بحاجة للبدء في رفض سيطرة الجن لعقلك. وفي حال خضوعك لهم، سيستمتعون أكثر وسيجعلونك تقع أكثر في المشاكل في جميع الأوقات. وتكون الشياطيين مسؤولة عن تغذيتنا بالأفكار السيئة والامنيات داخل عقولنا.

العرافون
عادة ما يمتلك العرافون شيطان واحد على الأقل لتحقيق أهدافهم.

كيف يكون القليل من الأشخاص قادرين على اخبارنا بماضينا وحاضرنا والعلاقات المستقبلية التي تخصنا؟ في العادة، يمتلك هؤلاء العرافون (المتكهنون بالغيب) القليل أو شيطان واحد جداً مخلص لهم وهو بدوره يتواصل مع شياطيين آخرين. وكما أسلفت الذكر لعدة مرات. دائماً ما يكون هناك العديد من الشياطيين في كل جميع المنازل او مكتب العمل أو حولنا. ويبقون حولنا لأجيال عديدة وهم يعلمون كل شيء عنا والعلاقات العائلية الخاصة بنا وما تحويها من مشاكل. وعندما يذهب أحد إلى العرافيين على اختلاف أنواعهم يقوم

tellers ask their demons to communicate with other demons that are around us or around those people. A fortune-teller's demons find information from our demons and transfer it to the fortuneteller. After that, the fortune-teller tells us about our past and current problems, affairs, and habits. And we are surprised when that fortune-teller knows everything about us. In this way, fortunetellers make money from us their demons, and communicate information about any person through hypnotism in their mind. These people collect information about people by the use of their demon. So simple, fortune teller's demon, communicate with our demon to collect information about us. And by hypnotism feed that information in the mind of that fortune teller. And fortune teller, use those information to impress us.

Can demons make anyone an extremist?

Normal people are always nonextremist. Demons are helpful and sincere with many people; however, they are basically naughty, and their base is negativism. Demons do not spread positive energy. Demons are negative energy, so they will always amplify negative activity or negative energy. Demons are behind extremeness, regardless of the field or scope. Few people have extreme behavior about religion, and few are extremists in politics. Few are extremists because of race or language. Some have extreme behavior toward their spouse or beloved. Extreme behavior is a negative quality. And demons are behind this bad habit. Demons never give up. They boost and amplify extreme behavior by hypnotizing us. Usually, these kinds of people are under the influence of more than one demon. Even if we understand this point, even if we figure out that our extreme behavior is the result of a few powerful demons and those demons are controlling our mind by hypnotizing us, we still cannot do anything, because people who display extreme behaviors have weak minds. The only way to fix their problems is by resisting extreme behaviors. They need to practice a lot to control their emotions, intentions, and

هؤلاء العرافون بمطالبة شياطينهم للاتصال بشياطين اخرى من حولنا أو حول أشخاص معينين. ويجد شيطان العراف المعلومات من شياطين آخرين وينقل تلك المعلومات الى العراف. وبعد ذلك، يخبرنا العراف عن ماضينا والمشاكل التي تواجهنا في الوقت الحالي والعلاقات والعادات. ونتفاجأ عندما يعلم العراف كل شيء عنا. وفي هذه الحالة، يجني العرافون النقود منا. حيث يجمع هؤلاء الأشخاص المعلومات عن أشخاص آخرين باستخدام شياطين يسيطرون عليها. وبتلك البساطة، يتصل شيطان العراف بشيطان آخر يسيطر على عقلنا ويجمع المعلومات عنا. ويقوم ذلك الشيطان بتغذية المعلومات للعراف عن طريق التنويم المغناطيسي. ويستخدم العراف تلك المعلومات ليتفاجأنا.

هل بإمكان الجن جعل أي شخص متطرف؟

دائماً ما يكون الأشخاص العاديون غير متطرفين. ويساعد الجن ويخلص للكثير من البشر، علاوة على ذلك، فهم سخيفون وأساسهم سلبي. حيث أن الشياطين لا تنشر الطاقة الإيجابية. فهم يملكون طاقة سلبية. لذلك فهم دائماً ما يعززون النشاط السلبي والطاقة السلبية. فالشياطين تكون السبب وراء التطرف بغض النظر عن المجال. ويمتلك العديد من الأشخاص التصرف المتطرف حيال الدين وبعضهم الآخر متطرفون حيال السياسة. وهناك البعض متطرف حيال العرق أو اللغة أو المحبوبين. ويعتبر التصرف المتطرف هو سلوكا سلبي. وتقف جميع الشياطين وراء تلك العادات. ولا يستسلمون أبداً. فهم يعززون سلوك التطرف عن طريق التنويم المغناطيسي. وفي العادة، يخضع هؤلاء الأشخاص لتأثير أكثر من شيطان واحد. حتى لو أدركنا تلك النقطة، وحتى لو اكتشفنا بأن تصرف التطرف هو نتيجة لبعض الشياطين ذي القوى الخارقة وأن تلك الشياطين تتحكم في عقولنا عن طريق التنويم المغناطيسي، ولكننا نبقى عاجزون عن فعل أي شيء لأن الأشخاص الذين يظهرون سلوك التطرف يمتلكون عقول ضعيفة. وإن الطريقة الوحيدة لحل مشاكلهم هي مقومة سلوك التطرف. فهم بحاجة الي الممارسة كثيرة للتحكم بعواطفهم ونواياهم و

thoughts. And when they feel that they only have limited control of that extreme behavior, they need to contact someone like me who can help them exorcize those demons. Everything is possible. They just need a little bit more power to help.

The soul/spirit is a positive energy.
Demons are negative energy.

The soul or spirit is a permanent positive energy of a living body. Souls/spirits reside inside the body until the body is alive. Soul/spirit is completely positive energy. Soul/spirit has limited power to operate bodily functions. The soul/spirit keeps us alive. Soul/spirit is a combination of thousands of smaller positive energies. The combination of all positive energies is a soul/spirit within the body. In a living body, thousands of positive energies are individually responsible for performing different bodily functions. Keep in mind that the combination of all these positive energies is the soul/spirit.

All these positive energies in the living body are responsible for doing individual functions or operations. If we have five hundred kinds of different hormones in our bodies, then a positive energy is individually responsible for the function and operation of that hormone. The same applies to each bone, each joint, each muscle, each organ, and even our blood. All parts of the body have a positive energy. That positive energy is responsible for bodily functions. Positive energy is confined inside our body and has limited powers. We can increase the powers of positive energy by using or by adopting healthy rules of life. We can eat healthy, keep our body strong and healthy, and avoid bad and unhealthy habits. Keep a positive approach and avoid negative thinking. This is the only thing we can control to make our all positive energies stronger. As I said, the positive energy or energies of a normal person have limited powers, and they can function only within our living body. And as I explained earlier, each positive energy has a separate responsibility. For example, if a positive energy is responsible for producing insulin in our bodies, then this

وأفكارهم. وعندما يشعرون بأن سيطرتهم محدودة فيما يخص تصرف التطرف، سيحتاجون شخص آخر للاتصال به مثلي لمساعدتهم في التخلص من تلك الشياطين. كل شيء محتمل، وهم يحتاجون الى القليل من القوة للمساعدة.

الروح (النفس البشرية) هي طاقة إيجابية.
بينما يمتلك الجن طاقة سلبية.

إن النفس البشرية أو الروح هي طاقة إيجابية دائمة في الجسم الحي. فهي تسكن داخل الجسم وهي طاقة إيجابية خالصة وقوتها محدودة في إطار تنظيم وعمل الوظائف الجسدية. وهي تبقينا على قيد الحياة. وهي أيضاً اندماج من آلاف من الطاقات الإيجابية الصغيرة. بالإضافة الى تداخل جميع الطاقات الإيجابية في النفس البشرية للجسم. ويوجد هناك الآلاف من الطاقات الإيجابية في الجسم الحي وهي مسؤولة بشكل فردي في إنجاز الوظائف الجسدية المختلفة. ويجب الأخذ بعين الاعتبار بأن هذا الاندماج للطاقات الإيجابية يكون النفس البشرية/الروح.

إن جميع تلك الطاقات الإيجابية في الجسم الحي مسؤولة عن عمل الوظائف أو العمليات الفردية. وفي حال وجود خمس مئة نوع من الهرمونات في أجسامنا، فإن هناك طاقة إيجابية واحدة مسؤولة بشكل فردي عن وظيفة وعمليات ذلك الهرمون. والشيء نفسه ينطبق على كل عظمة في الجسم وكل مفصل وعضلة وعضو وحتى الدم الذي يجري في العروق. وتحتوي جميع أجزاء الجسم على الطاقة الإيجابية حيث أنها مسؤولة عن الوظائف الجسدية وهي محجوزة داخل أجسامنا ولديها قوة محدودة. فباستطاعتنا زيادة قوى الطاقات الإيجابية باستخدام أو تبني القواعد الصحية في الحياة. حيث أنه بإمكاننا أن نتناول طعام صحي ونحافظ على أجسامنا قوية وصحية ونتجنب العادات السيئة وغير الصحية. والحفاظ على الطريقة الإيجابية وتجنب التفكير السلبي. فهذه هي الطريقة الوحيدة للسيطرة والحفاظ على طاقاتنا الإيجابية أكثر قوة. وكما أسلف الذكر، إن الطاقة أو الطاقات الإيجابية للإنسان الطبيعي محدودة وبإمكانها العمل فقط داخل أجسامنا الحية. وأوضحت سابقاً أن كل طاقة إيجابية لها مسؤولية منفصلة عن غيرها. على سبيل المثال، إذا كانت طاقة إيجابية ما مسؤولة عن إنتاج الأنسولين في أجسامنا، فهي هي

is its job, and that's all it can do. This energy will not go to our knee joints and help operate the knee. In the same way, a positive energy is responsible for controlling the function of knee joints and their operations, and that energy will do only that. That positive energy will not go to the pancreas and control the production of insulin. Positive energies are only our internal energies. They keep us alive, and they have limited strength just to do the work/functions assigned to them. As compared to positive energies, all negative energies all external energies. External energies are not part of the soul or spirit. Negative energies are not helpful to run any of our body's functions or operations. These negative energies mainly consist of diseases, sicknesses, and demons.

Positive medications like vitamins, pills, and syrups are not positive energies. These positive medications are only a help to strengthen our internal positive energies so that they can do a better job and fight against external negative energies. In the same way, good food, workouts, and healthy habits increase the strength of internal positive energies. Any negative external energy (like disease or sickness or pain or demons) cannot damage any organ, cannot make us sick, cannot control our mind, cannot make us extra angry, cannot make us depressed/sad, cannot give us pain, cannot stop production of insulin hormone cannot damage knee joints or any other joint, cannot damage function of thyroid glands, cannot create health problems, and cannot damage livers or kidneys unless the external negative energy is more powerful than internal/positive energies.

Internal positive energies are strong enough to do the regular operations of organs, and they are powerful enough to save us from the attack of external energies. But internal positive energies have limited powers and are only responsible for performing particular functions. However, negative external energies have unlimited powers. We only feel pain or experience sickness—including production of insulin hormone or any other hormone, heartburn or stomach ulcers, mental sickness, arthritis or any joint pain, liver damage or kidney function failure, infections etc., as well as shortness of temper,

وظيفتها لعمل ذلك لا غير. ولن تقوم هذه الطاقة للمساعدة في عمل مفاصل الركبة أو الركبة ككل. وبنفس الطريقة، تكون هناك طاقة إيجابية تكون مسؤولة عن التحكم بوظيفة مفاصل الركبة وعملياتها. فلا تستطيع تلك الطاقة في عمل البنكرياس والتحكم في إنتاج الأنسولين. حيث إن الطاقات الإيجابية هي فقط طاقات داخل أجسامنا. وتبقينا أحياء ولديها قوة محدودة للقيام بالوظائف الموكلة لها. مقارنةً مع الطاقات الإيجابية، فإن الطاقات السلبية هي طاقات خارجية. وهذه الطاقات الخارجية ليست جزءاً من الروح أو النفس البشرية. وهي طاقات ضارة في حال التحكم في أي وظيفة من وظائف الجسم أو عملياته. وتحتوي تلك الطاقات بشكل رئيسي على الأمراض والسقم والشياطيين.

وإن الأدوية الإيجابية مثل الفيتامينات والحبوب والدواء المحلول لا تعتبر طاقات إيجابية. فهي فقط للمساعدة في تقوية طاقاتنا الإيجابية الداخلية للقيام بوظائفها بشكل أفضل ومقاومة الطاقات السلبية الخارجية. وبنفس الطريقة، تزيد الأطعمة الصحية والتدريبات والعادات الصحية من قوة الطاقات الإيجابية الداخلية. ولا تستطيع الطاقة السلبية الخارجية (مثل المرض والألم والجن) من تدمير أي عضو أو جعلنا مرضى أو التحكم في عقولنا أو جعلنا غاضبين جداً أو جعلنا مكتئبين/حزينين أو التسبب لنا بالألم أو ايقاف انتاج هرمون الأنسولين أو تدمير مفاصل الركبة أو أي مفصل آخر أو تدمير وظيفة الغدد الدرقية أو التسبب بالمشاكل الصحية أو تدمير الكبد والكلى إلا إذا كانت هذه الطاقة السلبية الخارجية أكثر قوة من الطاقات الإيجابية الداخلية.

إن الطاقات الإيجابية الداخلية قوية كفاية لعمل الوظائف المنتظمة للأعضاء وقوية أيضاً كفاية لحفظنا من هجمات الطاقات الخارجية. ولكن لدى الطاقات الإيجابية الداخلية قوى محدودة وهي فقط مسؤولة عن إنجاز وظائف محددة. علاوة على ذلك، فإن الطاقات السلبية الخارجية لديها قوى خارقة. نحن فقط نشعر بالألم أو المرض_ وما يشمله من انتاج الأنسولين أو أي هرمون آخر كحرقة المعدة وقرحة المعدة والسقم العقلي والتهاب المفاصل وآلام المفاصل وتلف الكبد أو فشل في وظائف الكلى والعدوى، الخ. بالإضافة الى ضيق المزاج

insomnia, extremism—when external negative energies beat our internal positive energies. Internal/positive energy never gives up as long as we are alive. Positive energy or in scientific language i.e. body immunity. If internal positive energy i.e. immunity is strong enough to protect our body from the attack of external disease/pain, we will stay healthy. If positive energy or immunity power will decrease /reduce then all kind of external negative energy i.e. sickness/pain, will come to our body and will keep us sick and damaged. So, when we take painkillers or other medications, they increase the strength of our internal positive energies so that we can fight against external negative energies. But external negative energies have more strength and can work against our body for a long time and damage them completely. If the organs or parts of the body are completely damaged, then the only thing that will help internal positive energy is replacing those damaged organs or parts. And we must keep taking the related medications to increase the powers of internal positive energies.

Every disease, sickness, and pain is fixable. But can anyone be sure about how long we can fix them? Internal positive energy has limited powers. If someone is using the right medication, then a person like me can help him or her by using powers to remove those external negative energies (demons) from his or her mind or body. I can only help to reduce the pressure of external negative energy, and I can easily remove that external negative energy; however, it is your responsibility to fix your organs and take proper medications to increase the strength of your positive internal energies so that they can function better.

My powers can control external negative energies within and around your bodies, and I can help until you have enough time to fix your internal injuries by using proper medication. I can clear your body of external negative energy, but the rest is your responsibility. God has not given me powers to regenerate any organ or body part or heal their damage—not yet at least. By now, you should understand that your positive internal energy is inside you and that all you can control are your workouts, your healthy eating habits, and your medication;

والأرق والتطرف ـ عندما تتغلب الطاقات السلبية الخارجية على طاقاتنا الإيجابية الداخلية. ولا تستسلم الطاقات الإيجابية الداخلية أبداً طالما نحن احياء. إن الطاقة الإيجابية تعني بلغة أوضح مناعة الجسم، وفي حال أن تلك المناعة قوية لحماية أجسامنا من هجمات الآلام والأمراض الخارجية، سنبقى صحيحين بدنيا وفي حال تناقص تلك المناعة/الطاقة الإيجابية فإن جميع أنواع الطاقات السلبية الخارجية مثل المرض/والألم ستأتي إلى أجسامنا وسنبقى مريضين. لذلك، عندما نتناول مسكنات الآلام أو أي نوع أخر من الأدوية، فإنها تقوم بزيادة قوة طاقاتنا الإيجابية الداخلية للمساعدة في مقاومة الطاقات السلبية الخارجية. ولكن الطاقات الخارجية السلبية تكون أكثر قوة وبإمكانها العمل ضد أجسامنا لفترة طويلة من الزمن وتدميرها بشكل كامل. وفي حال تم تدمير أعضاء أو أجزاء من الجسم، فإن الشيء الوحيد لمساعدة الطاقة الإيجابية الداخلية هو استبدال تلك الأجزاء أو الأعضاء التالفة. وعلينا الاستمرار في تناول الأدوية لزيادة قوة الطاقات الإيجابية الداخلية.

إن جميع الأمراض والآلام يمكن علاجها. ولكن هل بإمكان أي شخص أن يكون متأكداً من طول الفترة التي نحتاجها لعلاجها؟ إن الطاقات الإيجابية الداخلية لديها قوى محدودة, وفي حال قيام شخص ما استخدام الدواء الصحيح فإن ذلك الشخص يشبهني في المساعدة في استخدام القوى للتخلص من تلك الطاقات السلبية الخارجية (الشياطين)من عقله أو جسمه. فبإمكاني فقط المساعدة في تخفيف الضغط للطاقة السلبية الخارجية وأستطيع بكل سهولة التخلص من الطاقة الخارجية السلبية، علاوة على ذلك، أنت مسؤول عن علاج أعضاء جسمك وتناول الأدوية الصحيحة لزيادة قوة الطاقات الإيجابية الداخلية في جسمك حتى يعملن بشكل أفضل.

باستطاعة قواي التحكم في الطاقات السلبية الخارجية داخل وحول أجسامنا، وأستطيع أن أساعد حتى تمتلك الوقت الكافي لعلاج جروحك الخارجية باستخدام الأدوية الصحيحة. حيث منحني الله تلك القوى لإعادة تشغيل أي عضو من الجسم أو لعلاج التلف الحاصل به ـ ولكن ليس بع على الأقل. وحتى الآن، ينبغي عليك الإدراك أن طاقتك الإيجابية الداخلية هي في داخلك وما تستطيع السيطرة عليه هي تدريباتك وعادات الأكل الصحية وأدويتك

however, you cannot control external negative energy. I can help with that.

Do demons, disease, or pains have any restrictions?

This is a question that even I am confused about. Do these negative external energies have any restrictions or a particular schedule or list from God of the people whom they need to make sick? Or are they free to choose anyone anytime? God knows better.

Who is the boss of our minds?

We are the bosses of our minds. The only problem is that if we don't have strong minds, demons can easily hypnotize and use us however they like. Still, we are bosses of our minds, but demons amplify everything negative. If we are a little bit angry, they will make us angrier. If we are a little bit sad, they will make us more depressed and insist that we commit suicide, kill someone, or hurt someone. If we do not like someone, demons will increase that hate. Because of their nature of negativism, demons are compelled to take us on a negative path. Even though we are the bosses of our minds, we still follow their instructions unconsciously. Once we are aware that all extreme conditions are not coming from our minds but a demon playing with us, then we need to start practicing controlling our extreme behaviors. It is not easy for anyone to get rid of a demon from a body or mind, but once you figure out how to resist all extreme actions and temperaments, then you can at least attempt to fight these negative influences. If you try but still cannot control your mind and behavior, this is the time when you need someone like me who can move that demon away from you. Usually, demons have been around or inside you since your childhood, and these are tougher and resist a lot before they leave someone, because they think you are their property, toy, or residence. Once someone takes that demon away from you, you will have an empty place or a vacancy available for a new demon.

علاوة على ذلك، لا تستطيع السيطرة على الطاقة الخارجية السلبية. ولكن أنا أستطيع المساعدة في ذلك.

هل يوجد معوقات للآلام أو الأمراض؟

هذا السؤال يحيرني أنا. هل يوجد لتلك الطاقات السلبية الخارجية أي معوقات أو جدول معين أو قائمة منحها لها الله لأناس يحتاجون أن يمرضوا؟ أم أنهم أحرار في اختيار أي شخص وفي أي وقت؟ الله وحدة أعلم.

من هو مالك عقولنا؟

نحن من نملك عقولنا. ولكن المشكلة الوحيدة تمكن فيما إذا كنا لا نمتلك عقول قوية، فإن الشياطين تستطيع بكل سهولة تنويمنا واستخدامنا كيفما يشاؤون. ولكن ما نزال مالكين لعقولنا وتقوم الشياطين بضخ كل شيء سلبي داخل عقولنا. في حال كنا غاضبين قليلاً، ستجعلنا الشياطين أكثر غضباً. وفي حال كان حزينين قليلاً سيجعلوننا أكثر اكتئابا ويقنعوننا بالإقدام على الانتحار أو قتل شخص ما أو الحاق الضرر بأي شخص. وفي حال كنا لا نحب شخصاً ما، ستزيد الشياطين من تلك الكراهية. وبسبب طبيعتهم السلبية، فإنها تكون مجبرة على جرنا الى الطريق السلبي. وعلى الرغم من أننا نملك عقولنا، ولكننا نخضع لتعليماتهم بشكل غير واعي. وعندما ندرك كل تلك الظروف المتطرفة تكون غير قادمة من عقولنا وأن الشياطين هي من تلعب بها، نعلم حينها بأننا نحتاج الى البدء في التدرب على السيطرة على تصرفاتنا المتطرفة. وليس من السهل التخلص من شيطان ما واخراجه من عقولنا واجسامنا ولكن عندما تكتشف كيفية مقاومة جميع الأفعال المتطرفة، فإنه بإمكانك على الأقل المحاولة في مقاومة تلك التأثيرات السلبية. وفي حال كنت تحاول ولا تستطيع السيطرة على عقلك وتصرفاتك، فإنه هذا هو الوقت الذي تحتاج فيه لشخص آخر مثلي ممن يستطيع اخراج ذلك الجن بعيداً عن جسمك. وفي العادة، تكون الشياطين حولك أو داخلك منذ طفولتك، وهذه تكون أصعب للمقاومة قبل اخراجها من الجسم لأنها تعتقد بأنك ملكيتهم ودميتهم أو سكنهم الذي يعيشون فيه. وعندما يخرج شخص ما ذلك الشيطان من جسمك سيكون هناك مكان فارغ أو شاغر متوفر لشيطان جديد لكي يدخل الى جسمك.

But no one will have strong control on you if you keep practicing to control and reduce negative behaviors, lessen anger, and keep a cool temperament. I or someone like me can remove those demons from you to give you enough time to maintain control of your mind. Once you quit listening and quit following demons, they will not waste their time with you. They will find someone else more interesting for them. Finally, you can become the boss of your mind again!

How can you stop them so they do not enter your body?

This is impossible to stop them from entering a body. Even though I have good control, if a new demon comes around me, it still goes inside my body immediately. Usually, it is not hurtful or painful like diseases or sickness when a demon penetrates our bodies. Still, few people may experience a condition like low or high blood pressure, depending upon the power, size, and aggression of the demons. My senses developed differently than the normal person's. I can feel a demon's presence like you can touch or hug of another person. The way you don't feel comfortable if someone keeps holding your body, I can tolerate any demon inside or around me. It makes me really uncomfortable. There are several ways you can try to keep them away from you. But they penetrate inside the body so quietly even you will feel nothing. Slowly and steadily, you will experience some aggression and extremism.

Normal people cannot sense demons. Once you will be able to sense/feel them, you will not be able to tolerate them. You will be uncomfortable and disturbed until they leave your body. So, thank God that normal people have no clue or feelings when demons start residing inside their bodies. Trust me—it is not easy to get rid of any demon from your body. I went through so many problems. Finally, I gained a little bit of control over them, and they now listen to me most of the time. Otherwise, I am able to insist that they listen to me. Usually, they create some problems for me; however, once we have been introduced, they trust me, and they become better friends than

ولكن لن يمتلك أي شخص سيطرة قوية عليك إذا حافظت على التدرب بشأن التحكم وتقليل التصرفات السلبية، ويخفف الغضب والحفاظ على المزاج الهادئ. أستطيع أنا أو أي شخص مثلي اخراج تلك الشياطين من جسمك لمنحك الوقت الكافي للحفاظ على السيطرة على عقلك. وعندما ترفض الاستماع الخضوع للشياطيين، فلن يضيعوا وقتهم معهم. سيقومون بالبحث عن شخص آخر يثير اهتمامهم أكثر. وفي النهاية، تستطيع أن تصبح مالكاً لعقلك مرة أخرى.

كيف بإمكان ايقافهم حتى لا يدخلوا الى جسمك؟

من المستحيل ايقافهم من الدخول الى أي جسم. على الرغم من أنني أملك سيطرة جيدة نوعاً ما، ففي حال قيام شيطان جديد بالقدوم حولي يدخل الى جسمي مباشرة. وفي العادة، يكون الأمر غير مؤذي وغير مؤلم كالأمراض عند دخول وتغلغل الجن الى أجسامنا. ولكن، من المحتمل أن ينتاب بعض الناس شعور كارتفاع أو انخفاض ضغط الدم بالاعتماد على القوة وحجم وعدوانية الشياطيين. وقد تطورت أحاسيسي بشكل مختلف عن الشخص العادي. فباستطاعتي الشعور بوجود الشياطيين كأنك تلمس أو تخضن شخصاً ما. إن الطريقة التي لا تجعل بالشعور بالراحة في حال استمرار شخص ما مسك جسمك، أستطيع تحامل وجود أي شيطان داخل جسمي أو حولي. فهو يجعلني غير مرتاح. وهناك العديد من الطرق لمحاولة بقائها بعيداً عنك. ولكنها تتغلغل داخل الجسم بكل هدوء حتى لو لم تشعر بأي شيء. ببطء وثبات، ستواجه بعض العداء والتطرف.

لا يستطيع الأشخاص العاديون من الشعور بالشياطيين. وعندما تكون قادراً على الشعور/الإحساس بهم، فلن تكون قادراً على تحاملهم. ستصبح غير مرتاح ومنزعج حتى يغادروا جسمك. لذلك، الشكر لله بأن الأشخاص العاديون لا يعلمون أو يشعرون عند دخول الشياطيين الى أجسامهم. ثق بي-ليس من السهل التخلص من أي شيطان واخراجه من جسمك. وقد واجهت هذه المشاكل. وفي النهاية، حصلت على القليل من السيطرة عليهم وهم الآن يستمعون إلي معظم الأوقات. وبطريقة أخرى، فإنني قادر على اقناعهم بالاستماع إلي. وفي أغلب الأحيان، تسبب لي بعض المشاكل، علاوة على ذلك، عندما يقدمون أنفسهم، فإنهم يثقون بي ونصبح أصدقاء أفضل بدلاً من

human. They behave better than humans. They are less harmful than humans and animals. This is only true in my case. This is not true for everyone. So, remember that no one can stop demons from coming into our homes or our bodies, but by controlling our behaviors and minds, we can reduce their influence in our bodies and lives.

The simple rule is the following: We need to make ourselves less interesting for them. They like extremism, anger, depression, negativism, and bad habits like drinking and drugs. Quit the bad stuff and curb your bad temperament and they will be less interested in us and will look for someone more interesting for them.

Are animals a big cause of diseases?

The animals around us are an especially big cause of the spread of diseases. Given my knowledge and experience, I believe that demons do not favor any particular body to live in or damage. For them, all humans, insects, and reptiles are the same. They definitely don't want to struggle too much. That's why most of them prefer already damaged or sick bodies or organs, regardless if they belong to humans or other animals.

These days, we are finding and learning more and more about new diseases, pains, and sicknesses. The reason for this is because the population of everything is increasing. Most people are moving and traveling from one part of the world to another. And animal health is not as important in most areas of the world. One animal may get sick and die. After a few days, diseases come out from them. Demons in their bodies come out from them, and they do not go too far. Wherever they find damaged organs, they penetrate that body and start damaging them even more. If they do not find a damaged or sick body, they just go inside a healthy body and start damaging it.

I used to kill insects and reptiles frequently, but since I started sensing these demons, I have developed a lot of problem killing them, because

البشر. فهم يتصرفون بشكل أفضل من البشر. فهم أقل ضرراً من الإنسان والحيوان. فهذا صحيحاً في حالتي. وهو أيضاً غير صحيح لكل شخص. لذلك، تذكر بأن لا يستطيع أي شخص من ايقاف الشياطين من الدخول الى منازلنا أو أجسامنا، ولكن عن طريق التحكم بتصرفاتنا وعقولنا، بإمكاننا تخفيف تأثيرها في أجسامنا وحياتنا.

إن القاعدة ببساطة هي كالتالي: نحتاج الى جعل أنفسنا أقل اهتماماً بهم. فهم يحبون التطرف والغضب والاكتئاب والسلبية والعادات السيئة كشرب الكحول وتناول المخدرات. ابتعد عن العادات السيئة واكبح جماح مزاجك السيء وسيكونون أقل اهتماماً بك وسيبحثون عن شخص آخر أكثر اهتماماً.

هل تعتبر الحيوانات سبب كبير للأمراض؟

إن الحيوانات من حولنا اكبر سبب لانتشار الأمراض. وطبقاً لمعرفتي وخبرتي، أعتقد أن الشياطين لا تفضل أي شخص معين للعيش فيه أو تدميره. بالنسبة لهم، جميع البشر والحشرات والزواحف في نفس مستوى اهتمامهم. فهم لا يحبذون المقاومة كثيراً. لهذا السبب تفضل معظمهم الأجسام المريضة أو التالفة سابقاً بغض النظر حوال ما إذا كانوا ينتمون الى بشر أو حيوانات أخرى.

وفي هذه الأيام، نحن نكتشف ونتعلم الكثير عن الأمراض الجديدة والآلام والسقم. وإن السبب وراء ذلك هو أن عدد سكان العالم في تزايد مستمر. والكثير من الأشخاص يتنقلون ويسافرون من مكان الى آخر في هذا العالم. ولا تعتبر صحة الحيوان بأهمية صحة الأنسان في معظم أنحاء العالم. فمن المحتمل أن يمرض حيوانٌ ما ومن ثم يموت. وبعد بضعة أيام، تخرج الامراض منه والجن أيضاً يفعلون ذلك ولا يبتعدون كثيراً. وأينما يجدون أعضاء تالفة، يتغلغلون بذلك الجسم ويبدؤون بتدميره أكثر. وفي حال عدم عثورهم على جسم مريض وتالف، يدخلون داخل جسم صحي ويبدؤون بتدميره.

وقد اعتدت على قتل الحشرات والزواحف بشكل متكرر، ولكن من أن بدأت الشعور بتلك الشياطين، تطور لدي مشكلة قتلهم، لأنني

I do not want their demons or diseases to visit my body. In my case, I argue with them or insist that they go back to original body, or if that body is dead, I ask them to find something similar but not me. I am able to do it, but in normal people's cases, the best thing is to keep houses and workplaces insect-free and stay away from animals, especially sick animals. Or if you still want to keep animals, then take care of their health. I do not know if this is easy or possible for everyone. These insects, reptiles, rats, and other animals go everywhere and bring all kind of dirty and dangerous diseases to our homes and our bodies. This is a cycle, and someone needs to think about how to fix it. But sick animals of all kinds can easily spread diseases and sicknesses everywhere. I do not have any knowledge about the reproduction system of disease or demons; however, it is my assumption that they grow really fast, and as the growth increases, they need more bodies, which means more people will get sick. I am sure you understand that demons and diseases are all invisible things in the physical world and that they do not die easily. They are hundreds of years old. They are on a mission. After they kill one person, they choose someone else. And when they are in a body, they are damaging that body and its organs, and during that time, they are reproducing and increasing their numbers.

How do diseases and demons operate?

Disease and demons are different from each other in the way human and wild animals or poisonous reptiles are different from each other. When a lion kills a deer, that lion eats first. Once that lion is finished eating the deer, the second strongest animal will come and start eating the leftover meat of deer from lion. After that, the third strongest animal will eat the leftover meat. In this way, all these animals will eat. And lastly, all the small animals or insects will attack the leftover meat of the hunted deer. In the same way, once a disease attacks us, it comes with a group and keeps attacking our bodies until it has damaged us completely. In regards to damaged organs, we have to deal with a line of diseases, sicknesses, and pains. No one can kill

لا أريد تلك الشياطيين أن تقوم بالدخول الى جسمي. وفي تلك الحالة، أقوم بالتحدث معاك وأقنعهم بالتراجع والعودة الى الجسم الأصلي، وفي حال كان ذلك الجسم ميتاً، أطلب منهم البحث عن شيء آخر غير. فأنا قادر على فعل ذلك، ولكن في وضعية الأشخاص العاديون، إن الشيء الأفضل هو ابقاء المنزل وأماكن العمل خالية من الحشرات والابتعاد عن الحيوانات وخاصة المريضة منها. وفي حال رغبتك بالحفاظ على الحيوانات، اذن اعتني بصحتها. ولا أعلم اذا كان ذلك ممكناً لكل شخص. وتذهب تلك الحشرات والزواحف والفئران والحيوانات الأخرى الى كل مكان وتجلب جميع أنواع الأمراض الخطيرة والقذرة الى منازلنا وأجسامنا. وهذه تعتبر كدورة، ويحتاج الشخص الى التفكير حيال كيفية علاج تلك المشكلة. ولكن بإمكان جميع الأنواع المختلفة من الحيوانات المريضة نشر الأمراض بكل سهولة وفي كل مكان. ولا أمتلك أي معلومة حول نظام تكاثر الأمراض أو الشياطيين. علاوة على ذلك، تنص فرضيتي على أن تلك الامراض تنمو بسرعة كبيرة وبازدياد النمو، تحتاج تلك الأمراض الى أجسام جديدة وهذا يعني المزيد من الأشخاص سيتعرضون للمرض. وأنا متأكد من إدراككم بأن الشياطيين والأمراض هي مخلوقات لا ترى ومخفية في العالم ولا تموت بتلك السهولة. وهي تبلغ من العمر مئات السنين ولديها مهمة محددة وهي قتل البشر والانتشار. عند تواجدها في جسم ما، تقوم بتدميره وأعضائه وفي تلك الأثناء تقوم بالتكاثر وازدياد أعدادها.

كيفية عمل الامراض والشياطيين؟

تختلف الأمراض والشياطيين عن بعضها باختلاف الإنسان والحيوان، وتختلف الزواحف السامة عن بعضها البعض أيضاً. عندما قوم أسد بقتل ظبية، فإن الأسد من يأكل أولاً. وعندما ينتهي الأكل من أكل الظبية، يأتي ثاني أقوى حيوان ويبدأ بأكل ما تبقى من لحم الظبية وما خلفه الأسد. وبعد ذلك، يقوم ثالث أقوى حيوان بأكل ما تبقى من لحم الظبية. وبهذه الطريقة، تأكل جميع الحيوانات. وفي النهاية، تقوم جميع الحيوانات الصغيرة والحشرات بمهاجمة ما تبقى من لحم الظبية التي اصطادها الأسد. وبطريقة مماثلة، عندما يهاجمنا المرض، فإنه يأتي مع مجموعة من الأمراض ويبقى يهاجم بأجسامنا حتى يدمرها كلياً. وفيما يخص الأعضاء التالفة، علينا التعامل مع خط من الأمراض والآلام. ولا يستطيع أحد قتلهم

them. Only with luck, if we fix the symptoms and stay away from the source of the disease, we will be able to become 100 percent normal. Otherwise, once they make room in our bodies again, they can re-infect us. This is a lifetime problem like ulcers, migraines, liver damage, diabetes, kidney failure, hemorrhoid infections, other infections, and different kinds of cancers. Our sick bodies and damaged organs are their food. They eat our bodies and organs and damage them more and more every day. In modern science, we have very good healing medication to heal the damages caused by these diseases. But it is very difficult for that healing medication to move these diseases away from the wounded or damaged parts of the body. They do not leave. We take painkillers, antibiotic, and healing medication, but the demons damage us again. At this point, if someone is using very good healing medication, I can or a person like me can help them to remove those diseases from the damage body. After that, someone needs to use the right kind of healing medication to fix the damages.

Even if a demon or disease is a friend, why does it still hurt?

I had this crazy and unbelievable experience several times. Pains and a myriad of sicknesses have become my friends. But problem is that they are just like a fire, and fire burns. Diseases, pains, and sickness can stay out of the body. So, even they are acting or behaving like a friend. So, they can reduce the effects but still, their effect is pain, once they will go to a body, or part of that body, that part will feel the pain. This is all crazy, but I deal with this world all the time. And only those people who experience my power firsthand actually believe me. It is not difficult for me to prove anything. Almost every day, I find several people with different problems and help them by taking their pains away from them.

فقط من يحالفه الحظ، ففي حال علاجنا من أعراض المرض والابتعاد عن مصدره، فإننا سنكون قادرين على أن نبقى سليمي الصحة. وإلا، عندما نفسح المجال للأمراض في أجسامنا، فإنها ستقوم بعدوتنا مرة أخرى. فهي مشكلة الحياة كالقرحة وأمراض الشقيقة وتلف الكبد ومرض السكري وفشل الكلى والباسور والكثير من العدوى وأنواع مختلفة من السرطان. حيث أن أجسامنا المريض وأعضاءنا التالفة مصدر طعام للأمراض. وتقوم بأكل أجسامنا وتدميرها أكثر وأكثر كل يوم. وفي العلم الحديث، يوجد هناك أدوية معالجة جيدة جداً لعلاج التلف الحاصل بسبب تلك الأمراض. ولكنه من الصعب تلك الأدوية لإبعاد تلك الامراض عن الأجزاء التالفة من الجسم. فهي لا تغادرها، حيث أننا نقوم بتناول مسكنات الآلام ومضادات حيوية وأدوية علاج، ولكن تقوم الشياطين بتدمير أجسامنا مجدداً. وفي هذا الحالة، إذا قام شخص ما باستخدام دواء جيد، فباستطاعتي أو أي شخص متخصص مثلي مساعدة هذا الشخص في التخلص من الأمراض الموجود داخل الجسم التالف. وبعد ذلك، يحتاج ذلك الشخص الى استخدام الصنف الصحيح من الدواء لعلاج الضرر الحاصل في الجسم.

حتى لو كان الشيطان أو المرض صديق، لماذا يبقى مسبباً للأذى؟

كان لدي هذه الخبرة الفظيعة المجنونة في العديد من الأوقات. فقد أصبحت أعداد لا تحصى من الأمراض والآلام أصدقائي. ولكن تكمن المشكلة في أن تلك الأمراض تشبه النيران والنار تحترق. ويمكن للأمراض والآلام أن تبقى خارج الجسم. لذلك، فهتي تتصرف على أنها صديقة، ويمكنها تخفيف الآثار ولكن يبقى تأثيرهم مسبباً للآلام، وعندما يدخلون جسماً ما فإن ذلك الجسم سيشعر بالألم. وهذا كله جنون وبإمكاني التعامل مع هذا العالم طوال الوقت. وفقط الأشخاص الذين خضعوا لخبرة قواي بشكل مباشر هم من يصدقون ما أقول. وتقريباً في كل يوم، أجد العديد من الأشخاص لديهم مشاكل مختلفة وأساعدهم في التخلص منها.

Where do demons live?

Surely, they do not live in water, because their basic configuration is *fire*. That's why they do not like water. We are only talking about demons right now. They are everywhere, and they have extraordinary powers. Because I sense them and feel them, I know they live in the air. Sometimes they are very close to walls and ceiling if they are not flying in air. I also know that they live inside or on trees. Those kinds of demons are like vegetarians. I know that they can live inside any living body, regardless human, animal, insect, bird, or reptile. All these bodies are the same for them. They can choose any body and can switch whenever they want. But remember that though they live in the air, trees, and bodies, their qualities are still the same. If they are flying in air, they can easily go into any animal's body or start living inside it. This is true for all of them.

Can anyone communicate with demons?

Only demons need a language to communicate with us or other animals. And for all of them, they just have one language, and that language is hypnotism. On other hand, we do not need any special language to communicate with them. They listen to us all the time. They are very nosy. They keep information about us. If they are new to us, they can dig inside our memory and easily find out a lot of information about us. So, they listen to us, and they understand our language, regardless of whether we speak English or another language; however, that does not mean they will obey us when they can hear us. Most of the time, they do not obey us. But if they become sincere with us, they will do much for us. And once they decide to go against us, then they will bring many obstacle.

أين تعيش الشياطين؟

بكل تأكيد، فهي لا تعيش في الماء لأن تركيبها الأساسي هو النار. ذلك الشبب فهم لا يرغبون العيش في الماء. فنحن الآن نتكلم فقط عن الشياطين. فهم متواجدون في كل مكان ويمتلكون قوى خارقة. ولأنني أشعر بهم، أعلم بأنهم يعيشون في الهواء. وأحياناً ما يكونون قريبون من الجدران والسقوف عندما لا يكونوا طائرين في الهواء. وأيضاً أعلم بأنهم يعيشون داخل أو على الأشجار. وترغب تلك الأنواع من الشياطين الأكل النباتي. ولدى معرفة حول امكانية عيشهم داخل أي جسم حي بغض النظر سواءً كان انسان أو حيوان أو حشرات أو طيور أو زواحف. ويمكن لتلك الشياطين أن تختار أي جسم ويمكن أن تقوم باستبداله حينما يشاؤون. ولكن تذكر بأنه على الرغم من أنهم يعيشون في الهواء والأشجار والأجسام، إلا أنهم يملكون مزايا متشابهة. في حال كونهم طائرون في الجو، فهم قادرون على الدخول الى أي جسم حيوان والعيش بداخله. فهذا حقيقي لهم جميعاً.

هل بإمكان أي شخص التواصل مع الجن؟

إن الشياطين هي وحدها من تحتاج الى لغة للتواصل معنا أو مع حيوانات أخر. وبالنسبة لهم، فلديهم لغو واحدة وهي لغة التنويم المغناطيسي. ومن ناحية أخرى، فنحن لا نحتاج الى لغة خاصة للتواصل معهم. فهم يستمعون لنا طوال الوقت. فهم مزعجون ويخفون ويخفون المعلومات عنا. وفي حال كانوا غريبين عنا، يمكنهم الحفر داخل ذاكرتنا واكتشاف الكثير من المعلومات عنا بكل سهولة. لذلك، فهم يستمعون لنا ويفهمون لغتنا بغض النظر عن كوننا نتكلم الإنجليزية أو أي لغة أخرى. علاوة على ذلك، هذا لا يعني أنهم يخضعون لطاعتنا عند سماعهم لنا. وفي معظم الأحيان، لا يخضعون لطاعتنا. ولكن في حال أصبحوا مخلصين لنا، سيقومون بخدمتنا كثيراً. وعندما يقررون مقاومتنا، فإنهم سيجلبون لنا الكثير من المتاعب.

How do demons create obstacles for us?
How do demons resolve our problems?

Demons do not have as many liabilities as we do. I am talking about money, jobs, houses, insurance, among others. As far as problems and fights, demons have more fights and wars between themselves. The demon's language is hypnotism. If you understand hypnotism a little bit, then you know it is a trick. If someone uses it on you, then you do not necessarily know that someone is communicating with you or trying to influence you. If someone hypnotizes you, you will see whatever they want you to see. You will think only whatever they feed your mind. And if demons are hypnotizing you, you will not be able to beat them. We think only whatever they want us to think. We see whatever they want us to see.

If demons are all around us and they are our enemies, then what they can do? They can keep us misguided all the time by hypnotizing us. These demons can reach wherever we go before us and misguide other people by hypnotizing them. Wherever you go, whatever you do, you will face problems everywhere. If demons are friends of someone, then they clean up their paths everywhere. Those people have good luck everywhere. These groups of demons reach wherever they're going before them and hypnotize everyone and keep the person's path clear of all problems.

How do we see demons? Can dream tell us the location and/or the nature of a demon?

Almost all demons do not change their places. If they are living in a house, office, or shop, they live there for generations. They do not easily allow demons or other than their family in their particular places. A few live in our house, office, or shop, and a few travel with us. Demons are very nosy and take full interest in our affairs. I am sorry to say that we are totally under their control most of the time and that

كيف يسبب الجن المتاعب لنا؟
وكيف يقوم الجن بحل مشكلاتنا؟

لا يوجد للشياطيين الكثير من المسؤوليات كما يوجد لدينا. فأنا أتكل عن النقود والعمل والمنازل والتأمين وغيرها الكثير. وبالنسبة للمشاكل والصراع، فإن الشياطيين لديها الكثير من المشاكل والصراعات والحروب فيما بينها. ولغتهم هي لغة التنويم المغناطيسي. وفي حال فهمك لتلك اللغة قليلاً، فإنك تصبح على دراية أنها مجرد خدعة. وفي حال استخدمها شخص ما ضدك، فأنت لست بحاجة الى معرفة ذلك الشخص بأنه يحاول التواصل أو التأثير عليك. وفي حال قيام شخص ما بتنويمك مغناطيسياً، فإنك سترى ما هم يريدوك أن ترى. وستفكر فيما هم فقط غذوا عقلك به. ولن تكون قادراً على التغلب عليهم. وستفكر فيما يفكرون أو يريدوك أن تفكر وترى ما هم يريدوك أن ترى.

وفي حال تواجد الشياطين حولنا وهم أعداؤنا، إذن الذي باستطاعتنا فعله؟ فهم يبقونا مشوشون طوال الوقت عن طريق تنويمنا مغناطيسياً. ويمكن لتلك الشياطيين الوصول الى أي مكان قبل أن نصل نحن البشر إليه وتشتيت الأشخاص الآخرين عن طريق التنويم المغناطيسي. وأينما تذهب أو مهما فعلت، ستواجه المتاعب في كل مكان. وفي حال كون الشياطين أصدقاء لشخص ما، فيمكنهم تنظيف طريقهم في كل مكان. ويكون هؤلاء الأشخاص محظوظون في كل مكان أيضا حيث أن تلك المجموعات من الشياطيين تصل أينما يشاؤون هؤلاء الأشخاص وقبلهم وتقوم بتنويم كل شخص في تلك الأماكن وتحافظ على طريق الشخص خالية من المشاكل.

كيف يمكننا رؤية الشياطيين؟ هل يمكن للحلم أن يخبرنا عن مكان أو/وطبيعة الشياطيين؟

تقريباً كل الشياطيين لا تغير من أماكنها. وإذا كانت تعيش في منزل، او مكتب أو بقالة، فإنها ستبقى في تلك الأماكن لأجيال عديدة. فهم لا يسمحون لشياطيين من عائلات أخرى بأخذ الأماكن الخاصة بهم. حيث يعيش القليل منهم في المنزل والمكتب والبقالة والقليل الآخر يسافرون معنا. فهم مزعجين جداً ومهتمون كثيراً في علاقاتنا. وأنا آسف للقول بأننا تحت إمرتهم معظم الأوقات وأننا

we usually do what they want us to do. Regardless of the sincerity of demons, they are basically naughty and full of negativism. Demons use the power of hypnotism. They can show us anything while we are sleeping or while we are awake. When they show us something that isn't really there, we will call that a "trick of the eyes." And they can show us anything during sleep, and we call those "dreams."

We think we see whatever we recently had on our minds in our dreams. This is totally wrong. We see only whatever demons around us show us in dreams. Sometimes it happens, and we see whatever we had on our minds, but that's because demons are so much involved in our affairs and lives. Consequently, we think that those dreams are coming from our own minds, but in actuality, the demons around us are totally responsible for that. Usually, one dream does not come from two demons. One demon shows us one dream. If we have more than one demon around us, these demons usually take turns, depending on which is more powerful.

Demons usually show us dreams about our family problems, affairs, business problems, among others. If they are watching movies with us, they can show us the whole movie again. If we are around a jungle or wild animals or if we have poisonous reptiles inside or around our homes and demons come out from them and penetrate our bodies, our dreams will just be nightmares. These demons are not our regular demons that are usually involved in our lives or our affairs. These new demons usually come from other animals, and they do not have much material other than nightmares or scary dreams.

Always remember that if you want to really judge which kind of demon you have around you or from where a demon came, you need to analysis your dreams. If you have too many demons inside or around your house, then you will experience different dreams every night, especially if you have a lot of trees around your house, which could mean a significant population of demons. If you are completely possessed by a single demon, then that demon will have complete control, and it will be only one that shows you your dreams. But if

عادة ما نفعل ما يريد الجن أن نفعل؟ وبغض النظر عن إخلاصهم إلا أنهم بشكل أساسي سخيفين ومليئين بالسلبية. حيث أنهم يستخدمون قوة التنويم المغناطيسي، ويمكنهم أن يظهروا لنا أي شيء أثناء نومنا أو أثناء الاستيقاظ. وعندما يقومون بإظهارنا شيء ما غير حقيقي، فإننا ندعوه بـ"خداع العيون" وعندما يظهروا لنا شيء غير حقيقي أثناء النوم، ندعوه بـ"الأحلام".

ونعتقد أننا نرى اشياء مؤخراً في عقولنا قد رأيناها في أحلامنا. وهذا خطأ. في الحقيقة نحن نرى أشياء يرينا إياها الشياطيين في الأحلام. وهذا الشيء يحدث أحياناً أننا نرى ما يجول في خاطرنا ولكن ذلك لأن الشياطين تكون على اتصال في علاقاتنا وحياتنا. وبالتالي، نعتقد أن تلك الأحلام قادمة من عقولنا ولكن في الحقيقة إن الشياطيين من حولنا هو مسؤولة بشكل كامل عن ذلك. وعادةً ما لا يأتي حلو واحد من شيطانان، حيث يرينا شيطانان واحد حلم واحد فقط. وفي حال نرى أكثر من شيطان واحد حولنا، فإن تلك الشياطيين تتبادل الأدوار بالاعتماد على أكثرهم قوة.

وعادةً ما ترينا الشياطيين أحلاماً عن مشاكلنا العائلية والعلاقات ومشاكل العمل وغيرها الكثير. وفي حال مشاهدتها أفلاماً بصحبتنا، فيمكنها أن ترينا الفلم كاملاً مرة أخرى. وفي حال تواجدنا بجوار الأدغال أو الحيوانات البرية أو الزواحف السامة داخل أو حول منازلنا فإن الشياطين تخرج منها جميعاً وتتغلغل في أجسامنا وستصبح أحلامنا كوابيس. وتلك الشياطيين ليست بالشياطيين المنتظمة التي تتدخل في حياتنا وعلاقاتنا. وتأتي هذه عادةً من الحيوانات ولا يوجد لديها الكثير من الكوابيس أو الأحلام المخيفة.

وتذكر دائماً بأنك اذا كنت تريد الحكم على أي نوع من الشياطيين متواجد حولك أو من أي مكان جاء، عليك أن تقوم بتحليل أحلامك. وفي حال كان لديك الكثير من الشياطيين داخل أو حول منزلك، عليك أن تواجه أحلام مختلفة كل ليلة وخاصة في تواجد الكثير من الأشجار بجوار منزلك وهذا يمكن أن يعني عدد كبير من الشياطيين. وفي حال سيطرة شيطان واحد عليك سيكون مسيطر عليك بشكل كامل وسيكون الجن الوحيد الذي يريك أحلامك؟ ولكن في

you are a strong-minded person, then no single or permanent demon will be around you. You will be dealing with different demons all the time.

Anyway, if you are seeing dreams totally different than your thoughts and you are seeing dreams about lizards or cats or dog, that means the demon was likely inside those animals for long time and that's all it knows. That's why they are showing you these dreams. If your friend in a different country talks to you over the phone, that demon may choose you to visit you for some reason. This new demon will mostly show you dreams related to your friend or your friend's country, and it will show you dreams about your friend's affairs. In short, demons do not show us whatever we want to see. They always show us whatever they want to show us. This is their hobby. They do that for themselves, not for us.

You may not be able to, but I can ask demons around me to show me some particular dreams. I have different demons that visit every day or sometimes every hour, and that's why my dreams are different all the time. Sometimes, I have some complicated dreams, but you would be surprised, because sometimes I do not recognize any of the people in those dreams. I just assume that because I remove demons from different people in different part of the world, those demons come around me and show me dreams about the lives or affairs of their previous hosts.

Anyone can use these practices in regards to dreams. If you are experiencing and seeing really dangerous and scary dreams and you want them to stop, I can guide you in how to stop them. These nightmares do not come from our sincere demons. They usually come from demons we get from wild animals or reptiles. Showing us scary dreams is their hobby, and they really enjoy it when they scare us and see our reactions to those scary dreams.

When you have a scary dream, just remember that these demons are playing with you. Do not act like you are scared at all. Once you

حال كونك شخص ذو ذهن قوي، فلن يقدر شيطان أو عدة شياطيين من التواجد حولك. وستتعامل مع العديد من الجن طوال الوقت.

على أي حال، في حال رؤيتك لأحلام مختلفة تماماً عن أفكارك كرؤية سحالي أو قطط أو كلاب، فإن ذلك يعني بأن الشيطان داخل تلك الحيوانات لفترة طويلة وهذا ما هو يعرفه. وهو السبب وراء مشاهدتك لتلك الأحلام. وفي حالكان صديقك من دولة مختلفة ويتحدث معك عبر الهاتف، فمن المحتمل أن يقوم ذلك الجن باختيار زيارتك لسبب ما. ويريك هذا الجن الغريب أحلام متعلقة لصديقك أو الدولة التي يعيش فيها صديقك. وسيريك أحلام عن علاقات صديقك. وباختصار، لا ترينا الشياطيين من نريد نحن أن نرى. فدائماً ما ترينا ما هم يريدوننا أن نرى هي هوايتهم وهم يفعلون ذلك لأنفسهم ليس من أجلنا.

ربما لا تكون قادراً ولكن بمقدوري أن أطلب من الشياطيين من حولي أن يروني أحلاماً معينة. ولدي العديد من الشياطيين الذين يزورونني كل يوم أو حتى كل ساعة فإن ذلك السبب فإن أحلامي تتغير طوال الوقت. وأحياناً، تأتيني بعض الأحلام المعقدة ولكنك ستكون متفاجأ لأنه في أحيان أخرى لا أستطيع تمييز أي من تلك الأحلام. فقط أقوم بالافتراض لأنني اخرج الكثير من الشياطيين من الناس في جميع أنحاء العالم، فتأتي تلك الشياطيين حولي وتريني أحلاماً عن حياة وعلاقات أناس اخرين من العالم.

وبإمكان أي شخص التدريب على تلك الحوادث فيما يخص الأحلام. وفي حال مواجهتك ورؤيتك لأحلام خطيرة ومخيفة وتريد إيقافهم، يمكنني ان أرشدك الى كيفية إيقافهم؟ حيث ان تلك الكوابيس لا تأتي من شياطيننا المخلصة لنا. عادةً ما تأتي من شياطيين تأتينا من الحيوانات البرية والزواحف. حيث أن مشاهدتك لأحلام مخيفة تعتبر هواية للشياطين وتستمتع بذلك عند اخافتنا ورؤية ردود أفعالنا حيال تلك الأحلام المخيفة.

عند رؤيتك لحلم مخيف، فقط تذكر بأن تلك الشياطيين تريد اللعب معك. ولا تظهر لها بأنك خائف مطلقاً. وعندما تستيقظ

wake up from the nightmare, do not yell or act scared. Just look toward your left shoulder and say to the demon, "You are wasting your time. I am not scared of that dream, so please quit wasting your time with me and find someone else." However, you cannot lie to demons, because they can read deep inside our mind. If you really do not want to keep having nightmares, you need to control your feelings and fears. Once you are more in control of your feelings, you will display more confidence about whatever you are saying to the demons around you, namely you are not scared of the dreams and that they need to quit wasting their time and find someone else. Once the demons figure out that you are not really scared of their dreams, they will leave you alone, because they will essentially lose interest. And if you are not getting scared anymore, they will leave you alone and find someone else.

Can demons show us any photos or movies in mirrors, by hypnotizing us?

Usually, some demon's doctor uses their demons to hypnotize someone and show them any photo or movie, whatever they want to show us. Usually, people go to these kinds of people to find out if someone wants to kill them or kill their business. Those fortunetellers usually use their demons to show us a few photos or films from our mind. This happens when we are awake. This is not a surprise, because when demons hypnotize us during sleep in order to show us our dreams, then this is not difficult for demons to show a few photos or a film in a mirror by hypnotizing us. We always want to know, if there is someone behind our bad luck or our problems. Usually people go to demon's doctor (not me) to resolve their problems and issues.
Or at least they want to know, who their enemy is. Those demons' doctors take advantage of the situation. They use their demons. Their demon read the mind of those people by hypnotism. And then, those demons' doctors keep a mirror in front of that person. At that point those demons hypnotize that person again and show him the picture

من الكابوس، لا تصرخ أو تظهر بأنك خائف. فقط انظر باتجاه كتفك الأيسر وقل للشيطان "إنك تضيع وقتك. أنا لست خائفاً من ذلك الحلم، لذلك رجاءً لا تضيع وقتك معي وابحث عن شخص آخر غيري." علاوة على ذلك، لا يمكن الكذب على الشياطين لأنها تستطيع أن تقرأ ما يجول في بالك. وفي حال لم تكن تريد الاستمرار في رؤية الكوابيس، عليك أن تتحكم في شعورك وستظهر المزيد من الثقة حيال ما تقوله للشياطين من حولك وبشكل رئيسي أنك لست خائفاً من أحلامهم وأن عليهم أن يتوقفوا من تضييع وقتهم معك والبحث عن شخص آخر. وعندما تكتشف الشياطين أنك حقاً لست خائفاً من أحلامهم، سيغادرونك ويتركونك لوحدك لانهم فقدوا الاهتمام بك بشكل أساسي. وفي حال عدم خوفك بعد الآن، سيتركونك لوحدك ويبحثون عن شخص آخر.

هل يمكن للشياطيين أن ترينا صور أو أفلام في المرآة عن طريق تنويمنا مغناطيسياً؟

عادة، يستخدم بعض أطباء الجن شياطينهم لتنويم شخص ما مغناطيسياً ليريهم أي صورة أو فلم مما يشاؤون. وفي أغلب الأحيان، وعادة ما يذهب الناس الى هؤلاء الأشخاص (أطباء الجن) لمعرفة من يريد قتلهم أو افشال عملهم. وعادة ما يستخدم هؤلاء العرافون شياطينهم ليرونا بعض الصور أو الأفلام من عقولنا. ويحدث هذا عندما نكون مستيقظين. فهذه ليست بالمفاجأة لأنه عندما يقوم الجن بتنويمنا مغناطيسياً ليرونا أحلامنا ومن ثم إنه ليس من الصعب بالنسبة للشياطين أن يرونا بعض الصور أو فلماً ما في المرآة عن طريق تنويمنا مغناطيسياً. ودائماً ما نريد أن نعلم إذا ما كان هناك شخصاً ما وراء حظنا السيء أو مشاكلنا. ويذهب الناس في العادة الى هؤلاء العرافون (ليسوا مثلي) لحل مشاكلهم وقضاياهم. أو على الأقل يريدون معرفة من هم أعداءهم. ويستغل هؤلاء العرافون هذا الوضع باستخدام شياطينهم لمساعدتهم في قراءة أفكار هؤلاء الأشخاص عن طريق التنويم المغناطيسي. ومن ثم يضع هؤلاء العرافون مرآة أمام ذلك الشخص لتقوم الشياطين في تلك اللحظة بتنويم ذلك الشخص مغناطيسياً ويروه صورة

of few suspected enemies of that person in mirror. So, this is a very controlled hypnotism procedure by a demon doctor.

Are demons spirits or souls?

Demons are not positive energy. Demons are not responsible for keeping us alive and performing bodily functions and operations.
The soul/spirit is a positive energy that is limited and confined inside our bodies with a fixed strength. Demons and diseases are uninvited guests in our house (i.e., our body and environment). They are not a problem when they are outside of our house or our body, but they are a burden when they are inside our house or inside our body.

Demons and diseases are external negative energies that can go inside our bodies easily. And once they go inside our body, our soul/spirit or positive energy protects us from demon's negative actions. But positive energy is limited, and it works individually for separate parts of the body. Negative energy is external, and they can increase their power by using it or by inviting more demons or diseases into our bodies. Demons have no limits on their powers. They can increase their strength to defeat internal positive energy. Once negative energy beats the positive internal energy (i.e., our immunity system), we get sick and suffer pains like infections, heart attacks, paralysis, hemorrhages, and even organ failure. Doctors and medication are external influences that can help increase the powers of our internal positive energy to protect us from the actions of external negative energies (i.e., demons or diseases).

We are like trees. Our bodies and their damages are like nests for birds. And diseases are like birds in those nests.

Trees are alive like us. When birds use their sharp beaks to make holes in the stem of a tree or make a hole in any branch of the tree, they can

لبعض الأعداء المشتبه بهم في المرآة. لذلك، هذا اجراء تنويم مغناطيسي مسيطرة عليه جداً من قبل العراف.

هل الشياطيين نفس بشرية أم أرواح؟

إن الشياطيين ليسوا بالطاقة الإيجابية وهم غير مسؤولون عن إبقائنا أحياء أو انجاز المهام الجسدية والعمليات. وتعتبر الروح/النفس البشرية طاقة ايجابية محدودة ومحجوزة داخل أجسامنا مع قوة متفاوتة. والشياطيين والأمراض هي ضيوف غير مرحب بها في منازلنا (كأجسامنا والبيئة). وهم لا يشكلون مشكلة أثناء تواجدهم خارج منازلنا وأجسامنا ولكن يسببون التعب عند دخولهم الى المنزل أو الجسم.

إن الأمراض والشياطيين طاقات سلبية خارجية تستطيع الدخول الى أجسامنا بكل سهولة. وعندما يدخلون الى أجسامنا تقوم روحنا/نفسنا البشرية أو الطاقة الإيجابية بحمايتنا من الأفعال السلبية للشياطين. ولكن تكون الطاقة الايجابية محدودة وتعمل بشكل فردي لأجزاء منفصلة في الجسم. ولكن الطاقة السلبية هي طاقة خارجية ويمكنهم زيادة طاقاتهم باستخدامها أو باستدعاء المزيد من الشياطيين أو الأمراض الى داخل أجسامنا. وطاقات الجن غير محدودة. حيث يمكنهم زيادة قوتهم لهزيمة الطاقة الإيجابية الداخلية. وعندما تتغلب الطاقة السلبية على الايجابية (نظام المناعة في أجسامنا)، نتعرض للأمراض ونعاني من الآلام كالعدوى والنوبات القلبية والشلل والنزيف وحتى فشل الأعضاء. ويعتبر الاطباء والأدوية تأثيرات خارجية تساعد في زيادة قوة الطاقات الإيجابية الداخلية لحمايتنا من أعمال الطاقات السلبية الخارجية (الشياطين والأمراض).

نحن نشبه الى حد كبير الأشجار. حيث أن أجسامنا وتلفها تشبه أعشاش العصافير. وتشبه الأمراض العصافير المتواجد في تلك الأعشاش.

والأشجار كائنات حية مثلنا البشر. وعندما تستخدم العصافير مناقيرها الحادة لعمل الحفر في جذع الشجرة أو لعمل حفر في غصن الشجرة، فإنها

set up a nest in those holes. When birds make a hole in any part of the tree, birds don't care how much their actions will hurt a tree. We are exactly like trees, and these demons are like birds. These demons damage parts of our bodies so that they can eat. They do not care how much pain we must endure because of their actions. They do not care; they just make wounds/injuries in order to eat them or to live their lives. In the same way, if you go to that tree and clean the nest from the tree and remove the bird from the nest, what will happen after that? There will be no nest in that hole in the stem or branch of the tree. There will be no bird around that hole in the tree.

But if the hole is there in the stem or branch of the tree, another bird will find the hole, and this new bird will try to make a nest in that hole. And if new bird is bigger in size than the old bird was, then the new bird may try to make the hole even bigger, and that action will create more pain for the tree. But birds do not care about the tree. If tree is not going to fix that hole in the stem or branch, new birds will keep coming and hurting the tree. Similarly, our body will not be fixed by taking proper medication and surgery. New demons and diseases will keep coming and attacking our injured organs.

I can remove a pain, sickness, or disease from a person, but if symptoms persist and nobody takes care of those symptoms, another disease will come pretty quickly. But there is another thing, and we call that thing "bad luck." You may not have symptoms, but by bad luck—maybe you have to deal with someone or live with someone who is sick— these diseases will transfer to your body very easily. Maybe you do not feel any pain for few days, weeks, or months, but eventually, those diseases will damage part of our body by defeating your positive energies. And then a cycle of problems and sickness will start.

We do not need to be sick people or have wounds or injuries to invite demons inside or around us. Demons are always around us. Demons do not hurt like disease, but because of their negativism, everyone feels some mental sickness or extreme temperament.

تبنى عشاً لها في تلك الحفر. عندما تقوم العصافير بعمل حفر في الشجر لا تهم عن مدى الضرر الذي يلحق بالشجر. ونحن (البشر) نشبه الشجر الى حد كبير تقوم تلك الشياطين بتدمير أجزاء من أجسامنا حتى يأكلون. ولا يهتمون عن مدى الألم الذي نتعرض له من جراء فعل ذلك. فهم فقط يسبون الجروح من أجل الطعام والبقاء على قيد الحياة. وبنفي الطريقة، في حال ذهابك الى شجرة وتقوم بتنظيف الأعشاش من على ظهرها، ماذا سيحدث بعد ذلك، لن يكون هناك أعشاش في الحفر في جذع الشجرة أو الأغصان. ولن يكون هناك عصافير حول تلك الحفر.

ولكن في حال تواجد الحفر في الجذع أو الغصن، سيأتي عصفور آخر وسيجد الحفرة وسيحاول في بناء عش جديد له في تلك الحفر. وفي حال العصفور الجديد أكبر حجماً من المحتمل أن يحاول أن يكبر حجم الحفر هذا سينشأ عنه ألم للشجرة. ولكن العصافير لا تهتم كثيراً بالشجرة. ولن تقوم الشجرة بعلاج تلك الحفرة في الجذع أو الغصن وستبقى العصافير الجديدة تأتي وتؤذي الشجرة. وبشكل مشابه، لن يتم علاج أجسامنا عن طريق أخذ الادوية الصحيحة والعمليات. ستأتي الشياطين والأمراض الجديدة بالقدوم ومهاجمة اجسامنا وأعضاءنا المجروحة.

يمكنني التخلص من الألم والمرض وازلته من الشخص، ولكن في حال تغلغل المرض ولم يقم أي شخص بالعناية بتلك الامراض، سيأتي مرض جديد بسرعة. ولكن هناك شيء آخر وهو ما نطلق عليه "سوء الحظ" فمن المرجح أن لا يكون لديك أمراض ولكن بالحظ السيء- عليك الاتصال بشخص آخر مريض- وستنتقل الامراض من ذلك الشخص الى جسمك بسهولة. ومن المحتمل أن لا تشعر باي ألم لعدة أيام أو أسابيع أو شهور، ولكن في النهاية ستدمر تلك الأمراض جزء من جسمك بالتغلب على طاقاتك الايجابية, ومن ذلك تبدأ دورة المشاكل والامراض بالظهور.

فنحن لسنا بحاجة ان نكون مرضى أو مجروحون حتى نستقبل الشياطين داخل أجسامنا. فدائماً ما تكون الشياطين من حولنا. ولا يؤذينا كما تفعل الامراض، ولكن بسبب السلبية التي تمتلكها الشياطين، يشعر كل شخص بالمرض العقلي أو مزاج متطرف.

When I work on someone on a regular basis, I create a vacuum in his or her body.

We are not designed to have any demon or a disease inside our bodies. In a neutral condition, when no demons or diseases are inside our bodies, we feel extremely relaxed and comfortable. If I am not working on someone for a few days, I experience that relaxed and comfortable condition. But that is not possible for me all the time, because I am always busy helping someone, regardless of whether they are aware of that help or not. "Vacuum condition" means that the person is like a vacant house. We are not designed to have a demon or disease in our body. We live better without them, but demons are designed to find a medium where they can penetrate, expand, and start living. Demon are mean, and they are physical bodies; however, they are just like air, and to secure a medium, they choose anybody, regardless if they are human or another animal. They don't care how much they hurt/damage the medium or that body. After I work on someone and clean his or her body of these demons and disease, after that, his or her body has an empty space, which means demons and diseases can easily penetrate that clean body. So be careful and stay away from sick bodies.

People with any kind of mental sickness are being controlled by demons.

God has gifted demons with lots of powers to control minds through hypnotism. In rare cases, they act differently. Otherwise, they have no sympathy for human beings. They will generate all kinds of negative qualities in us, such as jealousy, greed, anger, intolerance, impatience, suspicion, mistrust, and sickness. I have a little control over them with help from God. I use different procedures to disrupt their control. I don't think this is possible for a normal person. Someone like me can reduce the pressure from a demon. The rest is in your hands, namely how easily and quickly you adapt and move toward a positive

عندما أعمل على شخص معين وفق قاعدة منتظمة، أنشأ فراغاً في جسمه/ا.

فنحن لسنا مصممون لقبول أي شيطان أو مرض في جسمنا. وفي الوضع الطبيعي، عندما لا يكون هناك شياطين ولا أمراض داخل أجسامنا، نشعر بارتياح شديد. وفي حال كنت لا أعمل على شخص لعدة أيام، أواجه الوضع الأكثر ارتياحاً. ولكن ذلك غير ممكن بالنسبة إلي في جميع الأوقات لأنني دائماً ما أكون مشغولاً في مساعدة شخص ما بغض النظر عن إدراكه بالمساعدة أو لا. وتعني "حالة الفراغ" إن الشخص عبارة عن منزل فارغ. ونحن لسنا مصممون لإدخال الشياطين أو الأمراض الى أجسامنا. ونعيش بشكل أفضل بدونهم. ولكن الشياطين مصممة للعثور على وسط يمكنا من التغلغل والتوسع والبدء بالحياة. وإن الشياطين قاسية وهم أجسام يمكن لمسها، علاوة على ذلك، فهم فقط كالهواء. ومن أجل تأمين وسط، يختارون أي شخص بغض النظر حول ما إذا كان إنسان أو حيوان. فهم لا يهتمون بمدى الضرر الذي يسببونه للجسم أو الوسط. وبعد أن أعمل على تنظيف جسم شخص ما من تلك الشياطين والأمراض، سيصبح بعدها جسمه فارغ، وهذا يعني أن الأمراض والشياطين يمكنها التغلغل في ذلك الجسم النظيف. لذلك عليكم الحرص والابتعاد عن الأجسام المريض.

إن الناس الذين يعانون من الامراض العقلية مسيطر عليهم من قبل الشياطين.

لقد منح الله الشياطين بقوى خارقة للسيطرة على العقول من خلال التنويم المغناطيسي. وفي حالات نادرة، يتصرفون بشكل مختلف. وهم لا يوجد لديهم شفقة للبشر. فهم يعملون بجميع أنواع الميزات السلبية ضدنا. كالغيرة والطمع والغضب والتعصب وعدم الصبر والشك وعدم الثقة والمرض. ولدي القليل من السيطرة عليهم بمساعدة الله. وأستخدم إجراءات مختلفة لتعطيل سيطرتهم. ولا أعتقد أن هذا ممكن للشخص العادي. ويمكن لشخص مثلي أن يخفف من ضغط الشيطان. والباقي بيدك/ وبشكل رئيسي مدى سهولة وسرعة تكيفك وتجاوبك مع طريقة إيجابية

approach and way of thinking. If you train yourself to behave and think positively, you will make it difficult for a demon to make you mentally sick person.

We always have positive and negative thoughts. Good thoughts come from our mind, bad thoughts fed by demons.

If you still have a choice to differentiate between good and bad, positive and negative, true and false, right and wrong, then you still have time to defeat a demon. If you are a normal person, all positive and good thoughts are coming from your mind. All negative and bad thoughts are coming from a demon around you. So, if you still want to beat a demon and regain your control, you need to start practicing right now. Start rejecting all bad and negative thinking. Stop getting too suspicious. Reduce jealousy. Try to reduce negative competition. Always be sure about positive decisions. This is a possible way to train a demon around you to be less negative. I am sure demons will not like this behavior, but this is your decision—whether you want to give your control to a demon and act crazy or keep your control and compel that demon to help you in your positive path. You will need a lot of practice. Simple, we reject bad thoughts means, we have more control over our mind. And if we accept bad thoughts means demons have more control of our mind.

l Demons can find extremism even in positive activities like studies/business, or they try to make us irresponsible and lazy, whatever work for demons.

Consider our responsibilities like going to job and making money, going to school and behaving like a responsible student, or caring and loving our families. All these responsible behaviors come from our mind. Demons are not helping us become more and more responsible. If you do not want to go to school or work, I'm lazy. I'm not doing a

من التفكير. وفي حال تدريب نفسك على التصرف والتفكير بشكل إيجابي، سيصبح من الصعب على الشيطان أن يجعلك مريض عقلياً.

دائما ما يكون لدينا أفكار إيجابية وسلبية. فالأفكار الجيدة تأتي من عقولنا أو الأفكار السيئة فيكون مصدرها الشياطين.

وفي حال كان لديك الخيار للتفريق بين الشر والخير، والسلبي والإيجابي والصح والخطأ، إذن سيكون لديك الوقت للتغلب على الشيطان. وفي حال كونك شخص عادي، تأتي جميع الأفكار الإيجابية والحسنة من عقلك. وتأتي الأفكار السلبية والسيئة من الشياطين من حولك. لذلك، وفي حال كونك تريد التغلب على الشيطان وإرجاع سيطرتك على نفسك، عليك البدء بالتمرين من الآن. بدأ برفض جميع الأفكار السيئة والسلبية. والتوقف عن الشك والتقليل من الغيرة. والمحاولة للتقليل من المنافسة السلبية. وتأكد دائماً من القرارات الإيجابية. وهذا ممكن لتدريب الشيطان من حولك أن يكون أقل سلبية. وأنا متأكد بأن الشياطين لن ترغب بذلك التصرف، ولكن هذا قرارك ـــ سواءً كنت تريد منح سيطرتك الى شيطان والتصرف بجنون أو الحفاظ على سيطرتك على نفسك واجبار ذلك الشيطان على مساعدتك في طريقك الإيجابية. وستحتاج الى الكثير من التدريب. وبكل بساطة، نحن نرفض الأفكار السيئة ولدينا سيطرة أكثر على عقولنا. وفي حال قبولنا للأفكار السيئة فإنه يكون للشياطين اكثر سيطرة على عقولنا.

وبإمكان الشياطين البحث عن التطرف حتى بالأفعال الإيجابية مثل الدراسة/والعمل، أو يحاولون جعلنا غير مسؤولين وكسولين، فذلك يخدم الشياطين.

خذ في الاعتبار مسؤولياتنا كالذهاب الى العمل والحصول على النقود والذهاب الى المدرسة والتصرف بمسؤولية، أو الاهتمام وحب عائلاتنا. حيث أن جميع تلك التصرفات المسؤولة تأتي من عقولنا. ولا تساعدنا الشياطين بأن نكون أكثر مسؤولية. وفي حال عدم رغبتك في الذهاب الى المدرسة أو العمل، فأنا كسول. ولا أعمل

good job. I'm not doing homework. All these irresponsible behaviors occur when we listen to demons instead of our own minds.

When there is healthy competition, regardless of the type, these come from our minds. But when competition crosses the line, when you feel hatred for your competitors and you're ready to kill them, demons are in charge of you at that point. When demons cannot stop us from doing good, they try to bring us to extremely negative competition. We can control this by acting more positive.

We can control and reduce any extreme passion, habit, or desire just by remembering we are being pushed by demons.

Demons are not busy people. They do not have to go to work. They do not have to cook. But competition for them is pretty similar to ours. We are their main hobby. Demons are not going to just stay around us and waste their time by letting us just do good stuff and act like a positive person. Demons are very pushy. They push us all the time to do negative stuff. The only way we can try to reduce their presence is by controlling our immediate desires. Sometimes you desire to do something, and you feel you need to do it immediately. But all these desires come from demons. If we slow down and do not fuel our extreme desires, we can reduce a demon's control on us, though it can be very difficult.

A love for any profession, hobby, or habit signals an extreme condition.

Demons want us to do whatever they want all the time, and their pressure never reduces. But in some ways, they are very helpful because they push us to some positive extreme levels. Like poets, demons push us to extreme love, grief, and sadness. These extreme conditions create great poetry and art. No one could do these

بشكل جيد. ولا أقوم بإنجاز وظيفتي البيتية. وتحدث كل تلك التصرفات الغير مسؤولة عندما نستمع الى الشياطيين بدلاً من الاستماع الى عقولنا.

عندما يكون هناك منافسة صحية، فإنها تأتي من عقولنا بغض النظر عن نوعها. ولكن عندما تتعدى المنافسة حدها الشرعي وعندما تشعر بالكراهية تجاه منافسيك وبأنك مستعد لقتلهم، فإن الشياطيين هي من تكون مسؤولة عن ذلك. وعندما لا يستطيع الجن ايقافنا عن فعل الصحيح، يحاولون جلبنا الى المنافسات السلبية للغاية. ويمكننا التحكم بذلك عن طريق التصرف بشكل أكثر ايجابية.

ويمكننا التحكم والتخفيف من أي شعور متطرف أو عادة أو رغبة عن طريق التذكر بأنه يتم دفعنا من قبل الشياطيين.

والشياطيين ليسوا بالأشخاص المشغولون. ولي يتوجب عليهم العمل. ولا يتوجب عليهم الطبخ. ولكن المنافسة فيما بينهم تشبه المنافسة بيننا الى حد كبير. ونحن هوايتهم المفضلة. ولا تبقى الشياطين حولنا تضيع وقتها بالسماح لنا بعمل الأفعال الحسنة والتصرف كأشخاص ايجابيين. فهم انتهازيون وتغطرسون. ويقومون بانتهازنا طوال الوقت لإجبارنا على عمل أشياء سلبية. وإن الطريقة الوحيدة التي يمكننا محاولة تقليل وجودهم بها هي التحكم برغباتنا المباشرة. وأحياناً يكون لديك رغبة في عمل شيء ما، وتشعر بأنك تحتاج الى فعل ذلك الشيء فوراً. وفي حال قيامك بالتمهل وعدم تغذية رغباتك المتطرفة، يمكننا التقليل من سيطرة الجن على كقولنا على الرغم من صعوبة ذلك.

حب المهنة والهواية والعادة هو إشارة على الوضع المتطرف.

يريدنا الجن فعل ما يشاؤون في جميع الأوقات، ضغطهم علينا لا يقل أبداً. ولكن في بعض الحالات، هي يساعدوننا لأنهم يدفعوننا لعمل أشياء على مستويات عالية جداً. كالشعراء، فيدفعنا الجن الى الحب المتطرف والحزن والألم. وتخلق تلك الأوضاع المتطرفة شعر وفن راقي. ولا يستطيع أحد من فعل تلك

dangerous activities with a mind unaffected by demons. But demons make us fearless and increase our courage by hypnotizing us. And we do incredible and extreme activities without fear of death or injury. Behind all extraordinary achievements, there is an extreme behavior and extreme effort. Demons are able to push us to that level. In a normal condition for a normal person, these behaviors and accomplishments can seem like impossible things.

Extra Passion about anything is external.

Extreme passion about anything, including politics or a love interest, is the result of demons. Passion is a craze and a push from one or more demons around us. It is a good behavior to love someone too much, but it is not when you love someone with extremely jealousy and make their life hell. That is a negative behavior. Indeed, to control this is to reduce pressure of demons around us. Extreme passion is the result of demons controlling us.

Love or hate or similar feelings of an extreme nature means demons are there.

Love is a positive behavior, but demons can turn this positive behavior to an extreme behavior when we become too much possessive about something we love. We have no tolerance if our mother or father loves our other brothers or sisters more. We have no tolerance if our boyfriend or girlfriend talks or mixes with someone else. We cannot tolerate it if our husband or wife is getting a little friendly with someone else. Love is a positive behavior, but very quietly, demons bring extremism to love. And after that, a lot of negative arguments, fights, and damages happen. So, be careful and keep your control by acting more tolerant and positive.

الأشياء الخطيرة بعقل غير متأثرة بسيطرة الشيطان. ولكن تجعلنا الشياطين غير خائفين وترفع من شجاعتنا عن طريق تنويمنا مغناطيسياً. ونقوم بعمل أشياء متطرفة وغير مصدقة دون خوف من الموت أو الإصابة. ووراء كل تل كالإنجازات الخارقة، هناك جهد أو تصرف خارق. والشياطين قادرة على دفعنا وانتهازنا الى ذلك الحد. وفي الوضع الطبيعي لشخص طبيعي، تكون تلك الإنجازات والتصرفات أشياء مستحيلة.

الشعور الزائد حيال أي شيء خارجي.

إن الشعور الزائد حيال أي شيء، كالسياسة أو الحب، هو سببه الشياطيين. فالعاطفة هي جنون وانتهاز من قبل واحد أو أكثر من الشياطيين من حولنا. حيث أن الحب تصريف حسن ولكن لا يكون كذلك عندما تقع في حب شخص ما بشكل يصل الى الغيرة القاتلة وتحويل الحياة الى جحيم. فهذا هو تصرف سلبي. وفعلاً، للسيطرة على ذل التصرف عليك التقليل من ضغط الشياطيين من حولك عليك. والعاطفة الزائدة هي ناتجة عن وجود الشياطيين التي تسيطر علينا.

وجود الحب أو الكره أو مشاعر مشابهة لطبيعة زائدة عن الحاجة يعني وجود الشياطيين هناك.

إن الحب هو تصوف إيجابية، ولكن يمكن للجن أن تحوله الى تصرف زائد عندما نصبح نعشق شيء ما الى درجة الملكية. ولا نسامح الأمهات والآباء إذا كان يحبون إخواننا أو أخواتنا أكثر منا. ولا نسامح إذا تكلم/ت صديق/ة أو اختلطت مع شخص آخر. ولا نسامح زوجتنا أو زوجنا في حال كان لطيفاً مع شخص آخر. حيث أن الحب هو تصرف إيجابي ولكن بشكل هادئ، وتجلب الشياطيين لنا التطرف الى الحب. وبعد ذلك، تحدث الكثير من المجادلات السلبية والمشاكل. لذلك، عليك الحذر الحفاظ على السيطرة على أنفسكم عن طريق التصرف بشكل اكثر إيجابي ومتسامح.

Sometimes, I feel that a demon's control on me keeps my life full of desires and that this is the attraction of life, for life without any desires doesn't seem worth living.

This may sound crazy, but sometimes I feel that these extreme desires that demons feed our minds make up the very attraction and beauty of life. I am not talking about terrorist activities. I am not talking about damaging or killing someone. I am talking a passion for things, ideas, and other people. When I was a normal person, I was running after my desires like crazy. But when no demon pushes me too much for any particular desire or person, I feel just like a dull person. With no desire, I have no ambition, and consequently, I can give up on anything.

Extra or over shy and extra or over bold is due to external demon's pressure.

Extra shy, extra bold, extra hate, extra love—all of these are extreme conditions, and we are compelled by demons through hypnotism. Feeling drunk when someone uses alcohol or drugs come from external sources. It will be very difficult for me to explain this to you, but whenever I work to remove the demons from someone's mind or body, if those people are under the influence of sleeping pills, alcohol, or other drugs at that time, regardless of whether they are in front of me or in another part of the world, I always feel extremely sleepy. Most of the time, it is very difficult for me to stand up and stay awake during these cases. That's why I am always careful when I have to work with someone who may be alcoholic or addicted to drugs.

وأحياناً ما أشعر بأن سيطرة الشيطان علي يجعلني مليء بالرغبات وهذا هو جاذبية الحياة، لأن الحياة بدون رغبات لا تبدو تستحق العناء والعيش.

ومن المرجح أن يكون ذلك جنوناً، ولكن أحياناً ما أشعر بأن تلك الرغبات المتطرفة والتي يغديننا إياها الجن تجعل الحياة أكثر جاذبية وجمالاً. ولا أتكلم عن الأنشطة الإرهابية أو تدمير وقتل الناس. فأنا أتكلم عن عاطفة الأشياء والأفكار والأشخاص الآخرون. كنت شخص عادياً وكنت أركض خاف رغباتي كالمجنون. ولكن عندما لا يقوم أي شيطان بدفعي لعمل ذلك، أشعر بأنني شخص فارغ. حيث أنني بدون رغبات لا يوجد لدي طموح وبالتالي يمكنني أن أستسلم حيال أي شيء.

الخجل الزائد أو الجرأة الزائدة تعزى الى ضغط الشياطيين الخارجي.

إن الخجل الزائد والجرأة الزائدة والكراهية الزائدة والحب الزائد هي حالات متطرف، ونحن مجبرون على ذلك من قبل الشياطيين التي تستخدم التنويم المغناطيسي لعمل ذلك.

إن الشعر بالثمل عند استخدام الكحول أو المخدرات يأتي من مصادر خارجية. وسيكون من الصعب بالنسبة لي توضيح ذلك لكم، ولكن عندما أعمل على إزالة الشياطيين من عقل أو جسم شخص ما وفي حال كانوا تحت تأثير حبوب النوم أو الكحول أو المخدرات في حينه وبغض النظر سواءً كانوا أمامي أو في مكان آخر في العالم، دائماً ما أشعر بالنعاس الشديد. وفي معظم الأوقات، من الصعب بالنسبة لي الوقوف والبقاء مستيقظاً خلال تلك الحالات. لذلك السبب دائماً ما أكون حذراً عند العمل مع شخص من المرجح أن يكون مدمن على الكحول أو المخدرات.

Sexual desires are similar to hunger, fever, depression, happiness, sadness, anger, among other feelings.

Eye twitching is a very naughty habit that demons use to harass us. Whenever your eye is twitching, keep your finger on that eye and say, "I know you are doing this, Mr. Demon, to harass me. Quit doing it. If you are alerting me about a danger by twitching my eye, then go and fix that problem for me. But quit harassing me." If you talk like this and your eyes stop twitching, it means that the demon is listening to you, but in regards to how long and how many times it will listen, I cannot give you any guarantee. You cannot just control demons. Demons listen to you only when you are somebody who can put pressure on them. In ordinary conditions from normal people, they hear us but do not listen to us. Even if we are busy doing something very important and have no time to think about anything else, demons will be the first ones to remind us that we are hungry and we need to eat something immediately.

Description of different inner feelings, or kaifiyat.

Kaifiyat is an Urdu word. I cannot find similar word in English, but I would say it is much like "inner feelings." Demons give us two things: extreme behaviors and different inner feelings. Different inner feelings include feelings of too much pride, self-praise, self-importance, superiority, and self-love. All of these conditions are brought from the influence of demons. I learned about these inner feelings because a demon from someone I was working on was inside me for at least twenty-four hours, during which time I was under influence of that demon. I thought that the whole world was thinking about me and watching me. After those twenty-four hours, I figured out what was going on with me. Usually these qualities/demons come out from women. Once I figured out that I was under influence of a demon, that demon left me immediately, I am sure the reason it left

تشبه الرغبات الجنسية الى حد كبير الجوع والحمى والاكتئاب والسعادة والحزن والغضب وغير الكثير من المشاعر.

إن عادة وخز العين هي عادة بذيئة يستخدم الجن لإيذائنا. وعندما تنخز عينك، ضع أصبعك عليها وقل "أعلم أنك تفعل ذلك سيد. شيطان لإيذائي. كف عن فعل ذلك. وفي حال تنبيهك لي حيال خطر ما عن طريق وخز عيني، اذهب وعالج تلك المشكلة لأجلي. ولكن كف عن إيذائي." وفي حال تفوهك بهذا الكلام وتحافظ على إبقاء عينك واقفة عن الوخز، فهذا يعني أن الشيطان يستمع إليك ولكن بخصوص إلى متى وكم من المرات سيستمع إليك. ولا يمكنني إعطاؤه أي ضمان. ولا يمكنك التحكم بالشياطين. ويستمع الجن إليك فقط عندما تكون الشخص الذي يمكنه الضغط عليهم. وفي الحالات الطبيعية، يسمعوننا لكن لا يطيعوننا. وحتى لو كنا مشغولين في عمل شيء ما مهم جداً ولا يوجد لدينا الوقت للتفكير حيال أي شيء آخر، يتكون الشياطين أول من يذكرنا بأننا جائعون ونحتاج لأكل شيء ما فوراً.

وصف مشاعر داخلية مختلفة، kaifiyat

Kaifiyat هي كلمة أوردية، ولم أستطع إيجاد كلمة مشابهة لها في الإنجليزية، ولكن بإمكاني القول بأنها تعني "المشاعر الداخلية" تمنحنا الشياطين شيئين: التصرفات المتطرفة والمشاعر الداخلية. وتشمل المشاعر الداخلية على التفاخر الزائد والثناء على النفس والاهمية الذاتية والسمو وحب الذات. جميع تلك الحالات تأتي من تأثير الشياطين. وقد تعلمت عن تلك المشاعر الداخلية لأن شيطان من شخص كنت أعمل معه كان في داخلي لمدة أربعة وعشرين ساعة على الأقل. وفي الأثناء كنت تحت تأثير ذلك الشيطان. واعتقدت بأن العالم كله كان يفكر بشأني ويشاهدني. وبعد مضي تلك الأربعة والعشرين ساعة، اكتشفت ما الذي حدث لي. وعادة ما تخرج تلك الشياطين من النساء. وعندما اكتشفت أنني كنت تحت تأثير شيطان، تركني فوراً وأنا متأكد من أن السبب وراء تركه لي هو

45

was because I was not a very suitable person for that demon or that kind of behavior.

Smoking, drinking, and using drugs have external sources.

Because of our limited knowledge, we often think that we are addicted to smoking, drinking, or using drugs. But from my experience, I have learned that a few demons like the smell or taste of tobacco, alcohol, and drugs. This is extremely strange theory, but I can prove it to anyone very easily. Demons can hypnotize us and show us dreams, both good and bad. Demons can bring us to any extreme condition, and in the same way, demons can insist that we use a few things they like. But why would we smoke or drink or use drugs for them? Maybe we these make us more relaxed and comfortable. So, demons are capable of giving us relaxed and comfortable feelings, but they do this only when they want something. And demons want us to smoke, drink, and use drugs for them so that they feel good. They do not care if those things are bad for our health. They give us relaxed and soothing feelings as a bribe so that we use those unhealthy and dangerous things frequently. In case someone realize that smoking tobacco or drinking alcohol or using drugs are not healthy habits and try to quit those habits, demons punish those people by giving them "withdraw symptoms" until that person decide to start smoking/drinking or drugs again.

I can sit in front of a smoker, alcoholic, and a drug addict, and whenever those people start feeling that withdraw from their demons, I can take those pains away. And after, I am sure they will feel 100 percent normal again. If you want to quit any of these bad habits, you can use my ideas wherever you are. If someone claims that he or she can communicate with demons or control them even a little, that person can remove the demon that is compelling you to smoke, use drugs, or drink alcohol, and if you do not listen to that demon, that demon will make your life hell by giving you all kind of pains. Willpower is another solution if you cannot find a person like me.

أنني لم أكن الشخص المناسب لذلك الشيطان أو ذلك النوع من التصرف.

هناك مصادر خارجية للتدخين وشرب الكحول والمخدرات.

بسبب معرفتنا المحدودة، عادة ما نعتقد أننا مدمنون على التدخين أو شرب الكحول أو تعاطي المخدرات. ولكن من نتاج خبرتي، فلقد تعلمت أنه هناك القليل من الشياطيين التي تحب رائحة أو طعم التبغ أو الكحول أو المخدرات. هذه حقاً نظرية غريبة، ولكن يمكنني اثباث ذلك لأي شخص بكل سهولة. حيث أنه بإمكان الشياطيين تنويمنا مغناطيسياً ويرونا الأحلام السيئة والجيدة. ويمكن للشياطين وضعنا في أي حالة متطرفة، وبنفس الطريقة، يمكن للشياطين اقناعنا باستخدام أشياء هو يرغبون بها. ولكن لماذا نقوم بالتدخين أو الشرب أو تعاطي المخدرات لأجلهم؟ ربما بأن تلك الأشياء تجعلنا أكثر ارتياحاً. لذلك، فإن الشياطيين قادرة على منحنا الشعور بالارتياح، ولكنهم يفعلون ذلك فقط لأنهم يريدون شيئاً ما. وتريدنا الشياطيين أن نقوم بالتدخين و شرب الكحول وتعاطي المخدرات لأجلهم حتى يشعروا بالارتياح. فهم لا يهتمون في حال كانت تلك الأشياء جيدة أو سيئة على صحتنا. فهم يمنحونا مشاعر ناعمة و مرتاحة كرشوة حتى نقوم باستخدام تلك الأشياء الغير صحية والخطيرة بشكل متكرر. وفي حال إدراك شخص ما أن التدخين أو شرب الكحول أو تعاطي المخدرات ليست بالعادات السليمة ويحاول تركها، تقوم الشياطيين بمعاقبته بمنحه "أمراض الانسحاب" حتى يقرر ذلك الشخص العودة الي التدخين/شرب الكحول أو تعاطي المخدرات مجدداً.

يمكنني الجلوس أمام مدخن أو مدمن على الكحول أو المخدرات وعندما يشعر هؤلاء الأشخاص بالانسحاب من شياطينهم، بإمكاني أخذ تلك الآلام بعيداً عنهم. وبعد ذلك، أكون متأكد بأنهم سيشعرون بأنهم أشخاص طبيعيون بنسبة 100%. وفي حال رغبتك في ترك أي من تلك العادات السيئة. يمكنك استخدام أفكاري أينما تكون. وفي حال ادعاء شخص ما بأنه يستطيع الاتصال بالشياطيين أ والتحكم بهم حتى ولو بنسبة قليلة، يمكن لذلك الشخص اخراج الشيطان الذي يقوم بإجبارك على التدخين وتعاطي المخدرات وشرب الكحول. وفي حال عدم استماعك للشيطان، سيجعل حياتك كالجحيم بالتسبب لك بجميع أنواع الآلام. وتعد قوة الإرادة حل آخر في حال عدم عثورك على شخص مثلي.

If you are experiencing any problem with your left ear, such as heavy feelings or whistling noises or deafness, it means that demons are using this path to reach our mind.

Outside our bodies, demons are really small flying objects. They are similar to visible insects! They are not like what we have seen in horror movies or scary pictures. They are totally harmless when they are flying in air around us. Sometimes I have seen several hundred demons flying around me in a very small room. Until now, I have never seen any of demons expanding their bodies when they are flying in the air, but demons can easily compressed and expend their sizes according to the body they penetrate or possess. They can very easily damage any nerve or organ of a body. They can easily go into any vein, artery, or tube and use their compressing/expanding qualities to block it. For demons, the left ear is the path toward our brains. Demons reach into our minds to hypnotize us by using our left ear. Anybody who has problems with his or her left ear could be under the influence of a demon.

Demons are the ones that discourage us from visiting doctors or religious people.

Demons are main cause of mental sickness within humans. Demons and diseases cause a lot of physical and mental disorders in our brains and our bodies. The mentally sick person is pretty much under the control of one or more demons. We can see if someone is acting crazy around us. Doctors and other normal people can easily judge that a particular person is exhibiting a mental illness, but that mentally sick person never realizes that he or she is talking and acting crazy. That is because that crazy person is under the control of a demon's hypnotism. Demons continuously convince that crazy and mentally ill person that he or she is not sick, that he or she is perfectly okay. This mentally ill person may believe that everybody else around him or her is wrong, crazy, or mentally sick. If you have experience around

وفي حال مواجهتك لأي مشكلة بأذنك اليسرى، المشاعر الثقيلة أو انزعاج تصفير أو الصم، فهذا يعني بأن تلك الشياطيين تستخدم تلك الطريقة للوصول الى عقلك.

وخارجاً عن أجسامنا، فان الشياطيين أجسام طائرة صغيرة. فهي تشبه الحشرات التي نراها! وهم ليسوا كالأجسام التي نراها في أفلام الرعب أو الصور المخيفة. فهم غير مؤذيين بشكل كامل عندما يكونون طائرين في الهواء من حولنا. وأحياناً ما كنت أرى المئات منها طائرة من حولي في غرفة صغيرة جداً. وحتى الآن، فلم أرى أي من الشياطين التي تتمدد أجسامها عندما يكونون طائرين في الجو، ولكن يمكنها بسهولة الانكماش والتوسع طبقاً للجسم الذي يقومون بالتغلغل فيه وامتلاكه. ويمكنهم بسهولة اتلاف أي عصب أو عضو في الجسم. وبإمكانهم الوصول الى الوريد والشريان بكل سهولة لاستخدامه في الانكماش/التوسع لإغلاقه. وبالنسبة للشياطيين، تعد الأذن اليسرى الطريق للوصول الى أدمغتنا. وتقوم الشياطين بالوصول الى أدمغتنا عن طريق تنويمنا مغناطيسياً واستخدام الأذن اليسرى. وأي شخص يكون لديه مشاكل في الأذن اليسرى فمن المرجح أن يكون تحت تأثير شيطان ما.

إن الشياطين هي من لا تشجعنا على زيادة الطبيب أو رجال الدين.

تعد الشياطين السبب الرئيسي في المرض العقلي عند البشر. حيث أن الشياطين والأمراض تسبب الكثير من الاضطرابات العقلية والجسدية. ويعتبر الشخص المريض عقلياً تحت سيطرة واحد أو أكثر من الشياطين. ويمكننا مشاهدة في حال تصرف شخص ما بشكل جنوني من حولنا. ويمكن للأطباء والناس الطبيعيون الحكم على ذلك الشخص بتعرضه لمرض عقلي بكل سهولة، ولكن لا يدرك ذلك الشخص المريض عقلياً بأنه يتحدث أو يتصرف بشكل جنوني أبداً. وذلك لأنه تحت سيطرة التنويم المغناطيسي للشياطين. وتقوم الشياطيين بشكل مستمر بإقناع الشخص المريض عقلياً بأن له ليس كذلك. ومن المرجح لذلك الشخص المختل عقلياً أن يصدق ذلك ويعتقد أن كل شخص من حوله مخطئ ومجنون ومريض عقلاً. وفي حال مواجهتك

a mentally sick person, you know how they do not want to take any medication, how they do not like doctors, and how they do not like the company of religious people. The reason is demons. Demons do not let this person take medication or go to doctors or religious people easily so that the individual stays sick for a long time.

Demons have a lot of resistance to medication and doctors, but demons cannot resist religious people and religious practices for a long time.

There is no perfect medication that can bring an abnormal or mentally sick person back to a normal mental condition. Doctors feed or inject sedatives into mentally sick people. Once the mentally ill person goes to sleep, the pressure from demons is usually reduced for a few days. This is the reason doctors regularly suggest those medications for the treatment of mentally ill people. Those medications keep mentally ill people relaxed and down most of the time. In that condition, demons cannot use that person completely. Do not think that those medications can remove that demon from the person. A slow or sleepy person is simply less useful to demons. That's why demons continuously hypnotize that person and insist that mentally ill person not take any medications. All of them resist taking medications because of the influence of demons. No medication has any effect on demons. Demons are completely resistance to medications. Medications are totally ineffective against demons. Only truly religious people can control the problems created by demons, not any medication.

Demons do not give up command of a human to another demon easily. It never happens without a fight?

We are not aware of this, but demons act like we are their property. Demons treat us as their toys. Demon use us however they want by hypnotizing us. But one demon will never let another demon take over the animal they possess unless the new demon is more

لشخص مريض عقلياً من حولك، فإنك ستعلم مدى عدم رغبتهم في تناول أي أدوية ومدي عدم رغبته في رؤية الطبيب ومدي عدم رغبتهم في مصاحبة رجال الدين. وإن السبب وراء ذلك هو الشياطين. ولا تسمح تلك الشياطين لذلك الشخص بتناول الأدوية أو الذهاب للطبيب أو رجال الدين بشكل سهل حتى يبقه ذلك الشخص مريض لأطول فترة ممكنة.

يوجد لدى الجن الكثير من المقاومة للأدوية والأطباء، ولكن لا يمكنها مقاومة رجال الدية لفترة طويلة.

لا يوجد هناك دوام مثالي لعلاج الشخص المريض عقلياً. ويمكن للأطباء اعطاء المسكنات في الأشخاص المريضين عقلياً. وعندما يذهب الشخص المريض للنوم، فإن ضغط الجن عليه ينخفض لبضعة أيام. ولهذا السبب يقترح الأطباء تناول تلك الأدوية بشكل منتظم. وتحافظ تلك الأدوية على الأشخاص المريضين عقلياً بالارتياح لمعظم الوقت. وفي تلك الحالة، لا يمكن للجن استخدام ذلك الشخص بشكل كامل. ولا تعتقد أن تلك الأدوية يمكنها ازالة ذلك الشيطان من الشخص. ويعد الشخص البطيء والنعس أقل فائدة للشياطين. ولهذا تقوم الشياطين بتنويم الشخص بشكل مستمر وتقنعه على عدم تناول الادوية. وجميعهم يقاوم تناول الأدوية بسبب تأثير الشياطين. ولا يأثر أي دواء على الشياطين. وهم مقاومين بشكل كامل للأدوية. وتكون الأدوية غير فعالة. فقط رجال الدين من يمكنهم من التحكم بالمشاكل المسببة من قبل الشياطين وليس الأدوية.

لا تستسلم الشياطين لأوامر الإنسان لأي شيطان آخر. ولا يحدث ذلك أبداً بدون صراع فيما بين الشياطين؟

فنحن غير مدركين لذلك، ولكن الشياطين تتصرف وكأننا ملكيتهم. وتعاملون الشياطين كأننا دمى لهم. ويستخدموننا على الرغم من تنويما مغناطيسياً. ولكن لا يسمح شيطان ما لشيطان آخر بالتغلب على الشخص الذي يملكه حتى يكون الشيطان الجديد أكثر

powerful. Some people are under the influence of more than one demon. The person who is under the influence of more than one powerful demon will become an extremely ill person with extreme behavior problems. Demons do not like cool, sensible, and normal people. Demons usually prefer possessing the body of short-tempered, stubborn, and extreme people. It is easy for demons to exploit these kinds of people. Honesty, it is not difficult for demons to make anyone crazy, but abnormally short-tempered individuals and people prone extreme behavior are an easy task for them. Demons usually have total control and command of that person. If another demon wants to take command of that person, those demons have to fight with each other to change the command.

Demons inside and around us continuously generate desires in our minds?

Demons cannot leave us in peace. Demons keep us disturbed all the time, but not because they are our enemies. The reason is that we are their hobby. They want us to entertain them. Demons continuously create desires and wishes in our minds. After that, demons continuously push us to run after those wishes and desires. Demons keep us very unhappy and angry when we cannot get whatever we desire. They feel better when they have control over us.

Once incident with me, when I was unable to feel the touch of demon but I was only able to smell it.

This is one of the worst incidents to happen to me. The refrigerator in my house was out of order one time. We started using a second unit. Nobody bothered to clean up the broken refrigeration. We had four packets of ground chicken in that refrigerator for almost a month. After one month, a technician came to fix that refrigerator, and before he fixed it, he cleaned it first. Along with some other stuff, he left three plastic-wrapped chicken packets in the backyard. When I came back

قوة. ويكون بعض الأشخاص تحت تأثير أكثر من شيطان واحد. ويكون عادة هذا الشخص مريض للغاية ولديه مشاكل في التصرف المتطرف. ولا ترغب الشياطين بالأشخاص العاديين والحساسيين والهادئين. وعادةً ما تفضل الشياطين السيطرة على أشخاص ذي الغضب السريع والعناد والأشخاص المتطرفون. ومن السهل على الشياطين استغلال تلك الأنواع من الشياطين. وبصراحة، ليس من السهل على الشياطين جعل أي شخص مجنوناً ولكن الأفراد السريعين الغضب والغير طبيعيين والأشخاص العرضة للتصرف المتطرف هم أهداف سهلة بالنسبة للجن. وعادة ما يسيطر الجن بشكل كلي على ذلك النوع من الأشخاص. وفي حال رغبة شيطان آخر في السيطرة على ذلك الشخص، تقوم تلك الشياطين بالصراع والاتصال مع بعضها البعض لتغيير السيطرة.

تولد الشياطين لدينا الرغبات بشكل مستمر في داخلنا ومن حولنا؟

لا يمكن للشياطين تركنا في سلام. وهي تبقينا متشتتين طوال الوقت، ولكن ليس لأنهم أعداءنا. حيث أن السبب هو أننا هوايتهم. ويرغبون في الترفيه معهم. وعادة ما تنشأ الشياطين الرغبات والأمنيات في عقولنا. وبعد ذلك، تدفعنا للركض وراء تلك الرغبات. وتبقينا غير سعداء وغاضبين عندما لا نصل الى الرغبة التي نريدها. ويشعرون بالراحة عند سيطرتهم علينا.

وقد حدثت معي حادثة، عندما كنت غير قادر على لمس الجن ولكن كنت فقط قادراً على شم رائحته.

وهي تلك أسوأ الحوادث التي جرت معي. فقد كانت الثلاجة متعطلة في يوم من الأيام. وبدأت باستخدام الثلاجة الاحتياطية. ولم يزعجني أي شخص في تنظيف الثلاجة المعطلة. فقد كان لدينا أربع صناديق مليئة بالدجاج في تلك الثلاجة لطيلة شهر تقريباً. وبعد شهر واحد، جاء التقني لإصلاح تلك الثلاجة، وقبل أن يقوم بإصلاحها، قام بتنظيفها أولاً. وبصحبته بعض العاملين، فقد ترك ثلاثة من حزم الدجاج الملفوفة بالبلاستيك. وعندما عدت الى

to the house, I saw three chicken packets in the backyard. For some reason, I decided to unwrap those chicken packets and feed the cats in my front yard. Once I opened those packets of ground chicken, I had to deal with an extremely bad smell. I picked up those packets and set them down in the far corner of the front yard. I washed my hand several times, but that smell moved with me. And within few minutes, something was inside my body. I cannot explain what happened to me in the next thirty minutes and how I handle that difficult problem. But somehow, I handled that problem. What I am trying to tell you is how that bad smell came from the ground chicken and how that demon became my friend after it tried to kill me for thirty minutes. After that day, that bad smell visited me at least seven to eight times as a friend without hurting me and without going inside my body. Usually, after two or three days, I ask everyone to leave my house. That smell was not the demon itself. After three days, that smell left my house. Since then, it had never visited me again.

Few people, their pain/sickness go away in seconds. And few very difficult? Why do people recover from pain at different rate?

The fact that people recover from sickness and pain at a different rate has always been a mystery to me. Sometimes I feel that the pain is not difficult and will leave that body easily, but during other times, I have to insist that the demons leave the body. Sometimes people have pains for several years, and it takes more time for the demon to leave that particular body. But most of the time, pain leaves the body immediately without too much struggle. God knows better about this mystery. Most of the time, I just feel, I am just a reason in many cases otherwise may be Go d already decided to take their pain away from those people. People suffering from arthritis pains and taking six or seven kinds of prescription pills to kill the pain for several years come around me, and then their pain leave their bodies and finds some other place to dwell. On a few times, the task is very easy, but it can consume a lot of time. I have two steps to communicate with

المنزل، شاهدت ثلاثة من حزم الدجاج في الساحة الخلفية. ولسبب ما، قررت عدم لف تلك القطع من الدجاج واطعامها للقطط في الساحة الأمامية للمنزل. وعندما فتحت تلك الحزم، كان علي التعامل مع رائحة سيئة جداً. وقمت بالتقاط تلك القطع من الدجاج ووضعها في الزاوية البعيدة من الساحة الأمامية للمنزل. وقمت بغسل يداي عدة مرات، ولكن الرائحة بقيت على يداي. وخلال دقائق، كان شيئاً ما داخل جسمي. ولا يمكنني تفسير ما حدث لي في الثلاثين دقيقة وكيفية تعاملي مع تلك المشكلة المعقدة. ولكن بطريقة ما، تعاملت مع تلك المشكلة. ما احاول قوله لكم هو كيفية تنقل تلك الرائحة السيئة من الدجاج الى كيفية تحول الشيطان الى صديق بعدما حاول قتلي في خلال تلك الثلاثين دقيقة. وبعد ذلك اليوم، جاءت الرائحة السيئة الي من سبع الى ثمان مرات على الأقل كصديق بدون إيذائي ودون الدخول الى جسمي. وعادة، بعد يومين أو ثلاثة، طلبت من شخص ما مغادرة منزلي. ولم تكن تلك الرائحة الشيطان نفسه. وبعد ثلاثة أيام أخرى، غادرت تلك الرائحة منزلي. ومنذ حينه، لم تزرني أبداً.

القليل من الناس من يغادر هم الالم/والمرض خلال ثوان. وبعضهم يصعب عليهم فعل ذلك؟ لما يشفى الناس من الآلام بنسبٍ مختلفة؟

في الحقيقة، أن شفاء الناس من المرض والألم بنسب متفاوتة دائماً ما كان مأساوياً بالنسبة إلي. وأحياناً ما أشعر بأن ذلك الألم ليس بالصعب وسيغادر الجسم بسهولة، ولكنه يؤذي في أحيان اخرى. وعلي أن أقنع تلك الشياطين مغادرة الجسم. وعادةً ما يكون أشخاص لديهم آلام لسنين عديدة، ويأخذ المزيد من الوقت لمغادرة الشيطان الجسم. ولكن في معظم الأوقات، يغادر الألم الجسم فوراً دون عناءٍ شديد. والله يعلم بشكل أفضل عن هذه المأساة. وعادةً ما أشعر بأنني انا السبب في العديد من الحالات عدا أن يكون هو الله من قرر بالتخلص من آلامهم. يتناول الأشخاص الذين يعانون ما آلام المفاصل سبعة أنواع من الحبوب لتسكين الألم لسنين عديدة، ومن ثم يغادر الألم أجسامهم ويبحث عن أماكن أخرى للعيش. وفي عدة أوقات، تكون المهمة سهلة للغاية، ولكن يمكن أن تأخذ الكثير من الوقت. ولدى خطوتين للاتصال مع

pains. First, I convince them to leave—if they listen to me. Otherwise, I insist these pains leave the body. Ninety-nine percent of the time, I am successful in my efforts.

Why do people recover from pain at different rates? Reasons for that maybe because

They have more damaged body or joint or organ so that pain is over their body.
2) Pain is more powerful demon/insect and giving a lot of resistance and not ready to leave. Like cancer, patients use more and more medications everyday but those insect never leave that part of the body and finally completely destroy the health of that person. My point I can move that insect from there but for how long, no idea.

Cold and flu are difficult viruses.

The flu and colds both are a little bit difficult and time-consuming to fix. The flu can completely come back within few minutes after I remove it from a body. Usually, I give up with flu easily. But if insist several times, it gets better, but it's not easy. Honestly, flu is not impossible for me, but it is very hard job. Colds are difficult jobs too. They come back again and again several times. But they are not impossible. I strongly feel that the flu is not a single thing. I feel that the flu is a group of diseases that operates together. These days, I suggest everyone start medication for the flu and colds immediately. During that time, I can help them reduce the pressure quickly. I've had to suffer the flu whenever I've helped someone to beat it, but not all the time.

الآلام. أولاً، أقنعهم بالرحيل- في حال استمعوا. عدا ذلك، أجبر تلك الآلام على مغادرة الجسم. وأنجح في تلك الجهود بنسبة 99% في معظم الأوقات.

لماذا يتعافى الناس من تلك الآلام بنسبة متفاوتة؟ إن الأسباب وراء ذلك ربما تكون

1) يكون جسم هؤلاء الأشخاص أكثر تلفاً لذلك يكون تأثير الألم أكبر عليهم.
2) ويكون الألم شيطان أكثر قوة ولدي مقاومة كبيرة ولا يغادر بسهولة. فعلى سبيل المثال، مرضى السرطان يستخدمون الكثير من الأدوية كل يوم ولكن تلك الحشرات لا تغادر أبداً وتقوم بإتلاف الجسم بشكل كامل. ووجهة نظري هي أنه بإمكاني اخراج تلك الحشرة من هناك ولكن ما المدة التي أحتاجها، أعتقد أنه لا يوجد لدي أدنى أي فكرة.

إن الإنفلونزا والبرد فيروسات صعبة

تعد فيروسات الإنفلونزا والبرد من الفيروسات الصعبة العلاج قليلاً وتستهلك الوقت لعلاجها. فيمكن للإنفلونزا أن تعود مجدداً إلى الجسم خلال بعض دقائق بعد أن أخرجها. وعادة، أستسلم من مقاومة الإنفلونزا بكل سهولة. ولكن في حال اصراري عدة مرات، أحسن الجسم من آلام الإنفلونزا، ولكن ليس تلك السهولة. وبصراحة، لا تمثل الإنفلونزا عقدة بالنسبة لي، ولكن أجدها مهمة صعبة وشاقة. ويعد البرد مهمة صعبة أيضاً بالنسبة لي. فهي تعود الى الجسم مراراً وتكراراً. ولكن ليس بالمهمة المستحيلة. وأشعر بأن الإنفلونزا هي مجموعة من الامراض تعمل مع بعضها البعض. وفي هذه الأيام، أقترح بأن يبدأ كل شخص بالعلاج لمرض الإنفلونزا والبرد مباشرة. وفي تلك الأثناء، يمكنني ان أساعده في التخفيف من الضغط بسرعة. وقد كان علي أن أعاني من الإنفلونزا حينما أساعد أي شخص للتغلب عليه ولكن ليس في كل الأوقات.

One time, when I was already suffering from some pains and sickness take out I decided to go underneath of a big tree.

We know that big fish eats small fish in seas and oceans. This is only my experience. I never tried to experience it again, either. In the beginning when I was trying to learn more about demons and the world of diseases, I was very bold and less careful. Day by day, I learned more and more, and I became more and more careful about demons and diseases. In the beginning, I frequently went underneath big trees at night without any fear. I still don't feel any fear going under the big trees in middle of night, but lately, I have had less courage. I used to start working on any kind of pain or disease in anyone without knowing any of the details about the problem. But these days, I am less bold and more careful. One time when I had different diseases and pains in my body, I went close to one big tree. Immediately, one demon jumped on me from that tree. I sensed that demon all around and inside my body for at least two or three minutes. After a few minutes, when that demon came out of my body, I felt perfectly all right. All the pains and sick feelings I had felt before just disappeared from my body. When I left that tree, I had no pain or sick feelings at all. But still, I will not recommend this to anyone, reason: How they will get rid of demons from trees in their bodies.

If you sometimes feel your cell phone vibrating in your pocket or hear it ringing but nothing is actually happening, this is not a problem.

This happens to everyone. Few people notice it, and many just ignore it. You may have your cell phone in your pocket and suddenly feel it vibrating only to find that you have no missed calls. Similarly, you may have your cell phone and suddenly hear it ringing but then find that it was dead silent the whole time. So what is this? These are demons around us. These demons are capable of showing us anything

وفي يوم من الأيام، عندما كنت مستعداً لمعاناة من بعض الآلام والمرض قررت الذهاب الى تحت شجرة كبيرة.

وكلنا يعلم بأن السمكة الكبيرة تأكل السمكة الصغيرة في البحار والمحيطات. وهذه هي تجربتي في الحياة. فلم أحاول أبداً أن أعيد التجربة مرة أخرى. وفي البداية، عندما كنت أحاول تعلم المزيد عن الشياطين وعالم الأمراض، كنت جريئاً جداً وغير حذر. ويوماً بعد يوم، تعلمت المزيد، وأصبحت أكثر حذراً بشأن الشياطين والأمراض. في البداية، ذهب مراراً الى تحت شجر كبير في الليل بدون أي خوف. ولكن لا زلت لا أشعر بالخوف عند الذهاب الى تحت الأشجار في منتصف الليل. ولكن مؤخراً، لم يكن لدي الشجاعة الكافية لفعل ذلك. وتعودت أن أبدأ العمل على أي نوع من الآلام دون معرفة أي تفاصيل عن المشكلة. ولكن في هذه الأيام، فأن أقل جرأة وأكثر حذراً. وفي يوم من الأيام وعندما كنت أعاني من أمراض وآلام مختلفة في جسمي، ذهب بالقرب من شجرة كبيرة. وفوراً قفز شيطان من تلك الشجر الى جسمي. وشعرت به في جميع أنحاء جسمي لدقيقتين أو ثلاثة على الأقل. وبعد بضع دقائق، وعندما خرج ذلك الجن من جسمي، شعرت بصحة جيدة جداً. واختفت جميع الآلام ومشاعر المرض التي شعرت بها. وعندما غادرت من تحت تلك الشجرة، لم يظهر أي ألم أو مشاعر مرض إطلاقاً. ولكن ما زلت لا أوصي أي شخص على فعل ذلك، والسبب هو أنه كيف سيتخلصون من الشياطين تحت الأشجار؟

وفي حال شعورك في بعض الأحيان بأن هاتفك النقال يعتز في جيبك أو تسمعه يرن ولكن لا يحدث أي شيء من ذلك في الحقيقة، هذه ليست مشكلة.

فهذا يحدث لأي شخص. وقد لاحظه القليل من الأشخاص. وتجاهله الكثيرون. ومن المحتمل أن يكون جهازك النقال في جيبك وفجأة تشعر بأنه يهتز فقط للتأكد من أنه لا يوجد مكالمات فائتة في جوالك. وبشكل مشابه، من المحتمل أن تسمع هاتفك النقال يرن ولكن تكتشف أنه كان في الوضع الصامت طوال الوقت. لذلك ما هذا؟ إنها تلك الشياطين من حولنا. حيث أنها قادرة على أن ترينا أي شيء

whenever they want. By hypnotizing us, demons can make us hear any noise or feel any sensation, even a ringing phone or a vibration. They have a lot of time to play with us all the time. This is fun for them. But we feel that we may be going crazy.

I do not find a single person without liver or stomach and intestine problems.

My senses and my body are programmed to be more sensitive to pains. That's why, even if I have any minor pains or sicknesses around or inside me, I start feeling them immediately. Usually, a normal person does not feel pain or sickness until their body has been sufficiently damaged. But I start feeling these immediately, and I must endure much more pain as compared to a normal person. Whenever I work on my family members and close friends, I usually cover each and every part of their bodies. Even if they feel nothing wrong in their livers, stomachs, or intestines, I always receive so many problems from those organs. I ask people if they are feeling much pain before I work on them, and most of the time, they say they were okay and don't feel any pain right now. Only God knows why some pains are not hurtful for them but extremely hurtful for me.

I don't need to go to someone to release them from demons.

In this world, only God knows about his system. I strongly feel that I am just a medium, but there is also the will of God. Even a photo or picture is enough for me to help a person. I am able to fix their pain over phone and sometimes without even contacting them. All I ask for is an update about their conditions. Sometimes it is so easy to fix major problems, but other times, it is very difficult to fix really minor problems. But I still try my best to help people; however, if God wants to punish someone, no one can help that person. In 99.9 percent of cases, I do not need to go to anyone. I can do a lot of positive activities

حينما تشاء. فيمكن للشياطين ،عن طريق تنويمنا مغناطيسياً، أن يجعلونا نسمع أي إزعاج أو الشعور بأي احساس حتى رنين واهتزاز الهاتف. فلديهم الكثير من الوقت للعب معنا. وهذا ممتع بالنسبة لهم. ولكن نشعر بأننا مجانين.

لم أجد شخص واحد بدون مشاكل في كبد أو معدة أو أمعاء.

إن حواسي وجسمي مبرمجان ليكونا أكثر تحسساً للآلام. لذلك السبب، حتى لو كان لدي آلام خفيفة، أشعر بها فوراً. وعادة، لا يشعر الشخص العادي بتلك الآلام حتى يدمر جسمه. ولكن أنا أشعر بها فوراً، وعلي تحمل المزيد من الآلام مقارنةً مع الشخص العادي. وحينما أعمل على أفراد عائلتي وأصدقائي المقربين، عادة ما أغطي كل جزء من أجسامهم. حتى لو لم يشعروا بأي شيء خاطئ في أكبادهم أو معدتهم أو أمعائهم. ودائماً ما أستقبل الكثير من المشاكل من تلك الأعضاء. وأسأل الأشخاص في حال كانوا يشعرون بالكثير من الآلام قبل علاجي لهم، ويقولون معظم الأوقات بأنهم بخير ولا يشعرون بأي ألم حالياً. فقط الله وحده يعلم لماذا تكون بعض الآلام غير ضارة ولكن تكون كذلك بالنسبة لي.

ولا أحتاج للذهاب الى شخص ما لتحريره من الشياطين.

في هذا العالم، فقط الله وحده يعلم بشأن هذا النظام. وأشعر بقوة بأنني فقط وسيط، ولكن هناك إرادة الله. حتى كل صورة كانت صورة كافية بالنسبة لمساعدة شخص ما. وأنا قادر على علاج آلام الناس عن طريق الهاتف وأحياناً دون الحاجة الى الاتصال بهم. كل ما أطلبه هو آخر الأحداث عن حالاتهم. وأحياناً من السهل علاج المشاكل الكبيرة ومن الصعب علاج الصغيرة منها. علاوة على ذلك، في حال أراد الله معاقبة شخص ما، لا يستطيع أحد مساعدته. وفي 99.9% من الحالات، لا أحتاج للذهاب لرؤية أي شخص. فباستطاعتي فعل الكثير من الأنشطة الإيجابية

to help people just by sitting in my office or home, regardless of where that person is in the world.

Demons and disease are better friends than human beings, if they become your friend.

It's true. It is not easy to communicate with them. Demons and diseases have only one direction, what they want from us. They do not care what we want. Most of us don't have any clue about the invisible world or what is happening within it. Once demons or diseases become friends, nobody can be better friends than they can be to you. Their sincerity is pure, not fake like some humans'. But it is not easy to become friends with them. It may be a little less difficult to become friends with a demon, but it is almost impossible to become friends with a disease. In my case, it is not difficult to become the friend of a demon or disease. Demons definitely listen to me more. In the case of diseases, they give me a hard time when they come out of a body. Sometimes I convince them to leave, and other times, I have to insist that they leave. But after this meeting, they are very easygoing with me. They listen to me immediately after the first time. A lot of times, they just figure out my intention and come out of that person, or they do not choose anyone around me or close to me. Anyway, demons and diseases are like fire, and even when fire is your friend, you cannot keep it close to you, because it burns.

Cutting or trimming a tree is very annoying to demons. Demons really get upset.

Green trees are just a house for demons. They live on trees for years. Hundreds or more just live on one tree. As we don't like anyone to destroy our houses, they do not like if someone messes with their tree. Cutting or trimming a tree is very annoying to demons. As I said, they are like us mentally, but they have better ways to hurt us and take revenge on us. A demon's revenge is not limited to one person.

لمساعدة الناس عند طريق الجلوس في المكتب أو البيت بغض النظر عن مكان ذلك الشخص في العالم.

تعد الشياطيين والأمراض أفضل أصدقاء بدلاً من البشر في أصبحوا أصدقائك.

هذا صحيح. فليس من السهل الاتصال بهم. حيث أن الشياطيين والأمراض لها اتجاه واحد فقط، وهو الذي يريدونه منا. فهم لا يهتمون بما نريد نحن. ولا يعرف معظمنا أي شيء عن العالم الخفي أو الذين يحدث فيه. وعندما تصبح الشياطيين أو الأمراض صديقة لنا، لا يمكن لأحد أن يكون صديقاً لنا أكثر منهم. حيث أن اخلاصهم نقي وليس مزيف كإخلاص بعض البشر. ولكن ليس من السهل أن نكون أصدقاء معهم. وربما من الصعب قليلاً أن نكون أصدقاء مع شيطان ما، ولكنه ليس مستحيل. وفي حالتي، ليس من الصعب أن نصبح أصدقاء مع شيطان أو مرض ما. وبكل تأكيد تستمع إلى الشياطيين أكثر. وفي حالة الأمراض، يمنحوني وقت صعب عند الخروج من جسمي. وأحياناً ما أقنعهم بالمغادرة وفي أحيان أخرى أجبرهم على فعل ذلك. ولكن بعد هذا الاجتماع، أصبحِوا متساهلين معي. ويستمعون إلي فوراً بعد المرة الأولى. وفي كثير من الأوقات، يكتشفون نيتي ويخرجون من ذلك الشخص، أو لا يختارون شخص آخر من حولي أو قريب مني. وعلى أي حال، تشبه الشياطيين والأمراض النيران عندما تكون النيران صديقتك، فلا تستطيع أن تبقيها بجانبك لأنها تحترق.

إن قطع أو تقليم شجرة يزعج الشياطيين كثيراً. وتصبح الشياطيين منزعجة.

تعد الأشجار الخضراء منزل للجن. فهم يعيشون على الأشجار لسنين. ويعيش مئات منهم على شجرة واحدة. وبما أننا لا نرغب أحداً بتدمير منزلنا، فإن الشياطيين أيضاً لا ترغب أحداً العبث بأشجارها. وقطع أو تقليم شجرة يزعج الشياطيين كثيراً. وكما قلت، فهم يشبهوننا من الناحية العقلية، ولكن لديهم طرق أفضل لإيذائنا والانتقام منا. وانتقام الشياطيين غير محدود بشخص معين.

Demons take revenge from generations. This may be sound crazy to you, but it may be helpful to reduce their anger just in case you need to cut or trim a tree. Before you cut any tree, just go close talk to tree: "Whoever lives on this tree, I need their permission to cut this tree." Just tell them your excuse of cutting that tree and tell them to move to another place. Give them at least fifteen days before you cut that tree down. Usually, they do not get too upset when we ask permission from them.

Demons are a mystery to everyone. I am sure I am a mystery to them!

I believe most people in this world do not believe in the concept of demons. Most people do not believe that there is a parallel world and that the population of that invisible world is much higher than the population of the visible world. Most people have no clue that this invisible world is involved in our lives and our affairs. Maybe after they have read this book, a few people will gain a concept of this invisible world. But for most of the people, this invisible world will remain an unsolved mystery. But on other hand, I strongly feel that though all demons and diseases are a mystery to human beings, I am a mystery to demons and diseases. I surprise them by informing them when they come close to me. I surprise them when I point my finger at them as they are flying in air. And I surprise them when I keep my eyes pointed straight at them.

I can easily invite any demon into me from any person in any part of the world. But trust me; it is not a fun at least first 24 hours.

This is a very strange concept but, it is possible to ask any demon possessing any human body in any part of the world to leave. I can convince them to leave that body, but sometimes I need to insist. Insisting is a procedure, and it takes some time. But during the

وتأخذ الشياطين بثأرها لأجيال. وربما يبدو ذلك نوعاً من الجنون، ولكن قد يكون ذي فائدة لتخفيف غضبهم في حال حاجتك لقطع أو تقليم شجرة ما. قبل قطعك لأي شجرة، اقترب وتحدث مع الشجرة: "أياً كان يعيش على تلك الشجرة، أحتاج تصريح لقطع الشجرة." فقط افصح لهم عن عذرك بقطع تلك الشجرة واطلب منهم الانتقال الى مكان آخر. وامنحهم على الأقل خمسة عشر يماً قبل قطعك لتلك الشجرة. وعادة، لا ينزعجوا كثيراً عند سؤالهم عن الإذن لقطع الشجرة.

تعد الشياطيين معضلة لكل فرد. وأنا متأكد من أنني أشكل معضلة لهم!

أعتقد بأن معظم الناس في هذا العالم لا يؤمنون بمفهوم الجن. ولا يؤمنون بأن هناك عالم موازي وأن سكان ذلك العالم الخفي أعلى بكثير من سكان العالم المرئي. ولا يعلم المعظم بأن هذا العالم الخفي متصل بحياتنا وعلاقاتنا. وربما بعد قراءتهم لهذا الكتاب، سيكسب ابعض مفهوم مفهوم العالم الخفي. ولكن المعظم، فإن هذا العالم الخفي سيبقى لغز معقد لا يمكن حله. ولكن من ناحية أخرى، أشعر وبقوة أنه على الرغم من أن الشياطيين معضلة للبشر، فأنا أشكل معضلة لهم. وأفاجئهم بإبلاغهم عندما اقترابهم مني. وأفاجئهم أيضاً عند أشير بإصبعي إليهم أثناء طيرانهم في الهواء. وأفاجئهم عندما أبقي عيني موجهة بشكل مباشر إليهم.

ويمكنني بكل سهولة دعوة أي شيطان إلي من أي شخص في أي جزء من هذا العالم. ولكن ثق بي؛ ليس بالشيء الممتع وخاصة في ل 24 ساعة الأولى على الأقل.

فهذا مفهوم غريب جداً ولكن من المحتمل مطالبة أي شيطان يسكن جسم إنسان ما في أي جزء من العالم مغادرة ذلك الشخص. ويمكنني ان أقنعهم بمغادرة ذلك الشخص، ولكن أحياناً أحتاج الى إجبارهم على فعل ذلك. والإجبار هو عبارة عن إجراء، ويأخذ بعض الوقت. ولكن أثناء

process of taking out a demon from a person, most of them come to me first once they decide to leave that person. They are usually very unhappy and angry with me during our first meeting. After twenty-four hours or less, they forgive me and become my friend. I usually ask everyone to leave my house on the second or third day, and they listen most of the time.

It is possible to move demons from a particular house or area, but usually, I avoid it.

Instead of a person, if I chose a particular house or a particular area, I was able to move all the demons in that house or area. I ask them to go to some other place, and most of them come to me. Not knowing how many demons are in that particular area or what kind of powers they have can be a problem for me, and handling numerous demons is really difficult. They are usually surprised, and I am surprised, too. And I need at least twenty-four hours so that they understand and learn about me before they leave. I performed this experiment several times, and the only thing I learned was that it is not a good idea to get involved or mess with so many demons at one time.

I don't think that one demon is around me more than once day.

Demons are the only ones that can show us dreams. Dreams do not come from our minds. Demons can easily read our minds and even find information deep inside our brains. Demons are the one that show us dreams by hypnotizing us. Normal people are usually under the influence of at least one demon. And that demon shows them dreams, sometimes to scare them, sometimes to harass them, and sometimes to reveal affairs around them. This is the hobby of demons, and our minds are just like toys for them.

عملية إخراج الشيطان من شخص ما، تدخل تلك الشيطان الى جسمي أولاً عندما يقرر مغادرة ذلك الشخص. وعادة ما يكونون غير سعيدين وغاضبين مني في أول لقاء لنا. وبعد ما حوالي 24 ساعة أو أقل، يسامحوني ونصبح أصدقاء. وعادة ما أطلب من واحد منهم مغادرة منزلي بعد يومين أو ثلاثة، وهم يستمعون إلي في معظم الأحيان.

ومن المحتمل نقل الشياطيين من منزل أو منطقة معينة ولكن عادة ما أتجنب فعل ذلك.

بدلاً من اختيار شخص ما، أختار منزل معين وأكون قادر على نقل جميع الشياطيين في ذلك المنزل أو المنطقة. وأطلب منهم الذهاب الى مكان آخر، ومعظمهم يأتي إلي. ولا أعلم كم عدد الشياطيين التي تكون في منطقة معينة وما نوع القوى التي تمتلكها فمن المرجح أن تكون مشكلة بالنسبة لي، وإن التعامل من الكثير من الشياطيين صعب للغاية. وعادة ما يكونون متفاجئون وأنا ايضاً. وأحتاج الى 24 ساعة على الأقل لكي يعلمون ويفهمون شخصيتي قبل مغادرتهم لي. وأنجزت تلك التجربة عدة مرات، وإن الشيء الوحيد الذي تعلمته أنها ليست بالفكرة الجيدة في التدخل أو العب مع العديد من الشياطيين دفعة واحدة.

ولا أعلم عدد الشياطيين من حولي.

إن الشياطيين هي الوحيدة القادرة على أن يرونا الأحلام. ولا تأتي الأحلام من عقولنا. ويمكن للشياطيين قراءة أفكارنا بكل سهولة واكتشاف المعلومات داخل عقولنا العميقة. حيث يقومون بتنويمنا مغناطيسياً. وعادة ما يقع الأشخاص العاديون تحت تأثير شيطان واحد على الأقل. ويرينا ذلك الشيطان الأحلام من أجل أن يخيفنا أو يؤذينا أ، لكشف علاقات من حولنا. فهذه تعتبر هوايتهم وإن عقولنا عبارة عن دمى في أيديهم.

If you are not seeing a dream, no demon is around you, or they are not playing with your mind when you are sleeping. These days, I have to deal with new demons. New demons treat me as a regular and normal person at first instead of digging up information from my mind. They try to show me dreams about the person, family, or area I pulled them out of. As a result, I see strange people, strange houses, and strange problems in my dreams. This is crazy, but it happens every day. By the time that demon learns about me, they do not bother to waste time with me by showing me more dreams. By then, however, I will have someone else's demon hanging around me.

A few diseases act individually, and a few act in groups.

A few animals live, hunt, and eat by themselves, but a few animals like to stay in big groups. And wherever these animals go, they go together. It's the same way in the invisible world, and the same rule applies to diseases. A few diseases stay and act by themselves, and a few stay and act together in a group. Individuals can often suffer from a great deal of symptoms. Moreover, if one person in a family is suffering, that pain can be easily transferred to a second person; however, it still hurts one person at one time. But a few diseases stay and act in a group. Sometimes a whole family, neighborhood, or community can suffer from the same disease at same time. All of these diseases are invisible to the naked eye, and they are not regular demons.

Pills and medications usually work on those areas that are affected or controlled by demons? In few cases, tastes and smells can be effective against pains and sicknesses.

Our nerves are very sensitive. Demons and diseases usually choose nerves in different areas of our body to give us pain. Usually, painkillers make those nerves relaxed or numb to reduce the pressure inflicted on us by demons.

وفي حال عدم رؤيتك لحلم، فاعلم أنه لا يوجد شياطيين من حولك. أو أنهم لا يريدون اللعب معك أثناء نومك. وفي هذه الأيام، علي التعامل مع شياطيين جديدة. حيث تعاملني كشخص عادي في البداية بدلاً من البحث عن المعلومات داخل عقلي. فهي تحاول أن تريني أحلاماً عن شخص أو عائلة أو منطقة قمت بإخراج شياطين منها. ونتيجة لذلك، أرى أناس غريبون ومنازل غريب ومشاكل غريبة في أحلامي. وهذا جنون، ولكنه يحدث كل يوم. وعندما تعلم الشياطين المزيد عني، لا يقومون بإزعاجي واضاعة الوقت معي بإظهار المزيد من الأحلام لي. ولكن يكون هناك شيطان لشخص آخر يعبث معي.

تتصرف بعض الأمراض بشكل فردي ويتصرف بعضها الآخر بشكل جماعي.

تعيش بعض الحيوانات وتصطاد وتأكل بنفسها، ولكن القليل من الحيوانات من ترغب البقاء في مجموعات. وأينما تذهب تلك الحيوانات، يبقون مع بعضهم البعض. وهي الطريقة نفسها في العالم الخفي. حيث أن هناك القليل من الامراض تبقى وتتصرف لوحدها، والبعض الآخر يبقى ويتصرف بشكل جماعي. ويمكن للأفراد أن يعانوا من الكثير من الأمراض. بالإضافة الى ذلك، في حال معاناة شخص واحد في عائلة ما، يمكن أن ينتقل ذلك الألم بكل سهولة الى الشخص الآخر في نفس العائلة. علاوة على ذلك، فإنه يؤذي شخص واحد دفعة واحدة. ولكن القليل من الأمراض التي تبقى وتتصرف كمجموعة. وأحيانا تعاني العائلة جميعاً، أو الحي أو مجموعة من الناس من نفس المرض في نفس الوقت. وتكون جميع تلك الأمراض خفية للعين المجردة وهي شياطيين غير طبيعية.

هل تنجح الحبوب والادوية في مثل تلك الحالات؟ يمكن للقليل من الحالات وكالذوق والرائحة أن تكون فعالة ضد الآلام والأمراض.

تعد أعصابنا حساسة جداً. وعادة ما تختار الأمراض والشياطيين الأعصاب في مناطق مختلفة من أجسامنا للتسبب لنا بالآلام. وعادة، ما تجعل مسكنات الآلام تلك الأعصاب مرتاحة أو مخدرة للتخفيف من الضغط الموجه من الشياطيين.

Infections are the damaged sections of the body, both internal and external. Small insects (i.e., disease) stay around that infected part of the body. Usually, antibiotics and other medications have tastes or smells that those diseases do not like. Within few days, all the diseases leave that wound. During this process, the positive energy of the body and the protective system of the body help in healing that wound.

Red meat carries more problems.

It is an experimental truth, a belief held by all spiritual people, that any kind of demon, or any kind of disease, always goes behind red meat.

Usually, red meat belongs to the cow or bull. Honestly, I do not have any problem with any kind of meat or any kind of food, but I am an abnormal person. I do not have any problem with demons. They listen to me, and they usually do not hurt me. But a normal person needs to avoid inviting demons or diseases, and demons and diseases live inside red meat and follow red meat, so be careful.

A migraine is fixable.

To me, the flu is the most difficult task, because it is not one disease or invisible insect. Flu is a combination attack. To fix this, one must fix all the individual symptoms several times. On the other hand, a migraine is the action of one demon. The migraine is not an invisible insect or disease. The migraine is a very powerful demon. Usually, migraine demons make their homes in particular places in the brain. It is very easy to fix a migraine. But migraine demons always leave some damages behind. Whenever another migraine demon comes close to that person, it doesn't have to expend as much energy, because there is already room for the new migraine demon in that brain.

وتعتبر الإصابة الأجزاء التالفة من الجسم داخلياً أو خارجياً. حيث تبقى الحشرات الصغيرة (على سبيل المثال) حول الجسم المصاب. وعادة ما يكون للمضادات الحيوية والأدوية طعم ورائحة لا ترغب بها تلك الأمراض. وخلال أيام معدودة، تترك تلك الامراض المنطقة المصابة. وأثناء تل كالعملية، تساعد الطاقة الإيجابية للجسم والنظام المناعي للجسم في شفاء ذلك الجرح.

يحمل اللحم الاحمر المزيد من المشاكل.

وفي حقيقة تجريبية، تبنى جميع الأشخاص الروحانيين معتقد، يقول بأن أي نوع من الشياطيين أو الأمراض دائماً يكون سببه اللحم الأحمر.

وفي الغالب، ينتمى اللحم الأحمر الى البقر أو العجل. وبصراحة، لا يوجد لدي أي مشكلة مع أي نوع من اللحم أو الطعام، ولكن أنا شخص غير طبيعي. فليس لدي اي مشكلة مع الشياطيين أيضاً. فهم يستمعون إلي ولا يؤذونني. ولكن يحتاج الشخص العادي الى تجنب استدعاء الشياطيين أو الأمراض، حيث تعيش داخل اللحم الأحمر. لذلك يجب عليك الحذر.

يمكن علاج الصداع النصفي

بالنسبة لي، إن عملية علاج الإنفلونزا هي أصعب مهمة لأنها تشتمل على أكثر من مرض أو حشرة خفية. وتعد الإنفلونزا هجوم مدمج. وعلاج هذا، على الشخص علاج جميع الأمراض الفردية عدة مرات. ومن ناحية أخرى، سبب الصداع النصفي هو عمل شيطان ما. حيث أن الصداع النصفي ليس مرض أو حشرة خفية. فهو شيطان قوي جداً. وفي الغالي، تنشأ شياطيين الصداع النصفي منازلها في مكان محدد من الدماغ. ومن السهل علاج الصداع النصفي. ولكن دائماً ما يترك أضرار خلفه. وعندما يأتي شيطان صداع نصفي آخر، فليس عليه أن يستهلك الكثير من الطاقة لأنه يوجد هناك مكان جاهز لشيطان الصداع النصفي الجديد في ذلك الدماغ.

The migraine is easily fixable, but after that, I need to take proper medication to heal the damages to avoid migraines in the future.

How do contagious diseases spread?

If these diseases leave one body, they immediately go to second body and then third and then fourth, which can make life hell. Contagious diseases are usually stubborn insects. These diseases do not leave particular areas or locations easily. A very simple example is the flu. The flu is not a demon. It is a combination of bunch of different invisible diseases. Flu has all kinds of sicknesses. Flu is not an action of one kind of invisible insects. It is a combination of a group of invisible insects with different effects. Plus, these insects come out from one body and go to another body immediately to make the next person sick. Why am I saying that this is the action of more than one invisible insect? Because when a sickness usually comes as the result of an action of one demon or one insect, it is easy to take it out, but when more than one or a bunch of invisible insects or diseases act together to create a sickness like the flu, it is difficult to take them out at one time. Even in this different kind of invisible insects or diseases, same kind of insects or disease also come as a group. It means: Few insects has effect of cold, few has effect of fever, some has effect of pain, etc. My point is that Flu disease has a group action of cold-fever-pain-insects together. But, I feel still they come in a group of cold insects, fever insects, and pain insects also. So, at same time they attack individually on several bodies to give them flu. This is the reason that they quickly attack more than one person. In regards to the flu, no doubt, their combined action is very powerful, but this group is still composed of physical but invisible insects. Their action is controllable as well, but it takes a longer time to control them. Other than injuries, I sometimes face difficulties in fixing the flu and bad coughs immediately. It is contagious because each group of insects attacks several persons at the same time.

وعملية علاج الصداع النصفي سهلة جدا. ولكن بعد ذلك أحتاج الى الدواء الصحيح لعلاج الأضرار الناتجة لتجنب حدوث صداع نصفي آخر في المستقبل.

كيف يمكن للأمراض المعدية أن تنتشر؟

في حال مغادر تلك الأمراض لجسم ما، فانها تنتقل فوراً الى جسم آخر وآخر. وهذا بدوره يحول الحياة إلى جحيم. وعادة ما تكون الامراض المعدية حشرات عنيدة. حيث لا تغادر مناطق أو مواقع معينة بسهولة. وهناك مثال بسيط جداً ألا وهي الإنفلونزا. فهي تعتبر شيطان. وهي مزيج من الكثير من الامراض الخفية المختلفة. ولديها جميع اشكال الأمراض. إنما هي مزيج من مجموعة من تلك الحشرات مع تأثيرات أخرى مختلفة. بالإضافة الى ذلك، تنتقل تلك الحشرات من جسم الى آخر فوراً. لماذا أقول بأن الإنفلونزا هي نتاج عمل أكثر من حشرة غير مرئية؟

لأنه عند قدوم المرض، فإنه يأتي نتاج لعمل شيطان أو حشرة، ومن السهل اخراجها، ولكن عندما تعمل أكثر من حشرة مع بعضها البعض فإنه ينشأ مرضاً مثل الإنفلونزا. حيث من الصعب علاجه دفعة واحدة. حتى في هذا النوع المختلف من الحشرات الخفية والأمراض، فإن النوع نفيه من الحشرات أو الامراض يأتي كمجموعة. ويعني هذا: بضع الحشرات تسبب البرد والبضع الآخر يسبب الحمى وبعضها الآخر يسبب الألم. ووجهة نظري هي أن الإنفلونزا مرض ناتج عن مجموعة من الأعمال كالبرد والحمى والألم كلها مع بعضها البعض. ولكن ، أشعر بأن تلك الأمراض تأتي كمجموعة من حشرات التي تسبب البرد وحشرات التي تسبب الحمى والحشرات التي تسبب الألم. لذلك، تهاج بشكل فردي العديد من الأجسام دفعة واحدة وتسبب الإنفلونزا. وهذا هو السبب وراء هجومها بسرعة على أكثر من شخص. وفيما يخص الإنفلونزا، لا يوجد هناك أي شك بأن عملها الممزوج قوي جداً ولكن هذه المجموعة تتكون من الحشرات الجسدية ولكن تكون خفية. ويتم التحكم بأفعالها أيضاً. ولكنها تأخذ المزيد من الوقت للسيطرة عليهم. وبالاختلاف عن إصابات أخرى، أحياناً ما أواجه صعوبات في علاج الإنفلونزا والسعال الشديد فوراً. فهو معدٍ لأن كل مجموعة من الحشرات تهاجم العديد من الأشخاص في نفس الوقت.

The causes of fevers and flus are physical creatures that are similar to demons.

Flu is a combination of bunch of diseases. This is the reason that flu is a difficult task for me. But compared to the flu, a fever is a very easy task and easily fixable. A fever is not a demon. A fever is not an invisible insect or disease. A fever is a *kaifiyat* or deep inner feeling. It is easily fixable.

Almost everyone experiences pressure on the chest during sleep and cannot yell or wake up?

Almost everyone experiences at least one of these actions by demons. You can sometimes feel a lot of pressure on your chest when you sleep, but the demon is controlling you by hypnotizing your mind. During all that drama, demons are completely controlling your body. Even if you want to move, you can't. Even if you want to yell, you have no control over yourself. With a strong willpower, most people can conquer this trap in few minutes. But sometimes a few people suffer heart attacks if they go to sleep after they have been heavily drinking alcohol. That alcohol can reduce their strength against that demon's actions, which can sometimes result in heart attacks.

Demons and diseases are physical.

Both demons and diseases are physical bodies but invisible to most of us. Both demons and diseases are similar to air. We cannot see air, but we can feel air. We cannot see demons and diseases, and most of us cannot feel them either; however, they are physical bodies like air. But almost all of us can feel their effects in shape of sickness or sick feelings or pains. Only physical bodies can create impact like this.

أسباب الحمى والإنفلونزا هي مخلوقات جسدية شبيهة بالشياطيين.

إن الإنفلونزا هي تكريب من الكثير من الأمراض. ولذلك السبب فإن علاج الإنفلونزا صعب. لوكن مقارنة معها، فإن علاج الحمى سهل. حيث أن الحمى ليست شيطاناً. فهي شعور داخلي وسهل علاجه.

يواجه تقريباً كل شخص الضغط في الصدر خلال النوم ولا يستطع الصراخ أو الاستيقاظ؟

يواجه كل شخص تقريباً اعمال الشياطيين. ويمكنك أحياناً الشعور بالكثير من الضغط على صدرك أثناء نومك، ولكن الشيطان الذي يسيطر عليك يقوم بتنويمك مغناطيسياً. وخلال ذلك الوقت، تتحكم الشياطيين بك بشكل كامل. حتى لو أنك تريد التحرك، لا تستطيع فعل ذلك. أو حتى لو كنت تريد الصراخ فأنت لا تمتلك السيطرة على نفسك. وبقوة الإرادة، يستطيع الكثير من الناس التغلب على هذه المصيدة خلال دقائق. ولكن أحياناً ما يعاني بعض الأشخاص من النوبات القلبية في حال ذهابهم للنوم بعد شربهم للكحول بشكل كبير جداً. حيث يقلل الكحول من قوة الأنسان ضد أفعال الشيطان الذي ينتج عنه أحياناً النوبات القلبية.

إن الشياطيين والأمراض هي جسدية (ملموسة)

تعد الشياطيين والامراض أجساما جسدية فيزيائية ملموسة ولكن خفية عن معظمنا. وكلاهما شبيهة بالهواء. فلا يمكننا رؤية الهواء ولكن يمكننا أن نشعر به. ولا يمكننا رؤية الشياطيين والأمراض، ولا يمكن لمعظمنا الشعور بهم أيضاً؛ علاوة على ذلك، هم أجسامنا فيزيائية ملموسة. ولكن معظمنا يمكن أن شعر بتأثيرها على شكل مرض أو مشاعر المرض أو الآلام. حيث أنه بإمكان الأجسام الفيزيائية فقط خلق تأثير كهذا.

Genetic diseases: Why kids get the same disease as their Parents

In the invisible world, we mainly have two things we have to deal with: demons and diseases. Demons are less responsible for damaging organs or blocking of hormones. Diseases are mainly responsible for all organ damage, organ failure, and hormonal problems. Diseases are totally negative and damage our body and health. As compared to us, the reproduction of these diseases is faster than humans can reproduce. During the birth of a child, or even after the birth of child, this reproduction process of diseases is responsible for genetic disease. One invisible insect or disease is responsible for stopping or blocking the production or extraction of insulin inside the body. The pancreas is situated by the liver. When there is no production of insulin, that person becomes diabetic. When this disease is creating the diabetic problem inside that person, it is also undergoing reproduction as well. I assume they leave their eggs inside that body as well. And when that woman becomes pregnant, those eggs with the diabetic disease transfer the disease to the body of the child. In this way, we receive diseases from our parents. Sometimes we inherit them during the pregnancy, but most of the time, we easily contract whatever diseases they are carrying inside their bodies because we are always around our parents. In this way, kids get genetic diseases from their parents. This is not fate. We can try to change it by using healthy rules and help from someone like me.

How do you know that you are under the influence a demon?

How can you know if you have any demon around you? It is very simple. If you are not dreaming during sleep, no demons are around you, but if you are dreaming during sleep, you have demon around you. If you are experiencing different kinds of dreams every night, then you are under influence of more than one demon. I strongly feel

الأمراض الجينية: لماذا يتعرض الأطفال لنفس الأمراض التي يتعرض لها آبائهم؟

في العالم الخفي، لدينا شيئان مهمان علينا التعامل معهما وهما: الشياطيين والأمراض. وتعد الشياطيين أقل مسؤولية عن تدمير الأعضاء أو تعطيل الهرمونات. والأمراض هي المسؤولة بشكل رئيسي عن الحاق الضرر بالأعضاء والمشاكل الهرمونية. وعادة ما تكون الامراض شلبية كلياً وتدمر أجسامنا وصحتنا. ومقارنةً معنا، فإن تكاثر تلك الأمراض أسرع من تكاثر الإنسان. وأثناء ولادة الطفل، أو حتى بعد الولادة، تكون هذه عملية التكاثر مسؤولة عن الأمراض الجينية. ويكون مرض ما مسؤول عن ايقاف أو تعطيل انتاج أو استخلاص الأنسولين داخل الجسم. ويتم تحديد وضعية البنكرياس عن طريق الكبد. وعندما لا يكون هناك انتاج للأنسولين، بأن ذلك الشخص يعاني من مرض السكري. وعندما يخلق هذا المرض مشكلة مرض السكري عند ذلك الشخص، فإنه أيضاً يخضع لعملية التكاثر أيضاً. وأفترض أنها تغادر بيوضها داخل الجسم كذلك، وعندما تحمل تلك المرأة. تنتقل تلك البيوض التي تحمل مرض السكري الى جسم جنينها؟ وبهذه الطريقة، نستقبل الأمراض من آبائنا. وأحياناً نورث تلك الأمراض خلال عملية الحمل، ولكن معظم الوقت، نستقبل أياً كان نوع المرض بكل سهولة لأننا دائماً ما نكون حول آبائنا. وبهذه الطريقة، يتعرض الأطفال للأمراض الجينية من آبائهم. وهذا ليس مصير. حيث يمكننا المحاولة في التغيير باستخدام القواعد الصحية والمساعدة من شخص ما مثلي.

كيف تعرف أنك تحت تأثير شيطان ما؟

كيف يمكنك أن تعلم إذا ما كان هناك شيطان ما حولك؟ هذا بسيط جداً. في حال عدم حلمك أثناء النوم، إذن لا يوجد هناك شياطيين من حولك. وفي حال مواجهتك لأنواع مختلفة من الاحلام كل ليلة، فاعلم أنك تحت تأثير أكثر من شيطان واحد. وأشعر بقوة

that anyone who is under the influence of more than one demon will become mentally sick sooner or later.

Diseases are mainly hungry and invisible insects. What can we expect from dangerous insects? They just eat our bodies and organs. Within a few days, they make wounds or injuries anywhere, including the stomach, liver, kidneys, intestines, or even the brain. Internal injuries and wounds do not heal easily, not even if we take medication regularly. Those invisible insects or diseases never leave us alone until they completely damage our organs and kill us.

On the other hand, demons are very sensible like us, but they are totally negative. They will keep or at least try to keep control of our minds. Demons will get more and more control of our minds. We will get closer to mental sickness. Once our minds are under the control of demons, we become mentally ill.

Usually, I pull any demon or disease related to my topic of interest and keep it around for few days. After at least twenty-four hours, they helped me write this book by providing information to my mind through hypnotism.

In writing this book, I got a lot of help from different demons feeding my brain at different times.

My life is mostly neutral these days, because I am not controlled by any demon all of the time.

I used to be different. I used to exhibit many extreme behaviors. But because demons cannot stay around me for a long time, I feel neutral

أن أي شخص تحت تأثير أكثر من شيطان واحد سيصبح مريض عقلياً عاجلاً أم آجلاً.

فالأمراض عادة تكون جائعة وحشرات غير مرئية. ماذا يمكننا أن نتوقع من الحشرات الخطيرة؟ فهي فقط تقوم بأكل أجسامنا وأعضائنا. وخلال بضعة أيام، يحدثون الجروح والإصابات في أي مكان بما في ذلك الدماغ. ولا تتعافى الجروح الداخلية بسهولة، ولا حتى في حال تناولنا الأدوية بشكل منتظم. ولا تتركنا تلك الأمراض والحشرات الخفية لوحدنا حتى تقوم بتدمير أعضائنا بشكل كامل وتقتلنا.

ومن ناحية أخرى، تعد الشياطين حساسة مثلنا، ولكنهم سلبيين للغاية. فهم يحاولون السيطرة على عقولنا. وسنصبح نحن قريبين من المرض العقلي. وعندما تصبح عقولنا تحت سيطرة الشياطين، نصبح مريضين عقلياً.

في الغالب، أسحب أي شيطان أو مرض له علاقة في موضوع اهتمامي وأبقيه في الجوار لعدة أيام. وبعد 24 ساعة على الأقل، يقومون بمساعدتي في كتابة هذا الكتاب بتزويدي بالمعلومات عن كريق التنويم المغناطيسي.

وفي كتابة هذا الكتاب، حصلت على الكثير من المساعدة من العديد من الشياطين التي تغذي عقلي بالمعلومات في أوقات مختلفة.

وحياتي متعادلة في هذه الأيام لأنني غير مسيطر عليه من قبل أي شيطان طوال الوقت.

وقد تعودت أن أكون مختلفاً. وتعودت أيضاً اظهار العديد من التصرفات الغريبة والمتطرفة. ولكن لأنه لا يمكن للشياطين البقاء حولي لفترة طويلة، أشعر بأنني شخص عادي

most of the time. Nowadays, I can easily withdraw from many things. I do not feel too much hate or love for anything or anyone. Overall, I am more responsible, but my extreme behaviors are reducing. These demons keep us going when they insist that we have hobbies, likes, dislikes, competitions, and desires all the time. On the one hand, a demon's negativism is extremely bad for us, but somehow, they keep us active and keep us running behind our wishes and desires, and I think that is the attraction of life.

Demon can make us hate or love someone.

Trust me, hypnosis is a very strong tool, and demons have this tool. They add different kinds of negative and positive thoughts toward people. Demons continuously convinced us about feelings for people through hypnosis. Sometimes it takes a long time, but eventually, a normal person will be convinced easily. By using hypnotism, demons can make us hate someone or love someone very easily.

Why do some people have pain in their calves once they go to bed to sleep?

Leg pain is a very common complaint from a bunch of people. In this way, demons or diseases torture people. Many people feel no pain during the whole day, but as soon as they go to bed, they start feeling pain in their calves. And that unbearable pain in their calves keeps them up the whole night. This is not the action of a regular demon. This is the action of a demon that's between the demon and disease classes. Some pains and problems are similar to this pain. These demons just do not rely on controlling us, but they want to keep us in pain either during certain parts of the day or the whole day. Examples of these torturous demons are migraines, high and low blood pressure, pains in calves, backbone and hipbone pains, sleep disorders, and even intolerance. I will keep these demons in the disease category.

معظم الأوقات. وفي هذه الايام، يمكنني الخروج من العديد من الأشياء. ولا أشعر بكراهية كبيرة أو حب عميق لأي شيء أو أي شخص. وبشكل عام، أكون شخص أكثر مسؤولية، ولكن تصرفاتي المتطرفة تقل. وتبقينا تلك الشياطيين مستمرين عندما يجبرونا على أننا هواياتنا ورغباتهم وكراهيتهم والمنافسات طوال الوقت. ومن ناحية، إن سلبية الشيطان سيئة جداً لنا، ولكن بطريقة ما، يبقونا فاعلين ونركض خلف رغباتنا وامنياتنا، وأعتقد هذه هي جاذبية الحياة.

يمكن للشياطيين أن تجعلنا نكره أو نحب شخص ما.

ثق بي، أن عملية التنويم المغناطيسي أداء قوية، ويمتلك الجن هذه الأداة. فهم يضيفون أنواع مختلفة من الأفكار الشيء والإيجابية تجاه الناس. وتقنعنا الشياطيين بشكل مستمر حيال مشاعر الناس عن طريق التنويم المغناطيسي. وأحياناً ما يستغرق ذلك فترة طويلة، ولكن عقلياً، سيتم اقناع الشخص العادي بكل سهولة. باستخدام التنويم المغناطيسي، يمكن للشياطيين أن تجعلنا نكره أو نحب شخصاً ما بكل سهولة أيضاً.

لماذا يعاني بعض الأشخاص من الآلام في سيقانهم عندما يخلدون للنوم؟

يعد ألم الرجل شكوى شائعة جداً من قبل الكثير من الأشخاص. وبهذه الطريقة، تقوم الامراض أو الشياطيين بتعذيب هؤلاء الأشخاص. والعديد منهم لا يشعرون بآلام أثناء النهار ولكن حالما يذهبون للنوم، يشعرون بآلام في بطون سيقانهم. ويبقى هذا الألم الغير محتمل طوال الليل. فهذا ليس عمل شيطان عادي. وإنما عمل شيطان يصنف بين الشياطيين والأمراض. وتكون بعض الآلام والمشاكل شبيهو بهذا الألم. فلا تعتمد تلك الشياطيين فقط على السيطرة علينا، ولكن يريدونا أن نبقى نشعر بألم حتى أثناء أوقات معينة من النهار أو طوال اليوم. هناك امثلة على الشياطيين التي تعذب كالصداع النصفي وارتفاع أو انخفاض ضغط الدم وآلام السيقان وآلام عظام الظهر والعظم الحرقفي واضطرابات النوم وعدم التسامح. وأصنف تلك الشياطيين في خانة الأمراض.

Do you have a sleep disorder? Are you tired but cannot go to sleep?

This is a very common problem when someone is tired and wants to go to sleep, but these demons keep them up by hypnotizing them. As I have already described, demons like the smell or taste of certain things like cigarettes, tobacco, tea, coffee, beer, wine, alcohol, drugs, and some sleeping aids. This is a very simple practice of demons. Either they keep us in pain or keep us hyper so that we use drugs, alcohol, cigarettes, or sleeping aids. Demons like these things, and they enjoy them. They keep us in pain if we try to quit any of these bad habits. All these habits are external and easily fixable.

Demons and diseases do not die. They just move from body to body.

Demons and diseases both live for several hundreds of years. Usually, they do not leave a body or person until the person struggles against them. During that struggle, they do not die. They just move to another body.

Demons do not like water.

Demons and diseases are basically fire. Their basic configuration is fire. Naturally, they do not have too much resistance to water. Usually, most demons are around or in our body. In that case, water is a trouble for them; however, if they penetrate our bodies like most diseases penetrate our bodies to damage our organs, they are out of our reach, and the use of water is less effective. Do not misunderstand me. I am not saying water can kill them. I am only saying that they do not like water. If you keep spraying water around and inside your house, it will keep them uncomfortable all the time. And they will

هل تعاني ما اضطرابات في النوم؟ هل انت متعب ولكنك لا تقدر على النوم؟

تعد هذه المشكلة شائعة جداً عندما يكون ما شخص متعب ويريد الخلود للنوم، ولكن تبقيه الشياطيين مستيقظاً عن طريق التنويم المغناطيسي. وكم وصفت مسبقاً، فإن الشياطيين ترغب برائحة وطعم بعض الأشياء كالسجائر والتبغ والشاي والقهوة والبيرة والخمر والكحول والمخدرات وبعض مساعدات النوم. فهذه عادة بسيطة جداً من الشياطيين . فغما أن يبقونا متألمين أو منتشين لكي نتعاطى المخدرات والكحول والسجائر ومساعدات النوم. فالشياطيين تحب تلك الأشياء وتستمع بها فتبقينا متألمين في حال محاولتنا ترك أي من تلك العادات السيئة. وكل تلك العادات خارجية قابلة للعلاج بكل سهولة.

الأمراض والشياطيين لا تموت. فهم فقط ينتقلون الى جسم الى آخر.

تعيش كلاً من الأمراض والشياطيين لعدة مئات من السنين. وعادة ما لا يغادرون أي جسم حتى يكافح الشخص ضدهم. وأثناء ذلك الصراع، لا يموتون. فهم فقط ينتقلون الى جسم آخر.

الشياطيين لا تحب الماء.

تتكون الأمراض والشياطيين من النار بشكل أساسي. وتركيبهم الأساسي هو النار. وبشكل طبيعي، فلا يستطيعون مقاومة الماء كثيراً. وفي العادة، تكون معظم الشياطيين حولنا أو داخل أجسامنا. وفي تلك الحالة، يعد الماء مشكلة بالنسبة لهم؛ علاوة على ذلك، في حال تغلغلهم الى أجسامنا كما تفعل الأمراض لتدمير أعضائنا، وهم خارج السيطرة ويعتبر استخدام النار أقل فعالية. لا تسيء فهمي. فأنا لا أقول بأن الماء يمكنه أن يقتل الشياطيين. في حال بقاؤك رش المياه تحت وحول منزلك، سيبقيهم غير مرتاحين طوال الوقت. ولن

not stay in or around those houses or people for a long time. Religious waters will definitely be more effective.

The travelling speed of demons or diseases is like the speed of light or sound.

I strongly feel that ignorance is a blessing. When I was not aware of all this crazy stuff, life was okay; however, now, even if I do not want to, I get more and more involved in the invisible world, and I'm learning more and more every day.

I can give you some examples of few things, and then you can decide about their traveling speed. Remember that some demons and diseases come out of us very easily, but some take some time. Whenever I communicate with the demons of a person on the telephone, those demons jump on me within a few seconds. What is their traveling speed? Can you guess?

Demons and disease are similar to electromagnetic fields.

Demons or diseases can easily travel through phone lines. If you want to perform an experiment, you can call someone who's sick or someone who at least has a cold or a headache problem. Make sure you are not sick at that time. Talk to any sick person, and you will likely receive the following sicknesses. Deafness, headaches, colds, heart problems, high or low blood pressure, burning eyes, or sore throats are transferred from being in contact with someone already sick. However, I feel that kidney, liver, stomach, hormone, and thyroid problems do not easily transfer from one person to another. The left ear is just like a transmitter and sucks or transfers a lot of diseases from one end to another. I cannot prove this to everyone; however, all these demons and diseases have some kind of field for traveling, and it acts similar to an electromagnetic field.

تبقى حول تلك المنازل أو الأشخاص لفترة طويلة. وعادة ما تكون المياه المقدسة أكثر فعالية.

تعادل سرعة انتقال الشياطين والامراض سرعة الضوء أو الصوت.

أشعر بقوة أن ذلك الكبرياء نعمة. عندما لا أكون مدركاً لكل تلك الأشياء الحمقاء، تكون الحياة جيدة؛ علاوة على ذلك، الآن وحتى في حال عدم رغبتي في فعل ذلك، أتعلق بالعالم الخفي أكثر وأكثر كل يوم.

يمكنني ان أعطيكم أمثلة لبعض الأشياء، ومن ثم يمكنكم أن تقرروا بشأن سرعة انتقالهم. تذكروا بأن بعض الشياطين والأمراض تخرج منا بكل سهولة، ولكن البعض الآخر يستغرق بعض الوقت. وحينما أتواصل معهم عن طريق الهاتف، تقفز تلك الشياطين علي خلال ثوانٍ. فما هي سرعتهم؟ هل بإمكانك التخمين؟

تشبه الامراض والشياطين المجالات الالكترو مغناطيسية.

يمكن للشياطين والأمراض التنقل بسهولة من خلال خطوط الهاتف. وفي حال أردت انجاز تجربة ما، يمكن أن تطلب من شخص ما مريض أو على الأقل يعاني من البرد أو صداع الرأس. تأكد من أنك لست مريضاً في ذلك الوقت. وقم بالتحدث من أي شخص مريض، وستستقبل الأمراض التالية. وهي الصم والصداع وزلات البرد ومشاكل القلب وارتفاع أو انخفاض ضغط الدم وحروق العينين أو التهاب الحلق، حيث تنتقل تلك الأمراض عن طريق الاتصال بشخص ما مريض مسبقاً. علاوة على ذلك، أشعر بأن الكلى والكبد والمعدة والهرمون ومشاكل الغدد الدرقية لا تنتقل بتلك السهولة من شخص الى آخر. وتعد الأذن اليسرى وسط ناقل حيث تقول بنقل الكثير من الأمراض من شخص الى آخر. ولا أستطيع اثبات ذلك لكل شخص؛ علاوة على ذلك، يوجد لدى جميع تلك الأمراض والشياطين بعض أنواع من التنقل، وتتصرف بشكل مشابه للمجال الالكترو مغناطيسي.

Gravity has a lot of influence on them.

Maybe demons and diseases do not follow exactly all rules of electromagnetic field, but they have something very similar to electromagnetic field. And I strongly feel that this electromagnetic field is responsible of their traveling through the phone lines and transferring from one place to another in seconds, regardless of the distance.

In the beginning, I faced a lot of pain and sickness because whenever I communicated with any pain or sickness inside another person, every demon or disease coming out of those people was stored inside my body. Instead of storing all these demons and disease inside my body, I did a few experiments. And after those experiments, I learned that during the process of taking out demons or disease from someone, if I was holding any metal or if I was keeping my bare feet on a concrete floor or if I was touching a brick wall, those demons and disease were not stored in my body. They were like a current passing from my body and going inside those metals, walls, cements, or ceramic floors. After that, I learned that these demons and diseases had something very similar to gravity. If they are traveling from one body to another body through telephone lines or through electromagnetic fields and if they come from one body and enter mine, then they will be stored inside my body. But during that whole process, if I am grounded properly, demons and diseases will pass from my body. Most of them will go into the ground as a result of the principle of gravity. After that, I started suggesting that people keep their feet or hands on any brick walls, the cement of ceramic floor, or various metals. This way, any demon or disease will go to ground. Try it several times a day, and you'll find that it helps.

التأثير الكبير للجاذبية على الشياطيين.

من المحتمل أن الشياطيين والأمراض لا تتبع جميع قواعد المجال الالكترو مغناطيسي بدقة، ولكن لديها بعض الأشياء الشبيهة للمجال الالكترو مغناطيسي. وأشعر بقوة بأن هذا المجال مسؤول عن تنقلهم خلال خطوط الهواتف من مكان الى آخر خلال ثوانٍ معدودة بغض النظر عن المسافة.

في البداية، واجهت الكثير من الآلام والأمراض لأنني عندما كنت أتواصل مع أي ألم أو مرض داخل أي شخص، رخج الشيطان من ذلك الرجل ويدخل الى جسمي. وبدلاً من تخزين جميع تلك الشياطيين داخل جيمي، قمت بعمل بعض التجارب. وبعد تلك التجارب، تعلمت أنه أثناء عملية اخراج الشياطيين من شخص ما، وفي حال حملي لأي معدن أو وفي حال البقاء عاري القدمين وواقفاً على أرضية خرسانة أو كنت ألمس جدار من الطوب، لا تختزن تلك الأمراض والشياطيين داخل جسمي. فهي عبارة عن تيار مار من خلال جسمي الى داخل تلك المعادن أو الجدران أو الإسمنت أو أرضيات السيراميك. وبعد ذلك، تعلمت أن تلك الأمراض والشياطيين تمتلك شيء مشابه للجاذبية الأرضية. وفي حال تنقلها من جسم الى آخر خلال خطوط الهاتف أو خلال المجال الالكترو مغناطيسي وفي حال خروجها من جسم ما ودخولها جسمي، إذن سيتم تخزينها داخل جسمي. ولكن أثناء تلك العملية، في حال اتصالي بالأرض بشكل صحيح، ستمرر الشياطيين من خلال جسمي الى الأرض كنتيجة لمبدا الجاذبية. وبعد ذلك، بدأت باقتراح أن يبقي الناس أقدامهم أو أيديهم موضوعة على جدران من طوب أو إسمنت أو أرضيات السيراميك أو معدان. وبهذه الطريقة، سيمر أي شيطان أو مرض الى الأرض. جرب تلك المحاولة عدة مرات في اليوم وستكتشف أنها تساعد في ذلك.

Usually, the same diseases attack the same organs or parts of the body when they transfer from one to another.

If we like something or if we have expertise in any field, we usually do the same thing again and again. I learn that whenever I communicated with any disease inside any person, that disease traveled from that person and almost always hit the same part of my body, the party from where I pulled it out from the other person. In the beginning, the pressure was great, but with time, it reduced.

If I was fixing someone's pain and they were in front of me, their pain or disease almost never hurt me. The demons still came inside my body, but their effects were very friendly. And they never stayed inside or around me for too long. But whenever I fixed someone's pain over the phone or from a distance, I almost always had to face their demons' anger. Usually, after twenty-four hours, they went away without hurting me badly. Sometimes, though, regardless of from which part of the body the demons came, if any part or organ is already damaged, they will jump into that damaged part or organ of the body instead of choosing the healthy part and damaging that.

The treatment against demons is a continuous process.

The population of demons and diseases is several hundred times greater than ours. The actual size of demons and diseases is much smaller than the size of humans. Sometimes, maybe two or three people live in a house, but in same house, you can easily find millions of demons and diseases. With so many demons and diseases around us, how come someone thinks that only one treatment will be enough? This is a continuous struggle and fight.

عادةً، تهاجم الأمراض نفسها نفس الأعضاء من الجسم عندما تنتقل من جسم الى آخر.

في حال رغبتنا في شيء ما أو عندما يكون لدينا خبرة في مجال معين، عادة ما نفعل الشيء نفسه مرات ومرات. وأتعلم أنه عندما أتصل بأي مرض داخل أي شخص، ينتقل ذلك المرض من جسم ذلك الشخص وغالباً يصيب نفس العضو من جسمي. في البداية، كان الضغط كبيرا ولكن مع مرور الوقت، الضغط انخفض.

وفي حال كنت أعالج ألم من شخص ما وكان الشخص أمامي، لا يؤذيني ألمهم أبداً. ستدخل الشياطين الى جسمي، ولكن تأثيرها سيكون ودي. ولا يبقون داخل جسمي أو من حولي لفترة طويلة. ولكن عندما أقوم بعلاج آلام شخص ما عن طريق الهاتف أو عن مسافة، غالباً ما أواجه غضب الشياطيين. وعادة وبعد أربعة وعشرين ساعة، تذهب تلك الشياطيين بعيداً دون إيذائي بشكل سيء. وأحياناً، بغض النظر عن أي جزء من الجسم الذي يدخل اليه الشيطان، سيقفزون الى ذلك الجزء من الجسم حتى لو كان تالفاً مسبقاً بدلاً من اختيار جزء صحي واتلافه.

العلاج ضد الشياطيين هي عملية مستمرة.

إن عدد الشياطيين والامراض يفوق عدد سكان البشر بمئات المرات. وإن الحجم الطبيعي للشياطيين والأمراض أصغر بكثير من حجم الإنسان. وأحياناً ما يكون هناك اثنين أو ثلاثة أشخاص يعيشون في منزل واحد، ولكن في نفس المنزل، يمكنك بسهولة ايجاد بأن الملايين من الشياطيين والأمراض تعيش فيه.

وبوجود الكثير من الامراض والشياطيين من حولنا، كيف يعتقد شخص ما بأن معالجة واحدة قد تكفي للتخلص من الأمراض والشياطيين؟ فهذا قتال وصراع مستمر.

My body is programmed to feel more pain compared to the normal person.

To, me, it makes no difference if someone has just a headache, a fever, cancer, or HIV. All these diseases or sicknesses are same for me. Once I start working on someone, there are no restrictions or limits. I cannot limit myself to someone's headache. I will disturb all sicknesses and diseases inside the body. I will be able to move them out of that person, but after that, if that person does not want to contract new diseases, he or she needs to fix the damages by taking the proper medication or undergoing the correct surgeries. I can help keep the negative energies of demons and diseases away from that person, but the symptoms still need to be fixed as soon as possible to avoid continuous invitations to diseases, infections, and sicknesses.

Diabetes and several other internal diseases are pain-free. Usually, people do not feel any pain from those diseases until they damage the organs badly. But in my case, my body is extremely sensitive to all these diseases. Whenever diseases, sicknesses, or demons come around me, they keep me in pain and very uncomfortable until they leave or I compel them to leave my body. I can feel or sense demons as clearly as I can feel a touch from a human being. When demons come close to normal people, these individuals do not feel anything. That is why they feel no problems. But because of my extra sensitivity, I stay very uncomfortable until demons and diseases leave my body.

That noisy whistling sound in the ear is fixable?

A whistling sound or a continuous noisy sound in the ear is a very common sickness. As far as I know, no medication can fix that. From the blessing of God, it is very easy for me to fix this problem in few minutes. But this whistling sound is also a damaging disease. Usually, people get this problem during middle age. When someone is suffering from this disease for many years, it may cause serious damages deep

تمت برمجة جسمي على الشعور بالمزيد من الآلام مقارنةً بالشخص العادي.

بالنسبة لي، لا يوجد هناك أي فرق حول إذا ما تعرض شخص ما لصداع أو حمى أو سرطان أو الإيدز. فجميع تلك الأمراض هي نفسها بالنسبة إلي. وعندما أبدأ بالعمل على شخص ما، لا يوجد هناك قيود. ولا يمكنني تقييد نفسي في صداع شخص ما. وسأقوم بإزعاج جميع الأمراض داخل أي جسم، وسأكون قادراً على نقلها خارج ذلك الجسم، ولكن بعد ذلك، في حال أن ذلك الشخص لا يريد التعرض لأمراض جديدة، فهو/ي يحتاج الى علاج جميع الأضرار عن طريق تناول الأدوية الصحيحة أو الخضوع لعمليات. ويمكنني أن أساعد في إبقاء على الطاقات السلبية لتلك الشياطين والأمراض بعيداً عن ذلك الشخص، ولكن تحتاج تلك الأمراض الى العلاك في أقرب وقت ممكن لتجنب الدعوات المستمرة للأمراض والعدوى.

إن مرض السكري والعديد من الأمراض الداخلية تكون خالية من الآلام. وعادة، لا يشعر الناس بأي ألم من قبل تلك الأمراض حتى تدمر أعضاء داخل الجسم بشكل سيء. وعندما تأتي الأمراض أو الشياطين حولي، يسببون لي الآلام وعدم الراحة حتى يغادروا أو أجبرهم على مغادرة جسمي. ويمكنني الشعور بالشياطين بوضوح كأني أشعر بلمس جسمي من قبل إنسان. وعندما تأتي الشياطين بقرب الأشخاص العاديين، لا يشعر هؤلاء الأشخاص بأي شيء. ولهذا السبب هم لا يشعرون بأي مشاكل. ولكن بسبب حواسي الخارقة، أبقى غير مرتاح حتى تغادر الأمراض والشياطين جسمي.

هل يمكن علاج صوت الصفير المزعج في الأذن ؟

إن صوت الصفير أو الصوت المزعج المستمر في الأذن هو مرض مستمر. وحسب معرفتي، لا يوجد هناك أي دواء لمعالجه ذلك المرض. ومن نعم الله علينا، من السهل بالنسبة إلي علاج هذه المشكلة خلال دقائق. ولكن صوت الصفير هو أيضاً مرض مدمر. وعادة، يتعرض الناس لهذه المشكلة أثناء أعمارهم المتوسطة. وعندما يعاني شخص ما من هذا المرض لسنين عديدة، مكن المرجح أن يسبب أضرار خطيرة

inside the ears. It is very easy for me to take this whistling sound away from any person, but that person needs to use proper medications to heal the damages caused by that disease. Otherwise, that person will get something new with the same symptoms pretty quickly. I hope you now understand that an injured body without treatment invites new sicknesses and diseases all the time.

Slow, calm, and even-tempered people are less likely to be under the influence of demons.

Negativism, violence, and extremism are the main qualities of demons. Basically, we are the bosses of our minds. Demons cannot change us easily. That's why people who already exhibit violence, short tempers, dishonesty, negativism, and extreme behavior are more popular among demons. Demons can easily use these people for negative activities. Most demons do not like even-tempered, slow, and calm people. But that still does not mean that these people are not under the influence of demons, but those demons may be less dangerous. It is a very good practice to keep calm and quiet. Stay cool and patient and nonviolent and non-aggressive to make yourself less interesting for demons.

Face redness is fixable.

Many people have extra redness in their face as compared to other parts of the body. This redness in the face is moveable. This problem is not easy to remove. With time, it can become part of the skin itself. It can do a lot of damages to face skin. It is fixable, but it can definitely be very time-consuming, and it can become a continuous struggle.

داخل الأذن. ومن السهل بالنسبة إلي التخلص من هذا الصوت من أي شخص يعاني منه، ولكن يحتاج ذلك الشخص الى الأدوية الصحيحة للتعافي من الأضرار المسببة من قبل ذلك المرض.

عدا ذلك، سيتعرض ذلك الشخص الى أمراض جديدة مع نفس الأعراض بسرعة كبيرة. وأعتقد أنك الآن تدرك بأن الجسم المصاب بدون معالجة سيستقبل أمراض جديدة في جميع الأوقات.

الناس الهادئين وذوي المزاج المتعادل أقل تعرضاً لتأثير الشياطيين.

إن السلبية والعنف والتطرف هي من أهم ميزات الشياطيين. بشكل أساسي، فنحن أسياد عقولنا. ولا يمكن للشياطيين أن تغيرنا بسهولة. لذلك السبب أن الأشخاص الذين يظهرون العنف السريعين الغضب والغير صادقين وأصحاب السلوك المتطرف والسلبي، هم الأشخاص المتعارف عليهم عند الشياطيين. ويمكن للشياطيين وبكل سهولة استغلال هؤلاء الأشخاص لأنشطة سلبية. ومعظم الشياطيين لا تحب الأشخاص الهادئين والبطيئين. ولكن لا يعني ذلك أن هؤلاء الأشخاص لا يقعون تحت تأثير الشياطيين بل هم أقل خطراً على هؤلاء النوع من الأشخاص. ومن الجيد التدرب للحفاظ على الهدوء. والبقاء صبورين وغير عنيفين وغير عدوانيين لجعلك أقل اهتماماً بالنسبة للشياطيين.

هل يمكن علاج احمرار الوجه؟

يوجد عند العديد من الأشخاص احمرار زائد في وجوههم مقارنةً بأجزاء أخرى من الجسم. وهذا الاحمرار قابل للتحرك. وليس من السهل علاج هذه المشكلة. وبمرو الوقت، يمكن أن تصبح جزءاً من الجلد نفسه. ويمكن أن تحدث الكثير من الأضرار لجلد البشرة، ولكن مكنها بكل تأكيد أن تكون استهلاكاً للوقت وتصبح صراع مستمر.

How did demon doctors treat people with demon problem?

You can find demon doctors everywhere, but most of them just take advantage of people. Most of them are fakes, but some have limited expertise. These doctors usually have a few demons that listen to them. Those demon doctors use their demons to control other demons. I have only one dispute with them. Demon doctors use demons to treat humans for diseases or sickness, but eventually, new demons will do the same thing with that human. My system is different. God gifted me to keep demons away from human as much as possible.

My point is: The nature of demon, you can change it completely. When a demon doctor traet or make his demon, the body guard of a human to save that human from other evil demons, then who can give you guarantee that, for how long that body guard demon will not be acting as an evil demon? So, that is why, this way of treatment is not a solution against demons to secure a human body from demons. I do not use any demons to treat any human. That is why, I am insisting medical Science to learn my way of treating people scientifically and invent machine similar to laser machine to treat and keep all invisible insects away from human body.

My observation of demons inside the body of cat and a lizard during hunting.

I was in my backyard when a cat started hunting a lizard. The demons in the cat and the lizard both jumped on me. The demon from the lizard escaping made sense to me because the lizard was dying, but why did the demon from cat's body leave its home? I feel demons gets scared easily and sometimes feel insecure, so whenever anything unusual happens, all demons leave those bodies. Both demons left their bodies because they felt insecure or scared, but why didn't they stay in the air for a few minutes until the hunting process was done completely? Why did those demons leave those two bodies and

كيف يمكن للعرافين علاج الناس بالشياطين؟

يمكنك أن تجد الكثير من العرافين في كل مكان، ولكن معظمهم يستغلون البشر. ومعظمهم خداعون ولكن بعضهم لديه خبرة محدودة. وعادة ما يكون لهؤلاء العرافون بعض الشياطين التي تستمع إليهم. ويستخدمون شياطينهم للسيطرة على شياطين آخرين. ولدى فقط نزاع واحد معهم. حيث يستخدم هؤلاء العرافون شياطينهم لمعالجة البشر من الأمراض، ولكن في النهاية، ستفعل الشياطين الجديدة الشيء نفسه مع ذلك الشخص. ونظامي يختلف عنهم. وفقد وهبني الله لإبقاء الشياطين بعيدة عن البشر بقدر الإمكان.

فوجهة نظري هي: طبيعة الشياطين حيث يمكنك تغيرها بشكل كامل. وعندما يعالج العراف أو يطلب من شيطانه، حارس جسم الإنسان لحفظه من الشياطين الأخرى الشريرة، إذن من سيمنحك الضمان لذلك، وما هي المدة التي يستغرقها ذلك الشيطان في حراس الجسم دون أن يكون شيطان شرير؟ لذلك، هذا هو السبب، فهذه الطريقة من العلاج ليست حلاً لحماية جسم أي إنسان ضد الشياطين. ولا أستخدم أي من الشياطين لمعالج أي إنسان. لهذا السبب، أصر على أن يقوم علم الطب على تعلم طريقتي في معالجة البشر بشكل علمي واختراع آلة مشابهة الى آلة الليزر لمعالجة وإبقاء الحشرات الخفية بعيداً عن جسم الإنسان.

ملاحظتي حول الشياطين داخل جسم القط والسحلية أثناء الصيد.

كنت في الساحة الخلفية لمنزلي عندما بدأت قطة في اصطياد سحلية. فقد قفزت الشياطين الموجود داخل السحلية وداخل القط الى جسمي. وشعرت بالجن الذي هرب من جسم السحلية لأن تلك السحلية كانت تحتضر، ولكن لماذا غادر الشيطان الموجود داخل جسم القط منزله؟ أشعر بخوف الشياطين بسهولة وأحياناً ما تشعر بعدم الأمان، لذلك عندما يحدث أي شيء غير اعتيادي، تغادر جميع الشياطين تلك الأجسام لأنها تشعر بالخوف وفقدان الأمن، ولكن لماذا لا تبقى في الهواء لبضع دقائق حتى تنتهي عملية الصيد بشكل كامل؟ ولماذا غادرت تلك الشياطين هؤلاء الأجسام و

jump on mine? From this incident, I gathered that those kinds of demons need bodies all the time. Anyway, it kills me when a demon comes inside my body from these animals. I have always thought that ignorance is a blessing.

Vibrations or shaking fingers is a demon's action.

Vibration and the shaking of muscles or fingers are the acts of demons or diseases. Demons control a person's nerves to create this disorder inside the body. It is very easy to control, but patients may need some medication to reduce the external pressure from demons. Instead of going for surgery, I prefer to help these people, but only if they are ready to help themselves by taking medication. I learn this because, sometimes demons are so powerful and their presence in our body creates this kind of problems. I experience these kinds of problems once in a while.

Rudeness, short tempers, and greed are all extreme conditions that are controlled by demons.

Rudeness, arrogance, pride, short tempers, greed, jealousy, and competition are all extreme conditions and come from external sources. With the proper planning and the adoption of positive outlook, we can be reduced these behaviors before we are controlled by them.

All demons are capable of penetrating, expanding, and hypnotizing, regardless of where they live.

All demons are different. Some have a few powers, and others have different powers; however, a few things are common between all demons. All of them are capable of penetrating bodies. All of them

دخلت الى جسمي؟ وبدأ من هذه الحادثة، اجتمعت مع تلك الشياطيين التي بحاجة الى أجسام للعيش فيها طوال الوقت. على أي حال، يقتلني عندما يدخل شيطان ما الى جسمي من تلك الحيوانات؟ ودائماً ما كنت أعتقد بأن الجهل نعمة.

هز الأصابع هي من أفعال الشياطيين.

يعد اهتزاز العضلات والأصابع من اعمال الشياطيين أو الأمراض. حيث تسطير الشياطيين على أعصاب شخص ما لخلق هذا الاضطراب داخل الجسم. ومن السهل التحكم بذلك، ولكن ربما يحتاج المرضى بعض الأدوية للتخفيف من الضغط الخارجي من قبل الشياطيين. وبدلاً من الخضوع لعملية، أفضل مساعدة هؤلاء الأشخاص، ولكن فقط إذا كانوا مستعدين لمساعدة أنفسهم بتناول الأدوية. وأعرف ذلك لأنه أحياناً ما تكون الشياطيين قوية جداً وحضورهم في أجسامنا يخلق هذا النوع من المشاكل. أواجه تلك المشاكل بين الفينة والأخرى.

الفظاظة وسرعة الغضب والطمع كلها حالات متطرفة مسيطر عليها من قبل الشياطيين.

إن الفظاظة والغرور والكبرياء وسرعة الغضب والطمع والغيرة والمنافسة كلها حالات متطرفة وتأتي من مصادر خارجية. وبالتخطيط السليم والتكيف مع التوقعات الإيجابية، يمكن تخفيف تصرفاتنا قبل أن يتم التحكم بنا من قبل الشياطيين.

إن جميع الشياطيين قادرة على التغلغل والتوسع والتنويم المغناطيسي بغض النظر عن مكان عيشها.

وتختلف جميع الشياطيين عن بعضها البعض. فالبعض لديه قوى قليلة، والبعض الآخر لديهم قوى اخرى؛ علاوة على ذلك، هناك القليل من الأشياء تكون مشتركة فيما بينهم. حيث أن جميعهم قادر على التغلغل في الأجسام. وجميعهم

able to expand themselves as much they want. All of demons are capable of hypnotism.

What else the possible effect of a demon other than pain, sickness and controlling mind in our body.

When demons are controlling minds, they create all kind of mental illnesses and violent behaviors. Diseases create all kind of sicknesses, pains, and illnesses. There is another thing. This third thing is an *inner feeling*. I cannot find a single word to explain it. Consider a sleep disorder when you are tired but unable to fall asleep. This is not a disease but some deep problem created by a demon. Intolerance is not a disease, but demons keep us impatient and intolerant all the time. They keep us away from our studies, and they keep us lazy. All these are not diseases but, we suffer all of these because of the control demons have over us.

Life is much better when demons are not around.

We will have less wild and crazy desires in our minds when demons are not around us. No one can hypnotize us when they are gone. Plus, there is no sickness or tension if demons are not around. I strongly feel that life would be very peaceful without demons.

Self-praise is an inner feelings, and it is controlled through hypnotism by demons.

I learned this when I got these feelings during my procedures on the sick. I always feel when a person is in love with him or herself. When I fix other diseases and sicknesses, I pull that inner feeling of self-praising from the person as well. That day, I end up thinking that I am the most important person in the world. It usually takes a whole day for me to figure out that I am under the influence of something

قادرون على تمديد أنفسهم كما يشاؤون. وجميعهم قادر على التنويم المغناطيسي.

ما هي التأثيرات الأخرى المتوقعة للشياطين بشأن الألم والمرض والسيطرة على عقولنا؟

عن سيطرة الشياطين على العقول، يسببون جميع أنواع الأمراض العقلية والتصرفات العنيفة. وتسبب الأمراض الآلام. وهناك شيء آخر. وهو المشاعر الداخلية. لا يمكنني ايجاد كلمة واحدة لشرح معناها. خذ في عين الاعتبار اضطراب النوم عندما تكون متعباً ولكنك لا تستطيع النوم. فهذا ليس مرضاً ولكن هناك مشكلة عميقة سببها الشيطان. والتعصب ليس مرضاً، ولكن تبقينا الشياطين غير صبورين وغير متسامحين في جميع الأوقات. فهم يبقونا بعيدين عن دراستنا ويبقونا كسولين. وجميع تلك ليست أمراضاً، ولكن نعاني منها بسبب سيطرة الشياطين على عقولنا.

الحياة ليست أفضل بدون وجود الشياطين.

ستكون رغباتنا أقل متعة عند عدم وجود الشياطين من حولنا. لا يمكن لأحد تنويمنا مغناطيسياً في حال عدم وجود الشياطين. بالإضافة الى ذلك، لا يوجد أي أمراض أو توتر في حال عدم وجود الشياطين من حولنا. وأشعر بأن الحياة ستكون مسالمة بدون الشياطين.

يعد الثناء على النفس من المشاعر الداخلية، وهو مسيطر عليه من خلال التنويم المغناطيسي للشياطين.

وقد تعرفت على ذلك عندما حصلت على تلك المشاعر أثناء اجراءاتي على المريض. ودائماً ما أشعر عندما يكون شخص ما واقعاً في حب شخص آخر. وعندما أقوم بعلاج أمراض أخرى، أسحب تلك المشاعر الداخلية للثناء على النفس من ذلك الشخص أيضاً. وفي ذلك اليوم، أنتهي بالتفكير بأنني أهم شخص في العالم. وعادة ما أستغرق يوماً كاملاً لاكتشاف بأنني تحت تأثير شيء ما

pushing me to think like this. Once I figure this out, the demons leave my body immediately.

Usually, I am not easily shocked.

I have always felt that I have a strong mind. I do not startle easily, not even at sudden noises. But during the process of fixing someone's pain, I can get an unusual feeling inside me. At least four days I encounter this feeling, I become jumpy and get scared by minor things. After five days with the feeling, I return to normal. *I can become impatient and intolerant.* This happens same way. When I am fixing heart problem, I can absorb that problem from someone else. I was extremely impatient for two days straight. I rudely hung up the telephone on people at least twenty times during those two days. Fortunately, those demons leave me as soon as I realize their effects.

How do kidney failure, heart attacks, and brain damage happen?

Two kinds of sicknesses or diseases can affect the kidneys. The first is a disease that eats organs. It can damage and create infections in the kidneys, and this is painful. The second disease does not eat organs or damage the kidneys. This disease just blocks all the tubes from the kidneys, and after some time, it completely impacts all kidney function. The heart is a very strong muscle. It is difficult to damage heart muscles. Diseases usually attack the heart just to try to block arteries and disrupt blood circulation. These demons and diseases are very good at expanding themselves. These diseases go inside the heart tubes and valves and expand themselves to block the tubes and stop blood circulation. The same thing can happen in the brain. These diseases can easily block tubes in the brain tubes to give someone an aneurysm.

يدفعني للتفكير في ذلك. وعندما أكتشف ذلك، تغادرني الشياطين فوراً.

عادة، لا أُصَدَم بتلك السهولة.

دائماً ما أشعر بأنه لدي عقل قوي. فلا أندهش بسهولة، ولا حتى بسبب الأصوات المزعجة المفاجأة. ولكن أثناء عملية علاج شخص ما، يمكنني أن أحس بشعور غير عادي. وينتابني هذا الشعور لأربعة أيام على الأقل. وأصبح عصبي وخائف من قبل الأشياء الثانوية. وبعد خمسة أيام والشعور يراودني، أعود الى الحالة الطبيعية. وأصبح غير صبور وغير متسامح. ويحدث هذا بنفي الطريقة. عندما أعالج مشاكل القلب، يمكنني ان ألاحظ تلك المشكلة من خلال شخص آخر. وكنت غير صبور للغاية ليومين. وقمت بإغلاق الهاتف بفظاظة عندما كان يتصل بي الأشخاص لأكثر من عشرين مرة في تلك اليومين. ولحسن الحظ، غادرت تلك الشياطين جسمي عندما أدركت تأثيراتها.

كيف يحدث فشل الكلى والنوبات القلبية وتلف الدماغ؟

هناك نوعان من الأمراض التي تأثر على الكلى. الأول هو المرض الذي يأكل الأعضاء. حيث يتلف ويحدث اصابات في الكلى وهذا النوع مؤلم. والمرض الثاني لا يأكل الأعضاء لا يتلف الكلى. فهو يقوم فقط بإغلاق جميع شرايين الكلى وبعد فترة من الزمن، يؤثر كلياً على عمل ووظائف الكلى. إن عضلة القلب قوية جداً. ومن الصعب إتلافها. وعادة ما تهاجم الأمراض القلب لمحاولة إغلاق الشرايين وتعطيل عملة الدورة الدموية. وتلك الامراض جيدة جداً في تمديد أنفسها. حيث تدخل الى شرايين القلب وصماماته وتمدد نفيها لغلق الشرايين وايقاف الدورة المدوية. ويحدث الشيء نفسه في الدماغ. حيث يمكن لتلك الأمراض اغلاق الأوعية الدموية في الدماغ بسهولة مما يسبب في تمدد الأوعية الدموية للشخص.

الشياطين تسمعنا طوال الوقت، ولكن اخضاعهم لكي يسمعوك ليس

Demons hear you all the time, but making them listen to you is not easy.

Demons and diseases around us are able to hear us all the time. We cannot hear them. To convey their wishes, they hypnotize our minds. They know our problems. They know they are responsible for our pains and sicknesses, but they do not care. It is very difficult to stop their negative activities. But you are capable of compelling then to cease their influence and stop their wrongdoing. Other than that, it is really difficult to control their activities.

Can you try to reduce their control?

If you want to reduce the control they have over your mind, they only thing you can do is make yourself less interesting to them. And how you can do it? You can reduce the negativism, violence, and extremism in your personality. Avoid short temperaments and do not become impatient. Do not get angry too easily. Avoid competition as well. If you control your negative qualities, they will definitely be less interested in you. They will look for someone else.

Sincere demons remind us if we forget things. They feed different feelings into our mind to make us suspicious about other people.

Many times, we forget things. Then suddenly, whatever we forgot comes to our minds, but who reminds us of all this forgotten stuff? The demons that feel suspicious things in our minds can make us suspect other peoples.

بالشيء السهل.

إن الشياطين والأمراض من حولنا تكون قادرة على سماعنا طوال الوقت. ولكن لا نستطيع نحن سماعهم. ولحمل أمنياتهم، يقومون بتنويمنا مغناطيسياً. فهم يعرفون مشاكلنا. وهم يعرفون أنهم مسؤولون عن التسبب بالآلام لنا، ولكن لا يهتمون. فمن الصعب ايقاف أفعالهم السلبية. ولكنك قادر على اجبارهم ايقاف تأثيرهم وايقاف أفعالهم الخاطئة. وبدلاً من ذلك، إنه حقاً من الصعب التحكم بأعمالهم.

هل يمكنك التخفيف من سيطرة الشياطيين؟

إذا كنت تريد التقليل من سيطرة الشياطيين على عقلك، فإن الشيء الوحيد الذي يمكنك فعله هو جعل نفسك أقل اهتماماً بهم. وكيف يمكنك فعل ذلك؟ يمكن التقليل من السلبية والعنف وسرعة الغضب وأن تكون صبوراً. لا تغضب بسرعة وتجنب المنافسة كذلك. وإذا سيطرت على ميزاتك السلبية، سيقللون الاهتمام بك. وسيبحثون شخص آخر.

الشياطيين المخلصة تذكرنا في حال نسينا شيئاً ما. فهم يغدوننا بالمشاعر المختلفة داخل عقولنا لجعلنا نشك بالأشخاص الآخرين.

في الكثير من الأحيان، ننسى أياءً عدة. ومن ثم فجأة، مهما يكن الشيء الذي نسيناه، يأتي الى عقولنا، ولكن من يذكرنا بكل تلك الأشياء المنسية؟ إن الشياطيين التي تشعر بالشك في عقولنا هي من تجعلنا نشك بالأشخاص الآخرين.

هل يوجد هناك طريق للإنسان العادي لإخراج الشيطان من جسمه؟

74

Is there any way for a normal person to take a demon out of his or her body?

No, it is practically impossible, but if you contact your religious leaders, they should be able to guide you on how to reduce the pressure of demons. They can easily guide you in ways to prevent problems from demons. In this system created by God, everything is possible. It is not difficult for me to keep demons away from anyone.

Impatience is an inner feelings and it has an external source.

Impatience is not an internal quality. Demons make us impatient. It is almost impossible for a normal person to control this bad quality. If you have a strong willpower, then I am sure everything is possible for you. Just keep convincing yourself that if you are getting angry all the time or showing impatience, it means that you are giving your control to a demon. Maybe this kind of thinking will change your temperament, and then you regain your control from a demon.

I am not sure, but I believe the demons that bring us sexual desires come from women's bodies.

Do not take this explanation very seriously, because I cannot explain this theory to anyone. I do not want to. It is a difficult topic for me, but just read it and keep an open mind. The demons that bring extreme sexual desire are not residing inside us. They are residing inside Women's bodies. This is why we do not feel the same way about all women. I strongly feel the demons that bring extreme sexual desire usually come from women and convince us that we want particular women. You can reverse this theory to understand how a woman feels about a man.

لا، فهذا مستحيل عملياً، ولكن في حال اتصالك بمسؤوليك الدينيين، فينبغي عليهم أن يكونوا قادرين على ارشادك حول كيفية التقليل من ضغط الشياطيين. يمكنهم بكل سهولة ارشادك الى الطرق لمنع حدوث المشاكل التي تسببها الشياطيين. وفي هذا النظام الذي خلقه الله، كل شيء ممكن. فليس من الصعب بالنسبة لي ابعاد الشياطيين عن أي شخص.

عدم الصبر هو شعورا داخليا ومسببه مصدرا خارجي.

فهو ليس ميزة داخلية. حيث أن الشياطيين هي من تجعلنا غير صبورين. ومن المستحيل لشخص عادي من التحكم في هذه الميزة السيئة. وفي حال كان لديك قوة الإرادة، فأنا متأكد من أن كل شيء ممكن بالنسبة لك. فقط قم بإقناع نفسك إنه في حال غضبك طوال الوقت أو عدم الصبر، فهذا يعني أنك تمنح سيطرة على نفسك للشياطيين. وربما هذا النوع من التفكير سيغير مزاجك، ومن ثم ستستعيد السيطرة على نفسك.

لست متأكداً، ولكن أعتقد بأن الشياطيين التي تجلب لنا الرغبات الجنسية تأتي من اجسام النساء.

لا تأخذ هذا التفسير على محمل الجد لأنني لا أستطيع تفسير هذه النظرية لأي شخص. ولا أريد ذلك. فهو موضوع صعب بالنسبة لي. إن الشياطيين التي تجلب لنا رغبات جنسية متطرفة تسكن داخلنا. فهم يسكنون داخل أجسام النساء. لهذا السبب لا نشعر بالطريقة نفسها بشأن كل الناس. وأشعر بقوة بأن الشياطيين التي تجلب لنا الرغبات الجنسية المتطرفة عادة ما تأتي من النساء وتقنعنا بأننا نرغب في امرأة معينة. يمكنك عكس هذه النظرية لفهم كيفية شعور المرأة حيال رجل ما.

يمتلك بعض الأشخاص شخصيات قوية للغاية. وفي تلك الحالات،

Some people have extremely strong personalities. In their cases, instead of controlling them, demons follow them.

Demons are very smart and intelligent. For most of them, their level of intelligence is equal to a twelve-years-old kid's. However, they are more innocent than we are. The only problem is that they are naughty and promote negativism, violence, and extremism. Otherwise, they are better friends than humans, and they are very easygoing. But a few human are extremely intelligent with very strong minds. Their intentions and goals are strong. In the case of these people, I strongly feel that demons just follow them. When this happens, demons help those people in their endeavors. But I am sure you can count those few examples on your fingers.

The help I give to people is useless if they do not fix the symptoms or if the physical damages are not fixable.

Regardless of the sickness or disease, doctors always try to treat patients. All demons and diseases are external things. Any pains or sicknesses can be removed easily, but if an organ or part of the body is extremely damaged and medication or surgery is not an option, my help will be useless, because significant symptoms or damages will only invite new diseases and pains into the body. But nobody should be hopeless. Never give up. Only God knows what he has written for us, so do not give up, keep trying.

When your eyes twitch, this is a demon's action.

When your eye twitches, a demon is likely harassing you. By hypnotizing us, demons feed into our minds portents of bad things, and that's when eyes usually start twitching. Demons harass us all the time. They do this for no apparent reason. You can harass yourself for rest of your life for nothing. Demons are naughty, and they will keep

بدلاً من السيطرة عليهم، تقوم الشياطيين باتباعهم.

تعتبر الشياطيين ذكية جداً. فلمعظمهم، يكون مستوى الذكاء لديهم يساوي طفل يبلغ من العمر اثنتي عشر سنة. علاوة على ذلك، فهم أكثر براءة منا. ولكن المشكلة الوحيدة هي أنهم سخيفون ويشجعون السلبية والعنف والتطرف. عدا ذلك، فهم أفضل الأصدقاء مقارنة بالبشر، وهم متساهلون جداً. ولكن بعض الأشخاص من البشر أذكياء جداً ويمتلكون عقول قوي جداً. وأهدافهم ونواياهم قوية. وفي هذا النوع من البشر، أشعر وبقوة بأن الشياطيين فقط تقوم باتباعهم. وعندما يحدث هذا، تقوم الشياطين بمساعدة هؤلاء الأشخاص في تحقيق مساعيهم. ولكنني متأكد بأنه بإمكانك عد تلك الأمثلة من البشر على أصابع يدك.

إن المساعدة التي أمنحها للأشخاص تكون بلا فائدة في حال عدم علاج هؤلاء الأشخاص لآثار التلف الجسدية.

وبغض النظر عن المرض، دائماً ما يحاول الأطباء معالجة المرضى. وتعد الشياطين والأمراض أشياء خارجية. ويمكن إزالة أي ألم أو مرض بشكل سهل، ولكن في حال كان عضو أو جزء من الجسم تالف جداً وعدم توفر خيار الأدوية أو العمليات الجراحية، ستكون مساعدتي بلا فائدة لأن الأعراض المهمة أو الأضرار ستقوم بدعوة الأمراض الجديدة للدخول الى الجسم. ولكن لا ينبغي لأي شخص أن يفقد الأمل. فلا تستسلم أبداً. فالله وحده يعلم ما كتبه لنا، لذلك لا تستسلم أبداً، وحاول مجدداً.

عندما ترتعش عيناك، فهذا من عمل الشيطان.

عندما تكون عيناك ترتعش، من المرجح أن الشيطان هو من يقوم بإيذائه. عن طريق تنويمنا مغناطيسياً، تغذي الشياطيين عقلك بأعاجيب الأشياء السيئة، وذلك عندما تبدأ العيون بالارتعاش. فتقوم الشياطيين بإيذائها طوال الوقت. فهم يعمل ذلك بدون أي سبب واضح. ويمكن ايذاء نفسك لبقية حياتك بدون أي شيء، فالشياطيين سخيفة وسيبقون

يؤذونكم بارتعاش عيونكم حتى تتجاهلها انت بشكل كامل. وعندما

harassing you by twitching your eyes until you completely ignore it. Whenever your eye starts twitching, keep your finger on that eye and talk to the demon. Tell it to quit harassing you, or tell it to fix the coming problem it is trying to warn you about. You need to be very confident whenever you talk to a demon. Demons can read your mind. Your confidence will compel that demon to listen to you.

Demons can be like us. They can be very aggressive or less aggressive. They can be very negative or less negative. Usually, we behave like our parents or grandparents because the same demons penetrate our bodies.

The chemistry of humans and demons are the same. Many human have different temperaments, different levels of aggression, and different levels of negativity, but you can expect at least some positive behavior from most humans. In the case of demons, it would not be easy to find a positive demon, at least not one who's positive toward everyone. Maybe many demons are positive with me, but I am sure they will not be positive with everyone. Human beings usually live under a hundred years, but demons live more than several hundred years. These demons that possess us were with our grandparents, and they were with our parents. They are with us now, and these demons will be with our kids and grandkids. This is one reason people from one family usually have similar temperaments, problems, and issues.

Diseases are either painful or painless.

We can describe disease in two categories:
1) *Painful diseases*: Invisible insects that eat body parts and organs damage the body parts and organs continuously. Regardless how many painkillers and medications we take, these invisible insects can kill. They can easily be moved from

تبدأ عيناك الارتعاش، ضع اصبعك على عينك وتحدث الى الشيطان. وقل هل أن يتوقف عن ايذائك، أو قل له أن يعالج المشكلة القادمة التي يحاول أن يحذرك بشأنها. ويمكن للشياطين أن تقرأ عقلك. وستجبر ثقتك أن يستمع أليك.

يمكن للشياطين أن تكون مثلنا. ويمكنها أن تكون عدائية جداً أو أقل عدائية. ويمكنها أ، تكون سلبية أو أقل سلبية. وعادة، ما نتصرف كآبائنا وأجدادنا لأنه نفس الشياطين تتغلغل داخل أجسامنا.

إن التركيب الكيميائي للبشر والشياطين هي نفسها. ويختلف العديد من البشر في المزاج والمستويات المختلفة من العدوانية والمستويات المختلفة من السلبية، ولكن يمكن توقع بعض التصرف الإيجابي لبعض البشر على الأقل. وفي حالة الشياطين، فلن يكون من السهل البحث عن شيطان ايجابي، أو على الأقل ليس واحداً لديه تصرف ايجابي مع كل واحد. وربما يكون شياطين ايجابية معي، ولكنني متأكد بأنهم لن يكونوا ايجابيين مع كل واحد. وعادةً ما يعيش البشر أقل من مئة سنة ولكن يعيش الشياطين أكثر من عدة سنين. تلك الشياطين أتي تسيطر علينا هي نفسها التي سيطرت على أجدادنا وآبائنا. وهم الآن معنا، وستكون تلك الشياطين مع أبنائنا وأحفادنا. وهذا هو سبب أن أشخاص من عائلة واحدة عادة يمتلكون مزاجات متشابهة ومشاكل وقضايا متشابهة.

إما أن تكون الأمراض مؤلمة أو غير مؤلمة.

يمكننا أن نصف المرض في نمطين:
1) الأمراض المؤلمة: إن الحشرات الخفية التي تأكل أجزاء الجسم وتدمه بشكل مستمر. وبغض النظر عن كمية مسكنات الألم والادوية التي نتناولها، فبإمكان تلك الحشرات الخفية تقتل. ويمكن ازلتها بكل سهولة من

one body, but they do not die. They will find another body and start damaging that body.

2) *Painless diseases*: These invisible insects also create a lot of sickness in our body, but they do not eat our body or our organs. They share our food. But they block or stop different hormones in our bodies. If they block insulin, they create diabetes. If these invisible insects block tubes in the kidneys, heart, or brain, they can cause kidney failure, heart attacks, or aneurysms.

What is telepathy and hypnotism?

Telepathy and hypnotism are not the same. Telepathy is a form of communication that allows you to privately talk with someone who is not in front of you. You can mentally communicate with anyone in any part of the world. Our soul/spirit is a positive energy that keeps us alive and operates our bodily functions. No one can communicate by using telepathy to access souls. We always communicate with the demon or demons around that person. By using telepathy techniques, we can give instructions to their demons, which can then cause their hosts to think something in particular. Demons do not use telepathy on humans or animals, but demons use telepathy to communicate with each other. Humans use telepathy to communicate with other humans. But we are not communicating with their minds directly. We are communicating with their demons and giving them instructions. After that, demons use hypnotism to control our positive energy and our minds. Hypnotism is a language that demons use to communicate with humans, animals, and insects. By using hypnotism, demons can show us whatever they want in our dreams. Demons are so good at using hypnotism that they can show us anything they want in the real world, too. This quality of controlling someone's mind and feeding him or her different thoughts, dreams, and/or emotions is hypnotism.

الجسم، ولكن لا يموتون. فإنهم سيجدون جسماً آخر ويبدؤون بتدميره.

2) الأمراض الغير مؤلمة: تخلق تلك الحشرات الخفية الكثير من الأمراض في الجسم، ولكن لا يأكلون أجسامنا. فهم يشاركونا الطعام. ولكن يقومون بإيقاف هرمونات مختلفة في أجسامنا. وفي حال تعطيل الأنسولين، فيسببون مرض السكري. وفي حال اغلاق تلك الحشرات الخفية في الكلى أو القلب أو الدماغ، يمكنهم أن يسببوا فشل الكلى والنوبات القلبية وتمدد الأوعية الدموية.

ما هو توارد الخواطر (اتصال عقل بآخر) والتنويم المغناطيسي؟

تختلف فكرة توارد الخواطر عن التنويم المغناطيسي. فتوارد الخواطر هو نموذج من التواصل الذي يسمح لك بالتحدث بشكل خاص مع شخص آخر لا يقف أمامك. ويمكنك الاتصال مع أي شخص من الناحية العقلية في أي جزء من العالم. حيث أن نفسنا البشرية عبارة عن طاقة ايجابية وهي التي تبقينا أحياء وتشغل وظائف الجسم. لا يمكن لأي شخص التواصل عن طريق استخدام الاتصال بعقل آخر للوصول الى الأرواح. ودائماً ما نتواصل مع الشيطان من حولنا. وباستخدام تقنيات توارد الخواطر، ويمكنك اعطاء التعليمات الى شياطينهم الذين يجعلون مضيفيهم التفكير بشيء ما خاص. ولا تستخدم الشياطين تقنية توارد الخواطر على البشر أو الحيوانات، ولكن يستخدمونا للتواصل مع بعضهم البعض. ويستخدم البشر استخدام تقنية توارد الخواطر للتواصل مع بشر آخرون. ولكن لم نتواصل مع عقولهم بشكل مباشر. فنحن نتواصل مع شياطينهم ونعطيهم التعليمات. وبعد ذلك، يستخدم الشياطين تقنية التنويم المغناطيسي للتحكم بطاقاتنا الايجابية وعقولنا. والتنويم المغناطيسي هي عبارة عن لغة يستخدمها الشياطين للتواصل مع البشر والحيوانات والحشرات. وباستخدام التنويم المغناطيسي، يمكن للشياطين أن ترينا ما يريدون في أحلامنا. وهم جيدون في استخدام التنويم المغناطيسي ليرونا أي شيء يريدونا أن نراه في العالم الحقيقي أيضاً. إن ميزة التحكم بعقل شخص ما وتغذيته بأفكار واحلام مختلفة هي عبارة عن التنويم المغناطيسي.

How do telepathy and hypnotism work? What are the easy and difficult parts?

Hypnotism is a procedure that demons use to feed something into the minds of living creatures. Think of the way we can play a DVD and then change disc and watch another movie. Hypnotism works in a similar way. The DVD could be considered our dreams, or demons can show us anything they want. The more we are under their control, the more we will observe whatever they want.

No man can perform hypnosis. Usually, hypnotism experts have very strong demons with them, and they just ask those demons to perform those operations. Telepathy is a normal mode of communication with demons. But when demons are around us, we do not need to use the powers of telepathy to communicate with them. We can just talk normally, and they can hear us easily. But when we need to communicate with someone who is not in front of us, we will need this communication skill. I have learned that telepathy is an effective way of communicating with demons, diseases, and pains. I am able to use this skill in any part of the world without any previous friendship with those demons, but normal people need to have more connection with those demons.

Can we communicate with demons without telepathy?

Yes, we can communicate with demons, diseases, and pains in a normal way, but they usually do not pay attention to normal conversation. For remote communication, one needs to practice telepathy. Usually, people never reveal how to really practice telepathy. I am not sure how many people are really capable of this form of communication. Normal people always think they are practicing communicating the mind of another human, but in actuality, they communicate with the demons of that person. Most telepathy experts usually send their demons around those people with whom they need to communicate,

كيفية عمل تقنيات توارد الأفكار والتنويم المغناطيسي؟ وما هي الأجزاء الصعبة والسهلة فيهما؟

يعد التنويم المغناطيسي إجراء يستخدمه الشياطيين لتغذية شيء ما الى داخل عقول المخلوقات الحية. وفكر بطريقة تشغيل القرص المدمج دي في دي وقم بتغيير القرص وفم بمشاهدة فليم آخر. ويعمل التنويم المغناطيسي بطريقة مشابهة. يمكن لقرص الي في دي أن يعتبر أحلامنا أو يمكن للشياطيين أن ترينا أي شيء يريدون. كلما كنا تحت سيطرتهم بشكل أكبر، كلما ما نلاحظ ما يريدون.

ولا يمكن لأي شخص أن ينجز عملية التنويم المغناطيسي. وعادة ، ما يمتلك خبراء التنويم المغناطيسي شياطيين أقوياء جداً، ويطلبون منهم إنجاز تلك العمليات. وإن تقنية توارد الخواطر هي وضع طبيعي للاتصال مع الشياطيين. ولكن عندما تكون من حولنا. لا نحتاج الى استخدام قوى توارد الخواطر للتواصل معهم. ويمكننا فقط التحدث بشكل طبيعي. ويمكنهم سماعنا بسهولة. ولكن عندما نحتاج الى التواصل مع شخص آخر لا يكون أمامنا مباشرة، سنحتاج الى مهارة التواصل. وقد تعلمت بأن تقنية توارد الخواطر هي طريقة فعالة في التواصل مع الشياطيين والأمراض والآلام. وأنا قادر على استخدام هذه المهارة في أي جزء من العالم دون أي علاقة صداقة مسبقة مع تلك الشياطيين، ولكن الأشخاص العاديون الى المزيد من الاتصال مع تلك الشياطيين.

هل يمكننا الاتصال بالشياطيين دون استخدام توارد الخواطر؟

نعم، يمكننا التواصل مع الشياطيين والأمراض والآلام بالطريقة العادية، ولكن عادة لا يعيروننا انتباه للتحدث. للاتصال عن بعد، يحتاج شخص ما التدرب على تقنية توارد الخواطر. وعادة، لا يكشف الناس أبداً عن كيفية التدرب على تقنية توارد الخواطر. ولست متأكدا عن عدد الأشخاص القادرين عن هذا النموذج من الاتصال. ودائماً ما يعتقد الناس بأنهم يتدربون على الاتصال بعقل إنسان آخر ولكن في الحقيقة، يتصلون مع الشياطيين ويرسلون شياطين الشخص الآخر. وفي الغالب ما يرسل خبراء تقنية توارد الخواطر شياطينهم الى هؤلاء الأشخاص مع من يريدون أن تواصلوا معه

and those demons start hypnotizing the people according to their host's instructions.

You do not need two demons to screws you up? Demon's action is so powerful to our mind. So even one is enough to screws you up.

When you are reading this book, everything may sound very easy, but be careful. Demons are not a joke. They are very powerful, and they do not give their control to anyone that easily. When most people practice telepathy or hypnotism, it usually means that they open their minds to those demons. This all depends on how strong your mind is. Most of the time, instead of a demon listening to our instructions, the opposite happens. These people usually either die because of some accident or they become extremely mentally ill. And remember that we are a favorite hobby for demons. I deal with thousands of demons all the time, but to a normal person, a single demon is enough to make that person mentally ill or crazy. When you decide to practice any of dangerous skills like telepathy or hypnotism, make sure you know about the side effects.

My theory and process of moving or detaching demons/pains

My theory for medical Science is simple. I will sit in front of any person who has headache or any kind of pain. I will do my action without touching that person to fix the pain in his body. Medical Science just needs to observe my mind/eyes and the area of pain of that patient, technically. And discover the connection between my mind and that pain i.e. some kind of rays, once they discover that, Science need to use those rays like laser machine and use that machine against demons and pains.

وتقوم تلك الشياطيين بتنويم الأشخاص مغناطيسياً طبقاً لتعليمات مضيفهم.

لا تحتاج الى شيطانان لتدميرك؟ فأعمال الشياطيين قوية جداً بالنسبة لعقلك. لذلك يكفي شيطان واحد لتدميرك.

عندما تقوم بقراءة هذا الكتاب، من المرجح أن يكون كل شيء سهل جداً، ولكن كن حذراً. فإن الشياطيين ليست مزحة. فهم أقوياء جداً، ولا يتركون سيطرتهم لأحد بتلك السهولة. وعندما يتدرب معظم الناس على استخدام تقنية توارد الخواطر أو التنويم المغناطيسي، يعني هذا أنهم يفتحون عقولهم لتلك الشياطيين. ويعتمد هذا كله على مدى قوة عقلك. وفي معظم الأوقات، بدلاً من استماع الشياطيين الى تعليماتنا، يحدث العكس. حيث إما أن يموت هؤلاء الأشخاص بسبب حادث ما أو يصبحون مرضين عقلياً. وتذكر بأننا هوايتهم المفضلة لديهم. وأتعامل مع الآلاف من الشياطيين طوال الوقت، ولكن بالنسبة لشخص عادي، فإن شيطان واحدة يكفى لجعل ذلك الشخص مريض عقلياً أو مجنون. وعندما تقرر التدرب على أي من المهارات الخطرة ك توارد المخاطر أو التنويم، تأكد من أنك تعرف عن تأثيراته الجانبية.

نظريتي عن عملية التنقل وفضل الآلام/الشياطيين.

نظريتي عن العلوم الطبية بسيطة. سأجلس أمام أي شخص يعاني من الصداع أو أي نوع من الآلام. وسأقوم بعملي دون لمس ذلك الشخص لعلاج الألم المتواجد في جسمه. ويحتاج فقط علم الطب لملاحظة عيوني/عقلي ومناطق الألم لذلك الشخص، بشكل تقني. واكتشف الاتصال بين عقلي وذلك الألم. فعلى سبيل المثال، هناك بعض الأنواع من الأشعة، وعندما يكتشفون ذلك، يحتاج العلم الى استخدام تلك الأشعة كآلة الليزر واستخدامها ضد الشياطيين والآلام.

Are there any side effects to practicing hypnotism and telepathy?

If these techniques were easy, almost everybody would be using them. Personally, I avoid using these techniques whenever they are unnecessary. When I usually use them, I am cleansing someone of diseases and pains. That's all. I totally avoid their other applications. Think of demons as bombs. Using these techniques just to hypnotize someone means you are sending a guided missile into their mind. You may need few things from that mind, but what that demon does next with that mind is anyone's guess. My procedure is very simple. I usually do not use these techniques to control anyone's mind, because I do not need anyone to do anything for me.

Use of metal dumbbells and rods during workout without wearing gloves and stay barefooted on metal floor, cement floor or marble or concrete floor is very effective.

Demons, diseases, and pains travel with a force very similar to electromagnetism. Technical term grounding is effective in case of demons and pains also. How we can get grounded if we are touching/holding any metal, or standing on a concrete floor bare footed. We receive demons pains and sickness all the time from atmosphere or from other bodies. So these demons/pain use a medium or a traveling path to live or reside. So if we are grounded properly and talking to someone on phone. If by chance we attract a demon/pain towards us through phone line. That demon/pain will go straight to ground instead of storing inside our body, if we are properly grounded at the moment. But during this process, if we are wearing an insulated shoe or sandal, then they do not go into the ground. They are stored in our bodies. And once demons and diseases are stored in our bodies, it is difficult to get rid of them. So, grounding is a healthy habit. So, it is

هل هناك أي تأثيرات جانبية أثناء عملية التدرب على التنويم المغناطيسي وتوارد الخواطر؟

في حال سهولة تلك التقنيات، فبإمكان تقريباً أي شخص استخدامها. وبشكل شخصي، أتجنب استخدام تلك التقنيات قدر ما أستطيع وعندما لا يكون هناك حاجة لاستخدامها. وعندما أستخدمها، فإنني أنظف شخصاً منا من الأمراض والآلام. هذا هو الهدف من وراء استخدامها. وأحاول تجنبها تماماً. إن الهدف من استخدام تلك التقيات فقط لتنويم شخص ما مغناطيسياً يعني بأنك ترسل صاروخاً موجه الى عقله. وربما تحتاج الى العديد من الأشياء من ذلك العقل، ولكن ما الذي يفعله ذلك الشيطان مع عقل ذلك الشخص فيما بعد؟ فالخطوات التي أتبها بسيطة جداً. وعادةً لا أستخدم تلك التقنيات للسيطرة على عقل شخص ما لأنني لا أحتاج الى أي شخص لعمل أي شيء لأجلي.

إن استخدام الدميل المعدني والقضبان أثناء التدريبات دون لبس القفازات وعاري القدمين على أرضية معدنية، أو أرضية سيراميك أو رخام أو أرضية خرسانة تكون فعالة جداً.

تتنقل الأمراض والشياطيين والآلام بقوة مشابهة لعملية النقل الالكترو مغناطيسي. إن المصطلح التقني "التأريض" فعال في حالة الشياطيين والآلام والأمراض. كيف يمكن أن يتم تأريضنا في حال لمسنا/مسكنا معدن أو الوقوف على أرضية خرسانة عارية القدمين. نستقبل الشياطيين والآلام والأمراض طوال الوقت من الجو أو من اجسام أخرى. لذلك فإن تلك الشياطيين تستخدم وسط ناقل أو طريق للتنقل من أجل العيش أو السكن. لذلك في حال تأريضنا بشكل صحيح ونتكلم لشخص ما على الهاتف. وفي حال انجذابنا لشيطان ما مصادفةً عن طريق خط الهاتف. سيذهب ذلك الشيطان مباشرة الى الأرض بدلاً من تخزينه داخل جسمك، في حال تم معاقبتنا في تلك اللحظة. ولكن أثناء تلك العملية، في حال ارتدائنا خذاء عازل أو صندل، فلا يذهبون الى الأرض. حيث يتم تخزينهم في أجسامنا. وعندما تخزن الشياطيين في أجسامنا، من الصعب التخلص منهم. لذلك، البقاء قريباً من الأرض عادة صحية. لذلك، من

healthy to slay bare footed on clean floor and use metal dumbles and rods without using gloves

When it comes to liver, kidneys, and intestinal diseases, do not wait for any symptoms, because almost everyone has these problems. There should be some medications for regular use.

According to my theories, modern medications and surgeries are secondary treatments. Modern scientists should be able to invent a machine that emits rays that will insist that demons, diseases, and pains leave people's bodies. This should be a priority. Modern science might also be able to create the perfect grounding solution. These rules can be used very easily to detached or separate a demon, disease, or pain from a body. After we remove all these demons, diseases, and pains from a body, we will need modern medications and surgeries to heal the damages. We may not even feel pain or problems until these diseases have already damaged our organs. For that reason, there should be medication for regular use to avoid these damages from diseases, and everybody should be able to use those medications, whether they are sick or not.

I think demons enjoy their lives by using or residing inside or around us. Most of the time, we obey them without the slightest clue.

We are just toys or mediums for demons. They live and enjoy their lives inside us. We have to adopt their temperaments. We have to follow their instructions. We have to smoke cigarettes for them. We have to drink beer or wine for them. We have to have sex for them. We have to get extremely angry to please them. We have to stay sad and depressed to please them. We have to become extremists so that they feel good. We have to act in negative ways so that they feel better. We have to use drugs and tobacco because they like it. We

الصحي البقاء عارقي القدمين على أرضية نظيفة واستخدام الدميل المعدني والقضبان دون استخدام القفازات.

وعندما تأتي أمراض الكبد والكلى والأمعاء، لا تنتظر حتى ظهور أي أعراض لأن كل شخص لديه مشاكل من ذلك النوع. وينبغي أن يكون هناك بعض الأدوية للاستخدام المنتظم.

وطبقاً لنظرياتي، تعتبر الأدوية الحديثة والعمليات الجراحية طرق ثانوية في العلاج. وينبغي على العلماء الحديثيين أن يكونوا قادرين على اختراع آلة تقوم بحذف الأشعة التي تجبر الشياطين والأمراض على مغادرة أجسام البشر. وهذا ينبغي أن يكون أولوية. ومن المرجح أن يكون العلم الحديث قادراً على إنشاء حل التأريض الأمثل. ويمكن لتلك القواعد أن تستخدم بكل سهولة وفصل الشياطين عن أجسام البشر. وبعد ازلتنا للشياطين والأمراض من الجسم. سنحتاج الأدوية الحديثة والعمليات الجراحية للتعافي من الأضرار. ومن غير المرجح الشعور بالألم أو المشاكل حتى تقوم تلك الأمراض والآلام تدمير الجسم كاملاً. ولذلك السبب، ينبغي أن يكون هناك أدوية للاستخدام المنتظم لتجنب تلك الأضرار الناتجة عن الأمراض، وينبغي على كل شخص أن يكون قادراً لاستخدام تلك الأدوية سواءً كانوا يعانون من الأمراض أو لا.

أعتقد بأن الشياطين تمتع حياتها باستخدام أو السكن داخل أو حولنا. وفي معظم الأوقات، فنحن نطيعهم دون أي أدنى دليل.

فنحن نعتبر دمى أو وسط ناقل بالنسبة للشياطين. فهم يعيشون أو يمتعون حياتهم بالسكن داخل أجسامنا. وعلينا التكيف مع مزاجهم. وعلينا أيضاً الخضوع لتعليماتهم. وتدخين السجائر لأجلهم وشرب البيرة أو الخمر لأجلهم وممارسة الجنس لأجلهم والغضب أيضاً من أجل أن يكونوا راضيين عنا. وعلينا أن نكون متطرفين من جل أن يشعروا بالرضى عنا. وعلينا أيضاً التصرف بشكل سلبي من أجل أن يشعروا بشكل أفضل. وعلينا تعاطى المخدرات والتبغ لأنم فقط يرغبوننا في فعل ذلك. علينا أن

have to do a lot of crazy stuff because demons want us to. They just hypnotize us, and we do whatever they want; however, before we act in any negative way, if we just convince ourselves that we are giving more and more control to these demons, we can start resisting their influence. It is difficult, but we are the bosses of our own minds. We can do anything.

Demons act like currents.

Current is not alive but demons are. Only traveling style is similar. So during phone conversation and some other time during the day, if we keep us grounded with a metal or concrete floor, power of gravity can pull them in ground from our body. And if by chance we are receiving them in our body from someone else and at that time our body is grounded with a metal. I am sure they will just pass from our body. Medical Science needs to pay attention to this theory.

Normal people cannot feel when demons spread all over their bodies. If we are properly grounded, electric currents will never be stored inside our bodies, and by using that grounding medium, this current will go into a ground. The same rule is applicable to demons, diseases, and pains. But most of the time, we are not grounded. That's why all these demons, diseases, pains are stored in our bodies. In the case of demons, diseases, and pains, grounding is effective only when these demons are entering our bodies. But during the transfer, if a person is not grounded properly then all these demons, diseases, and pains will be stored in our bodies. But still gravity and grounding is effective for our health. Someday, Science will understand.

Demons can penetrate our bodies from anywhere, but hypnotism can only done by means of the left ear.

Demons are capable of possessing our bodies from anywhere, but they cannot hypnotize us until they come close to our left ears. They

أن نقوم بالكثير من الأشياء الخرقاء لأن الشياطيين تريدنا أن نفعل ذلك. فهم فقط يقومون بتنويمنا مغناطيسياً، وعندما نقوم بأي شيء يريدوننا أن نقوم به، علاوة على ذلك، وقيل أن نقوم بالتصرف بأي طريقة سلبية، وفي حال أقنعنا أنفسنا بأننا نمنح الشياطيين سيطرة أكبر علينا، يمكننا مقاومة تأثيرهم. فهذا صعب ولكن نحن أسياد عقولنا. ويمكننا أن نقوم بأي شيء.

تتصرف الشياطيين مثل التيارات.

لا يعد التيار كائناً حياً وبينما تعد الشياطيين كائنات حية. فهم يتشابهون في كيفية التنقل لا أكثر. ذلك أثناء التحدث بالهاتف في وقت ما من اليوم، في حال أبقينا أنفضنا ملامسين للأرض باستخدام معدن أو أرضية خرسانة، يمكن لقوة الجاذبية سحب الشياطيين الى الأرض من أجسامنا. وفي حال استقبلنا تلك الشياطيين مصادفة في أجسامنا من شخص آخر وكان جسمنا في ذلك الوقت ملامس للأرض باستخدام معدن. فأنا متأكد بأن الشياطيين سيمررون من أجسامنا. ويحتاج العلم الحديث لإعارة الانتباه الى هذه النظرية.

لا يشعر الأشخاص العاديون بالشياطيين عند انتشارها في جميع أنحاء أجسامنا. وفي حال لامسنا الأرض بشكل جيد، فإنه لا يمكن للتيارات الالكترونية أن تُخَزَن داخل أجسامنا، وباستخدام وسط التأريض، سينتقل هذا التيار الى الأرض. وتنطبق نفس القاعدة على الشياطيين والأمراض والآلام. ولكن في معظم الأوقات، نكون غير ملامسين للأرض. لذلك السبب يتم تخزين الأمراض والشياطيين والآلام في أجسامنا. وفي حالة الشياطيين والأمراض والآلام، يكون التأريض فعالاً فقط عندما يدخل الجن الى الجسم. ولكن أثناء عملية النقل، في حال كون الشخص غير ملامس للأرض بالشكل الصحيح إذن سيتم تخزين جميع تلك الأمراض والآلام والشياطيين في أجسامنا. ولكن ما تزال الجاذبية والتأريض طرق فعال للصحة. ويوماً ما، سيتفهم العلم ذلك.

يمكن للشياطيين أن تتغلغل الى أجسامنا من أي مكان، ولكن يمكن للتنويم أن يتم باستخدام الأذن اليسرى.

إن الشياطيين قادرة على السيطرة على أجسامنا من أي مكان، ولكنا لا يمكنهم تنويمنا حتى يكونوا قريبين من أذننا اليسرى. فهم

do not need to go inside our left ears to hypnotize us. Usually, this control must have an external source.

Diseases and pains are parasites, and millions of them are around and inside us. Demons are not parasites, but they share our food with us. Diseases and pains are parasites insects—that's why they do not leave ever our organ or damaged body parts until they eat them completely. Cancer is one example of that.

Diseases and pains are parasites. They eat our bodies and organs. They are damaging and very harmful to humans. However, demons are not parasites. They share our food. They are capable of hurting us physically, but most of the time, they do not hurt us. They enjoy hypnotizing and controlling us, and they use us as toys for different negative activities and behaviors.

I am not a magician. I use the power of argument.

I do not have magical powers, but I am capable of convincing and insisting that demons, diseases, and pains leave a body. This is not magic. This is the power of argument. That's why I have to suffer the negative reactions of demons, diseases, and pains. I think this is just part of the game, but eventually, every one of them either becomes my friend or gives up on me.

I can prove that all pains, diseases, and sicknesses are physical bodies. How will modern medical science take advantage of my theory?

To proof and convince medical science and to, I am ready to prove my point so that medical scientists start researching different ways of

لا يحتاجون الى الدخول في أذننا اليسرى لتنويمنا. وعادة يجب أن يكون لهذا التحكم مصدر خارجي.

تعد الآلام والأمراض من الطفيليات، والملايين منا متواجدون داخل أجسامنا ومن حولنا. بينما الشياطين ليست بالطفيليات، ولكنهم يشاركوننا الطعام. وتعتبر الأمراض والآلام حشرات طفيلية ـ لذلك السبب لا يغادرون أي عضو حتى يأكلونه بشكل كامل. ويعبر السرطان واحد من الأمثلة على ذلك.

تعد الأمراض والآلام من الطفيليات. فهم يقومون بأكل أجسامنا وأعضائنا. ويقومون بتدمير وإيذاء البشر. علاوة على ذلك، لا تعتبر الشياطين من الطفيليات. فهم يشاركوننا الطعام. وهم أيضاً قادرون على إيذائنا بشكل جسدي ولكن معظم الوقت، لا يقومون بإيذائنا. فهم يستمتعون في تنويمنا مغناطيسياً والسيطرة علينا.، ويستخدموننا كدمى لأنشطة وتصرفات سلبية مختلفة.

أنا لست ساحراً (مشعوذاً). ولكن أستخدم قوة المناقشة والجدال.

لا املك فوة السحر، ولكنني قادراً على اقناع واجبار الشياطيين والأمراض والآلام على مغادرة الأجسام. فهذا ليس بالسحر. فهذه قوة الجدال. لذلك السبب علي أن أعاني من ردود الفعل السلبية للشياطيين والأمراض والآلام. وأعتقد بأن هذا جزء من اللعبة، ولكن في النهاية، كل واحد من تلك الشياطيين إما يصبح صديقاً لي أو يستسلم لي.

يمكنني أن أثبت بأن الآلام والأمراض عبارة عن أجسام فيزيائية. فكيف سيستغل علم الطب الحديث تلك النظرية؟

لإثبات واقناع العلم الحديث، أنا مستعد لإثبات نظريتي حتى يبدأ العلم الحديث البحث عن طرق مختلفة من

handling demons, diseases, and pains. *How will you prove your point?* You may wonder. They need to bring me fifty people with different pains. Some can appear in front of me. Others can communicate with me over the phone, and some can be placed in remote areas. I only need to know how they look and what kinds of pains they each have. I will communicate with the pains of all these people, and I am sure I will be almost completely successful in removing their pains just by communicating with their demons. I hope that medical science will believe me and will start researching these alternative ways to combat demons, diseases, and pains. Only medical Science needs to discover the medium or my communication path, to a demon, scientifically. To invent or discover that power to control demons and pains.

Medical science can take advantage of this theory. Why do I have millions of diseases and pains around me all the time but manage to keep them away from me?

Once medical science accepts my theory and starts researching ways of treating bodies to control and remove demons, diseases, and pains, I will then reveal how I am able to keep all these diseases, pains, and demons away from my body. I can offer proof for this as well, but that is the next step.

A few demon doctors confine demons in bottles of water and then throw these bottles into seas or rivers.

A few demon doctors use bottles of water to confine demons. Demons do not like water. They do not live in water. They stay away from water. But this does not mean water can kill them. This procedure by demon's doctor is true and effective. Those doctors use their powerful demons to confine regular demons inside the bottle of water. But because demons are physical bodies and they cannot go inside an already close bottle. So, those demons doctors just to show people that they are arresting demons in water bottle and taking them away is

التعامل مع الشياطين والأمراض والآلام. فكيف ستقوم بإثبات نظريتك؟ فربما تتساءل عن ذلك. يحتاج العلماء الى احضار خمسين شخصاً بآلام مختلفة. ويمكن للبعض أن يظهر أمامي. ويمكن للآخرين التواصل معي عن طريق الهاتف، وبعضهم الآخر يتم وضعهم في مناطق بعيدة. فقط أحتاج الى معرفة تفاصيل أشكالهم وأنواع الآلام التي يعانون منها. وسأتواصل مع آلام هؤلاء الأشخاص، وأنا متأكد بأنني سأنجح بشكل كامل في ازالة آلامهم فقط عن طريق التواصل مع شياطينهم. وأتمنى بان يؤمن علم الطب بما أقول وسيبدأ بالبحث عن تلك الطرق البديلة لمحاربة الشياطيين والأمراض والآلام. وما يحتاجه علم الطب فقط هو اكتشاف الوسط الناقل للشيطان بشكل علمي لاختراع أو اكتشاف تلك القوة التي تسيطر على الشياطيين والآلام.

يمكن لعلم الطب استغلال هذه النظرية. ولماذا لدي الملايين من الأمراض والآلام من حولي طوال الوقت ولكن أعلم كيف أبقيهم بعيدين عني؟

عندما يقبل علم الطب نظريتي ويبدأ بالبحث عن علاج تلك الأجسام للسيطرة وازالة الشياطيين والأمراض والآلام، سأكتشف حينها بأنني قادرا على أبعاد تلك الأمراض والشياطيين والآلام عن جسمي. ويمكنني أن أقدم دليلاً لهذا أيضاً، ولكن في الخطوة القادمة.

يقوم بعض العرافون بحبس الشياطيين في زجاجات من الماء ومن ثم يقومون برميها في البحار أو الأنهار.

يستخدم القليل من العرافون زجاجات الماء لحبس الشياطيين. والشياطيين لا تحب الماء. ولا يعيشون داخل الماء. ويحاولون البقاء بعيداً عن الماء. ولكن لا يعني هذا بأن بإمكان الماء أن يقتل الشياطيين. فهذه الخطوة التي يقوم بها العرافون صحيحة وفعالة. ويستخدم هؤلاء العرافون قوة شياطينهم لحبس شياطيين أخرى داخل زجاجة الماء. ولكن لأن الشياطيين أجساماً فيزيائية لا يمكنهم الدخول الى زجاجة مغلقة مسبقاً. لذلك، يستخدم العرافون تلك الطريقة لإظهار الناس بأنهم يقومون باعتقال الشياطيين في زجاجة مياه ويأخذونهم بعيداً

something tricky. Then those doctors use their demons to hypnotize people, so people can see ghost inside the bottle of water. This may be a hypnotism trick also. But even after all these tricky procedure, there are some people or demons' doctors, who use same procedure to capture the demons in bottle of water and even I observed by myself, those demons in that area were disappeared after that. So even this bottle of water may be just a trick, but still, there is some management to control and move away those demons from that area.
(I cannot do this)

How does telepathy allow one to read people's thoughts?

Telepathy can allow one to read the minds of other people. By using this technique, you can easily read the thoughts of other people. When someone makes a telepathy connection with another person, they usually send at least two demons to that person. One important part of telepathy is hypnotism, and only demons can perform hypnosis. There are two possible ways one can use telepathy to read people's
minds:

1) Send two demons to the person whose mind you want to read. Both demons will receive yours instruction when you communicate with them by using telepathy. Both of them will read the thoughts of that person's mind by using hypnotism. Once they get the information, one demon will keep reading the mind of the person, but the second will come back to you and feed all the new information into your mind through hypnotism. This way, one demon will continuously read the mind of that person, and the other demon will transfer all the information to your mind.

2) When you send two demons to one person, you need to make sure that those two demons have no conflicts with each other and that they can easily communicate with each other. Demons can communicate with each other by using magnetic fields and systems that also utilize electromagnetic fields. This is

لإظهار شيء ما كخدعة. ومن ثم يستخدمون شياطينهم لتنويم الناس، لذلك يمكن للناس رؤية شبح داخل زجاجة المياه. ومن المرجح أن يكون التنويم خدعة أيضاً. ولكن بعد كل تلك الخطوات الخادعة، هناك بعض الأشخاص من العرافون، الذين يستخدمون نفس الخطوات لحجز الشياطين في زجاجة المياه وحتى لاحظت بنفسي، تلك الشياطيين في تلك المنطقة اختفت بعد ذلك. ذلك حتى أن هذه زجاجة المياه من المرجح أن تكون خدعة، ولكن ما يزال هناك بعض الإدارة للسيطرة ونقل تلك الشياطين من تلك المنطقة (لا أستطيع أن أفعل هذا).

كيف يمكن لتقنية توارد الخواطر السماح بقراءة أفكار البشر؟

يمكن لتقنية توارد الخواطر السماح لشخص ما بقراءة عقول البشر. وباستخدام هذه التقنية، يمكنك بسهولة أن تقرأ افكار الأشخاص الآخرين. وعندما يقوم شخص ما بالاتصال عن طريق توارد الخواطر مع شخص آخر، عادةً ما يؤسلون على الأقل شيطانان الى ذلك الشخص. وهناك جزء مهم من تقنية توارد الخواطر وهو التنويم المغناطيسي، ويمكن للشياطيين فقط أن تنجز هذه العملية. وهناك طريقتان محتملتان يستخدمهما شخص ما لقراءة عقول البشر بتقنية توارد الخواطر:

1_ ارسال شيطانان الى شخص ما الذي تريد أن تقرأ عقل وأفكاره. وسيستقبل هؤلاء الشيطانان تعليماتك عندما تقوم بالتواصل معهم باستخدام تقنية توارد الخواطر. وسيقوم كلا الشيطانان بقراءة أفكار ذلك الشخص باستخدام التنويم المغناطيسي. وعندا يحصلا على المعلومات، سيقوم شيطان واحد بالاستمرار في قراءة أفكار ذلك الشخص، بينما سيعود الشيطان الثاني لتزويدك بالمعلومات عن طريق التنويم المغناطيسي. وبهذه الطريق، سيستمر أحد الشيطانان بقراءة أفكار ذلك الشخص، بينما ينقل الشيطان الثاني تلك المعلومات الى عقلك.

2_ عندما ترسل الشيطانان الى شخص ما، تحتاج الى التأكد من أن تلك الشيطانان غير متخاصمان مع بعضهما البعض. ويمكن للشيطانين بالاتصال ببعضهما البعض باستخدام المجالات المغناطيسية والذي يستخدم المجالات الالكترو مغناطيسية. ويعد هذا

86

almost similar to telepathy, but because this communication is happening between two demons, the traveling medium is different. Otherwise, the rules are same as they are for telepathy. In this procedure, one demon will read the mind of the person and transmit all the information to second demon near you. The second demon will decode all the information in your mind by using hypnosis. Now you understand that demons cannot hypnotize us from a significant distance. I have no interest in reading other people's minds, because I am not a very nosy person. Still, I get a lot of feelings all the time.

My problem with telepathy and hypnotism

As I have explained, I am extra sensitive to demons, diseases, and pains. When diseases are inside a normal person, that person does not feel any pain until those diseases do major damage. Once they come close to me, I always feel pain and discomfort until they go away. The touch of demons is almost similar to the touch of humans to me. When these demons stay around normal people, those people feel nothing. That's why most normal people are unaware of the existence of demons. If one or even one thousand demons stay around a normal person, that person will feel nothing until the demons try to make him or her sick. In my case, I cannot tolerate the feeling once demons come close to me. It makes me really uncomfortable. I continuously feel like some on sitting on my shoulders and head. I continuously feel like something is hanging on my body. As a result, I always ask them to maintain a certain distance from me. To perform telepathy and hypnotism, you need to keep demons very close to you all the time, and it is very difficult for me to even keep one demon close to my body. I feel demons from every part of the world all the time, but I have to move them away from me every day, because I cannot handle their pressure for a long time. Or if they still stay around me, they usually help me, and they maintain a certain distance from me.

مشابهاً لتقنية توارد الخواطر (الاتصال بعقل شخص آخر)، ولكن هذا الاتصال يحدث بين شيطانان، فإن الوسط الناقل يكون مختلفاً. عدا ذلك، فإن القواعد هي نفسها المستخدمة في تقنية توارد الخواطر. وفي هذه الخطوات، يقوم شيطان واحد بقراءة أفكار شخص ما ويقوم بنقل تلك المعلومات الى الشيطان الآخر. حيث يقوم الشيطان الثاني بترجمة تلك المعلومات وتغذيها في عقلك باستخدام التنويم المغناطيسي. ويمكن الآن فهم بأن الشياطيين لا تقوم بتنويمنا مغناطيسياً من مسافات بعيدة. ولا أهتم في قراءة أفكار الآخرين لأنني لست بالشخص المزعج. ولكن، ينتابني الكثير من المشاعر طوال الوقت.

مشكلتي مع تقنية توارد الخواطر والتنويم المغناطيسي.

كما وضحت مسبقاً، فأنا إنسان حساس للغاية للشياطين والأمراض والآلام. عندما تكون الأمراض داخل شخص عادي، لا يشعر ذلك الشخص بأي ألم حتى تسبب تل كالأمراض أضرار كبيرة في جسمه. وعندما يقتربون مني، دائماً ما أشعر بالألم وعدم الارتياح حتى يبتعدوا عني. وإن لمس الشياطيين يشبه الى حد كبير لمس البشر لجسمي. عندما تبقى تلك الشياطيين حول أشخاص عاديين، لا يشعرون بأي شيء لذلك الشبب يكون معظم الأشخاص العاديين غير مدركين بوجود الشياطين. وفي حال بقاء واحد أو ألف شيطان حول إنسان عادي، لن يشعر ذلك الإنسان بوجود تلك الشياطيين حتى تقوم تلك الشياطيين بمحاولة تعريضه للمرض. وفي حالتي، لا يمكنني تمحل شعور تواجد الشياطيين بقربي. فيجعلني غير مرتاح. وأشعر باستمرار تواجد بعض الشياطيين على كتفي أو رأسي أو تعلقهم بجسمي. ونتيجةً لذلك، دائماً ما أطلب منهم الحفاظ على مسافة معينة بيني وبينهم. ولإنجاز تقنية توارد الخواطر والتنويم المغناطيسي، تحتاج الى ابقاء الشياطيين قريبين منك طال الوقت، ومن الصعب بالنسبة لي أن ابقي حتى شيطان واحد قريب مني. حيث أنني أشعر بجميع الشياطيين من جميع أنحاء العالم طوال الوقت، ولكن علي ابعادهم عني كل يوم لأنني لا أستطيع التعامل مع ضغطهم لفترة طويلة من الزمن. أو في حال بقائهم حولي، يقومون في العادة بمساعدتي، ويحافظون على مسافة معينة بعيداً عني.

Usually, everyone has a demon or demons around or inside them, but I do not have any inside my body most of the time. Nobody can stop demons from going inside our bodies. They go inside my body but do not stay there for long. I remove can demons from bodies every day, but they are quickly possessed another. Demons are in and out of our bodies all the time, but in case of normal people, they have few permanent demons. So what I do, I just use any demon around any person in any part of the world, instead of keeping few permanent demons around me for this purpose. This crazy telepathy makes everything very easy for me. I just reach them, introduce myself, and threaten them sometime to move away from that person, if they will not listen to me. Most of the time, it is enough for them and they listen. Sometimes they visit me before they start obeying me, may be just to check, who is that crazy person is?

Demons cannot push or hit you physically, but they can badly hurt us anywhere they want, even inside our bones. They can also easily hypnotize someone else to punch you for no reason.

Yes, this is true. They can possess a body completely and can use that body physically against anyone. Demons are physical bodies, but they are not solid like us. Their physical bodies are like air, but they are not plain air. Their powers are extraordinary. Some people think demons are a special kind of gas that can be used as an energy source. They are completely wrong about that. Flying demons are totally harmless. They cannot hurt anyone. They cannot even hypnotize anyone. Their powers start working only when they penetrate a body. Once they come inside a body, they are able to expand themselves. If they are covering the bottom part of a body, they cannot hypnotize and control a mind from there. A demon needs to be around the head, specifically our left ear, to hypnotize and control the mind. During the process of hypnotism by demons, we usually have a big argument inside the mind, the stronger the person, the stronger the resistance to the demon's influence.

وفي العادة، كل واحد يسيطر على شيطان أو يوجد داخله أو حوله شياطين، ولكن لا يوجد شياطين داخل جسمي في معظم الأوقات. ولا يمكن لأي أحد ايقاف الشياطين من الدخول داخل أجسامنا. فهم يدخلون الى جسمي ولا لا يبقون لفترة طويلة. وأقوم بإزالة الشياطين من الأجسام كل يوم، ولكن يسيطرون على شخص اخر بسرعة. حيث تدخل وتخرج الشياطين من أجسامنا طوال الوقت، ولكن في حالة الأشخاص العاديين، يسيطر عليهم بعض الشياطين الذين يبقون للأبد. لذلك ما أفعله هو استخدام أي شيطان حول أي شخص في أي جزء من أنحاء العالم بدلاً من الحفاظ على بعض الشياطين الدائمين حولي لهذا الغرض. وتجعل تقنية توارد الخواطر هذه كل شيء سهل بالنسبة لي. ما أفعله هو فقط الوصول الى اليهم والتعريف عن نفسي وأهددهم بإبعادهم عن ذلك الشخص في حال عدم استماعهم لي. وفي معظم الأحيان، يستمعون إلي. وأحياناً أخرى يقومون بزيارتي قبل أن يخضعوا لسيطرتي، وربما ذلك للتأكد من هو ذلك الشخص المجنون؟

ولا يمكن للشياطين أن تدفعك أو تضربك بشكل جسدي، ولكن يمكنهم أن يؤذوك بشكل سيء للغاية في أي مكان هم يشاؤون، حتى داخل منازلنا. يمكنهم بكل سهولة تنويم شخصاً ما مغناطيسياً ليقوم بضربك بدون أي سبب واضح.

نعم، فهذه حقيقة. يمكنهم أن يسيطروا على أي جسم بشكل كامل واستخدامه بشكل جسدي ضد أي شخص آخر. والشياطين أجساماً فيزيائية (جسد)، ولكنهم ليسوا جامدين كأجسام البشر. فأجسامهم كالهواء ولكن ليسوا هواءً بسيطاً. وقواهم خارقة. ويعتقد بعض الأشخاص بأن الشياطين عبارة عن نوع خاص من الغازات التي يمكنها أن تستخدم في مصادر الطاقة. فهم مخطئين حيال ذلك. فالشياطين الطائرة غير مؤذيين بتاتاً. ولا يمكنهم أن يؤذوا أي شخص. وحتى أن ينوموا أحداً تنويماً مغناطيسياً . حيث تعمل قواهم فقط عندما يتغلغلون داخل الجسم. وعندما يتغلغلون، يكونوا قادرين على تمديد أنفسهم. وفي حال كانوا يغطون الجزء الأسفل من الجسم، لا يمكنهم أن يقوموا بتنويم أي أحد تنويماً مغناطيسياً والسيطرة على عقله. ويحتاج الشيطان لأن يكون بقرب الرأس وخاصةً بقرب أذننا اليسرى لتنويم الجسم مغناطيسياً والسيطرة على العقل. وأثناء عملية التنويم المغناطيسي من قبل الشياطين، عادةً ما نخوض جدال كبير داخل العقل، فإن الشخص الأقوى هو الشخص الذي يملك مقاومة أكبر لتأثير الشيطان.

Demons cannot hypnotize and control a human from a remote area.

Demons need to be very close to us, especially near our left ear, to hypnotize us. Demons cannot hypnotize us from a remote area by using telepathy. Once medical science invents a machine that can affect demons and diseases, doctors will be able to remove or pull these negative energies out of our bodies. When no demons are around us, they will have little control over our activities and behaviors. The future of our health is very bright. Medical science needs to consider my theories for research. After that, it will not take long to invent the proper machines for treatment. We already have modern medication to heal the damages.

If you are driving, demons cannot move or turn your steering, and they cannot push the breaks. They can, however, tickle you or badly hurt your body in seconds. They can easily make you asleep in seconds as well.

Demons are extremely powerful, but they cannot operate or steer cars by themselves. They all need bodies to fulfill these actions. Demons can also make us sleep when we are driving. They can hypnotize us and push us to commit suicide by running a car into a tree or pole, but demons always need bodies to fulfill their desires. If everyone increases their self-control, we should be able to reduce the presence of demons in our lives and minds.

Reason why we get involve with someone like crazy love sometimes, and then get change after sometime?

I have explained how demons switch bodies if they feel more secure with another. Demons always like to stay around secure bodies. These should not be confused with healthy bodies. Now if you are a man

لا يمكن للشياطيين تنويم الإنسان مغناطيسياً والسيطرة عليه من منطقة بعيدة.

وتحتاج الشياطيين لأن تكون قريبة منا، وخاصة بالقرب من الأذن اليسرى لتنويمنا مغناطيسياً. ولا يمكن للشياطيين تنويمنا مغناطيسياً من منطقة بعيدة باستخدام تقنية توارد الخواطر. وعندما يخترج علم الطب آلة يمكنها التأثير على الشياطيين والأمراض، سيكون بإمكان الأطباء قادرين على إزالة أو اخراج تلك الطاقات السلبية من أجسامنا. وعندما تكون الشياطيين من حولنا، سيكون لديهم سيطرة قليلة على أنشطتنا وتصرفاتنا. إن مستقبل صحتنا واضح تماماً. ويحتاج علم الطب أن يأخذ قفي عين الاعتبار نظرياتي لإجراء البحوث. وبعد ذلك، فلن يستغرق الكثير من الوقت لاختراع الآلات المناسبة لاستخدامها في العلاج. ولدينا أدوية حديثة لعلاج الأضرار.

وفي حال كنت تقود السيارة، لا يمكن للشياطيين أن تحرك المقود ولا يستطيعون الضغط على المكابح. علاوة على ذلك، يمكنهم أن يداعبوك أو يؤذوك بشكل سيء خلال ثوانٍ. ويمكنهم بسهولة أن يجعلوك نائماً خلال ثوانٍ أيضاً.

وتمتلك الشياطيين قوة خارقة، ولكن لا يمكنهم تشغيل أو قيادة السيارات بأنفسهم. فهم بحاجة الى أجسام لإنجاز أفعالهم. ويمكنهم أيضاً أن يجعلونا نائمين أصناء القيادة. ويمكنهم تنويمنا مغناطيسياً ودفعنا للانتحار عن طريق اصطدام السيارة بشجرة أو عمود، ولكن دائماً ما يحتاجون إلى أجسام لإنجاز أفعالهم. وفي حال ازدياد السيطرة الذاتية لشخص ما، ينبغي علينا أن نكون قادرين على التقليل من حضور الشياطيين في حياتنا وعقولنا.

الأسباب التي تجعلنا نتدخل في حياة شخص كالحب المجنون، وتغييرها فيما بعد؟

وقد أوضحت كيفية قيام الشياطيين بتغيير الأجسام في حال شعورهم بأمان أكثر. ودائماً ما ترغب الشياطيين البقاء حول الأجسام الآمنة. ولا ينبغي الاختلاط بين الأجسام الصحية. والآن، إذ كنت رجلاً

and you go around a woman. And a demon, who was around that woman since she was born. That demon was around that woman whole/all her life. Once that woman will go close to any man, usually, that demon from that woman will switch the body and will move to body of that man. As I have said, demons live inside our bodies. They cannot do anything physical, but they enjoy their lives when they are living in our bodies. As humans, we enjoy our bodies, but demons also enjoy their lives when they are living inside us. So, when that woman will go close to a man, demon will move to that man. Now that man is in love with this woman and that demon is also attached with that woman. So, in that kind of condition, usually people they love each other like crazy. They can be very possessive of each other. They cannot share their spouses with anyone. Jealousy is usually involved in those kinds of relationships. Demons are behind this, and all that intensity within the relationship will decrease when these demons decide to go to another body!

What is basic difference between hypnotism and telepathy?

Telepathy and hypnotism are both different, but they go together. It is practically impossible to find a human with the ability to hypnotize someone. To me it seems rather impossible. Almost all hypnotism experts use their demons to help them. People need a communication skill like telepathy to communicate with their demons. For example, if someone sends a demon to someone else who is one hundred miles away from him, this means he or she must have some demons under his or her control. If you have demons under your control and you send those demons to someone with instructions, those demons will go to that person and start doing their job. If you want to give your demons more instructions tomorrow to fulfill another task or you want them to leave that person and go to someone else, you need telepathy to send those instructions to your demons. This could be an extremely dangerous practice for weak and normal people. One

وتذهب بالقرب من امرأة. وهناك شيطان، الذي يكون بالقرب من تلك المرأة منذ ولادتها. وعندما تقترب تلك المرأة من أي رجل، عادة يقوم الشيطان الذي برفقة تلك المرأة بتغيير الجسم وسينتقل الى جسم الرجل. وكما أسلف، تعيش الشياطين داخل أجسامنا. ولا يمكن القيام بأي عمل فيزيائي، ولكن يمتعون حياتهم عندما يعيشون في أجسامنا. ونحن كبشر، تستمتع بأجسامنا، ولكن الشياطين يمتعون حياتهم بالعيش داخل أجسامنا. لذلك، عندما تقترب المرأة من رجل، سينتقل الشيطان الذي يرافقها الى جسم ذلك الرجل. والآن يصبح ذلك الرجل واقعاً في حب تلك المرأة ويصبح أيضاً ذلك الشيطان متصل بتلك المرأة. لذلك، في تلك الحالة، يقع الناس في حب بعضهم كالمهوسون. ويمكنهم أن يسيطروا على بعضهم البعض. ولا يمكنهم مشاركة الأزواج مع أي واحد. وتدخل الغيرة في تلك الأنواع من العلاقات. وتكون الشياطين وراء تلك الغيرة، وستقل كل تلك العلاقات عندما تقرر الشياطين الإنتقال الى جسم آخر.

ما هو الاختلاف الأساسي بين التنويم المغناطيسي وتقنية توارد الخواطر؟

تختلف كلتا التقنيتين عن بعضهما البعض، لكنها يعملان معاً. فمن الناحية العملية، من المستحيل العثور على إنسان يمتلك قدرة التنويم المغناطيسي لشخص آخر. وبالنسبة لي، فهذا مستحيل. حيث يستخدم معظم خبراء التنويم المغناطيسي شياطينهم لمساعدتهم. ويحتاج البشر الى مهارة التواصل كتقنية توارد الخواطر للتواصل مع شياطينهم. فعلى سبيل المثال، في حال ارسل شخص ما شيطان الى شخص آخر يبتعد عنه مئة ميل، فهذا يعني أن هنام بعض الشياطين الذين يسيطر عليهم . وفي حال هناك شياطين تحت سيطرتك وترسلهم الى شخص ما بإعطائهم التعليمات، سيذهبون الى ذلك الشخص ويفعلون ما أمروا به. وفي حال أردت أن تعطي شياطينك بعض التعليمات غداً لإنجاز مهمة أخرى وتريدهم مغادرة جسم شخص ما والانتقال الى جسم شخص آخر، فإنك تحتاج الى تقنية توارد الخواطر لإرسال تلك التعليمات الى شياطينك. ومن المرجح أن يكون هذا خطيراً جداً للأشخاص الضعفاء والعاديين.

demon can make a normal person mentally ill in just few days, so be careful.

Is hypnotism and telepathy possible from anywhere?

It really depends on how skilled you are and how powerful your mind is. This is all a game of minds. If you mind is powerful enough, everyone could be your slave, follow you, and listen to you. If your mind is weak, these demons will send you to a mental hospital. Telepathy allows one to control someone else's mind. Well, actually, one does not control the mind but feeds it instructions, and those instructions always come from demons. Once demons receive the instructions, they start their procedures immediately. Telepathy experts can easily access any mind anywhere in the world. This is all depends on how powerful your mind is. A powerful mind with these skills can control any mind in any part of the world. Hypnotism cannot be done from remote distance. And hypnotism can be done by only demons, not by a human. And that demon needs to close to you to hypnotize you.

Do we need a setup, or can we just start hypnotizing or using telepathy?

Maybe there is a difference between me and some other experts of telepathy and hypnotism. Usually, those people have to practice on particular people for a while before they can send instructions. Usually, that practice involves them sending out their demons. They give their demons some time to set up and feeding hypnotism into the minds of others. Usually, everyone already has a group of demons around them. Sometimes these demons are from their childhood. In my case, the only difference is that I do not have any control over any particular demon. My mind can fly anywhere in the world quite easily. I can convince any demon to take instructions from me, but this is not my field of interest.

ويمكن لشيطان واحد أن جيد شخص عادي مريض عقلياً خلال بضعة أيام، لذلك عليك أن تكون حذراً.

هل يمكن القيام بعملية التنويم المغناطيسي وتقنية توارد الخواطر من أي مكان في العالم؟

في الحقيقة يعتمد ذلك علي مدى المهارة التي تمتلكها وقوة عقلك. حيث إنها لعبة العقول. وفي حال كان عقلك قوي بما فيه الكفاية، يمكنك أن تجعل أي شخص عبداً عندك، ويخضع لك ويستمع إليك. وفي حال كان عقلك ضعيف، سترسلك تلك الشياطين الى مستشفى الأمراض العقلية. وتسمح لك تقنية توارد الخواطر السيطرة على عقل شخص آخر. حسناً، في الحقيقة لا يسيطر شخص واحد على عقلك ولكن يغديه بالتعليمات، ودائماً ما تأتي تلك التعليمات من الشياطين. وعندما تستقبل الشياطين تلك التعليمات، تبدأ بخطواتها فوراً. ويمكن لخبراء تقنية توارد الخواطر الوصول الى أي عقل في أي مكان من العالم. وهذا كله يعتمد على مدى قوة عقلك. ويمكن لعقل يمتلك تلك القوة أن يسيطر على أي عقل آخر في العالم. ولا يمكن للتنويم المغناطيسي أن يتم إجراؤه من مسافات بعيدة. ويمكن أن يتم إجراءه فقط من قبل الشياطين وليس البشر. ويحتاج ذلك الشيطان الاقتراب منك لتنويمك مغناطيسياً.

هل نحتاج الى الإعداد، أو هل يمكننا فقط البدء بعملية التنويم المغناطيسي أو تقنية توارد الخواطر؟

من المرجح أن يكون هناك فرق بيني وبين بعض خبراء تقنية توارد الخواطر و التنويم المغناطيسي. وعادةً، يحتاج هؤلاء الأشخاص الى التدرب على أشخاص آخرين لفترة من الزمن قبل أن تمكنهم من ارسال التعليمات. وتتعلق تلك التعليمات بإرسال شياطينهم. ويمنحون شياطينهم بعض الوقت لإعداد أنفسهم والقيام بعملية التنويم المغناطيسي في عقول الآخرين. ويكون لكل واحد منهم مجموعة من الشياطين حولهم. وفي بعض الأحيان يكون هؤلاء الشياطين متواجدين معهم من طفولتهم. وفي حالتي، إن الفرق الوحيد هو أنني لا أمتلك أي سيطرة على شيطان معين. ويمكن لعقلي الوصول إلى أي مكان في العالم بسرعة وبكل سهولة، ولكن هذا المجال ليس ضمن اهتماماتي.

How long do the effects of hypnotism last?

Our minds are very powerful, and we are the bosses of our minds. Our minds can come under the influence of demons, and they can keep us hypnotized. Once we are free of hypnotism, we return to normal, but most are not aware of demons and their hypnotism. That's why we feel like we were thinking our own thoughts whenever demons feed something into our minds. And when something keeps coming to our minds, it can become difficult to ignore that idea. Usually, demons feed stuff into our minds for few hours and then leave us alone to see our reactions to their efforts. Once mankind understands the power of demons and their influence on us, I am sure we will gain better control over our minds.

Positive energy or the soul/spirit cannot be dictated or controlled externally by telepathy or hypnotism. Positive energy just follows the job assigned to it by God to run and operate bodily functions.

This is true. The soul/spirit cannot be controlled or dictated externally by telepathy or hypnotism. They are not involved in the processes of telepathy and hypnotism. Those have external sources. We send instructions to demons by means of telepathy, and demons defeat positive energies and compel our minds to think certain things. And this is not difficult for demons. This is the language they use to communicate with any mind.

When we say that we are hypnotizing someone, demons are actually the ones performing the hypnosis for us!

If you are a hypnotism expert and you are trying to hypnotize someone, you are not really performing hypnosis. Your demons are really performing hypnosis for you!

كم تدوم تأثيرات التنويم المغناطيسي.

إن عقولنا قوية جداً، ونحن من نسيطر عليها. ويمكن لعقولنا الوقوع تحت تأثير الشياطين، ويمكنهم ابقاؤنا منومين مغناطيسياً. وعندما نكون أحراراً من التنويم المغناطيسي، نعود أشخاصا طبيعيين، ولكن معظمنا لا يدرك ما فعله الشيطان. ولهذا السبب نعتقد أننا كنا نفكر في أفكارنا عندما تغذينا الشياطين بشيء ما في عقولنا. وعندما يأتي شيء ما باستمرار الى عقولنا، يمكنه أن يصبح من الصعب تجاهله. وعادة ما تقوم الشياطين بتغذية المعلومات الى عقولنا لعدة ساعات ومن ثم تغادرنا لوحدنا لرؤية ردود فعلنا لجهودهم. وعندما يدرك الإنسان قوة تأثير الشياطين علينا، أكون متأكد من أننا سنكسب تحكم أفضل على عقولنا.

لا يمكن أن يتم التحكم أو السيطرة على الطاقة الإيجابية أو الروح/النفس البشرية بشكل خارجي عن طريق تقنية توارد الخواطر أو التنويم المغناطيسي. ويمكنها اتباع التعليمات الموجهة إليها من قبل الله لإدارة والقيا وظائف الجسم.

وهذا صحيح، لا يمكن التحكم أو السيطرة على الروح/النفي البشرية بشكل خارجي عن طريق التنويم المغناطيسي أو تقنية توارد الخواطر. فلا يوجد علاقة بينها وبين تلك العمليات. ويوجد لتلك العمليات مصادر خارجية. ونقوم بإرسال التعليمات الى الشياطين عن طريق توارد الخواطر، وتقوم تلك الشياطين بالتغلب على الطاقات الإيجابية واجبار عقولنا على التفكير بأشياء معينة. وهذا ليس صعباً على الشياطين. فهذه هي اللغة التي يستخدمونها للتواصل مع أي عقل بشري.

عندما نقول بأننا نقوم بتنويم شخص ما مغناطيسياً، فإن الشياطين حقيقةً من تقوم بإنجاز تلك العملية.

وإذا كنت خبير في عملية التنويم المغناطيسي وكنت تحاول تنويم شخصا ما مغناطيسياً، فإنك في الحقيقة لا تقوم بإنجاز تلك المهمة. حيث أن شياطينك هي من تقوم بتلك العملية نيابةً عنك!

Few people claim that they are able to see demons either in human shape or in a scary and ugly ghost shape.

We have millions of demons around us. Their small size allows millions of them to gather in a very small room. Usually, weak-minded people give total control of their minds to their demons. Demons are their true friends, and they are friends to demons. When demons get that much control over someone's mind, they usually do not want to leave the person because of the friendship they have developed. This happens to kids as well as people of all ages. Usually, demons hypnotize those people, and through hypnotism, they show the people whatever they want. This is an individual effort of a friend demon towards a demon's controlled human. Actual size and shape of demon will not bring any interest to any human. So, by using hypnotism, demons create an imaginary demon friend in shape of either a ghost or a human for that particular human. This way, some human talk to those humans or ghost shaped demon in their imagination, created by their friend demons for them. Those human thinks, they are really seeing and talking to real demon but actually it is all their open eyes dream world. You will see bunch of people talking to themselves. Actually they talk to their demon (not really demon but imaginary demon) all the time. Some way, they are able to see some human shaped demons also, in their imagination. I think this happened when a very powerful demon totally control a weak mind of a human.

I know this will be very difficult to believe, but when many pains come to my body, I just tell them, "No," just by using my finger. And they listen to me! And this is not difficult for me to prove.

This may sound crazy, but it's true. With 80 percent of diseases and pains, I just convinced them to leave a body, and they listen to me. In 20 percent of the cases, I have to insist that they leave, but it's still

ويدعي القليل من الأشخاص بأنهم قادرين على رؤية شياطينهم سواءً على هيئة إنسان أو على هيئة شبح مخيف وقبيح الوجه.

هناك الملايين من الشياطين من حولنا. حيث يسمح حجمها للملايين منها بالتجمع في مكان صغيرة. وعادة ما يستسلم الأشخاص من ذوي العقول الضعيفة لسيطرة شياطينهم. وتعد الشياطين أصدقاءهم الحقيقيين، وهم أصدقاءً للشياطين. وعندما يحصل الشياطين على الكثير من السيطرة على عقل شخص ما، عادة ما لا يريدون مغادرة ذلك الشخص بسبب الصداقة التي ينشئونها. وهذا يحدث للأطفال والأشخاص في الأعمار المتقدمة. وعن طريق التنويم المغناطيسي، تقوم الشياطين بعرض ما يريدون للناس. فهذا جهد فرديا من شيطان صديق باتجاه الإنسان الذي يسيطر عليه هذا الشيطان. ولا يجلب الحجم الحقيقي والشكل للشيطان أي اهتمام لأي إنسان؟ لذلك، باستخدام التنويم المغناطيسي، تقوم الشياطين بإنشاء خيال لشيطان صديق على هيئة إما شبح أو إنسان لذلك الشخص. وبهذه الطريق، يقوم بعض الأشخاص بالتحدث الى هؤلاء الشياطين الذين يكونون على هيئة إنسان أو شبح. ويعتقد هؤلاء الأشخاص بأنهم يتحدثون الى شيطان حقيقي ولكن في الحقيقة هذا خيال. وسترى الكثير من الأشخاص يتحدثون إلى أنفسهم. في الحقيقة هم يتكلمون الى شياطينهم (ليس شيطان حقيقي ولكن شيطان من وحي الخيال) في طوال الوقت. وبطريقة او بأخرى، فهم قادرون على رؤية شياطين بهيئة إنسان أيضاً في خيالهم. وأعتقد أن هذا حدث عندما يسيطر شيطان قوي جداً على عقل إنسان.

أعلم بأنه من الصعب تصديق ذلك، واكن عندما تأتي الكثير من الآلام الى جسمي، أقول لهم "لا،" باستخدام أصبعي. وهم يستمعون إلي! وهذا ليس بالشيء الصعب إثباته بالنسبة لي.

ويبدو ذلك ضرباً من الخيال، قمت بإقناع حوالي 80% من الأمراض والآلام على مغادرة الأجسام، ويقومون بالاستماع إلي ولكن ما يزال

possible to remove them through communication. Most of the time, when I get a pain in my body, I just use my finger, and it listens to me. All these diseases and pains are sensible and can hear us, but they do not listen to us all the time. I am presenting my theories now to convince scientists to invent and use modern machines against demons.

Who can see easily demons in different shapes other than real shape easily?

In the case of an individual with a weak mind, a demon could completely control him or her. When we are sleeping, we are weak and unconscious. This is perfect time for demons to become 100% in charge of our mind, hypnotize us and show us any dream they want. But when we are up, we reject their control and it reduces their effect on our mind. So many times, it happens with people when they see some big ghost or a shadow in their backyard or in dark part of their houses. So what is this? This is more and more control of a demon on our mind. So, we can call this disorder of mind also, but to me, this is a lot of control of a demon to a human weak mind, that's why a demon is successful to hypnotize a weak mind to really high level, where humans mind is able to dream or see when human is up. In that condition, what someone can do? When a woman/man/kid is seeing an imaginary character created by the hypnotism and that character is continuously is with someone and continuously talk up to them. What can they do? These people have weak mind and they are under control of a very strong demon. Just bad luck. Nothing else. Steadily, those people get more and more involved with that imaginary figure. But this is just a mental disorder created by a demon. Remember, when you are dreaming, this distortion of reality is normal, but when you are awake and still see imaginary character around you, demons may be trying to drive you mod. This is a symptom of mental illness and the increase of control a demon has over your mind. Try to avoid talking to them when you are awake. Otherwise, this disorder will slowly drive you crazy.

هناك احتمال على التخلص منهم عن طريق التواصل معهم. وفي معظم الأوقات، عندما يدخل جسمي الألم، فقط أقول باستخدام أصبعي ويستمع إلي ويغادر جسمي. فجميع تلك الأمراض والآلام حساسة ويمكنها سماعنا، ولكنهم لا يستمعون إليهم معظم الأوقات. وأقوم بعرض نظرياتي الآن لإقناع العلماء لاختراع واستخدام الآلات الحديثة ضد الشياطين.

من يمكن ان يرى الشياطين على هيئات أخرى بدلاً من رؤيتها على هيئتها الحقيقة بشكل سهل؟

في حالة الفرد ذو العقل الضعيف، يمكن للشيطان السيطرة عليه بشكل كامل. وعندما نكون نائمين، نكون ضعفاء وغير واعيين. وهذا هو الوقت الامثل بالنسبة للشياطين للسيطرة على عقولنا بنسبة 100%، ويقومون بتنويمنا مغناطيسياً وجلب الأحلام لنا. ولكن عندما نكون مستيقظين، نرفض سيطرتهم على عقولنا. وفي الكثير من الأوقات، يحدث هذا من أشخاص يروا شبح كبير أو ظل في ساحة منزلهم الخلفية أو جزء مظلم من البيت. لذلك ما هذا؟ إن المزيد والمزيد من سيطرة الشياطين على عقولنا. لذلك، يمكننا تسمية هذا باضطراب العقل، ولكن بالنسب لي، فهذا سيطرة كبيرة لشيطان على عقل إنسان ضعيف. ولهذا السبب ينجح الشيطان في تنويم عقل ضعيف مغناطيسيا إلى مستوى عال عندما يكون عقل الإنسان قادر على رؤية الأحلام عند استيقاظه. في تلك الحالة، ما الذي يمكن لشخص ما فعله؟ عندما يرى طفل/رجل/امرأة شخصية خيالية تنشأ نتيجة التنويم المغناطيسي وإن تلك الشخصية تكون مع ذلك الشخص باستمرار وتتحدث إليه. ما الذي يمكنه فعله؟ يمتلك هؤلاء الأشخاص عقول ضعيفة وهو تحت سيطرة شياطين قوية جداً. فهذا الحظ السيء يلازمهم. لا شيء آخر. وبثبات، يحدث المزيد والمزيد من رؤية الشخصيات الخيالية مع هؤلاء الأشخاص. ولكن هذا فقط اضطراب عقلي يسببه الشيطان. تذكر، عندما يكون تحلم، يكون تشويه الواقع شيء طبيعي، ولكن عندما تكون مستيقظاً وما زلت ترى شخصيات خيالية من حولك، ربما تحاول الشياطين جعلك مجنوناً. فهذه أعراض المرض العقلي وازدياد سيطرة الشياطين على عقلك. حاول تجنب التحدث إليهم عندما تكون مستيقظاً. وإلا، سيقودك هذا الاضطراب الى الجنون ببطء.

It is a very good idea to have water around wherever you go to keep your house and work free of demons.

Water will make all demons around and inside house leave. Outside the house, a sprinkler system can work well, but you need to find out a way to spray water inside your house, too. Spray water on regular basis inside house and outside house. Your house will be neat and clean in a few days. All the demons will go to some other place, because water makes them very uncomfortable.

Modern scientists could build a machine that might be able to suck demons, diseases, and pains with the use of gravity or some kind of grounding mechanism. That machine may also use a vacuum and a tank of water.

Modern scientists could build a machine that may be able to suck and compressed the demons, diseases, and pains in the air. This machine could use the effects of gravity and electrodynamics. Inside, the machine could have a quantity of water to control the demons.

Medical scientists should listen to me and research my theories, because new diseases, pains, and viruses are appearing every day and it's becoming difficult to find medication to fight them.

These days, we hear about different viruses and diseases all the time. In most cases, modern medicine is helpless. We may be living in the modern age of medical science, but we still do not have a cure for migraines or arthritis. We cannot take care of animals around us as much we can take care of humans. These invisible demons, diseases, and pains are free of race and gender. They treat everyone the same way, regardless of species. The population of everything is growing. More sick animals mean more and more growth and reproduction for

وإنها لفكرة جيدة ابقاء الماء من حولك أينما تذهب لإبقاء منزلك ومكان عملك خالي من الشياطين.

الماء يجعل جميع الشياطين من حولك وداخل المنزل مغادرتها. وخارج المنزل، ينجح الإعتماد على نظام الرش، ولكن تحتاج الى أيجاد طريقة لرش المياه داخل منزلك أيضاً. قم برش الماء على أساس منظم داخل وخارج المنزل. وسيكون منزلك أنيق ونظيف خلال بضعة أيام. وستذهب جميع الشياطين إلى مكان آخر لأن الماء يجعلهم غير مرتاحين.

ويمكن لعلماء العصر الحديث اختراع آلة تكون قادرة على امتصاص الشياطين والآلام باستخدام الجاذبية الأرضية وبعض أنواع آليات التأريض. ويمكن استخدام انبوب تفريغ أو خزان من المياه في تلك الآلة.

ويمكن لعلماء العصر الحديث أيضاً اختراع آلة لامتصاص وضغط الشياطين والأمراض والآلام في الهواء. ويمكن لتلك الآلة استخدام تأثير الجاذبية الأرضية والديناميكا الكهربائية. وفي الداخل، يمكنها أن تحمل كمية من الماء للسيطرة على الشياطين.

وينبغي على علماء الطب الاستماع إلي وبحث نظرياتي لأن الأمراض الجديد والآلام والفيروسات تظهر كل يوم وأصبح من الصعب اكتشاف الادوية الملائمة للسيطرة عليهم.

وفي هذه الأيام، نسمع عن الفيروسات المختلفة والامراض طوال الوقت. وفي معظم الحالات، لا يمكن للطب الحديث أن يساعد في الشفاء منها. ومن المرجح أننا نعيش في عصر حديث من علم الطب، ولكن لا زلنا لا نملك علاج للصداع النصفي والتهاب المفاصل. ولا يمكننا العناية بالحيوانات من حولنا بقدر العناية بالإنسان. وإن تلك الشياطين والأمراض والآلام الخفية خالية من العرق والجنس. فهم يعاملون كل شخص بنفس الطريقة بغض النظر عن الكائنات. فإن عدد كل شيء في تزايد مستمر. فالمزين من الحيوانات المريضة يعني المزيد والمزيد من النمو والتكاثر

these diseases and pains. I have always known that I am not a special or extraordinary person, but I do believe in these demons, diseases, and pains. I am sure that God wants to increase the knowledge of mankind. I am sure that I am just a source or a medium to bring this information to the attention of modern medical scientists so that they can find more ways to protect and help mankind against all these diseases and pains.

If I had started writing several years ago, I am sure I would have already written several books about my different kinds of experiences with demons. Years ago, when I started sensing demons, my life was full of adventures. It was a unique and strange experience for me, but on the other hand, demons had more problems once they found out that a human could sense and communicate with them. Nowadays, I strongly feel that the demon's world is somewhat aware of me. That's why I do not face incidences like I used to face in beginning years.

I do not think I even can convey all my knowledge or experiences to readers. I should have started writing all these things a long time ago. Now dealing with and handling demons is just normal. That's why nothing surprises me too much nowadays. Years ago, these experiences were making me crazy, and I am sure, demons felt strange about me as well. Consequently, I will try to describe a few of these experiences to give readers a comprehensive picture.

A few years ago, I had no faith in the invisible world. I never talked to anybody about demons or the invisible world. I was a regular person. I never thought about demons or the invisible world because I never had any experience of demons. I never had any knowledge of them. I never imagined the possibility of a parallel world. Why would I need to talk to anyone about these things when I had no knowledge or awareness of demons?

There was no discussion about demons because there were no demons anywhere. I used to watch movies about demons and ghosts and witches once in a while. These stories and concepts were complete

للأمراض والآلام. ودائماً ما كنت أعلم أنني لست شخص خاص أو خارق، ولكن أؤمن بتلك الشياطيين والأمراض والآلام. وأنا متأكد من أن الله يريد إغناء معرفة الإنسان. ومتأكد أيضاً بأنني فقط مصدر أو وسط لاستحضار المعلومات لانتباه علماء الطب الحديث حتى يتمكنوا من اكتشاف المزيد من الطرق لحماية ومساعدة البشر ضد الأمراض والآلام.

لو بدأت بالكتابة قبل عدة سنين، لكنت متأكدا بأنني قد كتبت العديد من الكتب عن الأنواع المختلفة من الخبرات مع الشياطيين. وقبل سنين، عندما بدأت بالإحساس بالشياطيين، كانت حياتي مليئة بالمغامرات. وكانت خبرة فريدة من نوعها وغريبة بالنسبة لي، ولكن من ناحية أخرى، كان لدى الشياطيين مشاكل اكثر عندما اكتشفوا بأن الإنسان لديه قدرة على الإحساس والتواصل معهم. وفي هذه الأيام، أشعر بقوة بأن عالم الشياطيين يعرف عني شيئاً ما. لهذا السبب لا أواجه حوادث كنت قد واجهتها في سنين ماضية.

ولا أعتقد أنه بإمكاني نقل معرفتي وخبرتي الى القراء. وكان ينبغي علي البدء بكتابة تلك الأشياء من زمن بعيد. والآن أصبح تعاملي مع الشياطيين طبيعي. لهذا السبب لا يفاجئوني شيء في هذه الأيام. وقبل سنين، كانت تجعل مني هذه الخبرات والمواجهات جنوناً، وأنا متأكد، بأن الشياطيين شعرت بالغرابة بشأن أيضاً. وبالتالي، سأحاول وصف بعض تلك الخبرات لإعطاء القارئ صورة موضحة عنها.

وقبل بضع سنين، لم يكن لدي أي إيمان بالعالم الخفي. ولم أتحدث أبداً مع أي شخص بشأن تلك الشياطيين أو العالم الخفي. وكنت شخصاً عادياً. ولم أفكر أبداً بتلك الشياطيين والعالم الخفي لأنه لم يكن لدي أي خبرة بالشياطيين. ولم أعرف عنهم أي شيء أو حتى لم أكن أتخيل إمكانية العالم الموازي. ولماذا أحتاج الي التحدث لأي شخص حيال تلك الأشياء حيث أنه لا يوجد لدي أي معرفة أو إدراك بشأن الشياطيين؟

ولم يكن هناك اي نقاش حول الشياطيين لأنه لم يكن هناك شياطيين في أي مكان. وقد تعودت على مشاهدة أفلام تروي قصصاً عن الشياطيين والأشباح والسحرة في فترة من الفترات. حيث كانت تلك الأفلام والقصص خيالية بحتة بالنسبة لي.

fictions to me. I had no idea that they were all real. That's why I never spent even a second thinking or talking about demons. By now, you should have an idea about me and my concept of the invisible world. As you can imagine, when a person like me was chosen for this kind of knowledge and power, I had a great deal of resistance and disbelief. During different times of the day, I started experiencing extreme heat. That heat was so powerful that I got sores on different parts of my body several times. Even at that time, I was not even close to understanding the invisible world. I used to be a normal person. After those incidents, my life was hell. Wherever I went, I passed through fire. At the time, I never disclosed those problems to anyone. I had a few friends back then. I tried to discuss my problems with them, but they thought I was crazy. Most of them started avoiding me, and it did not take too long for the friendships to slip away. I had no clue at that time, but later on, I figured out that I suffered these feelings once demons came close to me. That's when they started playing with me.

Demons were also aware of my problems, but they were not traveling with me. Whenever I went to the garage, bedroom, or dressing room, they refused to leave me alone. They were playing with me as much as they could. I usually did not go to many places, so I didn't experience too many problems. However, I suffered the fire feeling at work as well. At that time, I had a business in Columbus, Texas. I used to sit in my office all day long, but now I had no place to hide. My skin burned there as well. Even just walking thirty steps, I had to deal with that burning sensation. I was still in denial. I was lying to myself. I tried to tell myself that it was a temporary thing and that maybe I had some disorder. I had no concept of demons or the invisible world. Wherever I was, I had to rub different areas on my body because of the burning sensation. I watched the other cashiers to see if they were uncomfortable like me, but they all seemed quite normal. The customers were normal, too. They were coming and leaving. It was like a hell for me.

Demons that come out from the bodies of rats smell really bad.

لم يكن لدي أي أدنى فكرة عن حقيقة وجود تلك الشياطين. لذلك السبب لم أستغرق حتى ثانية في التفكير أو الحديث عن الشياطين. ولكن الآن، ينبغي عليك أخذ فكرة عني وعن مفهومي للعالم الخفي. بإمكانك التخيل أنه عندما تم اختيار شخص مثلي لهذا النوع من المعرفة والقوة، كان لدي مقاومة جبارة وعدم ايمان. وفي أوقات مختلفة من اليوم، كنت أواجه حرارة عالية جداً. وكانت تلك الحرارة قوية جداً حتى أنه كانت تظهر تقرحات في أجزاء مختلفة من جسمي عدة مرات. وحتى في تلك المرة، لم أكن أفهم العالم الخفي. وقد تعودت أن أكون شخصاً عادياً. وبعد تلك الحوادث، أصبحت حياتي كالجحيم. حيث أنني أينما ذهبت، كنت أمر بتلك النيران. ولم أكشف تلك المشاكل التي واجهتني لأي أحد. حيث كان لدي بعض الأصدقاء في حينه. وقد حاولت مناقشة مشاكلي معهم، ولكن اعتقدوا بأنني كنت جنوناً. ومعظمهم بدأ بتجنبي، ولم يستغرق الوقت كثيراً حتى قطعنا علاقة الصداقة التي بيننا. ولكن لم يكن لدي أي فكرة في حينه، ولكن فيما بعد، اكتشفت بأنني عانيت من تلك المشاعر عندما اقتربت الشياطين مني. وكان ذلك عندما بدأوا باللعب معي.

وكانت الشياطين على علم بمشاكلي، ولكن لما يكن يتنقلون معي. وعندما كنت أذهب الى المرأب أو غرفة النوم أو غرفة الملابس، كانوا يرفضون تركي لوحدي. وكانوا يلعبون معي بقدر استطاعتهم. ولم أكن أذهب الى الكثير من الأماكن، لذلك لما أواجه الكثير من المشاكل. علاوة على ذلك، شعرت بالنيران في العمل أيضاً، وكان لدي بعض الأعمال في كولومبس في ولاية تكساس في ذلك الوقت. وكنت قد اعتدت على الجلوس في مكتبي طوال اليوم، ولكن الآن لا أيوجد أي مكان لأختبئ فيه. وقد احترق جلدي هناك أيضاً وحتى بعد التقدم لثلاثين خطوة، كان علي التعامل ما احساس الحرقة. وكنت لا أزال في إنكار. وكنت أكذب نفسي. وقد حاولت أن أقول لنفسي بأن ذلك كان شيء مؤقت وربما كنت أعاني من بعض الاضطرابات. ولكن لم يكن لدي أي مفهوم عن الشياطين أو العالم الخفيين. أينما كنت، كان علي فرك مناطق مختلفة من جسمي بسبب احساس الحرقة. وشاهدت في كان أمينين الصناديق غير مرتاح مثلي، ولكن كلهم بدوا مرتاحين وطبيعيين. وكان الزبائن طبيعيون أيضاً. ولكنها كانت كالجحيم بالنسبة إلي.

وإن رائحة الشياطين التي تخرج مع أجسام الفئران تكون سيئة جداً.

All the time, we have two desires or arguments or choices. The heart may be endorsing one path, but the mind may be telling you to embrace another. Out of these two, one instruction is coming from your mind, and the second is coming from demons around and inside us.

We can cover our bodies with very thin, insulated plastic or rubber—from at least the neck to the ankle—to keep all invisible pains, diseases, and sicknesses away from our bodies. Scientists can (and should) perform some experiments with this theory, because I am confident about these instructions that I have mentally received again and again. Because of the frequency of these instructions, I know covering the body with plastic or rubber insulation will be effective in preserving health.

My body cannot tolerate demons around or close to me, so I have no choice. I have to convince or insist them to leave my places several times a day. I am sorry, but I do not have a choice.

Some demon doctors openly advertise that they can improve someone's business or financial condition; however, I would request that they not use demons to target innocent customers, because those demons directly attack people's minds and eventually make the people mentally and/or physically sick.

It is not difficult to assign one or more demons to a particular person to create/open doors of any particular disease/pain. It is very easy for those demons to keep inviting different kinds of diseases and pains to a particular body all the time. But compared to this, it is very difficult to keep a body clean of all demons, diseases, and pains. Because of this fact, medical science needs to weigh in during this war.

Always remember, it is not difficult for demons to hypnotize any human or animal and make one do any physical activity, such as punching someone, killing someone, or even turning on the faucet. We do these actions either during sleep or when we are awake, but

وفي جميع الأوقات، لدينا رغبتان أو خياران. وربما يتحمل القلب طريقاً واحداً، ولكن ربما يقول لك العقل بحض شخص آخر، نستنتج من ذلك، أن أول معلومة تأتي من العقل، والمعلومة الثانية تأتي من الشياطين التي داخلنا أو حولنا.

يمكننا أن نقوم بتغطية أجسامنا بغطاء بلاستيكي أو مطاطي سميك وعازل- من الرقبة الى الكاحل على الأقل- لإبقاء على الآلام الخفية والأمراض بعيدة عن أجسامنا. ويمكن للعلماء (وينبغي عليهم) إجراء بعض التجارب على هذه النظرية لأنني واثق من تلك التعليمات التي تعرضت لها بشكل عقلي عدة مرات. وبسبب تكرار تلك التعليمات، أعرف أن تغطية الجسم بغطاء بلاستيكي أو مطاطي سيكون فعالاً في الحفاظ على الصحة.

ولا يمكن لجسم تحمل وجود الشياطين من حولي أو قريبين مني، لكن ليس لدي أي خيار. وعلي أن أقوم بإقناع أو اجبار تلك الشياطين على مغادر أماكني عدة مرات في اليوم الواحد. وأنا متأسف، ولكن لا أملك أي خيار آخر.

ويعلن بعض العرافون بصراحة عن قدرتهم على تحسين عمل شخص ما أو حالته المالية؛ علاوة على ذلك، سأكلب منهم بأن لا يستخدموا الشياطين لاستهداف زبائن بريئين لأن تلك الشياطين تهاجم عقول البشر بشكل مباشر وفي النهاية تجعل هؤلاء الأشخاص مريضين عقلياً و/أو جسدياً.

وليس من الصعب تعيين شيكان واحد أو أكثر لشخص معين لفتح أبواب أي من الأمراض/الآلام عليه. ومن السهل على تلك الشياطين استدعاء أنواع مختلفة من الأمراض والآلام لجسم معين طوال الوقت. ولكن مقارنةً مع ذلك، من الصعب أيضاً الحفاظ على جسم ما خالي من الشياطين والأمراض والآلام. وبسبب تلك الحقيقية، يحتاج علم الطب للتفكير ملياً أثناء هذه الحرب.

وتذكر دائماً، ليس من الصعب على الشياطين القيام بتنويم أي شخص أو حيوان وإجباره على القيام بأي نشاط جسدي أو فيزيائي كمعاقبة شخص ما أو قتله أو فتح صنبور المياه. ونقوم بتلك الأفعال إما أثناء نومنا أو عندما نكون مستيقظين، ولكن

we may be totally unaware of them. That all depends on how weak our minds are. Sometimes animals or reptiles or birds around us do activities for demons.

Don't you think this invisible world is already hurting and killing us? And shouldn't we stop hurting and killing each other at least?

Demons, pains, and diseases can be transferred very easily through the phone line, especially from an overcrowded body. That's why I hate making and answering phone calls. No black magic or demon can defeat holy books or holy procedures. When we use a phone with the speaker on, these pains and demons coming through the phone line either move to the open atmosphere around us or go back to the source on other end of phone line.

The desire to eat again and again is an external problem. One time after I had treated someone, I was affected with this problem. I suffered for at least five days. I was continuously eating something every fifteen minutes. That much eating was killing me, but I controlled myself in a few days.

During times when a person is yelling, crying loudly, or expressing anger, the body will start absorbing more demons and pains from the atmosphere surrounding him or her. At that moment, the person's regular demons will feel insecure in the body. Because of overcrowding, some of the existing demons and pains may (either temporarily or permanently) jump to the closest secure body. The best way for a scientist to discover demons and pains and find a means of controlling them or curing people of these presences is by doing experiments during the times when a human kills a spider, a lizard, or any other living creature and When two people are talking on phone, medical scientists need to observe both ends of the travelling pathway.

A lot of business owners improve their businesses with the use of demon doctors. Demon doctors send demons to these businesses to

ربما نكون غير مدركين لذلك. ويعتمد ذلك كله على مدى ضعف عقولنا. وأحياناً تقوم الحيوانات أو الزواحف أو الطيور من حولنا بأفعال يكون سببها الشياطين.

ألا تعتقد بأن هذا العالم الخفي يقوم بإيذائنا وقتلنا؟ ولماذا لا نقوم بالتوقف عن إيذاء وقتل بعضنا البعض؟

يمكن أن يتم نقل الشياطين والأمراض والآلام بكل سهولة من خلال خط الهاتف، وخاصة من قبل جسم مليء بالشياطين. لذلك السبب أكره القيا بإجراء المكالمات أو الرد عليها. ولا يمكن لأي سحر أسو أو شيطان التغلب على الكتب المقدسة أو الخطوات الدينية. وعندما نستخدم السماعة الخارجية أثناء التكلم بالهاتف، فإن تلك الآلام والشياطين تنتقل من خط الهاتف الى الجو المحيط أو تعود الى المصدر في النهاية الأخرى من خط الهاتف.

إن رغبة الأكل مرات عديدة هي مشكلة خارجي. وفي ذات مرة وبعد أن قمت بمعالجة شخص ما، تأثرت بهذه المشكلة. وعانيت منها لخمسة أيام على الأقل. كنت آكل باستمرار شيء ما كل خمسة عشر دقيقة. وكان الأكل بتلك الكمية يقتلني، ولكن قمت بالسيطرة على نفسي خلال بضعة أيام.

عندما كان شخص ما يصرخ بشكل عالٍ أو التعبير عن غضبه، سيبدأ الجسم ملاحظة تواجد الشياطين والآلام من الجو المحيط بذلك الشخص. وفي تلك اللحظة، ستشعر شيطان لعدية لذلك الشخص بعدم الأمان في الجسم. وبسبب الاكتظاظ داخل الجسم، ربما تقوم بعض الشياطين أو الآلام المتواجدة في الجسم (إما بشكل مؤقت أو بشكل دائم) بالقفز إلى أقرب جسم آمن. وإن أفضل طريقة على العلماء اتباعها لاكتشاف تلك الشياطين والآلام والبحث عن وسائل للسيطرة عليهم أو علاج البشر كم تلك الشياطين هي إجراء التجارب عندما يقوم شخص ما بقتل عنكبوت أو سحلية أو أي مخلوق آخر وعندما يتلكم شخصان على الهاتف، يحتاج علم الطب الى ملاحظة نهايتا خط الهاتف.

الكثير من أصحاب الأعمال يحسنون أعمالهم باللجوء الى العرافون. ويقوم هؤلاء العرافون بإرسال تلك الأعمال الى

control and hypnotize customers, who will then purchase more and come again. But those demon doctors and business owners need to realize that those demons are guided weapons and that they directly affect the minds of their customers in negative ways. Those demons are 100 percent responsible for creating mental illnesses. I have observed business owners from particular countries who are too involved in the use of evil demons to improve their businesses. Every one of us needs to observe very carefully. If you repeatedly experience heavy feelings or pains when you go to a particular business, quit going.

It is very easy to receive or absorb demons from anywhere, but it is very difficult to get rid of them, especially those demons that attack the mind directly to hypnotize people and urge them to do something in particular because the demons are following the commands of demon doctor. Those demons are way more dangerous and harmful compared to regular demons.

In any part of the world, if anyone misses us too much or thinks about us too much, their demons come all the way to us and give us the hiccups either by themselves or through demons already around us. They sometimes show us dreams or feed us thoughts about other people.

When we are working, watching TV, or doing almost anything else and we fall asleep during the activity, the demons around us usually wake us up by hurting or pinching any part of our bodies. Sometimes we bite our tongue or scratch our body unconsciously during sleep. Demons are responsible for all of this behavior.

You can always look to your left shoulder and confidently request that your demons show you some particular dreams about some particular person or place. Trust me—they will listen to you if you show them your confidence about their existence and action. But tell them clearly what you would like and make sure to tell them what you do not like, too. If the demons want to become your friends, they will listen to you. Anyone has any question or need any explanation, email

للسيطرة وتنويم الزبائن، الذين سيقومون بشراء المزيد من تلك البضائع. ولكن يحتاج هؤلاء العرافون وأصحاب الأعمال الى إدراك أن تلك الشياطين عبارة عن أسلحة موجهة وأنهم يكومون بالتأثير على عقول زبائنهم بطريقة سلبية. وتكون تلك الشياطين مئة بالمئة مسؤولة عن التسبب بالأمراض العقلية. ولقد لاحظت بعض أصحاب الأعمال من دول معينة متورطون بشكل كبير في استخدام الشياطين الشريرة لتحسين أعمالهم. ويحتاج كل واحد منا ملاحظة ذلك بحرص. وفي حال واجهت مشاعر ثقيلة بشكل متكرر أو آلام تذهب الى مكان عمل معين، لا تذهب هناك أبداً.

ومن السهل استقبال وملاحظة الشياطين من أي مكان ولكن من الصعب التخلص منهم، وخاصة أن تلك الشياطين التي تهاجم العقل بشكل مباشر لتنويم البشر والتحدث معهم للقيام بشيء ما بشكل خاص سبب اتباع الشياطين لأوامر العراف. وتكون تلك الشياطين أكثر خطراً من الشياطين العادية.

وفي أي جزء من العالم، في حال يشتاق شخص ما إلينا أو يفكر بنا كثيراً، فإن شيطانه يأتي إلينا ويعطونا الحازوقة إما بأنفسهم أو يرونا الأحلام أو يغذوننا بأفكار عن أناس آخرون.

عندما نكون في العمل أو نشاهد التلفاز أو القيام بأي شيء آخر ونغرف في النوم أثناء تلك القيام بتلك الأفعال، عادة ما توقظنا الشياطين من حولنا عن طريق إيذائنا أو وخز أي جزء من الجسم. وأحياناً نقوم بعض لساننا أو حك جسمنا بشكل غير واعي أثناء النوم. وتعد الشياطين مسؤولة عن جميع تلك التصرفات.

ويمكنك دائماً النظر إلى كتفك الأيسر والطلب من شياطينك بكل ثقة أن يروك بعض الأحلام الخاصة عن شخص معين او مكان معين. ثق بي سيستمعون إليك في حال أظهرت لهم ثقتك عن مكان تواجدهم وافعالهم. ولكن قل لهم بكل وضوح ما الذي ترغب برؤيته وتأكد من القول لهم ما الذي لا ترغب به أيضاً. وفي حال أردت أن يكون الجن أصدقاؤك، فإنهم يستمعون إليك. وفي حال أراد أي شخص السؤال أو الاستفسار عن أي شيء، قم بمراسلتي

me your questions and I will answer your questions and explain you in my next book on same subject, soon.

It should now be clear that demons, pains, and diseases are three different invisible things with different actions.

1.) The actions of demons are different, and you can control them easily by using holy water properly (or electromagnetism in the future, when medical science discovers the rays of proper intensity).

2.) Pains work on our nerves, joints, muscles, etc. They stay in one particular part of the body and send pain signals to different body parts to create migraines, arthritis pain, vomiting, diarrhea, or high/low blood pressure. These pains can be easily controlled with electromagnetism through the use of the proper rays; however, medical science still needs to discover those rays.

3.) Now I am going to tell you how to control and defeat a disease, infection, or cancer. As I said before, these diseases are parasites. They are heartless, invisible insects that can swarm a person. Their direction of attack on us is at a ninety degree angle to our body's surface. I will say that 90 percent of attacks are from a horizontal direction to our body surface. If someone is suffering from breast cancer, liver cancer, prostate cancer, heart disease, heartburn, intestine or stomach infections, diabetes, thyroid disease, kidney infection, or any internal/external infection or cancer, that person *needs to do the following*:

    a.) Take a lot of antibiotic, antibacterial, anti-infection, or anticancer tablets on a regular basis until you defeat a particular infection or cancer completely. But remember that you should always eat the proper food before you take any tablets to reduce the side effects. Do not ever take any medication on an empty stomach. These medications just help you in healing the infection or cancer. As you

على الإيميل وسأقوم بالإجابة عن أسئلتكم وسأقوم بتوضيح كل شيء في كتابي القادم في القريب العاجل.

ينبغي أن يكون الآن واضحاً بأن الشياطيين والآلام والأمراض ثلاثة أشياء مختلفة وبأفعال مختلفة.

1) إن أفعال الشياطيين تختلف، ويمكنك السيطرة عليهم بكل سهولة عن طريق استخدام الماء المقدس بالشكل الصحيح (أو الالكتروني مغناطيسي في المستقبل عندما يكتشف علماء الطب أشعة الكثافة الصحيحة).

2) تعمل الآلام على أعصابنا والمفاصل والعضلات، الخ. وتبقى في جزء معين من الجسم وترسل إشارات الألم إلى انحاء مختلفة من الجسم للتسبب بالصداع النصفي وآلام التهاب المفاصل والتقيا والإسهال وارتفاع/انخفاض ضغط الدم. ويمكن لتلك الآلام أن يتم التحكم بها بسهولة باستخدام تقنية الالكترو مغناطيسي من خلال استخدام الأشعة الصحيح؛ علاوة على ذلك، ما زال علم الطب بحاجة الى اكتشاف تلك الأشعة.

3) الآن، أريد أن أقول لكم كيفية السيطرة والتغلب على الأمراض والعدوى أو السرطان. كما أسلف الذكر، تعد هذه الأمراض من الطفيليات. فهي قاسية ويمكنها التجمع داخل جسم شخص ما. ويكون اتجاه هجومها علينا من زاوية تسعين الى سطح الجسم. وسأقول 90% من هجمات تلك الأمراض تأتي بالاتجاه الأفقي الى سطح أجسامنا. وفي كل كان شخصاً ما يعاني من سرطان الثدي او سرطان الكبد أو سرطان البروستات أو أمراض القلب أو عدوى الأمعاء أو المعدة أو مرض السكري أو أمراض الغدة الدرقية أو عدوى الكلى أو أي عدوى داخلية/خارجية أو سرطان، يحتاج الى القيام بالتالي:

أ) تناول الكثير من المضادات الحيوية ومضادات البكتيريا ومضادات العدوى ومضاد للسرطان على أساس منتظمة حتى تتغلب على العدوى أو السرطان بشكل كامل. ولكن تذكر بأنه ينبغي عليك دائماً أن تقوم بتناول الطعام السليم قبل أخذ أي من الحبوب للتقليل من التأثيرات الجانبية. ولا تقم بتناول أي من الأدوية ومعدتك خالية. حيث تقوم تلك الأدوية بالمساعدة في الشفاء من العدوى أو السرطان فقط. وعندما تبدأ

start recovering, keep increasing the power or strength of your medication gradually. As per instruction of your physician/doctor, this healing medication is effective only if we stop continuous attacks of diseases or insects.

b.) In the second step, you need to use anti-infection, anticancer, antibiotic, antibacterial creams and ointments on the surface of your body, regardless of whether dealing with infections or cancers, at least four times a day. Keep gradually increasing the strength of the creams or ointments until you defeat the infection or cancer completely. In the case of breast cancer or prostate cancer, tablets will heal the internal injury, and the use of creams and ointments will kill, clean, and repel the stream of diseases. Otherwise, you will allow them to live on your skin and then penetrate your body and keep infecting you. Do not slow down or give up the use of anticancer or anti-infection creams, because if these insects keep going inside your body, the healing medication will not be as helpful against the continuous attacks of these insects. We need to stop them and not allow them to stay on our skin or penetrate our bodies. The use of anti-infection or anti-cancer cream will help a lot. Always ground yourself when you are applying these creams to your body. You can ground any of your body part to any metal or concrete floor to give these insects an easy path to leave your body.

b.) Now the third and most important part is learning how to isolate your body from the open atmosphere. Simple, clear, comfortable, flexible, thin but strong rubber or plastic can make for the perfect insulator against any substance. You'll need to wear this material for twenty-four hours. Full sleeves should cover from neck to the hip area and hip to knee or all the way to ankle, as needed. Make sure there are no holes or open stitching. This plastic or rubber dress will keep cancer insects away from our bodies. Most infection or cancer insects attack from a horizontal

بالتعافي، قبل بزيادة قوة أو طاقة الأدوية التي تتناولها بشكل تدريجي. بالإضافة الى تعليمات طبيبك الخاص، يكون هذا الدواء فعال فقط إذا قمنا بإيقاف الهجمات المستمر من الأمراض والحشرات.

ب) في الخطوة الثاني، تحتاج الى استخدام مضادات العدوى ومضاد السرطان ومضادات الجراثيم والكريمات والمرهمات على سطح جسم بغض النظر عن ما إذا كان التعامل مع العدوى أو السرطان، على الأقل أربع مرات في اليوم. وقم بزيادة قوة الكريمات والمرهمات بشكل تدريجي حتى تتغلب على العدوى أو السرطان بشكل كامل. وفي حالة سرطان الثدي أو سرطان البروتستات، ستقوم الحبوب بشفاء أو علاج الجروح الداخلية واستخدام الكريمات والمرهمات سيقوم بقتل وتنظيف وطرد الأمراض. عدا ذلك، ستسمح تلك الأمراض بالعيش على جلد جسمك والتغلغل داخل جسم . ولا تتباطأ أو تترك استخدام مضادات السرطان أو كريمات مضاد العدوى. ولأنه في حال استمرار تلك الأمراض الدخول الى جسمك، فلن يكون الشفاء بالأدوية مساعداً ضد الهجمات المستمرة لتلك الحشرات. ونحتاج الى اقاف تلك الحشرات وعدم السماح لها بالبقاء داخل أجسامنا أو التغلغل إليها. وسيساعد استخدام مضادات العدوى والمضادات السرطان كثيراً. ودائماً اجعل جسمك يلامس الأرض عندما تقوم بوضع تلك الكريمات على جسمك. . ويمكنك أن تلامس الأرض من خلال أي جزء من جسم الى أي معدن أو أرضية خرسانة لمنح تلك الحشرات طريقاً سهلاً لمغادرة جسمك.

ت) والآن، يعد الجزء الأهم والثالث هو تعلم كيفية عزل جسمك من الجو المحيد المفتوح. ويمكن لمطاط أو بلاستيك بسيط وواضح ومريح ومرن وسميك أن يجعلك عازل تام ضد أي مادة. وستحتاج الى ارتداد هذه المادة على مدار الساعة. ينبغي أن تغطي الأكمام الكاملة جسمك من الرقبة الى منطقة الورك ومن الورك الى الركبة او الى الكاحل حسب الضرورة. وتأكد من عدم وجود ثقوب أو تطريز مفتوح. وسيحافظ هذا اللباس البلاستيكي أو المطاطي على حشرات السرطان بعيدة عن أجسامنا. وتهاجم معظم العدوى أو حشرات السرطان من الاتجاه الأفقي.

direction. Once we wear this plastic or rubber clothing, we will be saved from these cancer insects. If you already have a lot of infection or cancer insects inside your body or on your skin, then the continuous use of anti-infection or antibacterial creams and tablets will be able to defeat, kill, and repel those insects. Healing medication can fix internal wounds, infections, and cancer easily. If we stop, however, the continuous attack of insects will damage the surface or internal organs. Hence, it is good to cover the entire body with medically prepared, thin plastic or rubber dress to keep cancer insects away from our bodies. Plastic or rubber dress needs to be tight enough to create as much vacuum as possible. You also need to apply anti-infection creams several times a day under this plastic dress if you are suffering from breast, liver, kidney, prostrate, or any other kind of cancer. If you adopt this behavior, I am 100 percent sure you will be able to defeat any cancer very easily.

Companies can make clothing for regular people or normal use, such as jeans or shirts with inner plastic or comfortable rubber layers. Remember, even for normal people, it is not enough just to wear this plastic undergarment. It is very important to use antibiotic or anti-infection creams all the time. During this process, if you feel any movement of insects, just rub the area with as much pressure as you can without removing the protective rubber clothing.

Once you starting wearing this dress from neck to feet for twenty-four hour periods, you will save yourself from the side effects of medication, such as vomiting, heart problems, and upset stomachs. You will be surprised with the improvement of your health condition. When these insects cannot attack your body at the covered areas, they will attack the areas above the neck. To determine how to protect our heads, we will need help from medical science. The concept is very clear. Cancer is very difficult to treat, but if someone uses all the above procedures, he or she will be able to defeat any cancer very easily.

وعندما نرتدي هذا اللباس المطاطي والبلاستيكي، سيتم حفظنا من السرطان. وفي حال كنت تتعرض للكثير من العدوى أو حشرات السرطان مسبقاً داخل جسمك أو الجلد، عليك استخدام مضاد العدوى أو مضاد الجراثيم والحبوب لتكن قادراً على التغلب وقتل ومقاومة تلك الحشرات. ويمكن لأدوية أن تعالج الجروح الخارجية والعدوى والسرطان بسهولة. وفي حال توقفنا، علاوة على ذلك، ستؤدي الهجمات المستمرة للحشرات بتدمير سطح أو الأعضاء الداخلية. لذلك، من الجيد تغطية الجسم كله بالمطاط أو البلاستيك المجهز طبياً والسميك لإبقاء حشرات السرطان بعيدة عن أجسامنا. ويحتاج اللباس المطاطي أو البلاستيكي أن يكون ضيقاً بما فيه الكفاية لإنشاء تفريغ من الجسم. وستحتاج أيضاً الى وضع كريمات مضادات العدوى عدة مرات في اليوم تحت اللباس البلاستيكي في حال معاناتك من سرطان الصدي أو الكبد أو الكلى أو البروستات أو أي نوع من أنواع السرطان. وفي حال اتباع هذا التصرف، فأنا متأكد مئة بالمئة بأنك ستكون قادر على التغلب على السرطان بكل سهولة.

ويمكن للشركات أن تقوم بصناعة لباس للأشخاص العاديين أو للاستخدام العادي كالجينز أو القميص من طبقات من المطاط الداخلي المريح. وتذكر، حتى للأشخاص العاديون، ليس كافياً لارتداء هذا اللباس البلاستيكي. ومنم المهم أيضاً استخدام المضادات الحيوية أو مضادات العدوى طوال الوقت. وأثناء تلك العملية، في حال شعورك بأي حركة للحشرات، فقط قم بتدليك المنطقة بضغط كافي دون تحريك اللباس المطاطي الحامي.

وعندما تبدأ بارتداء هذا اللباس من الرقبة الى القدم طوال الوقت، ستقوم بحماية نفيك من التأثيرات الجانبية للأدوية، كالتقيؤ ومشاكل القلب واضطرابات المعدة. وستفاجأ بالتحسن الذي سيطرأ على صحتك. وعندما لا تستطيع تلك الحشرات مهاجمة المناطق المغطية، ستقوم بمهاجمة مناطق فوق الرقبة. وللتقليل من ذلك، ستحتاج الى مساعدة من علم الطب. وهذه المفهوم واضح جلياً. ومن الصعب معالجة السرطان، ولكن في حال استخدم شخص ما جميع الإجراءات التي تم ذكرها في الأعلى، سيكون قادراً على التغلب على أي نوع من أنواع السرطان بسهولة.

The same principle applies to demons, pains, and diseases, but I am writing about pains and diseases right now. In the summer or spring seasons when the weather isn't so cold, diseases live everywhere— inside, outside, houses, bodies, trees, animals, reptiles, insects, everywhere. They use living bodies as mediums to live and eat. Trees, animals, reptiles, birds, and insects all have less sense than people, so you can say they are unable to fight against these pains and diseases. Trees, animals, birds, reptiles, and insects cannot go to doctors when they suffer from these pains and diseases. Usually, humans can help a few animals and provide medications, but even that is limited. Ninety-nine percent of animals have no choice. They just suffer and stay sick or die because of these pains and diseases. But like everybody else, these demons, pains, and diseases do not like cold weather. In the winter when trees, birds, animals, reptiles, and insects stay out in the open in the cold climate, these demons, pains, and diseases leave those cold bodies and look for a warm atmosphere and a warm body. Humans are able to maintain the temperature of their bodies and the atmosphere around them. In the winter season, human bodies make for better places for these pains and diseases to live. Humans fight against them by using medication, but these pains and diseases still move from one human to another for the winter season. Whenever seasons change, most of these diseases start living again in other animals. *Demons* and *pains* do not live on dead bodies. They immediately leave dead bodies and find another body in which to live. Diseases, however, live on dead bodies until they have completely eaten those bodies. Once there is nothing left for them to eat, they look for new bodies.

In my memory again and again. I am sure they choose undesired people, so I quit pulling data about their victims. And sometimes it takes long time and sometimes less, but I have fewer problems like those these days.

The third and last thing demons do is control victims by hypnotizing them. And under hypnosis, they are very successful in keeping their victims away from me. I will help some people once they tell me about

وينطبق نفس المبدأ على الشياطيين والآلام والأمراض، ولكن سأقوم بالكتابة عن الآلام والأمراض الآن. وفي فصل الصيف أو الربيع عندما يكون الطقس ليس باردأ، تعيش الأمراض في كل مكان-داخل وخارج الأجسام والأشجار والحيوانات والزواحف والحشرات. فهم يستخدمون الأجسام الحية كوسط للحياة والأكل. فالأشجار والحيوانات والزواحف والطيور والحشرات يكون لها احساس أقل من البشر، لذلك يمكنك القول بأنهم غير قادرون على مقاومة الآلام والأمراض. ولا يمكنهم الذهاب الى الأطباء ندما يعانون من تلك الآلام والأمراض. وعادة، يمكن للإنسان مساعدة بعض الحيوانات واعطائها الأدوية، ولكن حتى ذلك يكون محدود. و لا يمك 90% من الحيوانات الخيار. فقط هم يعانون ويبقون مرضى أو يموتون بسبب تلك الآلام والأمراض. ولكن كأي شخص آخر، لا ترغب تلك الشياطيين والآلام والأمراض بالطقس البارد. وفي الشتاء وعندما تكون الأشجار والطيور والحيوانات والزواحف في المناخ البارد، تغدر الشياطيين والآلام والامراض الأجسام الباردة وتنتقل الى جو دافئ وجسم دافئ. ويكون البشر قادرون على الحفاظ على درجة حرارة أجسامهم والجو المحيط بهم. وفي الشتاء يعتبر الإنسان مكانا ملائما للأمراض والآلام للعيش فيه. ويقوم الإنسان تلك الأمراض باستخدام الأدوية، ولكن تنتقل تلك الأمراض من شخص إلى آخر. وعندما يتغير الفصل السنوي، تبدأ معظم تلك الأمراض بالعيش مجدداً في أجسام الحيوانات. فهم يغادرون الأجسام الميتة مباشرة والبحث عن جسم آخر للعيش فيه. علاوة على ذلك، تتعايش الأمراض على الأجسام الميتة حتى تأكلها بشكل كامل. وعندما لا يبقى شيء لتناوله، يبحثون عن أجسام جديدة للعيش فيها.

وفي ذاكرتي، أنا متأكد من أنهم يقومون باختيار الأشخاص الغير مرغوب بهم، لذلك ترك سحب المعلومات عن ضحاياهم. وأحياناً يستغرق بعض الوقت وفي أحيان أخرى لا يستغرق، ولكن أواجه بعض من تلك المشاكل في هذه الأيام.

إن الشيء الأخير والثالث الذي تقوم به الشياطيين هو السيطرة على الضحايا باستخدام التنويم المغناطيسي. وبعد ذلك، ينجحون في إبقاء ضحاياهم بعيداً عني. وسأساعد بعض الأشخاص عندما يقولون لي عن

their problems or pains, but if demons are in total control of these people's minds and insist that they endure pain and turn away from me for any reason, then the victims of these demons will continue suffering and refuse to contact me.

Joseph used to live in Weimar, Texas, but now he lives in Houston. He was in the tree business. One day, he came to me to talk about selling his truck. He was limping badly. He told me that he had dropped a big tree branch on his foot. I asked him if he was taking any painkillers. He said he had been taking painkillers for the last twenty-four hours but that the pain was not reducing and the swelling was increasing. I asked him to show me his feet. His left foot was swelling badly, and all the veins were clearly visible. I then communicated with his pain, and thanks to God, that pain listened to me. But the swelling was still there, so I suggested that he use some cream to reduce the swelling. He was a very strong man. I do not think he used anything. Two days later, I asked him if he had any more pain, but he said he was okay even without using any medication. However, he should have used the proper medication to heal the injury and avoid an open invitation to other pains.

Mr. Krenak had snacks business. One day, he came with his daughter and mentioned that she had been doing his route because he had some paralysis in his right arm. His arm was extremely sore all the time, and he was not able to move it at all. Because of those problems, he was not able to pull or lift anything. That's why the doctor suggested that he stay home and quit working. I was behind the counter that day. I asked him if I could help, and he asked how. Instead of explaining my process to him, I immediately started communicating with his pain. During that communication, I heard his daughter laughing behind him. In three steps, his pain was completely gone and he regained 70 percent of the mobility in his hand within a few minutes. Still, he was not able to move his hand all the way to the top of head, but he verified that he was not having any pain. I suggested that he use some cream to relax his muscles. His daughter was very surprised when they left me that day.

مشاكلهم أو آلامهم، ولكن في حال كانت تلك الشياطين مسيطرة بشكل كلي على عقول هؤلاء الأشخاص ويجبرونهم على تحمل الآلام والبعد عني بدون أي سبب. ذلك سيستمر الضحايا بالمعاناة ورفض الاتصال بي.

وقد عاش يوسف في مدينة ويما، في ولاية تكساس الأمريكية، ولكنه الآن يقيم في مدينة هيوستن في ولاية تكساس الأمريكية. وكان يعمل في الأشجار. وفي يوم من الأيام، جاء إلي يتحدث عن بيع شاحنته. وكان يعرج بشكل سيء. وقال لي بأن غصن شجر كبير قد وقع على قدمه. وقد سألته حول أخذه لمسكنات الألم. وقال لي بأنه كان يتناول مسكنات الألم لأكثر من أربعة وعشرين ساعة ولكن لم يقلل من شدة الألم وكان الانتفاخ يزداد. وقد سألته بأن يريني قدمه. وكانت قدمه اليسرى تنتفخ بشكل سيء، وكانت جميع الأوردة ظاهرة جلياً. ومن ثم قمت بالتواصل مع ألمه، والشكر لله، لقد استمع الألم إلي. ولكن كان الألم لا يزال متواجد، لذلك اقترحت عليه بأن يستخدم بعض الكريمات لتخفيف الانتفاخ. وكان رجلاً قوياً. ولا أعتقد بأنه قام باستخدام أي شيء. وبعد يومين، سألته حول إذا ما اذا كان يتألم، ولكنه أخبرني بأنه بصحة جيدة حتى بدون استخدام أي نوع من الأدوية. علاوة على ذلك، كان ينبغي عليه استخدام الدواء السليم لعلاج الجروح وتجنب أي دعة مفتوحة لآلام أخرى.

وكان السيد كريناك يعمل في الوجبات الخفيفة. وفي يوم م الأيام، جاءني مصطحباً ابنته بأنها كانت تعمل في نفسه مجال عمله وقد شلت يدها اليمنى. وكانت ذراعه ملتهبة بشكل حاد طوال الوقت، ولم يكن قادراً على تحريكها مطلقاً. وسبب ذلك كله، لم يكن يستطع سحب او رفع أي شيء. لذلك السبب نصحه الطبيب بأن يبقى في المنزل وأن يترك عمله. وكنت خلف طاولة الاستقبال في ذلك اليوم. وسألته في حال كان بإمكاني تقديم المساعدة وسألني عن كيفية ذلك. بدلاً من توضيح العملية التي سأقوب بها، بدأ مباشرة بالتواصل مع ألمه. وأثناء ذلك التواصل، سمعت ابنته تضحك خلفه. وفي ثلاث خطوات، اختفى ألمه بشكل كامل واستعاد 70% من قابلية الحركة لذراعه خلال دقائق. وكان لا يزال لا يستطيع تحريك يده الى أعلى رأسه، ولكنه أكد بأنه لا يعاني من أي ألم. ونصحته باستخدام بعض الكريمات لإراحة عضلاته. وكان ابنته متفاجئة عندما غادروا في حينه.

In practical life observation, we observe a lot, when some people or their feelings, get up or ideas, change completely like someone was not a religious and suddenly become too much religious. Or someone was bad, alcoholic, drug addicted or some other bad habits or behavior towards people, they suddenly changed persons. To me either they come out from the influence of bad demon or old demon died or now they have more control on themselves and rejecting demons or maybe they are under influence of a different demon. (Always something).

Mr. Charles Jr. mowed grass in Columbus, Texas. He had the same kind of problem as Mr. Krenak had with his left arm and shoulder. He was not taking any medication, but his pain came out of his body right away. The symptoms and pains of a few people are sometimes worse than others, but they may leave those bodies very easily when I communicate with them. However, sometimes they take a little longer. Maybe it depends on their overall health, or maybe good or bad luck is involved.

I remember one time a man named Karam was in Weimar to find out if I was willing to sell the business. During our talk, he started telling me that he had interacted with demons and that he could use them to tell someone's future and past. No doubt, he was making fun of me and criticizing me as well. He thought everything I had done and said was all bullshit. I did not know what to tell him. He kept asking me about my date of birth and my mother's name so that he could tell me my past and future. I just told him, "If you are capable of doing anything, then just tell me without asking me anything." In response, he said that no one could do that and that to deal with someone, you had to know things about the person. At that time, I mentioned that I did not have any restrictions like that. I didn't need to know a person's name, date of birth, or mother's name to do my job. He then made some bad remarks. I just told him that I did not tell people their pasts or futures, because I felt it was just a waste of time but I said that I could remove if a person's pain or sickness without knowing any details about him or her.

وفي الملاحظة العملية، نلاحظ الكثير عندما تتغير مشاعر الناس أو أفكارهم بشكل كامل كشخص ما لم يكن متديناً وفجأة يصبح متديناً كثيراً. أو أن شخصاً ما كان سيء التصرف أو مدمن على الكحول أو تعاطي المخدرات أو بعض العادات السيئة الأخرى، وفجأة يتغيرون إلى أشخاص آخرين. بالنسبة إلي، فهم يتحررون من تأثير شيطان سيء أو شيطان توفي أو أنهم أصبحوا الآن أكثر تحكماً بأنفسهم ورفض الشيطانيين أو ربما كانوا تحت تأثير شيطا آخر (دائماً ما يكون هناك شيء ما).

وقام السيد شارلز جينير بقص العشب في مدينة كولومبس في ولاية تكساس. وكان يعاني من نفس المشكلة التي عانى منها السيد كريناك في ذراعه الأيسر والكتف. ولم يتناول أي من الأدوية، ولكن خرج الألم من جسمه مباشرة. وتكون أعراض وآلام بعض الأشخاص أسوأ من الآخرين، ولكن ربما تخرج من أجسامهم بكل سهولة عندما أتواصل معهم. علاوة على ذلك، قد يستغرق من الوقت أطول قليلاً. ومن المحتمل انه يعتمد على ظروف صحة الأشخاص، أو الحظ السيء أو الحسن.

وأتذكر رجلاً اسمه كرم، كان يقيم في مدينة ويمار للبحث في حال كوني أردت بيع بعض الاعمال. وأثناء حديثنا، أخبرنه بانه يتواصل مع الشياطين ويمكنه استخدامه لقراءة مستقبل أو ماضي شخص ما. وبدن أي شك، كان يسخر مني وينتقدني أيضاً. اعتقد بأن كل شيء قمت به وقلت كان هراء. ولم أكن أعلم ما أقول له؟ واستمر بسؤالي عن تاريخ ميلادي واسم أمي حتى يمكنه إخباري عن ماضيي ومستقبلي. وقلت له "في حال كونك قادراً على فعل أي شيء، إذن أخبرني بدون سؤالي عن أي شيء." وفي المقابل، قال بأنه لا يستطيع أحد من فعل ذلك، عليك معرفة أشياء عن شخص معين. وفي ذلك الوقت، ذكرت له بأنه لا يوجد أي قيود علي مثل التي ذكرت. ولا أحتاج الى معرفة اسم الشخص، وتاريخ ميلاده، أو اسم أمك للقيا بما أقوم به. ومن ثم قام ببعض الإشارات السيئة. وقلت له بأنني لا أقول للناس عن ماضيهم ومستقبلهم لأنني كنت على علم بأنه مضيعة للوقت ولكن قلت بأنني قادر على تخليص الشخص من آلامه أو مرضه دون معرفة أي تفاصيل عنه.

When I communicate with demons, pains, or diseases, I do not use my tongue. I talk to demons and diseases in their language. No human can hear me. You won't see my lips moving, but demons, pains, and diseases can still hear me easily.

The same thing happened with this guy. I just ask him if he had any pain so that I could proof my point. Immediately, he mentioned that his ankle hurt all the time. Right away, I communicated with that ankle pain, and his ankle pain was gone in under four minutes. After that, he was surprised. He did not argue with me at all after that. He said one thing before he left: "I've never seen anything like this. Never even heard about any powers like this."

Mr. Bubila is my friend. He lives in Austin, Texas. I fixed his sinus problems two or three times over the phone. In the end, he always asked, "How did you do that?"

One time, I was in ACE Mart at Chimney Rock in Houston, Texas. During checkout, the assistant manager was complaining to the cashier about her neck and shoulder pain. Because of this pain, she was unable to move her neck properly. I just told her that I could fix her pain if she wanted. She thought I was kidding. She asked me, "How will you do this?" Instead of answering that question, I just asked her where she had pain. At that time, At least ten people, mostly other customers and employees, were between us, but I did not care and immediately started communicating with her pain. Within a few minutes, her pain was gone. She was extremely surprised and thankful.

Dora worked in Weimar Texas for few days. On several occasions, she complained of toothaches, headaches, and knee pain. She asked me for help. Each time, I communicated with her pains, and every time, those pains listened to me and left her body.

Crystal used to work with me in Weimen, Texas. One time when I went to the store, she was sitting on a chair behind the counter, and few

عندما أقوم بالاتصال مع الشياطين أو الآلام أو الأمراض، لا أستخدم لساني. حيث أقوم بالتحدث الى الشياطين والأمراض في لغتهم. ولا يستطيع أي إنسان أن يسمعني. ولن تستطيع أن ترى شفتاي تتحركان، ولكن الشياطين والآلام والأمراض يمكنهم سماعي بكل سهولة.

والشيء نفسه حدث مع هذا الشاب. فقط قمت بسؤاله إذا ما كان يعاني من آلام حتى أتمكن من التأكد من وجهة نظري. وفوراً، أخبرني بأن كاحله يؤلمه طوال الوقت. وحالاً، تواصلت مع ألم ذلك الكاحل، واختفى ذلك الألم في أقل من أربع دقائق. وبعد ذلك، تفاجأ. فلم يناقشني بعد ذلك مطلقاً. وقال لي شيئاً واحداً قبل أن يغادر: "لم أرَ في حياتي قط أي شيء من ذلك. حتى أنني لم أسمع عن أي من تلك القوة من قبل."

إن السيد بوبيلا صديقي. ويقيم في أوستن في ولاية تكساس. وقمت بعلاج مشاكل التجويف مرتين أو ثلاثة عن طريق الهاتف. وفي النهاية، دائماً ما كان يسألني "كيف قمت بفعل بذلك؟"

وفي يوم من الأيام، كنت في مطعم اي سي إي وارت في شارع شمني روك في مدينة هيوستن الواقعة في ولاية تكساس الأمريكية. وأثناء خروجي من المطعم، كان تشتكي مساعدة المدير لأمين الصندوق من آلام في رقبتها وكتفها. وبسبب هذا الألم لم تكن قادرة على تحريك رقبتها بشكل سليم. وأخبرتها بأنه بإمكاني علاجها من الألم في حال أرادت ذلك، واعتقدت بأنني كنت أمزح. وسألتني بالقول، "كيف يمكنك فعل ذلك؟" فبدلاً ما اجابتها، فقط قمت بسؤالها عن موضع الألم. وفي تلك اللحظة، كان هناك على الأقل عشرة أشخاص، معظمهم من الزبائن الموظفين يفصلون بيني وبينها ولكنني لم أعر اهتماماً وبدأ على الفور التواصل مع ألمها. وخلال بضعة دقائق، اختفى الألم. وكان مندهشة للغاية وشاكرةً لي أيضاً.

أما دورا فقد كانت تعمل في ويمار في ولاية تكساس الأمريكية لبضعة أيام. وفي عدة مناسبات كانت تشتكي من ألم الأسنان والصداع وألم الركبة. وطلبت من مساعدتها. وفي كل وقت، كنت أتواصل مع ألمها وفي كل مرة كانت تلك الآلام تستمع إلي وتغادر جسمها.

واعتادت كريستال العمل معي في وينمين في ولاية تكساس. وفي ذات مرة عندما ذهبت الى المتجر، كانت تجلس على كرسي خلف طاولة الاستقبال، وكان بعض

customers were waiting for her to help them. When I went inside, she mentioned that she had some joint problems and that all of her knee and hip joints locked up once in a while, which made it practically impossible for her to walk. With her permission, I communicated with her diseases. Her knee and hip joints soon became normal. Within a few minutes, she was okay. She was very thankful for my help.

Rushana used to work in Columbus. One time, she had a stomachache, and she asked for my help. Her stomach pain was fixed easily. One time, she had the flu. I fixed her flu that day, but I still told her to take medication, because flu is a continuous attack of many diseases; however, she was allergic to those medicines. I removed her flu from her body, but the next day, she was sick again. Since then, I did not get involved with people if they have the flu or coughing problems, because they never followed my instructions about taking medication. Honestly, the flu and colds are problems for me. I can remove them from the body, but it can be time-consuming, especially when it comes to the flu. I need to communicate with the disease several times for at least two days to keep them away from body.

Another lady named Lauren had had a tooth pulled, and when she was at work at day, she had to suffer swelling and pain. I had to communicate with her pain several times. She was completely out of pain after at least two hours.

Now I will mention a few people without using their names. One of my friends had problem with dry lips all the time. I was not sure lip dryness is an external disease, but I learned that it could be. I communicate with that disease several times, and finally, it came out from that body. After that, I suffered dry lips for several weeks. Finally, I asked that disease to come out from my lips, and it eventually listened to me; however, that was not as easy to deal with as headaches or knee or back pains were.

الزبائن ينتظرونها لتقدم لهم المساعدة. وعندما دخلت، أخبرتني بأنها تعاني من بعض المشاكل في المفاصل وكأن مفاصل ركبتها وركها متصلبة، حيث جعلتها من الصعب عليها المشي. وبعد أن أذنت لي، قمت بالتواصل مع ألمها. و بعد فترة أصبحت ركبتها ومفاصلها طبيعية خلال بضعة دقائق وكانت على ما يرام. وكانت شاكرة على مساعدتي لها.

وكانت روشانا تعمل في مدين كولومبس. وفي ذات مرة، كانت تعاني من ألم في المعدة وطلبت مني ان أساعدها. وتم علاج ألم معدتها بكل سهولة. وفي ذات مرة، كانت تعاني من الإنفلونزا، ولكن اخبرتها بتناول الأدوية لأن الإنفلونزا عبارة عن هجوم مستمر للعديد من الأمراض، علاوة على ذلك، كانت تعاني من الحساسية لتلك الأدوية. وقم بتخليص جسمها من الإنفلونزا ولكن في اليوم التالي، مرضت مرة أخرى. ومنذ ذلك الوقت، لم أتدخل في مرضى يعانون من الإنفلونزا أو مشاكل السعال لأنهم لا يقومون باتباع تعليماتي بشأن تناول الأدوية. وبصراحة، تعد الإنفلونزا والبرد مشكلة بالنسبة لي. ويمكنني التخلص منها، ولكن يمكن أن يكون مضيعة للوقت وخاصة عندما يتعلق الأمر بالإنفلونزا؟ وأحتاج للتواصل مع المرض لعدة مرات لمدة يومين على الأقل لإبقائها بعيدة عن الجسم.

وكانت سيدة أخرى اسمها لورين تعاني من أسنان منزوعة، وعندما كانت في العمل خلال النهار كانت تعاني من الانتفاخ والألم. وكان علي التواصل مع ألمها لعدة مرات. وكانت خالية من الألم بشكل كامل بعد أقل من ساعتين على الأقل.

والآن، سأقوم بذكر بعض الأشخاص دون ذكر أسمائهم. حيث كان أحد أصحابي يعاني من مشكلة جفاف الشفتين طوال الوقت. ولم أكن متأكداً من أن جفاف الشفتين يأتي من مصدر خارجي، ولكن عرفت بأنه يمكن أن يكون كذلك. وتواصلت من ذلك المرض لعدة مرات، وفي النهاية، تخلص من المرض. وبعد ذلك، عانيت من مرض جفاف الشفتين لعدة أسابيع. وأخيراً، طلبت من ذلك المرض الخروج من جسمي، وفي النهاية استمع إلي، علاوة على ذلك، لم يكن من السهل التعامل معه كالتعامل من الصداع وآلام الركبة والرقبة.

The flu and colds are different with different people. One time, my mother called me when she was suffering from the flu. I removed her flu very easily, but it took a great deal of time. For colds, I need to communicate with the disease several times but it is still time-consuming.

Another time, a friend had a problem with dark circles under the eyes. That was an experiment as well. It was not difficult to move those dark circles away from the eye, but every time I worked on them, they always came to me. Anyway, I was surprised when I figured out that these dark circles under the eyes were diseases and fixable. I only worked on one person for this just for testing purposes.

Another person had mouth sores. I was surprised when I communicate with those mouth sores and found out that they were diseases and easily fixable. A few times, my mother and my sister had the same problem, and I communicated with their disease and convince them to leave their mouths.

One time, I worked on two people who had some kind of fungus problem in their mouths. I tried to communicate with that white fungus, and it was not difficult at all. That white fungus easily left both of those people. In both cases, I learned that both of these people had sick dogs in their houses and that those dogs had the same problems in their mouths. Those fungus diseases were coming from their sick dogs.

Another time, a man had pains in his feet. I communicated with both of his feet. It was not difficult to remove those pains from his feet. Before I worked on that pain, I thought that this would be like a regular pain. Whenever I worked on feet, I received those pains directly in my feet. I had never experienced of foot pain ever in my life. Honestly, that foot pain was not a pain. It was like a fire in my feet. It was a very bad experience. It was not difficult for me to move that pain away from me, but the only problem was that it was moving back and forth. I had to work and deal with that pain for long time.

وتختلف الإنفلونزا والبرد باختلاف الأشخاص. وفي ذات مرة، دعتني أمي عندما كانت تعاني من الإنفلونزا. وأزلت الإنفلونزا من جسمها بكل سهولة، ولكنه استغرق معي الكثير من الوقت. وأما بالنسبة، للبرد، أحتاج الى التواصل مع المرض عدة مرات ولكن لا يزال مضيعة للوقت.

وفي وقت آخر، كان يعاني صديقي من وجود دوائر سوداء تحت العينين. وكانت تلك تجربة بالنسبة لي أيضاً. ولم يكن من الصعب ازالة تلك الدوائر السوداء، ولكن في كل مرة أعمل على ازالتها، يتنقل ذلك المرض إلي. على أي حال، كنت مندهشاً عندما اكتشفت أن تلك الدوائر السوداء عبارة عن أمراض يمكن علاجها. وفقط عملت على شخص واحد لأهداف الفحص.

وكان يعاني شخص آخر من تقرحات في فمه. وكنت أيضاً مندهشاً عندما تواصلت مع تقرحات فمه واكتشفت بأنها أمراض ومن السهل علاجها. وبضع مرات، عانت أمي وأختي من نفس المشكلة وتواصلت مع مرضهم وأقنعته بالخروج من أفواههم. وفي ذات مرة، كنت أعالج شخصين كانوا يعاني من الفطر في أفواههم. وحاولت التواصل مع ذلك الفطر الأبيض، ولم يكن من الصعب ازالته. وفي كلتا الحالتين، عرفت بأن هؤلاء الشخصين كان لديهم كلاب مريضة في منازلهم كانت تلك الكلاب تعاني من نفس المشكلة في أفواههم. حيث أنا هؤلاء الأشخاص استقبلوا مرض الفطر من الكلاب الموجودة في منازلهم.

وفي ذات مرة، كان رجلاً يعاني من آلام في قدميه. وتواصلت مع كلتا قدميه. ولم يكن من الصعب ازالة تلك الآلام. وقبل أن أعمل على ذلك المرض، اعتقدت بأنه سيكون ألم عادي. وعندما عملت على علاج قدميه، استقبلت نفس الألم في قدمي. ولم يكن لدي أي خبرة بآلام القدم قط في حياتي. وبصراحة، ألم القدم لم يكن ألماً. بل كان نار في القدم. وكانت تجربة سيئة بالنسبة لي. ولم من الصعب علي ازالة ذلك الألم بعيداً عني، ولكن كانت المشكلة الوحيدة هي الذهاب والقدوم.(حيث كانت الآلام تأتي وتذهب عدة مرات). وكان علي التعامل مع ذلك الألم لفترة طويلة.

109

Finally, I figured out that the pain was not a single pain. I was sure that pains were grouping together and attacking the same person.

Sometimes it surprises me that particular diseases have their own focus. I never feel foot pain come out of one person and jump into the stomach of another person. I learned that foot pain was the same for everyone. Foot pain comes out of one person, and that pain usually chooses the feet of the nearest available person.

In the same way, if a kidney or heart disease comes out of one person, that disease will target the same place in another person. But why are these diseases assigned particular jobs? This remains a mystery to me.

I have removed heartburn or stomach ulcers from people uncountable times, but the proper medication to heal the ulcer or wound is very important. Otherwise, the stomach walls will release acid again, and the ulcers or stomach wounds will become inflamed. This wound or ulcer in the stomach is a continuous invitation for diseases. Wounds or ulcers are really a part of the body, specifically the stomach, but heartburn or pain in the stomach is a disease. This stomach disease is easily movable, but if the person does not want to invite these pains into their stomach again, they need to use all possible healing procedures and medications. This stomach disease is orchestrated by invisible insects, and they just eat our wounds. The same problems occur in the liver, kidneys, and intestines.

I deal with liver problems in many people. Honestly, I do not know any single person without liver and stomach problems. These damages happen so quietly and continuously that it's too late to fix the symptoms by the time we find out about them.

I work on so many people without feeling any problems in their livers, but whenever I focus on their livers, I find that most people have some problems there. As I have described several times, my body is extremely sensitive to all demons, diseases, and pains. Just

وأخيراً، اكتشفت بأن ذلك الألم لم يكن لوحده. وكنت متأكداً بأن الآلام تجتمع مع بعضها وتهاجم الشخص نفسه.

وأحياناً ما كان يدهشني بأن بعض الأمراض لها تركيزها الخاص بها. ولم أكن أشعر بألم القدم أثناء خروجه من شخص ما والقفز الى معدة شخص آخر. وعرفت بأن ألم القدم هو نفسه عند أي شخص. عندما يخرج ألم القدم من شخص معين، يختار أقدام أقرب الشخص الموجود.

وبنفس الطريقة، في حال خروج أمراض القلب والكلى من شخص واحد، سيستهدف ذلك المرض نفس المكان في شخص آخر. ولكن لماذا تعين مهمات مخصصة لتلك الأمراض؟ هذا يبقى لغزاً بالنسبة لي.

وقمت بإخراج مرض حرقة المعدة وقرحة المعدة من الأشخاص لمرات لا حصى، ولكن الدواء الصحيح لعلاج القرحة أو الجرح مهم جداً. عدا ذلك، ستقوم جدران المعدة بإطلاق حوامض مرة أخرى، وستصبح تقرحات أو جراح المعدة مثارة. وهذه القرحة أو الجروح في المعدة تعتبر دعوة مستمرة للأمراض. وتعتبر التقرحات والجروح جزءاً من الجسم وخاصة المعدة، ولكن حرقة المعدة أو الألم في المعدة عبارة عن مرض. وهذا المرض من السهل إزالته، ولكن في أن الشخص لا يريد دعوة تلك الآلام الى معدهم مرة أخرى، ويحتاجون لاستخدام إجراءات العلاج الممكنة والأدوية. ومرض المعدة مخطط له من قبل الحشرات الخفية، ويقومون بأكل جروحنا، وتحدث نفس المشكلة في الكبد والكلى والأمعاء.

وأتعامل مع مشاكل الكبد عند العديد من الأشخاص. وبصراحة، لا أعرف أي شخص لا يعاني من مشاكل في الكبد والمعدة. وتحدث تلك الأضرار بكثرة وبشكل مستمر وقد فات الأوان لعلاج تلك الأمراض عندا اكتشافها.

وأعمل على علاج العديد من الأشخاص دون الشعور بأن مشاكل في كبدهم، ولكن عندما أركز على كبدهم، أكتشف بأن معظم الأشخاص يعانون من مشاكل هناك. وكما وصفت عدة مرات، فإن جسمي حساس للغاية ضد الشياطين والأمراض والآلام.

to test someone, I usually invite their disease into me to find out if they have any symptoms of a damaging disease. And my experience has been that 99 percent of people are under the influence of liver, stomach, and intestinal diseases. I strongly feel that there should be medication that can be taken just to keep these organs healthy and strong instead of waiting until someone start feeling pain. We all know that pain always starts when these organs are already too damaged to heal fully.

Many researchers say that most people are affected by heart disease and die because of heart attacks. Trust me, heart disease was very easy for me to remove from any heart. I learn that heart disease does not necessarily damage the heart but does block the vessels valves. But it is not enough to clean someone's heart one time and then leave him or her alone. This needs to be done on a regular basis.

I have had good experiences with heart pain and diseases. Once they become my friends, they visit me for few seconds whenever I encounter them. And if they stay for longer, I have to ask them to come out. I do remember one heart disease that was so powerful its touch felt like over ten thousand volts. The heart pain/disease never went inside my heart but always touched me from outside. Thankfully, it is not around me anymore.

Many people usually have headache or migraine pains, but these are very easy to fix. One time, I had a different kind of headache. That pain was in the skin of the head. It can take a little longer to remove that disease/pain from the skin of the head. Always remember, when these kinds of pains stay in the skin of the head for a while, it means that that pain will leave some major damages in the skin. If there are any symptoms or damages, use medication to heal it. Otherwise the symptoms or damages will invite new pains and diseases.

One time, I promised someone that I would fix his thyroid problem. I have communicated with thyroid diseases on several occasions. Finally, I found out that a thyroid problem is a physical disease as well.

ولفحص شخص ما، عادة ما أقوم بدعوة أمراضه بالدخول إلي لاكتشاف في حال كانوا أي أعرض لمرض مدمر. وكانت تجربتي أن 99% من الأشخاص كانوا تحت تأثير أمراض الكبد والمعدة والأمعاء. وأشعر بقوة بأنه ينبغي أن يكون هناك دواء لإبقاء تلك الأعضاء صحية وقوية بدلاً من الانتظار حتى يشعر شخص ما بالألم. وجميعنا يعلم بأنه ما دائماً تظهر الآلام عندما تكون الأعضاء مدمرة مسبقاً.

وذكر الكثير من الباحثين بأن معظم بالأشخاص يتأثرون بأمراض القلب ويموتون بسبب النوبات القلبية. ويق بي، من السهل علي ازالة أمراض القلب من قلب أي شخص. وتعلمت بأن مرض القلب ليس بالضرورة يقوم بتدمير القلب ولكن يغلق صمامات القلب. ولكن ليس كافياً لتنظيف قلب شخص ما مرة واحدة ومن ثم تركه. فهذا يحتاج الى أن يتم على أساس قاعدة منتظمة.

ولقد كان لدي تجربة مع ألم القلب وأمراضه. وعندما تصحب تلك الأمراض أصدقاءً معي، يقومون بزيارتي لعدة ثوان عندما أواجههم. وفي حال بقوا لوقت أطول، علي أن أطلب من هم الخروج من جسمي. وأتذكر بأن مرض قلب كان قوياً جداً وشعرت بأن لمستها كانت تزن أكثر من ألف فولت. ولم يذهب أي ألم/مرض في القلب الي قلبي ولكن دائماً ما يلامسني من الخارج. والحمد لله، هو ليس بجواري بعد الآن.

وعادةً ما يعاني الكثير من الأشخاص من الصداع أو الصداع النصفي، ولكن تلك سهلة العلاج. وفي ذات مرة، كان لدي صداع، وكان ذلك الألم في جلد الرأس. ويمكن أن يستغرق وقتاً أطول لإزالته. وتذكر دائماً، عندما تبقى تلك الأنواع من الأمراض في جلد الرأس لفترة، يعني ذلك أن ذلك الألم سيترك أضراراً جسيمة في الجلد. وفي حال كان هناك أي من الأعراض أو الأضرار، قم باستخدام الأدوية للشفاء منه. عدا ذلك، ستقوم تلك الأضرار بدعوة آلام جديدة.

وفي ذات مرة، وعدت شخصاً بأن أعلج مشكلة الغدد الدرقية. وتواصلت مع مرض الغدد الدرقية عدة مرات. وفي النهاية، اكتشفت أن مشكلة الغدد الدرقية هي مرض جسدي أيضاً.

It is not difficult to clean disease from thyroids, but either the same one or a new one will come to the same place pretty quickly. Like a kidney and liver disease, a thyroid problem is pain-free. So, when a patient is not feeling any problem, it means he or she will never tell me about that problem, and I will not be able to work on his or her problems. I do not know the logic behind these quiet diseases.

I have a list of people on whom I work on regular basis. Most of them are either very important people to me or part of my experiments to further my knowledge. I have also worked and communicated with burning eyes. I am able to fix burning eyes. I am also able to fix focus problems or nearsightedness. I learned this when I invited those eyes problems from someone to myself by communicating with these diseases. Nearsightedness and focus problems are continuous as well. I can communicate with them very easily, and they will come out very easily; however, I do know how long it will take before a new one occupies that empty place.

All these disease/pains that live inside us always need a medium or body. They do not live in the air or water. They travel in the air, but they do not stay in the air for a long time. A healthy body is a body without all these pains, diseases, sicknesses, and demons. A sick body, whether completely or partially sick, can become a healthy body after I communicate with its demons and cleanse it of all its pains, sicknesses, and diseases.

Are there any problems after I cleanse a body? Both healthy and newly cleansed bodies have the same problem, and the problem is that these healthy bodies are like vacuums.

Medical science has a very clear theory of contiguous and noncontiguous diseases, but my theory is different. Usually, diseases or invisible insects do not leave that wound or injured organ easily. Wounded organs or injured parts of the body have more attraction for those invisible insects, pains, and diseases. That's why healthy bodies do not get those invisible insects easily. According to me, this

وليس من الصعب تنظيف الغدد الدرقية من المرض، ولكن إما ستتعرض الغدد الدرقية لنفس المرض أو لمرض جديد وبسرعة؟ تماماً كما يحدث في امراض الكلى والكبد، فإن مشكلة الغدد الدرقية هي مشكلة خالية من الأمراض. لذلك، عندما لا يشعر المريض بأي مشكلة، يعني ذلك بأن لن يخبرني ابداً عنها. ولا أعلم الهدف من تلك الأمراض الصامتة.

ولدي قائمة بالأشخاص الذي أعمل معهم على أساس قائدة منتظمة. ومعكمهم إما أشخاص مهمون بالنسبة إلي أو يكونوا جزء من تجاربي لإثراء معرفتي. وقمت بالعمل والتواصل أيضاً مع حرقة العيون. وأنا قادر على علاج تلك الحرقة. وقادر أيضاً على معالجة مشاكل التركيز وقصر النظر. وعرفت ذلك عندما دعوت مشاكل العيون تلك من شخص الى جسمي بالتواصل مع تلك الامراض. إن مشاكل التركيز وقصر النظر مشاكل مستمرة أيضاً. ويمكنني التواصل معهم بكل سهولة، حيث يخرجون بسهولة. إن الجسم الصحي هو الجسم الذي يبقى في خالياً من تلك الآلام والأمراض والسقم والشياطيين. بينما الجسم المريض، سواءً مريض بشكل كامل أو بشكل جزئي، يمكن أن يكون جسماً صحياً بعد أن اتواصل مع شياطينه وأقوم بتنظيفه من جميع الآلام والأمراض.

هل يكون هناك مشاكل بعد أن أقوم بتنظيفه. تعاني الأجسام الصحية والمنظفة حديثاً من نفس المشكلة، وهي أن تلك الأجسام تشبه أنابيب التفريغ.

لدى علم الطب نظرية واضحة حول الأمراض المعدية وغير المعدية، ولكن نظريتي تختلف. عداة، لا تترك الأمراض أو الحشرات الخفية العضو المجروح بسهولة. وتعتبر الأجزاء المجروحة من الجسم أكثر جاذبية لتلك الحشرات الخفية والآلام والأمراض. لذلك السبب، لا تتعرض الأجسام الصحية لتلك الحشرات بتلك السهولة. وبالنسبة لي، فإن

contiguous and noncontiguous theory is outdated. Everything is possible, and it's just bad luck when these disease or pains leave one body and immediately choose another nearby body. They do not like to travel too much. You never know who will be their next victim. These demons, pains, diseases, and sicknesses have populations that are several hundred times greater than the human population. They live for several hundred years, too. If things continue this way, one human will be surrounded by one million disease and pains in near future.

So, if modern science accepts on my theory of the physical existence of all these pains, diseases, and sicknesses, they should try to invent different tools and weapons to control these disease and pains like medications and sprays to heal damages and keep demons away from our bodies.

Different people use demons for different purposes. For example, magicians use demons to show us their magic. And demons show us whatever the magician wants to show us by hypnotizing the audience. Some magicians will show us levitating or cutting themselves in two three pieces. We may be amazed, but in actuality, it is all hypnotism. Hypnotism is the language of demons.

I have always felt that I am not any extraordinary person, but my exposure to the invisible world and experience with demons should help compel modern scientists to develop more technology to help mankind stay safe and healthy. I know it is very difficult to believe my theory. That's why I am always ready and willing to demonstrate my capabilities to any scientist who wants to research ways of controlling these invisible diseases to help mankind.

When a healer sends a demon to someone to cleanse a body of pains and diseases, are there any side effects to this action? The demon may cleanse diseases from a body, but afterward, that demon will simply possess another body. And nobody can keep demons positive for a long time. This goes against the nature of demons.

نظرية الأمراض المعدية وغير المعدية قديمة. وكل شيء محتمل، وإنه فقط الحظ السيء عندما تترك تلك الأمراض والآلام جسماً وتختار جسماً آخر فوراً. ولا يرغبون بالتنقل كثيراً. ولا تعلم أبداً من سيكون الضحية التالية. وتمتلك تلك الشياطين والآلام والأمراض أعداداً تفوق مئات المرات من أعداد البشر. ويعيشون لعدة مئات من السنين. وفي حال استمرار الأشياء بتلك الطريقة، سيحاط إنسان واحد بمليون مرض في المستقبل القريب.

لذلك، في حال قبول العلم الحديث نظريتي حول الوجود الفيزيائي لتلك الآلام والأمراض، ينبغي عليهم المحاولة في اختراع أدوات وأسلحة مختلفة للسيطرة على تلك الأمراض والآلام كالأدوية والرشاشات لعلاج الأضرار وابقائه بعيداً عن أجسامنا.

ويستخدم مختلف الأشخاص الشياطين لأهداف مختلفة. فعلى سبيل المثال، يستخدم السحرة الشياطين ليرونا سحرهم. وترينا الشياطين ما يريده السحر بتنويمنا مغناطيسياً. ويرينا بعض السحرة يرفعون أو يقسمون انفسهم الى قسمين أو ثلاثة أقسا. وربما نكون مندهشين، ولكن في الحقيقة، إن كل ذلك تنويماً مغناطيسياً. فهو لغة الشياطين.

ودائماً ما شعرت بأنني لست شخصاً خارقاً، ولكن اكتشافي للعالم الخفي وتجربتي مع الشياطين ينبغي أن تساعد علماء العصر الحديث في تطوير تقنية لمساعدة البشر في الحفاظ عليهم آمنين وصحيين. وأعلم أنه من الصعب التصدق بنظريتي. لذلك السبب دائماً ما أكون مستعداً لإظهار قدراتي لأي من العلماء الذين يريدون البحث في طرق السيطرة على الأمراض الخفية لمساعدة البشر.

عندما يرسل المعالج شيطاناً لشخص ما لتنظيف جسمه من الآلام والأمراض، فهل هناك أي تأثيرات جانبية لهذا الفعل؟ ربما يقوم الشيطان بتنظيف الجسم من الأمراض. ولكن بعد وقت، سيسيطر الشيطان ببساطة على جسم آخر. ولا يمكن لأي شخص ابقاء الشياطين ايجابية لفترة طويلة. وهذا يعتبر ضد طبيعة الشياطين.

I talked to many demon doctors and few healers, and all of them had to work hard to gain some knowledge and powers. All of them use demons to do whatever they want. Usually, their demons perform everything for them. But their knowledge and information about the invisible world, diseases, and demons like it comes from books or teachers. And when they use their demon's power to perform any healing or magic, they are completely safe and healthy. In my case, I never had any faith in demons or the invisible world or any knowledge or information about physical existence of pain and diseases when I started. I never tried to learn from any teachers about demons or the invisible world. It just start happening to me, and day by day, I learned more and more. Now I know so much, even though it is hard to convince people about the existence of the invisible world.

The only difference between me and other demon doctors is they use demons, and because of the involvement of demons, they do not get hurt. In my case, I do not use any demon. I only use the powers of my mind to cleanse people of demons, diseases, and pains. I use my powers to cleanse any area or house of demons, diseases, and pains. The only problem is that I am not protected. Whatever demon, disease, or pain I remove from people, it comes straight to me. They hurt me sometimes. I cannot bear them for too long. Because of this problem, I have limited myself.

There is still one thing I have not clearly revealed, and this is how I am able to keep myself safe from these diseases, pains, and demons. This should be the next step of medical research, because once medical science can pull out these problems from a body by using magnetic fields and rays, how, people will be able to protect themselves once they leave the hospitals and go back to their normal lives.

These days, I experienced new diseases and pains every day. It is very hard for me to just do nothing once I know someone is in pain or sick, especially when it comes to people around me or individuals who are important to me. Most of the time, I am okay, but once in a while, I have to suffer a little bit. I get the same pain or sickness whenever I

وتحدثت الى الكثير من العرافيين والمعالجين، وجميعهم كان عليهم العمل بجد لجلب بعض المعلومات والقوى. وجميعهم يستخدم الشياطيين لعمل ما يريدون. وعادة، تنجز شياطينهم كل شيء لهم. ولكن معلوماتهم ومعرفتهم عن العالم الخفي والأمراض والشياطيين تأتي من الكتب والمعلمين. وعندما يستخدمون قوة شيطانيهم لإنجاز أي علاج أو سحر، يكونوا آمنين وصحيين بشكل كامل. وفي حالتي، لم يكن لدي أي إيمان في الشياطيين أو العالم الخفي أو عن وجودها الفيزيائي للآلام والأمراض. ولم أحاول قط التعلم من أي من المعلمين بشأن الشياطيين أو العالم الخفي. فقط حدث لي يوماً بعد يوم. وتعلمت الكثير. والآن، أعراف الكثير، على الرغم من أنه من الصعب اقناع البشر عن وجود العالم الخفي.

وإن الفرق الوحيد بيني وبين العرافون هو أنهم يستخدمون الشياطيين، وبسبب تدخل الشياطيين، لا يتأذون. وفي حالتي، لا أستخدم الشياطيين. ما أستخدمه فقط هو قوة عقلي لتنظيف الأشخاص من الشياطيين والأمراض والآلام. وأستخدم قواي لتنظيف أي منطقة أو منزل من الشياطيين والأمراض والآلام. وإن المشكلة الوحيدة هي أنني لست محمياً. حيث أن الشياطيين والأمراض والآلام التي أقوم بإزالتها من البشر، تأتي إلي مباشرة. ويقومون بإيذائي أحياناً. ولا أستطيع أن أحتملهم لفترة طويلة. وبسبب تلك المشكلة، قمت بتقييد نفسي.

وما زال هناك شيءٌ لم أذكره بوضوح، وهو كيف لي أن أكون قادراً على ابقاء نفسي آمناً من تلك الأمراض والآلام والشياطيين. وهذا ينبغي أن تكون الخطوة القادمة للبحث الطبي، ولأنه عندما يكون علم الطب قادراً على سحب تلك المشاكل من الجسم باستخدام المجالات المغناطيسية والأشعة، كيف ذلك؟ سيكون البشر قادرون على حماية أنفسهما يغادرون المستشفى والعودة الى حياتهم الطبيعية.

وفي هذه الأيام، واجهت أمراض وآلاماً جديدة. ومن الصعب علي فقط عدم القيام بأي شيء عندما أعلم أن شخصاً ما متألماً أو مريضاً، وخاصة عندما يتعلق بأشخاص من حولي أو أعزاء علي. وفي معظم الوقت، أنا على ما يرام، ولكن خلال لحظة، يجب علي أن أعاني قليلاً. حيث أتعرض لنفس الألم أو المرض عندما أقوم

114

remove one from a person, but these have only hurt me badly on a few occasions. Most of the time, I am able to control them.

I am really able to see demons and diseases unlike others who claim to see them in human shape, but that means they are just under the influence of a demon's hypnotism when they are not seeing anything. They are seeing whatever their demons are showing them. As a result, it will be a big help to medical science when scientists start using magnetic fields or technology to snatch diseases and pains from a body. Those scientists may not be able to see the results of their efforts, but I will be able to see. I can help any scientist who wants to do research in this field. I can easily tell them if their machines can snatch diseases and pains from a body. I have a lot of information that can help medical scientists invent these machines. Plus, they can use different kind of patients in their experiments to find out the exact kind of magnetic fields and rays needed.

Demon doctors will use anything to save us from demons or their negativism like nails and screws, but always remember that those nails and screws are nothing. They are only powerful because demon doctors assign some of their demons to them.

Plain or handwritten papers, stones, threads, ropes—whenever these are used by a demon doctor, they work. But remember that those demon doctors assign demons to those things, which means demons will become slaves of those stones or threads or pieces of paper. Wherever those things go, demon will go and do their job or resolve the problems. But remember that no one can keep a demon positive for too long. The effects of those things will have side effects. Usually, demons are pretty much like us, so when they stay around us or we keep them around us, they possess us and take control of our minds. That's why these things may be effective in the beginning, but they may have bad side effects in the long run.

Demons are way powerful and intelligent as compared to diseases and pains. Demons are not parasites. Demons are not positive energies,

بازلة المرض من أي شخص، ولكن يؤذيني كثيراً في بعض المناسبات. وفي معظم الأوقات، أكون قادراً على السيطرة عليهم.

وإنني حقاً قادراً على رؤية الشياطيين والأمراض ليس كالآخرين الذين يدعون بأنهم يرون الشياطيين بهيئة إنسان، ولكن يعني ذلك بأنهم تحت تأثير التنويم المغناطيسي للشياطيين عندما لا يرون أي شيء فهم يرون ما تريد الشياطين أن تريهم. ونتيجةً لذلك، ستكون مساعدة كبيرة لعلم الطب عندما يبدأ العلماء باستخدام المجالات المغناطيسية أو تقنية لانتزاع الأمراض والآلام من الجسم. ربما يكون هؤلاء العلماء غير قادرين على رؤية نتيجة جهودهم، ولكني سأكون قادراً على فعل ذلك. ويمكنني مساعدة أي عالم يريد أن يقوم بإجراء بحث في هذا المجال. ويمكنني أن أخبرهم بسهولة في حال قدرة تقنياتهم في انتزاع الأمراض والآلام من الجسم. ولدي الكثير من المعلومات التي يمكنها مساعدة علم الطب في اختراع تلك الآلات. بالإضافة الى ذلك، يمكنهم استخدام أنواع مختلفة من المرضى في تجاربهم لاكتشاف النوع المراج من المجالات المغناطيسية والأشعة المطلوبة في الشفاء من تلك الآلام والأمراض.

سيستخدم العرافون أي شيء لحمايتنا من الشياطيين أو تصرفاتهم السلبية كالأظافر والمسامير، ولكن دائماً تذكر بأن تلك الأظافر والمسامير لا تساوي أي شيء. فهي فقط قوية بسبب تسليط العرافون لبعض الشياطيين عليهم.

إن استخدام الأوراق المكتوبة باليد أو القماش أو الأحجار أو الخيوط أو الحبال من قبل العرافون فإنها تنجح. ولكن تذكر بأن هؤلاء العرافون يسلطون الشياطيين على تلك الأشياء، ويعني ذلك بأن الشياطيين ستصبح عبيد لتلك الأحجار أو الخيوط أو قطع الورق. وأينما تذهب تلك الأشياء، ستذهب الشياطيين وتقوم بعملها أو تحل المشاكل. ولكن تذكر أيضاً بأنه لا يستطع أحد الحفاظ على ايجابية الشيطان لفترة طويلة. فإن لذلك تبعات وتأثيرات جانبية. وعادة، فغن الشياطيين تشبه البشر كثيراً، لذلك عندما يبقون حولنا او نبقيهم حولنا، يقومون بالسيطرة علينا والتحكم بعقولنا. لذلك السبب من المحتمل أن تكون تلك الأشياء فعالة في البداية، ولكن ربما يكون لها تأثيرات جانبية على المدى البعيد.

تعد الشياطيين أقوى وأذكى من الأمراض والآلام. فهي ليست كالطفيليات، ولا يملكون طاقات إيجابية،

because demons can be used either way. But demons really like to do negative things and actions. We can use demons for good stuff, but not for long time. Demons can do positive actions and things, but just for few hours or days. Positive energies are our souls or spirits and angels, which only follow God's commands. Demons can befriend any human or animal, and once demons become sincere friends with someone, they will follow that person's commands without asking any questions.

As I have explained, almost all demons stay in big groups or tribes, and usually, there are bosses within those tribes or groups. All demons in a group or tribe follow the commands of boss demon. Once that head demon becomes a friend to any human, that human can use that whole tribe of demons however he or she wants just by passing commands to the head demon. And the head demon will pass the same command to the rest of its group or tribe of demons. Once that human nears death, he or she can transfer that friendship with demons to another human, and the same group of demons will start following the commands of the new human. No human can compel or push demons to do his or her bidding. This is all about friendship and sincerity.

Different humans use groups of demons for different purposes. I already described a few, but let me describe a few more. A few demon doctors use demons for healing purposes. Demons are way more powerful than diseases and pains. When a human healer passes a command to his or her demons to cleanse someone's body of all diseases and pains, the demons will cleanse the body in seconds. But remember, demons cannot do positive things for a long time. Now I will explain how this process works and the pluses and minuses of using demons to remove sickness, diseases, and pains from human bodies. Medical science may be able to invent machines that treat diseases and pains the way a healer treat them, but I will say that my procedure is better, because I do not use any demons to cleanse pains or diseases. My procedure involves pure electromagnetic rays and fields. And I will keep requesting and insisting medical and modern

لأنه يمكن استخدام الشياطين بالطريقتين، الإيجابية والسلبية. ولكن الشياطين ترغب في انجاز الأعمال السيئة. ويمكننا استخدام الشياطين لإنجاز الأعمال الحسنة، ولكن ليس لفترة طويلة من الزمن. ويمكن للشياطين القيام بأعمال ايجابية ولكن لعدة ساعات أو أيام. إن الطاقات الإيجابية هي أرواحنا أو نفوسنا البشرية والملائكة، التي تتبع فقط أوامر الله عز وجل. ويمكن للشياطين أن تكون ناصرة للإنسان أو الحيوان، وعندما تصبح الشياطين أصدقاء مخلصين مع شخص ما، سيقومون باتباع أوامر ذلك الشخص دون الاستفسار عن أي سؤال.

وكما أوضحت سابقاً، تعيش معظم الشياطين في جماعات كبيرة، وعادةً يكون هناك مسؤولون في تلك الجماعات. حيث تقوم جميع الشياطين في مجموعة واحدة أو قبيلة واحدة باتباع أوامر الشيطان المسؤول. وعندما يصبح الشيطان المسؤول صديقاً لأي إنسان، يمكن لذلك الإنسان استخدام جميع أفراد القبيلة عن طريق تمرير الأوامر الى الشيطان المسؤول. وسيقوم الشيطان المسؤول بتمرير تلك الأوامر الى كافة أفراد قبيلته. وعندما يقترب ذلك الإنسان من الموت، يكون قادر على نقل صداقته مع الشياطين الى إنسان آخر، وستقوم الشياطين من نفس المجموعة باتباع أوامر ذلك الإنسان الجديد. ولا يمكن لأي إنسان أجبار أو دفع الشياطين على انجاز طلبه. فهذا كله يتعلق بالصداقة والإخلاص.

ويستخدم البشر مجموعات من الشياطين لأهداف مختلفة. ولقد قمت بوصف ذلك مسبقاً، ولكن دعوني أوصف المزيد. يستخدم القليل من العرافون الشياطين لأهداف علاجية. حيث أن الشياطين أكثر قوة من الأمراض والآلام. وعندما يقوم معالج إنسان بتمرير الأوامر الى شياطينه لتطهير جسم شخص ما من الأمراض والآلام، سيقوم ذلك الشيطان بفعل ذلك خلال ثواني. ولكن تذكر، لا يمكن للشياطين القيام بالأشياء الإيجابية لفترة طويلة من الزمن. والآن، سأقوم بشرح مبدأ عمل هذه العملية في ازالة الأمراض والآلام من أجسام البشر. يمكن لعلم الطب أن يكون قادراً على اختراع آلات تقوم بمعالجة الأمراض والآلام بالطريقة التي تقوم بها المعالج، ولكن سأقول بأن طريقتي أفضل في علاج الأمراض لأنني لا استخدام الشياطين لتطهير الأجسام من الأمراض والآلام. وتتعلق طريقتي باستخدام المجالات والأشعة الإلكترو مغناطيسية. وسأقوم بالاستمرار في طلب والإصرار على أن يقوك علم الطب الحديث

science invent machines to clean a human's body from all invisible insects, diseases, and pains by using rays and electromagnetic fields.

We could snatch or pull out all of these invisible insects or diseases by using a magnetized room or walls. Medical science needs to invent those machines that utilize powerful magnetic fields. Whenever a human walks between those walls or into that room, the electromagnetic field should be able to suck, snatch, or pull out all those sicknesses, diseases, and pains from that body. Once those invisible insects, diseases, pains come out of the human body, we could condense those diseases and pains and either store them or find a way to keep them away from the open atmosphere.

A healer can pass commands to demons to cleanse bodies, and the demon will listen to that human; however, you should remember that the healer can reverse the procedure and make those demons infect a body with bunch of different diseases and/or pains. And this is easier for demons to do. Plus, they like all kinds of negative activity. Healers may not be reliable, and they may not offer a permanent solutions, so medical science needs to *step in* and find a permanent solution for these diseases and pains. This is very easy for me. We already have all kinds of healing medications and surgeries. This is just the second step.

Modern science only needs to research a few things: Scientist can find out kind of rays can insist that these diseases or pains leave particular bodies. Strong magnetic fields could work like gravity and suck demons out of our bodies and send them to a storage unit after these fields condense them. Patients can use healing medications and surgeries to become completely normal. Once that patient is released from that hospital, he or she will need to come back frequently and walk between those magnetic walls or rooms so that he or she can cleanse the body again. Houses and offices should have those rooms so that people can go in them by themselves and purify their bodies when needed.

لاختراع آلات لتطهير جسم الإنسان من جميع الحشرات الخفية والأمراض والآلام باستخدام الأشعة والمجالات الإلكترو مغناطيسية.

ويمكن سحب جميع تلك الحشرات الخفية باستخدام غرفة مجهزة بالمجالات الإلكترو مغناطيسية. ويحتاج علم الطب لاختراع تلك الآلات للاستفادة من المجالات المغناطيسية. وعندما يمشي الإنسان بين تلك الجدران أو الى داخل الغرفة، ينبغي على المجال الإلكترو مغناطيسي من امتصاص أو سحب تلك الأمراض والآلام من ذلك الجسم. ومكننا التخلص من تلك الأمراض والآلام إما بتخزينها أو ايجاد طريقة لإبقائها بعيدة عن الجو المفتوح.

ويمكن للمعالج أن يقوم بتمرير الأوامر الى الشياطيين لتطهير الاجسام، وستستمع تلك الشياطيين الى ذلك الشخص؛ علاوة على ذلك، ينبغي عليك تذكر بأنه يمكن للمعالج عكس الخطوات وجعل الشياطيين أن تقوم بإصابة الجسم بمختلف الأمراض والآلام. وهذا يعتبر أسهل للأمراض لإنجازه. بالإضافة الى ذلك، فهم يرغبون بجميع أنواع الأنشطة السلبية. ولا يمكن أن يكون المعالج موثوق به، وربما لا يعرضون حلولاً دائمة، لذلك يحتاج علم الطب للتدخل وايجاد الحل الدائم لتلك الأمراض والآلام. وهذا سهل بالنسبة لي. فنحن لدينا جميع أنواع الادوية والعمليات الجراحية. فهذه هي فقط الخطوة الثانية من التخلص من الأمراض والآلام.

ويحتاج علم العصر الحديث فقط إلى إجراء البحوث على القليل من الأشياء: حيث يمكن للعلماء اكتشاف أنواع من الأشعة يمكنها المساعدة في التخلص من تلك الأمراض والآلام. ويمكن للمجالات المغناطيسية القوية أن تعمل كالجاذبية وتقوم بامتصاص الشياطيين الى خارج الجسم وترسلهم الى وحدة تخزين بعد أن تتخلص منها تلك المجالات. ويمكن للمرضى أن يتعافوا باستخدام الأدوية والعمليات الجراحية ليصبحوا طبيعيين. وعند اخراج المريض من المستشفى، سيحتاج الى العودة بشكل تدريجي والمشي بين تلك الجدران أو الغرفة المغناطيسية حتى يتسنى له تطهير جسمه من الأمراض والآلام. وينبغي أن تحتوي المنازل والمكاتب على تلك الأنواع من الغرف حتى يتسنى للأشخاص الذهاب اليهم بأنفسهم وتنقية أجسامهم عند الحاجة.

Now how it happen when a healer passes a command to head/boss demon to do anything. Few times only really demons go to everyone and fulfill the command. Otherwise, demons use their communicating system by using magnetic fields all around the world and around us, and pass the message to those demons who are already around us. And because of those messages, demons around us follow the commands. Healers can also go against you. Demons can go against us. Instead of depending on healers or demons, we need to invent new machines to handle these problems. I am confident because I am the only one who is not using any demon to purify bodies from diseases and pains. This is done with my mind, and the rays come out from mind to control different diseases, pains, sicknesses, and demons. But I am a human, and I am not using demons, so I cannot do too much. I am learning how to use the gift God has given me. And this is the time when medical science needs to step in and control this invisible world of pains.

Sometimes healers pass some commands to stones, papers, or places. And their commands usually are for demons. They may say, "If someone touches this stone, then you need to help them." And these healer and demon doctors usually want to make money from their powers. Maybe that's why nobody has ever guided medical science properly.

There will be no end to this book if I keep describing each and every person. We are lucky. We live in the modern age with so many effective medications, skilled surgeons, and medical machines, and these are all effective in the healing process. Until now, modern science has not believed in invisible world. Modern science has no concept of invisible insects that are responsible for making us sick in innumerable. Personally, I was never interested in medical science. That's why I graduated with a degree in electrical engineering and a bachelor's in law. Years ago, if someone had told me what I am telling you right now, I might have just laughed and moved on without even listening. Doctors often tell someone that they cannot help with migraines, back pain, or any arthritis pain after medications and

والآن كيف يحدث ذلك عندما يمرر المعالج الأمر الى مسؤول الشياطين لعمل أي شيء. وفي قليل من الأحيان ما يقوم الشياطين بإنجاز الأمر. عدا ذلك، تستخدم الشياطين نظام التواصل الخاص بها باستخدام المجالات المغناطيسية في جميع أنحاء العالم ومن حولنا، ويقومون بتمرير الرسالة الى تلك الشياطين الذين يكونون مستعدين لإنجاز ذلك الأمر. وبسبب تلك الرسائل، تقوم الشياطين من حولنا باتباع الأوامر. ويمكن للمعالج أيضاً أن يضرك أيضاً. ويمكنهم التسبب في إيذائنا أيضاً. وبدلاً من الاعتماد على المعالجين أو الشياطين، نحتاج الى اختراع آلات جديدة للتعامل مع تلك المشاكل. وأنا واثق من نفسي لأنني الوحيد الذي لا يستخدم الشياطين لتنقية الأجسام من الأمراض والآلام. ويتم ذلك من خلال عقلي، وتخرج الأشعة من عقلي للسيطرة على الأمراض المختلفة والآلام والياطيين. ولكنني إنسان بطبيعتي، ولا أستخدم الشياطين ولا يمكنني إنجاز الكثير. وأنا أتعلم كيفية استخدام هبة الله التي منحني إياها. وقد حان الوقت لعلم الطب للتدخل والسيطرة على هذا العالم الخفي من الآلام.

واحياناً ما يقوم المعالجون بتمرير بعض الأوامر الى الحجارة والأوراق والأماكن. وعادة ما تكون أوامرهم موجهة للشياطين. ويمكنهم القول، "في حال قام شخص ما بلمس هذا الحجر، فإذن عليك مساعدته." وعادة ما يريد العراف أو المعالج الحصول على النقود باستخدام قواهم. وربما ذلك هو السبب وراء عدم ارشاد أي شخص علم الطب بالشكل الصحيح.

ولن تكون هناك نهاية لهذا الكتاب في حال بقائي وصف كل شخص. فنحن محظوظون لأننا نعيش في العصر الحديث بوجود الكثير من الأدوية الفعالة والجراحون الخبراء والمهرة والآلات الطبية، وكلها فعالة في عملية الشفاء من الأمراض والآلام. وحتى الآن، لم يؤمن العلم في العصر الحديث في العالم الخفي. ولا يوجد لديه مفهوم للحشرات الخفية المسؤولة عن جعلنا مرضى بأعداد لا تعد ولا تحصى. وشخصياً، لم أهتم أبداً في علم الطب. لذلك السبب تخرجت بشهادة في الهندسة الإلكترونية وشهادة بكالوريوس في القانون. وقبل سنين، في حال أخبرني شخص ما بما أخبركم به الآن، لكنت ضحكت وغادرت دون مجرد الاستماع إليه. وعادة ما يخبر الأطباء شخصاً ما بأنهم لا يمكنهم مساعدتهم في علاج الصداع النصفي وألم الظهر أو آلام التهاب المفاصل بعد أن

surgical techniques have been exhausted. I cannot fix damages to the organs or bones of the body. We need medication and surgery for that. But whatever is beyond the limit of medical science, whatever doctors can't fix or see, I am capable of fixing it.

Pains are relatively easy for me, regardless of its source. I have difficulty dealing with infants because they cannot give me an update. I can have problems dealing with pain-free diseases or painless diseases like kidney failure, thyroid problem, liver diseases, or diabetes. I have no way of knowing if the disease is still there or not. Only solution for these kinds of diseases is to keep working on them nonstop. That is definitely possible for a few people, but because of time constraints, it is practically impossible to help many individuals.

But when an organ or a part of the body is not completely damaged and those people can get the proper medical care to fix the damages, I am sure I can remove those diseases or insects responsible for those diseases. I am not a magician. I need to clearly understand the places of the damages or pains to help someone. HIV, any kind of cancer, or simple pains—they are all the same to me. Because once I cleanse someone of these demons or diseases, I will move all the negative energies away from their bodies but; if they will not take proper medication and surgery, negative energy will come back to them, after sometime.

I can work hard to help anyone defeat diseases and cancers, if they are willing to use the proper medication to heal the damages afterward. My e-mail is aruba74@hotmail.com.

Anyone can send me his or her picture along with details about his or her problems. In case of any kind of pain, I don't need to contact anyone. I will just need an e-mail update to make sure his or her problem is resolved. Before I communicate to people's pains, I will give them an exact time so that they notice the difference. In case of visible cancers, I will need to know which kind of medications, ointments, creams, and syrups the people are employing to fight

استنزاف تقنيات الأدوية والعمليات الجراحية. ولا يمكنني علاج أضرار الأعضاء أو عظام الجسم. فنحن نحتاج الى الأدوية والعمليات الجراحية. ولكن ما يكون في غير متناول قيود علم الطب، وما لا يستطيع الأطباء علاج أو رؤيته، فأنا قادر على علاجه.

ونسبياً فإن الأمراض سهلة المتناول بالنسبة لي بغض النظر عن مصدرها. ولدي صعوبة في التعامل مع الأطفال الرضع لأنهم لا يستطيعون إخباري عن آخر التطورات . ولدي مشاكل في التعامل مع أمراض الخالية من الآلام أو الأمراض الغير مؤلمة كأمراض الكبد وفشل الكلى ومشاكل الغدد الدرقية ومرض السكري. ولا يوجد لدي طريقة لمعرفة إذا ما كان المرض لا يزال موجود هناك أم لا. حيث ان الحل الوحيد لتلك الأنواع من الامراض هو إبقائها العامل من دون توقف. وذلك بكل تأكيد ممكن لبعض الأشخاص، ولكن بسبب ضيق الوقت، فذلك عملياً مستحيل لمساعدة الكثير من الأشخاص.

ولكن عندما لا يكون جزء من الجسم تالفاً بشكل كامل ويمكن لهؤلاء الأشخاص تناول الدواء الملائم لعلاج الأضرار، فإنا متأكد من ازالة تلك الأمراض أو الحشرات المسؤولة عن تلك الأمراض. فأنا لست بساحر. حيث أنني أحتاج الى معرفة أماكن الضرر أو الآلام لمساعدة الشخص. يعد مرض نقص المناعة المكتسبة الإيدز وأي نوع من أنواع السرطان أو الآلام البسيطة هي نفسها بالنسبة لي. ولأنني أقوم بتطهير شخص ما من تلك الشياطيين أو الأمراض، سأقوم بإبعاد جميع الطاقات السلبية بعيداً عن الأجسام، ولكن في حال عدم تناولهم الدواء المناسب واجراء العمليات الجراحية، ستعود الطاقة السلبية الى أجسامهم بعد فترة من الزمن.

ويمكنني العمل بجد لمساعدة أي شخص للتغلب على الأمراض والسرطان في حال رغبتهم في استخدام الأدوية الصحيحة للتعافي من الأضرار الناجمة. وهذا هو بريدي الإلكتروني:
aruba74@hotmail.com
حيث بإمكان أي شخص ارسال صورته ملحقة بالتفاصيل بشأن مشاكلها. وفي حالة أي نوع من الآلام، لا أحتاج الى الاتصال بالشخص. ما أحتاجه فقط هو اخباري عن آخر التطورات عن طريق الإيميل للتأكد من حل مشكلتها. وقبل التواصل مع آلام الأشخاص، سأقوم بمنحهم وقت دقيق حتى يلاحظوا الفرق. وفي حالة السرطان المرئي، سأحتاج الى معرفة نوع الأدوية والمرهمات والكريمات والعصائر التي يتناولها المريض لمقاومة

those cancers. After that, I can guide them with my help. In regard to depression, high blood pressure, anxiety attacks, and other similar issues, I can help only when someone is suffering from that problem at that specific time.

Several times when I was helping people fix their headache, I started receiving different kinds of diseases and pains from them. That's why I do not do any calculation anymore. I am always ready to deal with any problem that comes out of those people.

It is my strong believe that demons and diseases already know that they are not visible to us. They just watch us struggle and fight against pains or the damages caused by them. If medical scientists start to believe this theory, I am sure they will find cures for all the pains and diseases caused by these invisible demons or diseases. To prove my point and convince medical scientists about demons and their activities, I will demonstrate my skills and capabilities whenever they want.

The beings of the invisible world cannot go throw wall or glass doors. They need to have an entrance to come in or go out. I see this every day, especially when I ask them to leave my office and they leave through doors. But I strongly believe that they do not need much room to enter anywhere. If air can go somewhere, they can go there too. But they have the additional quality of penetrating and expanding themselves in our bodies.

Demons or diseases do not easily listen to anyone, not even me. Someone needs to have the ability to convince them not to do something. And if the demons do not listen, someone needs to be capable of putting some pressure on them or insisting that they listen to someone. I do that all the time. I am sure that some of them get upset with me because I am taking their toys or food away from them. I am sure a few of them work against me so that they can hurt me, but I do not know what to do about that.

تلك الأنواع من السرطانات. وبعد ذلك، يمكنني ارشادهم لمساعدتي. وبخصوص الاكتئاب وارتفاع ضغط الدم ونوبات الغضب وقضايا أخرى مشابهة، يمكنني مساعدتهم فقط عندما يعاني شخص ما من تلك المشكلة في وقت محدد.

وفي عدة مرات وعندما أكون أساعد الأشخاص في علاج صداعهم، أبدأ باستقبال أنواع مختلفة من الأمراض والآلام من تلك الأجسام. لذلك السبب لا أقوم بأي حساب بعد الآن. ودائماً ما أكون مستعداً للتعامل مع أي مشكلة تنشأ من هؤلاء الأشخاص.

إنه إيماني العميق بأن الشياطين والأمراض تعلم جيداً بأنهم ليسوا ظاهرين بالنسبة لنا. فهم فقط يقومون بمراقبتنا نتصارع ونقاتل ضد الآلام أو الأضرار الناتجة عن تلك الأمراض. وفي حال بدأ علماء الطب في تصديق هذه النظرية، فأنا متأكد بأنهم سيجدون العلاك لجميع الآلام والأمراض المسببة من قبل تلك الشياطين الخفية. ولإثبات نظريتي ولإقناع علماء الطب بشأن الشياطين وأعمالهم، سأظهر مهاراتي وإمكانياتي عندما تتطلب الحاجة الى ذلك.

لا يمكن لكائنات العالم الخفي الخروج من خلال الجدران أو الأبواب الزجاجي. فهم يحتاجون الى مدخل للدخول ومخرج للخروج. وأشاهد ذلك كل يوم، خاصة عندما أطلب منهم مغادرة مكتبي فهم يغادرون من خلال الأبواب. ولكن أؤمن بقوة بأنهم لا يحتاجون الى حيز كبير للدخول إلى أي مكان. وفي حال تمكن الهواء من الدخول في مكان ما، يمكن للشياطين أيضاً فعل ذلك. ولكن يملكون ميزة إضافية وهي التغلغل والتمدد بأنفسهم في أجسامنا.

ولا تستمع الشياطين والأمراض الى أي شخص بسهولة حتى إلي. ويحتاج شخص ما الى القدرة على إقناعهم على القيام بشيء ما. وفي حال عدم استماع الشياطين، يحتاج الشخص الى أن يكون قادراً على الضغط أو إجبارهم على الاستماع إليهم. وأقوم بذلك طوال الوقت. وأنا متأكد بأن بعضهم يغضبون مني لأنني آخذ دماهم أو طعامهم بعيداً عنهم. وأنا متأكد أيضاً بأن بعضهم يعمل ضدي حتى يتمكنوا من إلحاق الأذى بي، ولكن لا أعلم ما يمكنني فعله حيال ذلك الأمر.

One time, I treated a kid with blood cancer; however, that kid was only one year old, and his treatment was very difficult because the kid was in the last stage of the cancer in a foreign country. But I got the chance to learn a few things from that experience. The disease responsible of creating the blood cancer was sitting on the neck bone of the boy's body and in his mouth as well. And from there, that disease was creating and controlling the boy's whole body and spreading the blood cancer. I still do not feel confident that I am able to control a blood or bone cancer in some people, especially when it's in its last stages. The only problem I had when I was treating that kid was the bombardment of attacks. Every time I work on him, I pulled negative energies from his body. My actions reduced his fever. I fix his mouth and gum infections several times. I tried to fix his bleeding nose several times, but that kid only felt better for few hours before he was under attack again. I also experienced all of his pains and problems. I was in pain for few days, and that was very difficult. From that day on, I decided not to treat infants anymore, because they cannot tell me where they have problems. That was a very bad experience.

One time, someone asked me to work on their bone marrow. I tried several times. Every time I worked on them, I always felt something coming out of the bone marrow. After that, I tried to work on all the bones, but the only noticeable diseases came out from chest bones and bone marrow. Another time, I treated someone who was complaining about swallowing and breathing problems. I learned from that experience that a negative energy can block the tubes responsible for transferring food or liquid to the stomach. That was not difficult to treat.

The appendix is just an extra tube between the small and large intestines. Negative energy can go inside that tube and expand itself to damage the tube. Once this tube is damaged, surgery is necessary to clean up the mess and poisonous discharges.

وفي ذات مرة، قمت بمعالجة طفل كان يعاني من سرطان الدم؛ علاوة على ذلك، كان يبلغ ذلك الطفل من العمر عشرين عاماً، وكان من الصعوبة علاجه لأنه الطفل في المرحلة الأخيرة من السرطان في دولة أجنبية. ولكن اغتنمت الفرصة وتعلمت بعض الأشياء من تلك التجربة. ويكون المرض مسؤول عن التسبب في سرطان الدم الموجود في عظام الرقبة لجسم الطفل وفي فمه كذلك. ومن هناك، تسبب ذلك المرض وسيطر على جميع أجزاء الجسم مسبباً انتشار سرطان الدم. ولكن لا أشعر بالثقة بقدرتي على السيطرة على سرطان الدم أو العظام عند بعض الأشخاص، وخاصة عندما يكون السرطان في مراحله الأخيرة. إن المشكلة الوحيدة التي واجهتني عندما كنت أعالج ذلك الطفل هي انفجار الهجمات. في كل مرة أعلم فيها على مرض الطفل، كنت أخرج طاقات سلبية من جسمه. وقد قللت أعمالي الحمى لديه. وقمت بعلاج فمه ولثته من العدوى عدة مرات. وحاولت علاج نزيف الأنف عدة مرات، ولكن شعر الطفل بتحسن لعدة ساعات قبل أن يتعرض لهجوم مرة أخرى. وواجهت آلامه ومشاكله. وتعرض للألم لعدة أيام، وكان ذلك صعباً بالنسبة لي. ومنذ ذلك اليوم، قررت عدم معالجة الرضع بعد الآن لأنهم لا يمكنني اخباري أين تمكن مشاكلهم. حيث كانت تجربة سيئة بالنسبة لي.

وفي مرة أخرى، طلب مني شخص ما معالجة نخاع العظم، ولكن خرجت الأمراض التي يمكن ملاحظتها من عظام الصدع والنخاع العظمي. وفي مرة أخرى أيضاً، قمت بمعالجة شخص ما كان يعاني من انتفاخ ومشاكل في التنفس. وعرفت من تجربتي بأن الطاقة السلبية يمكنها أن تقوم بإغلاق الشرايين المسؤولة عن نقل الطعام أو السوائل الى المعدة. ولم يكن ذلك صعباً علاجه.

تعد الزائدة الدودية أنبوب زائد يقع بين الأمعاء الدقيقة والغليظة. ويمكن للطاقة السلبية الدخول الى ذلك الأنبوب وتمديد نفسه لتدمير الأنبوب. وعندما يتم اتلاف ذلك الأنبوب، فمن الضرورة اجراء عملية جراحية لتنظيف الفوضى والمخلفات السامة.

To use medical language, we call this problem a "gastric problem." These negative energies go to any tube or another part of the body and expand themselves, and they can sometimes kill someone. This expanding quality can prove that all these demons and diseases are actually physical creatures but invisible to us.

Maybe my theories will challenge medical science, but I am ready to proof my point. I will do anything to prove my theories to medical scientists, so that they eventually start working to find ways to reduce the effects of negative energies on our health.

All the creatures in the invisible world use doors, as I have stated, they have physical bodies similar to air. A sick person should keep using medication to heal damage organs or other parts of the body, but in the case of internal wounds or ulcers, there may be no cure. The invisible insects of diseases number in the millions, and they are all free to go inside our bodies and keep eating and damaging our organs. If it is possible to somehow isolate these kinds of patients and keep them in an isolated chamber where it would be impossible for these invisible insects and diseases to return to that injured body or organ, then the only problem will be removing those invisible insects or diseases already inside the body.

If this idea to keep negative energy from away from us works sometime in the future, hospitals, houses, and maybe even cars can be built to utilize this technology. I am sure that once medical science considers my theory and scientists start their research, they will find a way to keep negative energy away from our bodies and how to get rid of these diseases when the body is infected.

I have never seen anything like a fairy, a ghost, a witch, or any demon in the shape of a human being. I always see them in their original shape, small flying objects in different shapes. Some are round. Some are like threads. Some are similar to stars, and several are other shapes. But they are all very small in size, and they all fly in the air. If someone says that there are demons in the shape of humans or

ولاستخدام اللغة الطبية، نسمي هذه المشكلة ب "مشكلة في المعدة" حيث تدخل الطاقات السلبية الى أي أنبوب وتتمدد، ويمكنهم أحياناً قتل الإنسان. وميزة التمدد هذه يمكنها اثبات بأن جميع تلك الشياطيين والأمراض هي مخلوقات فيزيائية ولكنها غير مرئية بالنسبة لنا.

وربما ستقوم نظرياتي بخلق التحدي لعلم الطب، ولكن مستعد لإثبات نظريتي. وسأقوم بعمل أي شيء لإثبات نظرياتي لعلماء الطب، حتى يتسنى لهم في النهاية البدء في العمل على ايجاد طرق للتقليل من تأثيرات الطاقات السلبية على صحتنا.

وتستخدم جميع المخلوقات في العالم الخفي الأبواب كما ذكرت سابقاً، حيث لديها أجسام فيزيائية مشابهة للهواء. وينبغي على الشخص المريض الاستمرار في استخدام الادوية للتعافي من الأضرار في الجسم، ولكن في حالة الجروح الداخلية أو القرحة، ربما لا يكون هناك علاج لها. وتبلغ أعداد أمراض الحشرات الخفية بالملايين، وهم أحرار في الذهاب الى أي مكان وأكل وتدمير أي جسم. وفي حال يكون هناك امكانية نوعاً ما لعزل هؤلاء المرضى وابقائهم في غرف معزولة حيث يكون من المستحيل لتلك الحشرات الخفية والأمراض العودة الى ذلك الجسم المجروح، ولكن تبقى المشكلة الوحيدة في ازالة تلك الحشرات الخفية أو الامراض الموجودة اصلاً في الجسم.

وفي حال كون هذه الفكرة لإبقاء الاقة السلبية بعيداً عنا تعمل في بعض الأحيان في المستقبل والمستشفيات والمنازل، وربما السيارات ليتم تصميمها للاستفادة من هذه التقنية. وأنا متأكد بأنه عندما يعتمد علك الطب نظريتي واخذها في عين الاعتبار وعندما يبدأ العلماء بإجراء بحوثهم، سيجدون طريقة ما لإبقاء الطاقة السلبية بعيداً عن أجسامنا وكيفية التخلص من تلك الأمراض عنما يتعرض الجسم لها.

ولم ارى في حياتي قط أي شيء كجنية أو سبح أو ساحرة أو أي شيطان على هيئة انسان. ودائماً ما أراهم على هيئتهم الحقيقة، حيث أنها أجسام طائرة صغيرة ذو أشكال مختلفة. وبعضها يكون مستديرة وبعضها الآخر يشبه الخيوط وبعضها يشبه النجوم أو أشكالا اخرى مختلفة. ولكن أحجامها جميعاً صغيرة وطائرة في الهواء. وفي حال ادعاء شخص ما بوجود شياطيين على هيئة إنسان أو

fairies or that these creatures are twenty feet tall, ugly, black things with long teeth, red eyes, and long arms, these are all fictions. If ever I see anything similar to those fictions, I will not take one second to disclose this information. There is no doubt that these flying demons are very powerful once they possess our bodies, but when they are just flying in air, they are as harmless as air.

The heart usually is affected by the blocking and expanding of negative energy. Expending negative energy can increase the size of heart. And because of this expanding quality, these diseases can block the blood vessels and interrupt blood circulation.

Kidneys are usually affected by two kinds of negative energies or diseases. One blocks, and the other expands. The first disease just blocks the major tubes in the kidneys to disrupt their functions. The second kind of kidney disease is the result of invisible insects that eat and directly damage the kidneys. Consequently, people get kidney infections and sometime kidney stones.

If a demon is living in the body of a lizard and you kill that lizard, that demon will immediately go inside your body. And because the demon's world was based on the experience of the lizard, it will show you dreams about lizards. This is not true for normal people because they usually have a few permanent demons for their whole lives, but in my case, and people close to me or some other people with whom I frequently work, I remove their demons frequently all the time. Whenever they go here and there, some new demons possess their bodies; these new demons can come from other family members, from the workplace, from trees, from insects, from animals, or from sick people. Now remember that a normal person can only figure out whose demon is in his or her body by analyzing the symptoms or one's dreams. This is a very simple way of judging the mentality and background of your demon.

I do not have any permanent demon these days, but once I go to sleep, they come to me and show me dreams according to their

جنيات أو تلك المخلوقات التي يبلغ ولها عشرون قدماً، وقبيحة المنظر وأشياء سوداء، وعيون حمراء وأذرع طويلة، حيث ان جميع تلك الأشياء قصصاً خيالية. ولن آخذ وقتاً ولو حتى ثانيه لتفنيد تلك المعلومات. وليس هناك اي شك بأن الشياطين الطائرة قوية جداً عندما يسيطرون على أجسامنا، ولكن عندما يكونون طائرين في الهواء، فهم لا يؤذون أحداً.

ويتعرض القلب في العادة للإغلاق والتمدد للطاقة السلبية. ويمكن لتمدد الطاقة السلبية زيادة حجم القلب. وبسبب ميزة التمدد تلك، يمكن لهذه الأمراض اغلاق صمامات الدم وتقطع الدورة الدموية.

وتتعرض الكلى الو نوعين من الطاقات السلبية أو الامراض. الأول يقوم بإغلاق الشرايين والثاني يقوم بعملية التمدد. حيث يقوم المرض الأول بإغلاق الأنابيب الرئيسية في الكلى لقطع عملهم ووظائفهم. ويعتبر المرض الثاني نتيجة للحشرات الخفية التي تأكل وتدمر الكلى بشكل مباشر. وبالتالي، تصاب كلى الإنسان بالعدوى وأحياناً حصوة الكلى.

وفي حال اقامة الشيطان في جسم سحلية وتقوم بقتل تلك السحلية، سيقوم بالدخول الى جسمك مباشرة. ولأن عالم الشياطين يعتمد على تجربة السحلية، سيقوم بإظهارك أحلاماً بشأن السحالي. وهذا ليس صحيحاً بالنسبة لشخص طبيعي لأن لديهم شياطين دائماً الوجود طوال فترة حياتهم، ولكن في حالتي، والأشخاص القريبون مني أو أشخاص آخرون الذين يعملون معي بشكل متكرر/ أقوم بإزالة شياطينهم طوال الوقت. وعندما يذهبون هنا وهناك، تسيطر بعض الشياطين الأخرى على أجسامهم، ويمكن لتلك الشياطين القدوم من عائلات أخرى أو مكان عمل أو أشجار أو حشرات أو حيوانات أو أشخاص مريضون. والآن تذكر بأن الشخص الطبيعي يمكنه اكتشاف فقط شياطينه بتحليل الأعراض والأحلام. وهذا سهل جداً للحكم على عقلية وخبرة شيطانك.

ولا يوجد لدي أي شيطان دائم هذه الأيام، ولكن عندما أخلد للنوم، تأتي الى وتريني أحلاماً طبقاً خبرتها

backgrounds and knowledge. Some show me lizards or other bad stuff in my dreams. In that case, I immediately get up and complain to them, "What the hell are you showing me? Please show me good dreams." But I do not know about their knowledge or what they think is good or bad. The best thing to do whenever your demon is showing you bad dreams is to immediately look toward your left shoulder and tell your demon that you do not like these dreams and then tell it exactly what do you want to see in your dreams. Trust me, most of the time, they will listen to you. Only you need to act very confident, so demons believe that you are aware about them and their actions.

Now I can explain two more parts of same theory about demons. According to modern science, our eyes and ears have some limitations. We cannot see or hear more or less than those particular limits. In the same way, I believe that demons, diseases, and pains are physical bodies like air or rays. We are not able to directly see demons and diseases or pain right now because nobody has ever tried to invent a machine to reveal them, but I am sure once medical science will invent it one day. I can only give scientists guidelines on how to do their experiments. I adamantly insist it is possible to see demons, diseases, and pains because I am capable of seeing them right now. Because I am able to see them, I am sure it is possible to invent artificial eyes or machines to see or watch these demons. Remember, even if you use artificial eyes or machines to see demons, diseases, or pains, you'll only be able to see them either when they are flying in the air or leaving a body and transferring to another. It will be very difficult to notice them when they are already inside a body. I can sense demons both inside and outside the body because I have been given a gift from God.

Let me summarize how someone can perform experiments to invent artificial eyes or machines to see demons, diseases, and pains. Always remember to perform these experiments in an open atmosphere where you have trees, grass, and all kind of insects and reptiles. You can target a few lizards, rats, cats, dogs, and birds. Targeting them does not mean killing them. It means you need to focus your machines

ومعرفتها. ويرينا بعضها سحلي وأشياء أخرى سيئة. وفي تلك الحالة، أنهض بسرعة وأشكوهم "ما الذي تريني إياه؟" رجاءً، أريني أحلاماً جيدة." ولكن لا أعلم عن معرفتهم أو ماذا يفكرون سواءً كان جيداً أو سيئاً. وإن الشيء الأفضل للقيام به عندما يريك شيطانك أحلاماً سيئة هو النظر مباشرة الى كتفك الأيسر وقل لشيطانك بأنك لا ترغب في رؤية تلك الأحلام وقل له ما تريد رؤيته في أحلامك. ثق بي، في معظم الاوقات، سيستمعون إليك. ما تحتاجه فقط هو التصرف بكل ثقة، لذلك تعتقد الشياطيين بأنك مدركاً حيال أفعالهم.

والآن، يمكنني توضيح جزئيين آخرين من نفس النظرية حيال الشياطيين. وطبقاً لعلم العصر الحديث، هناك قيود في عويننا وآذاننا. ولا يمكننا رؤية أو سماع المزيد أو القليل عن تلك القيود. وبنفس الطريقة، أؤمن بأن الشياطيين والأمراض والآلام هي أجساماً فيزيائية كالهواء أو الأشعة. ونحن غير قادرون على رؤيتهم مباشرة لأنه لم يحاول أحداً قط اختراع آلة لإخبارهم، ولكني واثقٌ بأن علم الطب سيخترع تلك الآلة في يوم ما. ويمكنني أن اعطي العلماء المبادئ التوجيهية حول كيفية عمل تجاربهم. وأصر بعناد حول امكانية رؤية الشياطيين. لأنني قادر على رؤيتهم الآن. ولأنني قادرٌ على رؤيتهم، فأنا متأكد من امكانية اختراع عيون صناعية أو آلات لرؤية الشياطيين والأمراض والآلام. وستكون قادراً فقط على رؤيتهم سواءً كانوا طائرين في الهواء أو أثناء مغادرتهم لجسم ما والتنقل الى جسم آخر. وسيكون من الصعب ملاحظتهم عندما يكونوا داخل جسم ما مسبقاً. ويمكنني الإحساس بالشياطيين داخل وخارج الجسم بسبب منحي لهبة من الله.

دعوني أقوم بتلخيص كيفية تمكن شخص ما من انجاز تجارب لاختراع عيون صناعية أو آلات لرؤية الشياطيين والأمراض والآلام. ودائماً تذكر أنه لإنجاز تلك التجارب في جو مفتوح حيث وجود الأشجار والعشب وجميع انواع الحشرات والزواحف. يمكنك استهداف القليل من السحلي والجرذان والقطط والكلاب والطيور. ويعني هذا أنك بحاجة الى أن تركز آلتك على

on those animals. Always remember that demons will move from one body to another whenever they feel insecure. They always jump or transfer themselves to the most secure or most available body. For example, if you focus your machine eyes on a cat and a lizard (i.e., one weak and one strong animal), remember that whenever a cat tries to hunt a lizard, the demon in the lizard will jump into the cat's body. This is the time to observe the invisible image of demons. You need to trust me. Everybody is possessed by these demons. You can also ask a man to kill a spider or a lizard. He may not really need to kill the animal, but his action will definitely make the demons in the spider or lizard feel insecure. Within seconds, those demons will come out the body of the spider or lizard and jump into the body of that man. During this experiment, you can watch for the demons when they are transferring themselves from one body to another. Even if a man just scares an animal, its demons will do same thing. They will immediately leave the less secure body and probably go straight to that man's body because his will be the most secure one for demons at that time.

Next, we should try to invent a machine that utilizes lasers. The rays from that machine should be able to convince or insist the invisible insects, diseases, pains, and demons to leave a body or leave an infected or damage organ. That machine should be able to communicate with whatever pain from which the person is suffering. Now, you must be wondering how someone will be able to invent such kind of machine. To develop this technology, medical scientists need to watch and observe me, and to help mankind, I will demonstrate my capabilities as many times as needed.

They need to observe and watch how I communicate with pains without opening my mouth. Usually, I close my eyes when I'm helping someone. Medical scientists need to observe the kinds of rays coming from my mind when I am communicating with someone's pain. And then they need to observe that pain leaving the body and going somewhere else. With the proper artificial eyes or machines, they can find or discover which kind of rays are coming from my

على الحيوانات. وتذكر دائماً بأن الشياطيين تنتقل من جسم الى آخر عند شعورهم بالخوف. ودائماً ما يقفزون أو ينتقلون الى الجسم المتوفر والأكثر أمناً. على سبيل المثال، في حال تركزت آلتك على عيون قطة أو سحلية (حيوان ضعيف وآخر قوي)، تذكر بأنه عندما تحاول القطة اصطياد سحلية، سيقفز الشيطان الموجود في جسم السحلية الى جسم القطة. وحان الوقت لملاحظة الصورة الغير مرئية من الشياطيين. وتحتاج الى أن تثق بي. كل شخص مسيطر عليه من تلك الشياطيين. ويمكن سؤال رجل أن يقتل حيواناً، ولكن فعله هذا سيجعل الشياطيين في العنكبوت أو السحلية تشعر بعد الأمان. وخلال ثوان معدودة، ستأتي تلك الشياطيين الى جسم ذلك الرجل. وأثناء تلك التجربة، يمكنك ملاحظة الشياطيين عندما ينتقلون بأنفسهم من جسم الى آخر. وحتى في حال أخاف الرجل حيواناً، ستقوم شياطيين ذلك الحيوان بفعل الشيء نفسه. وسيغادرون الجسم الأقل أمناً ومن المرجح أن ينتقلون مباشرة الى جسم ذلك الرجل لأن جسمه سيكون الأكثر أمناً لتلك الشياطيين في ذلك الوقت.

وفي الخطوة القادمة، ينبغي علينا المحاولة في اختراع آلة للإستفادة من الليزر. وينبغي على تلك الأشعة الصادرة من الآلة أن تكون قادرة على اقناع أو إجبار الحشرات الخفية والأمراض والآلام والشياطيين على مغادرة الجسم. ويجب ان تكون تلك الآلة قادرة على التواصل مع أي ألم في جسم أي شخص يعاني منه. والآن، يجب أن تتساءل كيف يمكن لشخص ما أن يكون قادراً على اختراع مثل تلك الآلة. ولتطوير هذه التقنية، يحتاج علماء الطب الى ملاحظتي ومراقبتي ولمساعدة جنس البشر. وساقوم بإظهار امكانياتي في حال اقتضت الضرورة.

يحتاجون لملاحظة ومراقبة كيف أتواصل مع الآلام دجون أن أقوم بفتح فمي. وعادة، أقوم بإغلاق عيني عندما أقوم بمساعدة شخص ما. ويحتاج علماء الطب أيضاً مراقبة جميع أنواع الأشعة القادمة من عقلي عندما أتواصل مع آلام شخص ما. ومن ثم يحتاجون الى مراقبة ذلك الألم يغادر الجسم ويذهب الى مكان آخر، ويمكنهم ايجاد أو اكتشاف أي نوع من الأشعة القادمة من عقلي

mind and going to those pains or demons and convincing them or insisting them to leave the body of that human. They can also observe when that demon or disease leaves that body to catch the image of them in these cameras or artificial eyes. Once they have these images and the figures for the intensity of the rays, I am sure they will be able to invent a machine whose rays will be able to convince or insist any pain, sickness, disease, or demon leave damage bodies and organs. I think we should first cleanse the body and damage organs from these pains and diseases. And once this is done, we can start prescribing healing medications and surgeries. To me, these should be secondary procedures, but we have all kinds of effective medications and surgeries. Hopefully, my theories and ideas will encourage some medical scientists to start researching this area. Maybe not immediately, but I am hopeful that it will happen soon.

Most of the time, demons are not completely inside the body. Somehow, they surround the body. In this way, they are inside the body, but some parts are also above the skin. Whenever demons travel through the telephone lines, they are usually stuck in our ears, heads, and necks, especially our left ears. At that moment, demons have not completely penetrated our bodies. At that time, they sit on top of us and dig inside our minds by using the path of the left ear most of the time to learn more about us or use their hypnotizing powers. If a medical scientist observes a normal person who is on phone with a sick person who has a very short temper or someone who is an extremist in any field, I am sure that demons will travel via the phone lines and possess the other person. Medical science can use modern machines to detect the rays and signals. Once medical science is able to detect demons or diseases, I am sure they will be able to easily find the cures that normal people can use against them.

Always remember that demons and diseases/pains are not the same things. Demons are different. They do not hurt us, but they use us as toys. They control our minds, and most of the time, we do what they want us to do. Most of the time, we think whatever they want us to think. You may ask me, "What do demons get from this?" The

والمتوجهة الى تلك الآلام والشياطيين لإقناع تلك الآلام الشياطيين أو اجبارهم الى مغادرة الجسم. يمكنهم أيضاً مراقبة أثناء مغادرة الشيطان أو الأمراض لجسم الإنسان لالتقاط صورة لهم عن طريق استخدام الكاميرات والعيون الصناعية. وعندما يحصلون على الصور واكتشاف كثافة الأشعة المطلوبة لرؤية الشياطيين، أنا متأكد بأنهم سيكونون قادرين على اختراع آلة تكون أشعتها قادرة على اقناع أو اجبار أي ألم أو مرض أو شيطان مغادرة الأجسام المدمرة. وأعتقد بأنه يجب علينا تطهير الجسم والأعضاء التالفة من تلك الآلام والأمراض. وعندما يتم ذلك، يمكننا البدء بوضع الوصفات للأدوية العلاجية والعمليات الجراحية. وبالنسبة لي، يجب أن تكون تلك الأدوية إجراءات ثانوية. وكلي أمل، أن تقوم نظرياتي وأفكاري مشجعة لبعض علماء الطب للبداء بإجراء البحوث في هذا المجال. وربما ليس مباشرة، ولكن أتمنى أن يحدث ذلك في القريب العاجل.

وفي معظم الأوقات، لا تكون الشياطيين داخل الجسم بشكل كامل. ونوعاً ما، يقومون بإحاطة الجسم. وبهذه الطريقة، يكونون داخل الجسم ولكن بعض من أجزائه تكون موجود فوق الجلد. وعندما تسافر الشياطيين من خلال خطوط الهاتف، فهي تكون عالقة في آذاننا ورؤوسنا ورقابنا خاصة آذاننا اليسرى. وفي تلك اللحظة، لا تتغلغل الشياطيين بشكل كامل الى داخل الجسم، فهم يجلسون على فوق رؤوسنا وتقوم بالحفر داخل عقولنا باستخدام طريق الأذن اليسرى معظم الوقت لتعلم المزيد عنا واستخدام قواهم في التنويم المغناطيسي. وفي حال مراقبة علماء الطب شخصاً عادياً يتحدث بالهاتف مع شخص مريض الذي يعاني من سرعة الغضب أو شخصاً آخر متطرف في أي مجال، وأنا متأكد من تلك الشياطيين ستنتقل عن طريق الهاتف وتسيطر على أشخاص عاديين. ويمكن لعلم الطب أن يقومون باستخدام الآلات الحديثة لكشف الأشعة والإشارات. وعندما يكون علم الطب قادراً على الكشف عن الشياطيين والأمراض، فأنا متأكد من أن العلماء سيكونون قادرين على ايجاد العلاج بكل سهولة.

وتذكر دائماً بأن الشياطيين والأمراض والآلام لا تشبه بعضها البعض. فالشياطيين تختلف، ولا يقومون بإيذائنا ولكنهم يستخدمونا كدمى في أيديهم. ويقوم بالسيطرة على عقولنا. ونقوم بعمل ما يريدونه في معظم الأوقات. وأيضاً نحن نفكر فيما هم يريدونا أن نفكر. ويمكن سؤالي: "ما الذي تجنيه الشياطيين من ذلك كله؟"

simple answer is that this is their hobby and we are their toys. They have nothing else to do. They live their lives around or inside us; they get involved in our affairs and families, so they make decisions about what we need to do. They keep us angry and make us perform all kinds of negative acts. Practically, it is not possible to disrupt the demon's control. If someone like me takes the demon around you or inside you out, another will possess you within a few days or maybe a few hours. Demons can see that you are free of them and that no others are claiming ownership over you. Whatever demon is more powerful will come to you and will make room around and inside you within a few seconds. And you will never know about these changes because all demons pretty much act the same way. Your dreams may be different, but that may be the extent of the change.

On the other hand, diseases or pains do not hypnotize us in order to control our minds. They do not get involved in our family or business affairs. Diseases and pains are pure parasites. They eat our bodies and organs. They do not care if they hurt or kill us.

Modern science could potentially detect the demons, diseases, pains, or sicknesses that plague us. Medical scientists can use anyone, but if I have to help, I will. My techniques are very simple. I can talk to any person who has any kind of pain so that medical scientist can use their equipment to observe my procedure. I can use my power to pull the pain out of that sick person, and that pain will travel to me through whatever medium we use to communicate. I can do this as many times as needed. If I receive any demons or pains through the telephone, I can easily take them out of my body so that I am ready again for the experiments. In this very simple way, medical scientist can observe what is coming out from the sick person and traveling through phone lines and going into my body. According to my theory, once medical science is able to detect those rays, they will be able to find cures for all kind of sicknesses and diseases by just removing the invisible bodies from someone.

وإن الجواب البسيط على ذلك هو أنها هوايتهم ونحن دمى في أيديهم. ولا يوجد شيء آخر يقومون به. ويعيشون حياتهم داخل أجسامنا ومن حولنا. ويتدخلون في علاقاتنا وعائلاتنا، لذلك يقومون باتخاذ القرارات حول ما نحتاج القيام به. ويبقونا غاضبين وننجز جميع أنواع الأعمال السلبية. وبشكل عملي، من غير المحتمل كسر سيطرة الشياطين. وفي حال شخص ما مثلي يقوم بإخراج الشياطين من حولك أو داخل جسم، سيقوم شيطان آخر بالسيطرة عليك خلال أيام قليلة او ساعات قليلة. ويمكن للشياطين رؤيتك خالياً منهم ولا يوجد شياطين أخرى تدعى ملكيتها عليك. وعندما يكون هناك شيطان أكثر قوة، فإنه سيأتي إليك وسيجد مكان حولك أو في جسمك خلال ثوان معدودة. ولن تعرف عن تلك التغييرات لأن جميع الشياطين تتصرّف بنفس الطريقة. ويمكن لأحلامك أن تكون مختلفة، ولكن ربما أن يكون ذلك حجم التغيير.

ومن ناحية أخرى، لا تقوم الأمراض أو الآلام بتنويمنا مغناطيسياً للسيطرة على عقولنا. ولا يتدخلون في عائلتنا أو علاقات العمل. حيث أنها طفيليات نقية. يقومون بأكل أجسامنا ولا يهتمون في حال تأذينا أو قتلنا.

وباستطاعة علم العصر الحديث اكتشاف الشياطين والامراض والآلام التي تزعجنا. ويمكن لعلماء الطب استخدام أي شخص، ولكن في حال كان يجب علي المساعدة، سأقوم بذلك. حيث أن تقنياتي بسيطة جداً. ويمكنني التحدث الى أي شخص يعاني من أي نوع من الآلام حتى يتمكن علماء الطب من استخدام معداتهم لمراقبة خطواتي. ويمكنني استخدام قوتي لسحب الألم خارج الشخص المريض، وسينتقل ذلك المرض الي من خلال أي وسط ناقل نستخدم للتواصل. ويمكنني فعل ذلك الكثير من المرات حسب الحاجة. وفي حال تلقيت أي شيطان أو ألممن خلال الهاتف، يمكنني بسهولة اخراجه من جسمي حتى أكون مستعداً من جديد لتجاربي. وهذه طريقة بسيطة جداً، حيث يمكن لعلماء الطب مراقبة ما يخرج من جسم المريض وينتقل من خلال خطوط الهاتف ويدخل جسمي. وطبقاً لنظرياتي، عندما يكون العلم قادراً على اكتشاف تلك الأشعة، سيكونون قادرين على ايجاد العلاج لجميع أنواع الأمراض والآلام عن طريق ازالة الأجسام الخفية من شخص ما.

As I explained, I am capable of pulling out any demon or pain from anyone's body, regardless of their location in the world, even if someone is in Italy and I am in the United States. However, I should know that person and should have seen that person in some way. Now if this person in Italy has headache I will remove that pain from that person without using any phone line or any other device for communication. Most of the time, those pains come out of one body and find someone else close to that person, but I will try to bring that pain to me in the United States. With that pain, I will also try to pull out his demons as well. Usually, demons come straight to me. This should make for a very interesting observation. By observing both of us in these different areas, a scientist could easily detect the presence, motion, and traveling speed of these demons.

Now I am going to talk about another new theory, and I am ready help any medical scientist who wants to discover the cure for all these invisible pains and diseases. By chance, if medical scientists find out the rays of these diseases, pains, and/or demons, they will need to verify all of their conclusions by performing more experiments. However, I already know that these all travel through a field similar to an electromagnetic field. During travel, they act like rays, and that electromagnetic field provides them with medium to travel over great distances quickly. But there is no proof or evidence right now. That's why I am giving everyone these guidelines. For now, assume that medical scientists will be able to detect the rays and electromagnetic traveling system. Once medical science discovers all these details, the next challenge from them will be uncovering the ways to control these entities.

I can help with this as well. I am able to communicate with demons and pains, and I am capable of convincing demons and pains to do or not do something. If they do not listen to me, I am capable of insisting that they do something. Medical science just needs to observe me and find how I can interact with them. Once medical science understands this process, scientists will be able to invent machines with the same capabilities.

وكما أوضحت سابقاً، فأنا قادر على سحب أي شيطان أو ألم من جسم أي شخص بغض النظر عن مكان تواجدهم في العالم، حتى في حال تواجد شخص ما في إيطاليا وأنا في الولايات المتحدة. علاوة على ذلك، ينبغي علي معرفة ذلك الشخص ورؤيته بأي طريقة. والآن في كان ذلك الشخص المتواجد في إيطاليا يعاني من صداع في الرأس، سأقوم بإزالة ذلك الصداع بدون استخدام الهاتف أو أي جهاز للتواصل معه. وفي أغلب الأحيان، تخرج تلك الآلام من جسم وتبحث عن جسم آخر قريب لذلك الشخص، ولكن سأحاول جلب الألم الى جسم في الولايات المتحدة. وبالاستعانة بذلك الألم، سأحاول أيضاً اخراج الشيطان من جسمه. وفي العادة، تأتي الشياطين بشكل مباشر إلي. وينبغي أن يكون مراقبة مثيرة للاهتمام. وبمراقبة كلانا في مناطق مختلفة، يمكن للعالم وبسهولة اكتشاف وجود وحركة وسرعة تنقل تلك الشياطين.

والآن، سأتحدث عن نظرية جديدة أخرى، وأنا مستعد لمساعدة علماء الطب الذين يريدون اكتشاف علاج لجميع أنواع الآلام والأمراض. بالصدفة، في حال اكتشاف العلماء لأشعة لعلاج تلك الأمراض والآلام والشياطين، سيحتاجون الى تأكيد نتائجهم بإجراء المزيد من التجارب. علاوة على ذلك، أعلم بأن تلك الشياطين تنتقل من خلال مجال ما يكون مشابه للمجال الإلكترو مغناطيسي. وأثناء التنقل، يتصرفون كالأشعة، ويزود المجال الإلكترو مغناطيسي بالوسط الناقل للمسافات البعيدة وبسرعة. ولكن لا يوجد هناك أي دليل حالياً. لذلك السبب أقوم بمنح كل شخص تلك الإرشادات. لنفترض بأن علماء الطب سيكونون قادرين اكتشاف الأشعة ونظام التنقل الإلكترو مغناطيسي. وعندما يكتشفون جميع تلك التفاصيل، فإن التحدي القادم أمامهم سيكون باكتشاف الطرق للسيطرة على تلك الكيانات.

ويمكنني المساعدة في هذا كذلك. حيث أنني قادر على التواصل مع الشياطين والآلام، قادر ايضاً على اقناع الشياطين والآلام للقيام بفعل شيء أو عدم القيام بفعل أي شيء. وفي حال عدم استماعهم لي، فأنا قادر على اجبارهم على ما سيقومون به. ويحتاج العلماء لمراقبتي واكتشاف كيف يمكنني التفاعل معهم. وعندما يتفهم علم الطب هذه العملية، سيكون العلماء قادرون على اختراع آلات بالإمكانيات نفسها.

Once I see medical science start moving in this direction and assess their achievements, I will reveal more information so that they can perform more experiments and find out the answer of following question: Why do these angry and dangerous demons, diseases, and pains leave other bodies that they were damaging? How it is possible for one to keep them away from the body? What can I do to protect myself? I will reveal the answers to these questions when I see more research in this field.

Before I move forward, let me tell you a few things that will help you to understand the last topic of this book. There is no limit to the diseases or pains inside or around our bodies. Diseases and pains are parasites. They do not easily leave our bodies. They need mediums like our bodies all the time. Diseases and pains do not control our minds by hypnotism. They do not fight with each other. They share our wounds, injuries, and damages with each other.

On the other hand, demons are not parasites. They share the food in our house or around us. Several demons live in our houses, cars, and workplaces. Usually, they do not travel with us, or only one will usually travel with us. They do not stay inside our bodies all the time. They are in and out all the time. They usually live in the least used, darkest, quietest areas of houses. If they are not inside us, then they are either flying in air or flying around us. Usually, one demon is inside our body at one time. Remember two basic rules or habits of demons: (1) If they feel a little bit insecure inside specific bodies, they will jump to most secure bodies immediately, and (2) most of the time, demons are very attached primary persons or animals. Consequently, even if one goes to a second body, it will try to use that second body to stay close to its primary body.

Are demons part of the problems between men and women? A demon inside or around the body of a woman is able to sense danger long before the woman does. Around a man, there are three kinds of women. One kind of woman is not scared of some specific man at all, like a mother; grandmother; elder sister; old, bossy woman boss;

وعندما أرى تقدم علم الطب في هذا المجال ونقيم انجازاتهم، سأذكر المزيد من المعلومات حتى يتمكنوا من اجراء المزيد من التجارب واكتشاف الجواب للسؤال التالي: لماذا تغادر تلك الشياطيين والأمراض والآلام الغاضبة والخطيرة الأجسام التي يتم تدميرها؟ وكيف يكون ذلك ممكناً لأي شخص ابقائهم بعيداً عن الجسم؟ وما الذي يمكنني فعله لحماية نفسي؟ وسأقوم بذكر الأجوبة لتلك الأسئلة عندما أرى المزيد من الأبحاث في هذا المجال.

قبل أن أنتقل، اسمحولي أن أخبركم بعض الأشياء التي تساعدك على فهم الموضوع الأخير من هذا الكتاب. لا يوجد هناك أي قيود على الأمراض والآلام داخل أو حول الأجسام. وتعد الأمراض والآلام من الطفيليات. ولا يغادرون الأجسام بتلك السهولة. ويحتاجون الى وسط ناقل كأجسامنا طوال الوقت. ولا تسيطر الأمراض والآلام على عقولنا عن طريق التنويم. ولا يتقاتلون مع بعضهم البعض. ويتاركون جراحنا والأضرار مع بعضهم البعض.

ومن ناحية اخرى، لا تعتبر الشياطيين من الطفيليات. فهم يتشاركون الطعام في منازلنا أو من حولنا وتعيش العديد من الشياطيين في منازلنا وسياراتنا وأماكن عملنا. وفي العادة، لا ينتقلون معنا، أو يقوم واحد منهم فقط التنقل معنا. ولا يبقون داخل أجسامنا طوال الوقت. فهم في داخل وخارج أجسامنا معاً طوال الوقت. وعادة ما يعيشون في البيوت الأكثر هدوءً الأقل استخداماً والأكثر ظلمة. وفي حال عدم تواجدهم داخل أجسامنا، فإما أن يكونوا طائرين في الهواء أو من حولنا. وعادة، يكون هناك شيطان واحدة داخل أجسامنا في ذات الوقت. وتذكر قاعدتين أساسيتي أو عادتين للشياطيين: (1) في حال شعور الشياطيين بعد الأمان ولو قليلاً داخل جمس معين، سيقفزون الى اجسام أكثر أمناً مباشرة، و(2) في معظم الأوقات، تكون الشياطيين ملتحقة بشخص أو حيوان رئيسي. وبالتالي، حتى في حال انتقالهم الى شخص آخر، ستحاول الشياطيين استخدام الجسم الثاني للبقاء بالقرب من الجسم الرئيسي.

هل تعتبر الشياطيين جزءً في المشاكل الحاصلة بين الرجاء والنساء؟ إن الشياطيين المتواجدة داخل أو حول جسم المرأة يكون قادراً على الإحساس بالخطر قبل أن تشعر المرأة به بفترة. وحول الرجل، هناك ثلاثة أنواع من النساء. فهناك نوع لا يخشى الرجال أبداً، كالأم مثلاً أو الجدة أو الأخت الكبيرة أو المرأة الكبيرة في العمر أو المتسلطة،

or someone who is really not a good-looking woman. I hope you will be able to understand, regardless of whether you're a man or a woman, why we feel too much attraction for someone, even if they are not too much different in looks. Sometimes we have some ugly people around us. And even we have no attraction for them. Or we do not want to close to them. But suddenly, either dream or some time just thought, come to over mind, if we need to kiss or hug (or more) with that person? We all know, we all immediately reject that idea and almost in response almost every day say "what the hell, I am thinking?: So, this is not us. This is either our demons or that ugly person's demons. Regardless two of those people do not like each other, but maybe their demons like each other. That's why maybe they are trying to use two bodies. I am not saying that we do not have feelings or emotions, but behind all pushes and extreme conditions, demons are always involved. If you feel too much of anything, just try to control yourself. You just need a little bit of practice. You will observe that your extreme behaviors will slowly change in all matters concerning your life.

[[insert picture 001 here]]

Regardless if that man stays around those kinds of women for any amount of time, the demons from those kinds of women do not feel insecure about that man. Demons do not come out from the bodies of those women and do not jump on the bodies of these men. Those women are not scared of these men, so their demons feel more secure in the bodies of those women.

Second case: when a scary woman is in a room and a strange man is in that room, if the overall atmosphere is scary and dangerous, regardless of how long a demon is inside or around the body of that girl or woman, as soon as those demons around/inside the woman will feel a little bit insecure, they will not from these. They will look for the most secure bodies around them. And in that situation, that man is strongest person. The demons from that woman will jump on the body of the man. If the situation calms down and nothing bad

او أي امرأة حقيقةً لا يوجد لديها جمال المنظر. وأتمنى بأن تكونوا قادرين على تفهمي بغض النظر عن كونك رجلاً أو امرأة، ولماذا نشعر بجاذبية كبيرة لشخص ما حتى لو أن هذا الشخص لا يبدو مختلفاً في المنظر؟ أحياناً هناك بعض الأشخاص القبيحين من حولنا. ولا يوجد جاذبية لهم. أو لا نريد الاقتراب منهم. ولكن فجأة، إما حلماً أو أحياناً فكرة تخطر على البال، أننا بحاجة الى تقبيل أو حضن (أو اكثر) ذلك الشخص؟ وجميعنا يعلم، بأننا مباشرة نرفض تلك الفكرة وربما نرد بالقول: "ما الذي أفكر به بحق الجحيم؟" لذلك هذا ليس نحن. فإما ان يكون هذا شياطيننا أو شياطين ذلك الشخص القبيح المنظر. بغض النظر عن عدم رغبة شخصيين اثنين لبعضهما البعض، ولكن ربما يرغب شياطينهما ببعضهما البعض. لذلك الشبب ربما يحاولون استغلال كلا الجسمين. ولا أقول بأننا لا نشعر أو نتعاطف، ولكن وراء كل دافع والظروف المتطرفة دائماً ما تتدخل الشياطين. وفي حال شعورك بشيء ما كثيراً، فقط حاول السيطرة على أنفسهم. وتحتاج أيضاً فقط الى القليل من التدريب. وستلاحظ بأن تصرفاتك المتطرفة ستتغير ببطء في جميع مناحي الحياة الخاصة بك.

[[قم بإدخال الصورة 001 هنا]]

وبغض النظر عن بقاء ذلك الرجل حول تلك الأنواع من النساء للحظة من الوقت، فإن شياطين تلك الأنواع من النساء تشعر بالأمان باتجاه ذلك الرجل. ولا تخرج الشياطيين من أجسام تلك النساء ولا تقفز الى أجسام هؤلاء الرجال. ولا تخاف تلك النساء من هؤلاء الرجال، لذلك تشعر الشياطيين بالمزيد من الأمان في أجسام تلك النساء.

أما الحالة الثانية: عندما تكون امرأة خائفة في غرفة مع تواجد شخص غريب وفي حال كان الجو العام مخيف وخطير بغض النظر عن مدة تواجد الشيطان في داخل أو حول جسم تلك البنت او المرأة، ولطالما ستشعر تلك الشياطين في داخل أو حول المرأة/البنت بعدم الأمان قليلاً، سيقومون بالبحث عن أجسام اكثر أماناً من حولهم. وفي تلك الحالة، يكون ذلك الرجل الشخص الأقوى. وستقوم الشياطيين بالقفز من تلك المرأة الى جسم ذلك الرجل. وفي حال هدوء الوضع ولا يوجد أي شيء سيء

happens around them, some demons in that room will jump on the body of that woman in the room. Now that man has an extra demon around him or inside him from that woman. The demons from that woman cannot go back to that woman's body because new demons already possess that body now. Especially when new demon is more powerful.

Usually, demons are very involved with their own humans or animals. Always remember that demons came out from some other body. Even though they moved to new bodies, they still do not forget about the previous people or animals they possessed. In this case when a demon was originally in the body of a woman for long time but is now inside the body of a man, this demon will keep hypnotizing or pushing that man to think about the woman all the time. So, demon can keep that man close to that woman.

Do not ever think the approach of a demon is ever positive. By nature, they are negative, and they like negative activities. That man may have been okay before this demon from the woman penetrated his body, but now that demon will continuously hypnotize and push that man to keep thinking about this woman. I am not saying that men are faultless or blameless, but that demon is very responsible of intensifying the situation between that man and woman.

In another case, imagine few women are in the room, regardless of whether there is one or ten—same thing, in the same room—and there is one man or there are five men. In this case, I am not talking about insecure feelings for any demon. But those men are continuously watching and thinking about at least one woman all the time. In this case, demons from the woman's body penetrate a particular man's body and insist they keep thinking about that particular woman. Even woman is sitting totally unaware of some particular man. But either demon from woman or demon from both decide to bring them together. In that case regardless ten women are sitting in that room but one particular man is just worried about only one particular woman at that time. If man is thinking about only one particular

يحدث حولهم، ستقوم بعض الشياطين المتواجدة في الغرفة بالقفز الى داخل جسم تلك المرأة الموجود في الغرفة. والآن لدى الرجل شيطان زائد حوله أو داخل جسمه مقارنةً بالمرأة. ولا يمكن للشياطين التي كانت متواجدة داخل المرأة العودة الى جسمها لأن الشياطين الجديدة قامت بالسيطرة على جسمها الآن. وخاصة عندما يكون الشيطان الجديد أكثر قوة.

وفي العادة، تتدخل الشياطين بالبشر أو الحيوانات التي يسيطرون عليهم. وتذكر دائماً بأن تأتي من أجسام أخرى. على الرغم من تنقلها للجسم الجديد، إلا أنها لا تزل تتذكر الأشخاص السابقين الذين سيطروا عليهم من قبل. وفي هذه الحالة، عندما يكون شيطان ما دخل جسم امرأة في الأصل لفترة طويلة لكنه الآن داخل جسم رجل، سيقوم هذا الشيطان بتنويم الرجل مغناطيسياً أو دفعه عن تلك المرأة طوال اليوم. لذلك، يبقي شيطان ذلك الرجل قريباً من تلك المرأة.

لا تفكر أبداً بطريقة الشيطان أنه ليس ايجابي. فهو، بطبيعته، سلبي ويحب الأعمال السلبية. وربما لكان ذلك الرجل بحالة جيدة قبل أن يتغلغل الشيطان من تلك المرأة الى جسمه، ولكن الآن يقوم الشيطان بشكل مستمر من تنويم ذلك الرجل مغناطيسياً ودفعه للاستمرار في التفكير بتلك المرأة لا أقول بأن الرجل غير مذنب أو لا يلام، ولكن يعد ذلك الشيطان مسؤولاً عن تكثيف الوضع وتسخينه بين ذلك الرجل وتلك المرأة.

وفي حالة أخرى، تخيل عدة نساء في غرفة بغض النظر عن وجود شيء أو عشرة أشياء في نفس الغرفة وهناك رجل أو خمسة رجال. وفي هذه الحالة، لا أتكلم عن المشاعر الغير آمنة لأي شيطان. ولكن يقوم هؤلاء الرجال باستمرار مراقبة والتفكير بمرأة واحدة على الأقل. لذلك يتغلغل كل شيطان من تلك النساء الى جسم رجل واحدة ويجعلهم يفكرون بمرأة معينة. حتى لو كانت المرأة جالسة وغير مدركة وغير مهتمة لرجل معين. ولكن إما شيطان المرأة أو شيطان الرجل هو من أراد أن يقربهما من بعضهما. وبغض النظر عن تواجد عشر نساء ولكن رجل واحد فقط يفكر وقلق بشأن امرأة واحدة . وفي حال تفكير الرجل بامرأه واحدة فقط

woman, demon is involved in this. But if man is thinking about all ten women, then demon from woman is not involve in this activity. When a particular man is thinking and observing all ten women then, demon of that particular man is involved in all this activity.

In this and the previous situations, I do not know what these demons get out of these trade-offs. But this is their hobby. They hypnotize us and push us to act in negative ways. I do not know what they get from all that, but their influence does create and spread more negativism. However, you can reverse this situation with discipline and practice.

Whenever we feel strongly pushed toward a man or a woman, when we feel too much love or too much hate toward someone, when we just want to eat something immediately, when we just have a desire to have sex as soon as possible, remember that demons 99 percent responsible for all of these impulses!

What are some cures for the problems caused by demons?

At that time, I refused to believe that there was something invisible around me. Honestly, I had no clue about demons at that time. I still thought that I had some problems. I was just experiencing demons then. There were no diseases or pains or sicknesses around me. I was sensing and feeling only a burning sensation at this point. Once I moved from a particular place or area, the pain or sickness usually subsided. Most of the time, those burning feelings moved with me wherever I stayed close. Life was horrible at that time. At that time, I experienced this burning in only a few places, but most of the time, I was relaxed, especially after I moved away from those places, such as my office, behind the counter at the store in Columbus, and my garage, where I used to exercise. I had no problems in other places. In my garage, I suffered from that burning sensation after twenty to twenty-five minutes.

فإن الشيطان المسؤول عن ذلك، وفي حال كان الرجل يفكر في جميع النساء العشر، فإن شيطان المرأة ليس له أي علاقة. وعندما يقوم رجل معين بالتفكير ومراقبة النساء العشر فإن شيطان ذلك الرجل هو المسؤول عن أفعاله.

وفي هذه الحالة والحالات السابقة، لا أعلم ما الذي تجنيه تلك الشياطين من هذه المقايضات. ولكن هذه هي هواياتهم. حي يقومون بتنويمنا مغناطيسياً ودفعنا للتصرف بطرق سلبية. ولا أعلم ما الذي يجنيه الجن من ذلك كله، ولكن تأثيرهم يتسبب في نشر المزيد من السلبية. علاوة على ذلك، يمكنك عكس هذا الوضع بالانضباط والتدريب.

عندما نشعر بأننا منجذبين باتجاه رجل أو امرأة بقوة، ونشعر بالكثير من الحب أو الكراهية اتجاه شخص ما وعندما نريد أن نأكل شيئاً ما فوراً وعندما يكون لدينا رغبة في ممارسة الجنس بأقرب وقت ممكن، تذكر بأن الشياطيين مسؤولة عن ذلك بنسبة 99% عن تلك الدفعات.

ما علاج المشاكل التي تسببها الشياطيين؟

في ذلك الوقت، رفضت بأن هناك شيئاً ما غير مرئي من حولي. وبصراحة، لم أكن أعلم بشأن الشياطيين في تلك الأوقات. وكنت لا أزال أفكر بأنني أعاني من بعض المشاكل. وكنت أواجه الشياطيين في حينه. ولم يكن هناك أمراض أو آلام من حولي. وكنت أشعر وأحس بالحرقة في تلك الفترة. وعندما انتقلت الى مكان معين أو منطقة، فإن الآلام والأمراض تهدأ. وفي معظم الأوقات، انتقلت هذه الحرقة معي أينما أقطن. وكانت حياتي رهيبة في حينه. وواجهت هذه الحرقة فقط في بضع أماكن، ولكن في معظم الأوقات كنت هادئاً وخاصة بعد أن انتقلت بعيداً عن تلك الأماكن كالمكتب خلف طاولة الاستقبال في كولومبس، ومرابي حيث كنت أتدرب. وفي المراب، عانيت من احساس بالحرقة بعد عشرين الى خمسة وعشرين دقيقة.

And once that burning started, there was no way to stay where I was. When I would come back inside the house, the burning would stop, and I was okay after that; however, after a while, the burning started moving with me from my garage. Once I made it to the restroom, I left okay. This was happening every day. By that time, I was extremely scared all the time, especially of going to a few places. I was always surprised whenever I went behind the counter at the store in Columbus and I was unable to stand there because of this burning, and my cashiers and customers were perfectly all right. I used to watch their faces to see if I could feel any kind of problem, but they seemed normal. Usually I was okay when I was working, but as soon as I got ready to leave the office, the burning would start again. And I literally ran from that office so many times that I started leaving office door unlocked. That fire burning was playing with me. I was scared of these invisible attacks from invisible creatures and they were scaring me. After a while, the same problem started occurring in my dressing room. Usually, nothing happened for a few minutes, but as soon as I started changing, the burning would make me run from the room.

One day, I was driving toward Hellettsville from Eagle Lake when I saw that I needed some gas. Just before Hellettsville on the right side on Highway 90A, there was a small CITGO gas station. I parked my car by the gas pump and went outside. As soon as I stepped outside my car, my whole body immediately started burning. I jumped back inside my car to save myself from the fire. I was okay once I got back inside the car. That was the first time I had experienced the burning problems outside of my house and business. I was really scared to get out of my car again. I don't remember how long I stayed parked there or how I got gas and left from that place. But in that moment, I decided to discuss my problem with someone, maybe even a doctor.

I started searching for religious and spiritual people who could help me. But I soon learned that even the people who claimed that they knew a lot about the demon world were just talk. I could not find a single person who could help me—nobody. My family was not

وعندما بدأت الحرقة، لم يكن لدي أي خيار للبقاء في ذلك المكان. وعندما كنت أعود الى المنزل، كانت الحرقة تتوقف وكنت على ما يرام بعدها؛ علاوة على ذلك، بعدها بفترة بدأت الحرقة بالانتقال معي من المراب. وعندما وصلت الى غرفة النوم، شعرت بتحسن. وكان يحدث ذلك كل يوم. وكنت في حينه خائفاً جداً وخاصة من الذهاب الى بعض الأماكن. وكنت متفاجأ دائماً عندما أذهب الى الوقوف خلف طاولة الاستقبال في المتجر في مدينة كولومبس ولم أكن قادراً على الوقوف هناك بسبب الحرقة، كانوا زملائي أميني الصناديق والزبائن على ما يرام. وتعودت على مشاهدة وجوههم لرؤية إذا ما شعرت بأي نوع من المشاكل، ولكن كانوا يبدو لي طبيعيين. وعادة، كنت بخير عندما أعمل، ولكن طالما أستعد لمغادرة المكتب، تبدأ الحرقة مرة أخرى. وكنت أغادر المكتب مسرعاً في الحقيقة حتى أنني كنت أنسى الباب مفتوح. وكانت الحرقة تعبث معي ,لقد كنت خائفاً من تلك الهجمات الخفية من المخلوقات الخفية. وبعد غترة، بدأت تحدث نفي المشكلة معي في غرفة الملابس. وعادة، لم يحدث أي شيء لبضع دقائق، ولكن حالما بدأت بتغيير ملابسي، تجعلني الحرقة أن أغادر الغرفة مسرعاً.

وفي ذات مرة، كنت أقوم السيارة باتجاه هيليتسفيل قادماً ما ايجل ليك عندما شاهدت بأن السيارة تحتاج لملأها بالوقود. وقبل هيليتسفيل على الجانب الأيمن على الطريق السريع 90أي، كان هناك محطة وقود سيتغو. وأوقفت سيارتي بالقرب من مضخة الوقود وخرجت من السيارة. وحالما نزلت من السيارة، بدأ جسمي كله بالاحتراق. وقفزت الى داخل السيارة للحفاظ على جسمي من النيران. وأصبحت على ما يرام عندما دخلت السيارة مرة اخرى. كانت تلك المرة الأولى التي أتعرض فيها للحرقة خارج منزلي مكان عملي. وكنت حقاً خائفاً من الخروج من سيارتي مجدداً. ولا أتذكر كم هي المدة التي بقيت فيها واقفاً في المحطة وكيفية تعبئتي للسيارة بالوقود ومن ثم غادرت. ولكن في تلك اللحظة، قررت مناقشة مشكلتي مع شخص ما، وربما الطبيب حتى.

وبدأت بالبحث عن رجال الدين والروحانيين على أمل تقديم المساعدة لي. ولكن تعلمت بأن هؤلاء الأشخاص الذين يدعون بأنهم يعلمون الكثير عن عالم الشيطان كان هباءً. ولم أستطع العثور على شخص واحد يمكنه مساعدتي – لا أحد. ولم تكن عائلتي

aware of my problems. I knew someone who had a ranch at Oak Ridge, which was between Columbus and Weimar. I used to go there sometimes, but one time when I was there, I had an incident. Outside the building, the owners had few swing chairs in the open. I decided to sit down on one of them, but I had to jump from that chair as soon as I sat down. That chair was hot like an oven, and within seconds, the fire was inside my body. But once I moved away from that area, I was okay. After a few days, I went back to that ranch, and I sat down on the same chair; however, I didn't have any problems that day. Until that time, I was not ready to accept that I had some mental sickness or illness. I was not yet aware of the invisible world of demons at that time, and I didn't even think about that pain at all.

After few days, when I was leaving my house, I had to deal with this firestorm in my yard. I almost ran from my entrance to my car. I ran almost forty steps. After that day, I ran toward my car every day. I felt the fire burning my body everywhere, and that burning left clear sores all over my body. Those were pure demons, and my life would become hell once they came close to me. But they were not giving me any kind of sicknesses. That's why I always say that demons and diseases are two different things. The only commonality between them is that they are both invisible to the naked eye. Another incident happened when I was going to a bakery inside Savoy Shopping Center in Houston. I had an attack of fire again when I was leaving that bakery, and I had to deal with that problem until I got back to my house in Columbus. That was a pretty bad experience.

Nobody can imagine how scared I was at that time. Around then, my family decided to leave the country for a few months. Now I was alone in my house every night. I still was not ready to disclose my problems to anyone. I do not remember how many nights I just sat straight on one chair all night long without going in the different parts of the house. I didn't go close to any windows in my house. I just sat on one chair all night long and watched TV. In those days, I usually went to sleep around 9:00 a.m. in morning every day. I remember those nights when I was in my house all by myself, and at those times, I was the most terrified person in the whole world.

على علم بمشكلتي. وعرفت شخصاً كان له مزرعة في أوك ريج، بين مدينة كولومبس وويمار. وقد تعودت على الذهاب الى هناك أحياناً، ولكن في ذات مرة عندما كنت هناك، تعرضت لحادث. وخارج البناية، كان هناك مالكين لديهم القليل من كراسي سوينغ فب الخلاء. لذلك قررت الجلوس على احداها، ولكن كان علي القفز من تلك الكرسي حالما أجلس. وكان الكرسي حارة كالفرن، وخلال ثوان معدودة، كانت النار داخل جسمي. ولكن عندما أبعدت عن تلك المنطقة، كنت أشعر بخير. وبعد عدة أيام، عدت الى تلك المزرعة، وجلست على نفس الكرسي؛ علاوة على ذلك، لم أكن أعاني من أي مشاكل في ذلك اليوم. وحتى في حينه، لم أكن مستعداً لقبول أنني أعاني من أمراض عقلية. ولم أكن مدركاً للعالم الخفي للشياطيين في حينه، ولكن أكن حتى أفكر بذلك الألم مطلقاً.

وبعد عدة أيام، وعندما كنت مغادراً منزلي، كان علي أن أتعامل هذه العاصفة في الساحة الخاصة بمنزلي. وغالباً ما كنت أركض من مدخل البيت الى السيارة. تقدر المسافة بحوالي أربعين خطوة. وكنت أشعر بالحرقة في جميع أنحاء جسدي وخلفت الحرقة تقرحات واضحة في جميع أنحاء جسدي. وكانت تلك هي الشياطيين، وكانت حياتي كالجحيم عندما يقتربون مني. ولكن لم يكونوا يسببوا لي أي نوع من الأمراض. لذلك السبب دائماً ما كنت أقول بأن الشياطيين والأمراض مختلفان. إن الشيء الشائع والمشترك بينهم هو أنهما غير مرئيان ولا يمكن رؤيتهما بالعي المجردة. ووقع حادث عندما كنت ذاهباً الى مخبر في مركز سوفوي التسويقي في مدينة هيوستن الأمريكية. وتعرضت لهجوم من النار عندما كنت اغادر المخبر، وكان علي أن أتعامل مع تلك المشكلة حتى عودتي الى منزلي في كولومبس. وكانت تلك تجربة سيئة جداً.

ولا يمكن لأحد تخيل كم كنت خائفاً في حينه. وبعد ذلك، قررت عائلتي مغادرة المقاطعة لعدة أشهر. وكنت وحيداً في المنزل كل ليلة. ولم ان مستعداً لكشف مشاكلي لأحد. ولا أتذكر كم عدد الليالي التي جلست على الكرسي طوال الليل دون الذهاب الى أي زاوية من البيت. ولم أكن اذهب لإغلاق المنافذ في منزلي. وكنت أجلس على الكرسي طوال الليل وأشاهد التلفاز. وفي تلك الأيام، كنت أخلد للنوم حوالي الساعة 9:00 صباحاً كل يوم. وأتذكر تلك الليالي عندما كنت في منزلي لوحدي، وفي تلك الأوقات كنت بأنني أكثر شخص مرتعداً في العالم كله.

134

In those days, I used to have a friend with whom I discussed my problems, but that friend eventually left me. After that, I decided not to disclose everything to anyone. I suffered like that for several months, and the pain was getting worse and worse day by day. Wherever I went, I had to deal with that firestorm, and I had no choice about it. My body hurt all the time because of this burning sensation. During those days, I prayed to God and kept asking the following questions: "What is going on with me? How will I live my life like this?" Then, one night, I had a dream. Someone guided me in how to talk or communicate with those firestorms whenever they were hurting me. I needed to follow these instructions. That was the turning point in my life. I was shocked and surprised. I could communicate for the first time with these firestorms. As I said earlier, I was facing even more challenges each day, even. I am revealing only 1 to 5 percent of the incidents in this book.

Anyway, when I started communicating with them, they were more surprised than I was. Each day, I had to deal with different kinds of demons. Almost everyone was surprised. Some were convinced immediately, and some took a few days to convince. Until that point, I had been very unhappy because of these burning effects. Finally, I started complaining about how much I would get hurt when they came close to me. Most of them quit coming close to me after that, but then I didn't know if they were around me or not. Plus, when I had to deal with new demons, they still burned me. They did not listen to me until they became my friends, but during that period, that burning was killing me. I was complaining every day, and finally, the burning changed to a real touch. And from that day forward, I did not feel any burning. I could feel demons like a human touch on my body. I could sense them exactly like I could sense a human's touch.

Every day, I learned new things from them. They were feeding me all kinds of information through hypnotism. But even though they were acting friendly or becoming friendlier after a few days, the feeling that a thirty-foot-tall demon was around me kept me somewhat scared most of the time.

وكان لدي صديق كنت أناقش مشاكلي معه، ولكنه تركني. وبعدها، قررت عدم كشف أي شيء لأحد. وعانيت من ذلك لعدة شهور، وكان الألم يزداد سوءً يوماً بعد يوم. وأينما كنت أذهب، كان علي التعامل مع تلك العاصفة من الحرقة لوم يكن لدي أي خيار بشأن ذلك، وكان جسدي يؤلمني طوال الوقت بسبب هذه الحرقة. وخلال تلك الأيام، كنت أصلِ لله أطلب منه الأسئلة التالية: "ما الذي يحدث معي؟" كيف يمكنني العيش في مثل هذا الوضع؟" ومن ثم، في ذات ليلة، كان لدي حلم. حيث أرشدني شخص حول كيفية التحدث أو التواصل مع تلك الحرقة عندما يؤذونني. واحتجت الى اتباع تلك التعليمات. وكان ذلك نقطة تحول في حياتي. وكنت مصدوماً متفاجأ. وكان يمكنني التواصل مع تلك الحرقة لأول مرة. وكما أسلفت سابقاً، كنت أواجه المزيد من التحديات كل يوم، وقد ذكرت ما نسبته 1-5 بالمئة من الحوادث في ذلك الكتاب.

وعلى أية حال، عندما بدأت بالتواصل معهم، كانوا متفاجئين أكثر مما كنت أنا. وفي كل يوم، كان علي التعامل مع أنواع مختلفة من الشياطين. وكان معظم الأشخاص متفاجئين. وقد اقتنع البعض بشكل مباشر، وبعضهم استغرق عدة أيام للاقتناع. وحتى في تلك النقطة، كنت غير سعيداً بسبب تأثيرات الحرقة. وفي النهاية، بدأت بالاشتكاء بشان مدى الالم الذي أشعر به عند اقترابها مني. ولكن بعدها لم أعلم إذا ما كانوا حولي أم لا. بالإضافة الى ذلك، عندما كان علي التعامل مع شياطيين جديدة، كان يحرقونني. ولم يكونوا يستمعون إلي حتى يصبحوا أصدقائي. ولكن أثناء تلك الفترة، كانت الحرقة تقتلني. وكنت أشتكي منها كل يوم. وفي النهاية، تغيرت الحرقة الى لمس حقيقي. ومنذ ذلك الوقت، لم أشعر بأي حرقة وكنت أشعر بالشياطيين كلمسة الإنسان على جسدي. وكنت أحس بهم بالضبط كما أحسس بلمسة إنسان.

وكل يوم، تعلمت أشياء جديدة منهم. وكانوا يغدونني بجميع أنواع المعلومات من خلال التنويم المغناطيسي. ولكن على الرغم من أنهم كانوا يتصرفون بودية وأصبحوا اكثر أصدقاءً بعد عدة أيام، كان الشعور بشيطان يبلغ طوله ثلاثين قدماً يخيفني في معظم الأوقات.

135

And then things changed one day. Suddenly, I was able to see them all around me. I was surprised to see them, but they were more surprised that I could see them than I was. With more and more time and experience, I learned that they did not look like the ones we see in pictures or movies. They are just very small, flying objects of different shapes with the power of hypnosis and the power to possess bodies. Once I started seeing them, life became very easy. I was no longer scared. I learned a lot about demons during this period. I still learn new things about them every day, and I am sure that I will keep learning new things from them all the time. But I chose to write this book so I could share my knowledge with everyone and normal people could know more about them. My communication skills also developed further every day. Then I learned how to convince these demons to leave bodies. Then I learned how to insist that they leave certain bodies if they were not listening to me. This all seemed very crazy, but it was happening. After demons, I started dealing with different kinds of pains, diseases, and sickness. I learned something new, and I did not think there would be an end to learning about invisible world.

Remember that demons and diseases are different. Demons live around us or in our house or on trees, and they do not create pain, sickness, and disease. They hypnotize us to control us, use us in the way they desire, and show us dreams. Some demons live inside our bodies and create certain sicknesses within us like migraines, high and low blood pressure, anxiety attacks, bipolar disorders, and mental illnesses, among others.

But the third kind includes pure diseases, pains, and sicknesses. These are just like invisible animals or poisonous reptiles or insects. They are the main creators of pains, sicknesses, and diseases inside our body. But up to certain limit, all demons and diseases listen to me most of the time. Controlling them is very easy if the bodies or organs are not damaged or if the person is taking the proper medication and the healing process has begun. It can still be easy if damages are more

وفي يوم من الأيام تغيرت الكثير من الأشياء. وفجأة، كنت قادراً على رؤية جميع الشياطيين من حولي. وكنت مندهشاً لرؤيتهم، ولكن كانوا هم أكثر اندهاشاً بشأن قدرتي على رؤيتهم. وبعد وقت والمزيد من التجربة، علمت أنهم لا يشبهون الذين نراهم في الصور أو الأفلام. فهم صغيرو الحجم وأجسام طائرة بأشكال مختلفة ذوي قوة تنويم مغناطيسي وقوة السيطرة على الأجسام. وعندما بدأت برؤيتهم، أصبحت حياتي أسهل بكثير. ولم أعد أخاف، وتعلمت الكثير عن الشياطيين خلال هذه الفترة. وما زلت أتعلم أشياء جديدة كل يوم، وأنا متأكد بأنني سأبقى أتعلم منهم طوال الوقت. ولكن اخترت أن أقوم بكتابة هذا الكتاب حتى أقوم بمشاركة معرفتي مع الجميع والأشخاص العاديين لمعرفة المزيد عنهم. وتتطور مهارات اتصالي بالشياطيين كل يوم. لذلك تعلمت كيفية اقناع تلك الشياطيين على مغادرة الأجسام. ومن ثم تعلمت كيفية اجبارهم على مغادرة أجسام معينة في حال عدم سماعهم لي. ويبدو هذا نوعاً من الجنون، ولكنه كان يحدث معي. وبعد الشياطيين، بدأت بالتعامل مع شيء جديد، ولم أكن أعتقد بأنه سيكون هناك نهاية للتعلم حيال العالم الخفي.

وتذكر بأن الشياطيين والأمراض تختلف عن بعضها البعض. حيث تعيش الشياطيين حولنا أو في منازلنا أو على الأشجار، ولا يسببون الآلام أو الأمراض. فهم يقومون بتنويمنا مغناطيسياً والسيطرة علينا، ويستخدموننا بالطريقة التي يرغبون أن يستخدمونا بها ويرونا الأحلام. وتعيش بعض الشياطيين داخل أجسامنا ويسببون امراضاً معينة مثل الصداع النصفي وارتفاع أو انخفاض ضغط الدم ونوبات الغضب والاضطرابات الثنائي القطبية والأمراض العقلية غيرها الكثير.

ولكن يشتمل النوع الثالث على الأمراض الصافي والآلام والسقم. وتلك هي حيوانات غير مرئية أو زواحف سامة أو حشرات. فهم المسببون الرئيسيون للآلام والامراض داخل أجسامنا. ولكن الى حد معين، تستمع الشياطيين لي في معظم الأوقات. والتحكم بهم سهل جداً في حال أن الاجسام غير تالفة أو في حال كان الشخص يتناول الأدوية الصحيحة وبدأ بعملية التعافي. ويمكن أن تكون أيضاً سهلة في حال كانت الأضرار أكثر

extensive, but new discascs may inhabit those damaged bodies after the previous ones leave.

However, I only have control over external negative energies, such as demons, diseases, pains, and sickness. Damages these leave inside the body or organs need either positive healing energies or medications or surgeries. If these measures are not taken, new negative energies will come to those bodies and will start living/eating and damaging their hosts even more. For a long time, I thought I could fix only headaches. So, I started doing experiments on different people. I had no confidence in what I was doing or what I was saying at all. All this was so crazy and unbelievable that even I had hard time believing that it was actually happening. My procedure was very simple. I asked people which kinds of pains they had. Then I closed my eyes and communicated with the pain. Most of the time, the pains listened to me and left those bodies. If they did not listen and stayed in those bodies, I would have to insist that they leave the bodies. The insisting process is usually short, but sometimes, it depends on the nature of the pain and sickness. As I said, I once thought I could fix only headaches. One time, a person asked me if I could help his mother with a continuous pain in her left arm, but I told him that I could only remove headaches. Once I removed a migraine pain from one employee in Columbus for the very first time. She had been in the hospital for four days because of migraine pain. She came back to work after several days. She was working, but she was still sick. At around 4:00 p.m., the store maintenance person mentioned her sickness and told me that she had already taken six Advils in last three hours; however, her migraine pain was still getting worse. I asked him to ask her if she would let me attempt to help her with her migraine. I asked the maintenance person to stay with me. I went to cashier counter and closed my eyes and asked to the migraine pain to come out of her head. During this, the maintenance man kept laughing because it looked funny and crazy to him. When I asked her about her pain, she was surprised after few seconds. She just said, "It is weird, but most of the pain is gone. But there is still some left over." I communicated with the pain one more time, and she was okay after

كثافة، ولكن ربما تقوم أمراض جديدة بالعيش في تلك الأجسام التالف بعد مغادرة الأمراض السابقة.

علاوة على ذلك، لدي فقط السيطرة على الطاقات السلبية الخارجية كالشياطين والأمراض والآلام. وتحتاج الأضرار إما طاقات تعافي سلبية أو أدوية أو عمليات جراحية. في حال عدم إتباع تلك الإجراءات، ستأتي طاقات سلبية جديدة الى تلك الأجسام وستبدأ بالعيش وأكل وتدمير مضيفهم بشكل أكبر. ولفترة طويلة، اعتقدت أنه بإمكاني علاج الصداع فقط. لذلك، بدأت بإجراء تجارب على أشخاص مختلفين. ولم يكن لدي الثقة في ما كنت أفعله أو ما كنت أقوله مطلقاً. وكان ذلك كله نوعاً من الجنون ولا يمكن تصديقه حتى أنني واجهت أوقاتاً عصيبة لتصديق ما كان يحدث معي. وكانت خطواتي بسيطة جداً. وسألت أشخاصاً أي نوع من الآلام التي كانوا يعانون منها. وفي معظم الأوقات، كانوا يستمعون إلي ويغادروا (الأمراض) أجسام هؤلاء الأشخاص. وفي حال عدم استماعهم وبقائهم داخل أجسامهم، كنت أجبر هم على مغادرة الأجسام. وهذه العملية قصيرة. ولكن أحياناً، تعتمد على طبيعة الألم والمرض. وكما قلت سابقاً، اعتقدت لولهة من الزمن بأنه بإمكاني علاج الصداع فقط. وفي ذات مرة، سألتني شخص حول قدرتي على مساعدة أمه لعلاج ألم مستمر في ذراعها الأيسر، ولكن أخبرته بأنه يمكنني فقط علاج الصداع. وقد أزلت ألم الصداع النصفي من أحد زملائي الموظفين في كولومبس للمرة الأولى. وكانت موجودة في المشفى لأربعة أيام بسبب ألم الصداع النصفي. وعادت للعمل بعد عدة أيام. وكانت تعمل على الرغم من أنها كانت ما زالت مريضة. وفي حوالي الساعة 4 عصراً، أخبرتني مختصة الصيانة في المتجر بأنها قامت بتناول ستة حبات من الأدفلن في اخر ثلاث ساعات. علاوة على ذلك، كان الم الصداع النصفي عندها يزداد سوءً. وسألته بالاستفسار منها إذا ما أرادت السماح لي بالمحاولة في مساعدتها في علاج ألم الصداع النصفي الذي تعاني منه. وطلبت من متخصصة الصيانة في المتجر بالبقاء معي. وذهبت الى طاولة أمين الصندوق واغلقت عيني وطلبت من ألم الصداع النصفي بالخروج من رأسها. وأثناء ذلك، ضحك متخصص الصيانة لأن ذلك بدا مضحكا ونوعاً من الجنون بالنسبة له. وعندما سألتها عن الألم، كانت مندهشة بعد عدة ثوانٍ. وقالت فقط: "هذا شيءٌ غريب، ولكن جزء كبير من الألم قد اختفى ولكن هناك القليل منه." وتواصل مع الألم لمزيد من الوقت. وكانت على ما يرام بعد

the second try. I was really happy that day, because that had been my first experiment with migraine pain and I had been successful. After a few months, she called me one more time because of some migraine pain, but by that time, I was able to communicate with her migraine pain over the telephone. Even then it was easy to remove her migraine pain when I was on the phone with her. Her case was very easy because she had been continuously taking medication for migraines. After that, I just started trying to fix pains or sicknesses wherever I encountered them.

Most things in the invisible world are parasites, and they need mediums to live. However, demons are not parasites. Demons live around us. Demons share our food in different ways, but demons are not parasites. Other than demons, the rest of the invisible world are invisible reptiles and mostly invisible insects, and they are all parasites. If these invisible parasites are vegetarian, they live around and inside the trees and eat parts of the trees. If invisible parasites are carnivorous, then they live inside animals or humans. Even demons, when they are outside bodies, are very small in size, but demons have the ability to expand themselves to spread out into any host body. Compared to demons, diseases and pains are much smaller. All diseases and pains need mediums or bodies to live and eat. They live on or inside our bodies, and they do not share our food. They eat our body parts and organs. We have studied parasites in trees and human bodies but only those that are visible. Like all other parasites, these invisible diseases and sicknesses do not care how much they hurt us, how much they damage us, and how much they make us sick, because they are cruel like other parasites. The only problem with invisible diseases and sicknesses is that they are not visible. That's why we are more susceptible to their damages.

Once I figured out that I was able to communicate with migraine pain, I decided to inform my older sister, who lived outside of the United States. I tried to explain to her what I was capable of doing. She listened to me very carefully and asked me, "How long have you been suffering from that problem?" I was pretty much ready for that.

المحاولة الثانية. وكنت سعيداً ذلك اليوم لأنها كانت تجربتي الأولى لعلاج الصداع النصفي وكانت تجربة ناجحة. وبعد عدة شهور، اتصلت بي مجدداً بسبب معاناتها من ألم الصداع النصفي، ولكن في ذلك الوقت كنت قادراً على التواصل مع ألمها عن طريق الهاتف. وكان من السهل ازالة ألم الصداع النصفي الذي كانت تعاني منه. وكانت عمليتها سهلة جداً لأنها كانت تتناول الأدوية باستمرار. وبعد ذلك، بدأت بمحاولة علاج آلام أو أمراض أينما أواجهها.

تعد الكثير من الأشياء في العالم الخفي من الطفيليات، ويحتاجون الى وسط ناقل للعيش. علاوة على ذلك، لا تعتبر الشياطين من الطفيليات. فهم يعيشون حولنا. ويشاركوننا كعامنا بطرق مختلفة، لكن معظمهم ليس من الطفيليات. أما باقي كائنات العالم الخفي كالزواحف الخفية والحشرات الخفية تعد من الطفيليات. وفي حال كانت تلك الطفيليات الخفية نباتية، فإنهم سيعيشون حول وداخل الأشجار وتأكل أجزاء منها. وفي حال كونها من اللواحم، فإنها ستعيش داخل الحيوانات والإنسان. وحتى الشياطين، عندما يكونون خارج اجسامنا، يكونوا بأحجام صغيرة جداً، ولكن يكون لديهم القدرة على التمدد للانتشار داخل الجسم المضيف. مقارنةً مع الشياطين، تعد الأمراض والآلام أصغر حجماً بكثير. حيث تحتاج جميع الأمراض والآلام الى وسط ناقل أو أجسام للعيش فيها ولأكلها. فهم يعيشون داخل اجسامنا ولا يشاركونا الطعام. فهم يأكلون اجسامنا. وقمنا بدراسة الطفيليات التي تعيش على الأشجار وجسم الإنسان ولكن تلك كانت مرئية ويمكن رؤيتها بالعين المجردة. وكغيرها من الطفيليات، لا تهتم الأمراض بمدى إيذائها لنا أو تدميرنا أو جعلنا مرضى لأنهم قاسيون كغيرهم من الطفيليات. وإن المشكلة الوحيدة للأمراض أنها غير مرئية. لذلك السبب نكون اكثر عرضة للتدمير الذي يسببونه.

وعندما اكتشفت بأنني قادر على التواصل مع ألم الصداع النصفي، قررت إبلاغ أختي الأكبر التي كانت تعيش خارج الولايات المتحدة. وحاولت الشرح لها حول قدرتي. واستمعت إلي بكل حرص وسألتني، "كم من الوقت استغرقت وأنت تعاني من هذه المشكلة؟" وكنت مستعداً لذلك بشكل جيد.

Next, she mentioned that I had a daughter and that I should not disclose this problem to anyone else. She also wanted me to go to a doctor for checkup. After her speech, I tried to change the subject. I asked her if she had any pain in her body. First, she flatly refused to be a part of my experiment, but when I insisted, she mentioned that she had always had a pain in her right arm. I put her on hold and tried to communicate with her shoulder pain. After exactly two minutes, I asked her if she felt any difference. At first, she immediately said no, but just after that, she started saying that she felt weird, like the pain was moving from one place to another. Almost a minute later, she said that 60 percent of the pain was gone, but she still had some. I put her on hold again. This time, I communicated with her pain for almost one minute. When I talked to her then, she was extremely surprised and shocked. She said she had had that pain for several years and that she had been taking painkillers too. Then she started telling me about the different pains her kids suffered from. That day, I learned that I was able to communicate with shoulder pain as well.

That was just the beginning. At that time, I was not aware that all these invisible pains and sicknesses would come behind me. Before that, I was dealing with demons only, so I was not experiencing any pains or sicknesses because I was surrounded by demons. But dealing with pains and diseases was a different business. Diseases and pains need bodies or mediums. They are not going to keep flying in the air. They leave one body and jump into the next one immediately. At that time, I never had any problems because I did not have any pains and sicknesses the way I do right now. After a few days, I tried talking to my younger sister, but she was already aware of my problem because she had spoken to my older sister. She also lived outside of the United States. She mentioned to me that she had fallen on the floor a few years ago, and since then, her hip bone had hurt. She had visited several doctors, and she had used different medications; however, her hip bone still hurt her. Finally, she said that the doctor had told her that her condition would fluctuate. Sometimes the pain would reduce, but the pain would always be there. I put her on hold and started trying to communicate with the pain in her hipbone. I took

وفي المرة الثانية، قالت الى بأن لدي ابنة ولا ينبغي عليه كشف هذه المشكلة لأحد. وطلبت مني الذهاب الى الطبيب للفحص. وبعد خطابها، حاولت تغيير الموضوع. وسألتها إذا كان هناك ألم في جسمها. أولاً، رفضت بشكل قاطع أن تكون جزءً من تجاربي، ولكن عندما أصرت على ذلك، أخبرتني بأنها كانت دائماً ما تعاني من ألم في ذراعها الأيمن. ووضعتها على قائمة الانتظار في الهاتف وحاولت التواصل مع ألم كتفها. وبعد دقيقتين بالضبط، سألتها إذا ما شعرت بتحسن أم لا. في البداية، قالت فوراً لا، ولكن بعد ذلك مباشرة، بدأت بالقول بأنها شعرت بشيء غريب كأن الألم ينتقل من مكان الى آخر. وبعد دقيقة احدة فقط، قالت بان ستين بالمئة من الألم اختفى، ولكن ما زالت تعاني مبعض الألم. حالياً، تواصلت مع ألمها لمدة حوالي دقيقة من الزمن. وعندما تحدثت إليها، كانت مندهشة للغاية ومصدومة. وقالت بأنها كانت تعاني من ذلك الألم منذ عدة سنين وكانت تتناول مسكنات للألم. ومن ثم بدأت بإخباري عن آلام مختلفة كان يعاني منها أطفالها. وفي ذلك اليوم، علمت بأني قادر على التواصل مع ألم الكتف أيضاً.

وكانت تلك البداية فقط، وفي حينه لم أكن مدركاً جميع تلك الآلام والأمراض يمكنني تجاوزها. وقبل ذلك، كنت أتعامل مع الشياطين فقط، لذلك لم أكن أواجه أي آلام أو أمراض لأنني كنت محاطاً بالشياطين. ولكن التعامل مع الآلام والأمراض كان عملاً مختلفاً. وتحتاج الآلام والأمراض أجساماً أو وسط ناقل. ولا يستمرون في الطيران في الجو. فهم يغادرون جسماً وينتقلون الى جسم آخر فوراً. وفي ذلك الوقت، لم أكن أعاني من أي مشكلة لأنني لم أكن أعاني من أي آلام وأمراض بالطريقة التي أعاني منها الآن. وبعد بضعة أيام، حاولت التحدث الى اختي الصغيرة، ولكنها كانت على علم بالمشكلة لأنها تحدثت الى اختي الكبيرة. وكانت تعيش أيضاً خارج الولايات المتحدة الأمريكية. وأخبرتني بأنها وقعت على الأرض قبل عدة سنين، ومنذ ذلك الوقت، لا تزال عظم فخدها يؤلمها. وفي النهاية، قالت بأن الطبيب اخبرها بأن وضعها متذبذب. واحياناً كان الألم يقل ولكن كان لا يزال الألم موجوداً. ووضعتها على قائمة الانتظار في الهاتف وبدأت بمحاولة التواصل مع ألمها في عظمة الفخذ. واستغرقت

a few minutes, and after that, her pain was fixed. She called again after one week when she had the pain again in the same spot. On the second time, I fixed her pain again, but this time, I asked her to use some healing creams and ointments to fix the damages or symptoms that pain had created in her body.

There is no way that an external insect, visible or invisible, can go inside our bodies or bones and damage nothing. They damage a lot, but our positive healing systems work on our damages all the time, unless the speed or amount of damage is too great.

After a few days, I tried my mother. She was already aware of my activities, and she was unhappy about them. She started warning me and said, "Even your father had some mental disorder before he died. So you'd better be careful and do not get involved in these kinds of problems." Anyway, I listened to her advice, and then I asked her if she had any pains or sicknesses.

She mentioned that she would hear some whistling noises in her left ear all the time. She had gone to several doctors and had taken different kinds of medications, but that noise was still always there. And since she had developed that problem, her hearing ability had been decreasing continuously in her left ear.

That was my first time working on an ear. Within two minutes, she was okay, but she was still complaining about some abnormal sounds. Anyway, after a small struggle, the whistling noise disappeared, but her hearing was still not perfect. Then I talked to her every third or fourth day and asked her about her improvement. She said that the whistling noise would keep coming back every week. So, I suggested that she call me whenever she had problem. Plus, I asked her to use some eardrops to fix the damages in her ear. Nowadays, she is okay. She does not hear the whistling noise anymore. She stays in contact with me more frequently these days. Whenever she feels any kind of sickness or pain, she asks me to take care of it. And I am happy to help. At least she believes me these days. Every morning when I

بضع دقائق وبعدها عالجت الألم. واتصلت بي مرة أخرى بعد أسبوع عندما كانت تعاني من نفس الألم في نفس المنطقة من الجسم. وفي المرة الثانية، عالجت الألم مرة اخرى، ولكن هذه المرة سألتها باستخدام بعض الكريمات المعالجة للتعافي من الأضرار التي سببها ذلك الألم في عظمة الفخذ.

ولا يوجد هناك أي طريق يمكن الحشرات الخارجية والمرئية والخفية بالدخول الى أجسامنا وتدميرها. فهم يقومون بتدمير الكثير ولكن أنظمة التعافي الإيجابية فينا تعمل على علاج الأضرار طوال الوقت إلا إذا كانت سرعة وكمية الضرر كبيرة.

وبعد عدة أيام، حاولت الاتصال بأمي وكانت على علم بأعمالي، وكانت غير سعيدة بذلك. وبدأت بتحذيري وقالت: "حتى أباك كان يعاني من خلل عقلي قبل أن يموت. لذلك يجب عليك الحذر ولا تتدخل في هذه الأنواع من المشاكل." على أي حال، استمعت الى نصيحتها وبعدها سألتها إذا ما كانت تعاني من آلام أو أمراض.

ذكرت بأنها كانت تسمع صفير ضوضائي في أذنها اليسرى طوال الوقت. وذهبت الى العديد من الأطباء وتناولت العديد من الأدوية، ولكن لا يزال هناك ضجيج في أذنها. ومنذ حدوث ذلك، أصبحت قدرتها على السمع تقل باستمرار في أذنها اليسرى.

وكانت تلك المرة الأولى التي عالج فيها ألم الأذن. وخلال دقيقتين، كانت تشعر بخير، ولكن كانت تشتكي من بعض الأصوات الغير طبيعية على أي حال، بعد صراع صغير، اختفى الصفير الضوضائي، ولكن لم يكن سمعها في أفضل حال. وكنت تحدث إليها كل ثلاثة أو أربعة أيام وسألتها عن آخر التطورات. قالت بأن صوت الصفير لا يزال يعود كل أسبوع. لذلك اقترحت عليها بالاتصال علي عندما تشعر بالصوت. بالإضافة إلى ذلك، طلبت منها استخدام قطرة الأذن لعلاج الأضرار في أذنها. في هذه الأيام، هي بخير. ولا تسمع صوت الضوضاء والصفير بعد الآن. وبقيت على اتصال بي بشكل متكرر هذه الأيام. وعندما تشعر بأي نوع من الألم أو المرض، كانت تطلب مني أن أتعامل معه. وأنا سعيد جداً للمساعدة. فهي على الأقل تصدقني هذه الأيام. وكل صباح

wake up, I always think that all of these strange occurrences were just the result of a dream or a nightmare, but there was no dream. Everything was real and true. My mind was getting more trained with each day.

I am very happy, because I am not using any medium to communicate and influence a pain, sickness, disease, or demon. If there is a medium, I am not aware of it. To help someone fix some pain, I do not need to go to them, and they do not need to come to me. No phone call needed either. I can reach anyone anywhere. But my system is very complicated. Who wants to leave their houses or their food? I only need to talk to someone on the phone. Then I can save my time and help them quickly. I just need an update so I can move on. I am very thankful to God, because he gave me these powers. I do not need to ask any spirit or demons to help me. My mind flies everywhere and tries to help others just by communication with demons, sicknesses, and diseases inside those people.

Whenever I have time and I find someone who deserves help, I work on him or her without notifying the person. Without knowing their medical history, I can still try to move some invisible problems away from them. But always remember that these invisible parasites number in the millions and that their size is extremely small. Moreover, they are very powerful, and they live for hundreds of years. And I am not a magician, God gifted me with some powers to convince them to leave people, but behind them, millions are already in line, waiting. Anyway, what I am trying to say is this: If someone has migraine or arthritis pains and even if he or she is going to doctors and taking medications, I can be of help because I can convince migraines or arthritis pains to leave the body. After that, it is the individual's responsibility to fix his or her damages or symptoms by using medications. I will try to describe a few incidents concerning problems I tried to fix. The sequence will be random, and I will not write about two people with the same problems.

عندما أستيقظ، دائماً ما أفكر بأن كل تلك الحوادث الغريبة كانت فقط نتيجة حلم أو كابوس، ولكنها لم تكن كذلك. كل شيء كان حقيقة وصحيحاً. وكان عقلي يتمرن أكثر كل يوم.

فأنا سعيد جداً لأنني لم أستخدم أي وسط للتوصل والتأثير على الألم أو المرض أو الشيطان. وفي حال كان هناك وسط ناقل، فلا أكون مدركاً له. ولمعالجة شخص ما من الألم، لا أحتاج الى الذهاب اله ولا يحتاج للقدوم إلي. ولا حتى هناك حاجة الى مكالمة هاتفية. أستطيع أن أصل أي شخص في أي مكان. ولكن نظامي معقد جداً. من يريد أن يغادر منزله أو طعامه؟ أحتاج فقط الى التحدث مع شخص على الهاتف. وأحتاج الى معرفة آخر التطورات حتى يمكنني المساعدة بسرعة. وأنا شاكرٌ لله تعالى بسبب منحه لي تلك القوى. ولا أحتاج الى سؤال أي روح او شيطان لمساعدتي. حيث أن عقلي يطير في كل مكان ويحاول مساعدة الآخرين عن طريق التواصل مع الشياطيين والأمراض داخل هؤلاء الأشخاص.

عندما كان لدي الوقت لمساعدة أي شخص يستحق المساعدة، أقوم بذلك دون ابلاغ ذلك الشخص. ودون معرفة تاريخه الطبي، يمكنني أن أحاول أن اخرج المشاكل الغير مرئية بعيداً عنه. ولكن تذكر دائماً بأن تلك الطفيليات الغير مرئية يبلغ عددها بالملايين وحجمها صغير للغاية. بالإضافة الى ذلك، فهم قويون جداً، ويعيشون لمئات السنين. وأنا لست بساحر، فقد منحني الله بعد القوى لإقناع الشياطيين بالخروج من أجساد البشر، ولكن هناك الملايين وراءهم. على أي حال، ما أحاول قوله هو أنه: في حال معاناة شخص ما من الصداع النصفي أو آلام التهاب المفاصل وحتى في حال ذهابك الى الأطباء وتناول الأدوية، يمكنني أن أساعدك لقدرتي على إقناع آلام التهاب المفاصل والصداع النطفي على مغادرة الجسم. وبعد ذلك، تقع المسؤولية على الفرد نفسه لمعالجة الأضرار التي تعرض إليها جسده نتيجة استخدام الادوية. وسأحاول وصف بعض الحالات المتعلقة والتي قمت بمعالجتها. وسيكون التسلسل عشوائي، ولن اكتب بشأن شخصين يعانون من نفس المشكلة.

This incident concerns a short temperament. Donisha was working in Columbus at this time. Two things were very noticeable about her. She was extremely short-tempered and irritated all the time. The second thing was that she was extraordinarily good in keeping, maintaining, and organizing the store. One day during her work hours when I was standing in front of her, I asked her if she wanted me to take this temperament out of her body. She was having a hard time understanding what I was talking about. Anyway, even though I never communicated or convinced anyone to come out of her body, a demon suddenly came out of her and penetrated my body. I immediately mentioned this to her. She hadn't realized anything. After she heard me talking in air, she started telling me that she had been feeling a lot of pressure on her chest during sleep. And during that pressure, yelling or getting up often proved impossible for her. That day, her demon came out of her. During the next several days, she mentioned that she felt normal. Her short temper was gone. In the next few days, she asked me to fix a few more problems like a cramp in her stomach, some arthritic pain, and a sinus problem. One by one, I communicated with her problems, and one by one, they came out of her. The whole time, she kept saying, "This is all crazy." She worked there for a while after that, and she never complained about these problems. She was not acting like a short-tempered person for a while. After some time, she moved to another town and took another job.

Another time, a woman name was Edna in Columbus found out about me and asked me if I could help her reduce or remove a pain starting from her right kidney and going all the way to her right knee joint. That was the very first time I dealt with that kind of pain. And she was crying at that time because of the pain. I communicated with those pains in three steps, and thanks to God, all of them listened to me. She was okay after five minutes. She called me one more time after one week to help with the same kind of pain. I was at home at that time. This time, I communicated with her pain over the phone. Again, I was able to convince the pain to leave her body. After several months, she came to my business in Weimar, and this time, her complaint was different. She told me that she had quit drinking alcohol several

يتعلق هذا الحادث بخصوص المزاج السريع الغضب. كانت دونيشا تعمل مدينة كولومبس في هذا الوقت. وكان هناك شيئيان بارزان بشأنها. كانت سريعة الغضب غاضبة طوال الوقت. وكان الشيء الثاني بأنها خارقة في حفظ وصيانة وترتيب المتجر. وفي يوم من الأيام وأثناء عملها عندما كنت واقفاً أمامها، وسألتها إذا ما تريد اخراج هذا المزاج من جسمها. وكانت تعاني من اوقات عصيبة في فهم ما كنت أتحدث عنه. على أي حال، على الرغم من أنني لم أقم بأقناع أي شيطان للخروج من جسمها، تفاجأ الشيطان بالخروج من جسدها والدخول الي جسدي. وفوراً أخبرتها بذلك. ولم تدرك أي شيء. وبعدما سمعتني أتحدث في الهواء، بدأت بإخباري بأنها كانت تشعر بالكثير من الضغط على صدرها أثناء النوم. وأثناء ذلك الضغط، كانت تصرخ أو تستيقظ. وفي ذلك اليوم، خرج شيطانها منها. وبعد بضعة أيام، أخبرتني بأنها شعرت بخير. واختفى مزاجي السريع الغضب. وفي الأيام القليلة التالي، سألتني لمعالجة القليل من المشاكل كمغص في معدتها وألم التهاب المفاصل ومشكلة التجويف. ويوماً بعد يوم، تواصلت مع مشاكلها وخرجوا واحداً تلو الآخر. وطوال الوقت، استمرت في القول "إنه لشيء جنوني". وعملت هناك لفترة ولم تشتكي من تلك المشاكل. وكانت تتصرف على أنها سريعة الغضب. وبعد وقت قليل، انتقلت من المدينة وحصلت على وظيفة جديدة.

وفي حالة أخرى، كان هناك امرأة ادنا في مدينة كولومبس وعرفت بشأني وسألتني إذا ما يمكنني مساعدتها للتقليل أو إزالة ألم يبدأ من الكلى اليمنى حتى يصل إلي مفصل الركبة اليمنى. وكانت تلك المرة الأولى التي أتعامل مع هذا النوع من الآلام. وكانت تبكي في حينه بسبب شده الألم. وتواصلت مع تلك الآلام في ثلاث خطوات، والشكر لله، جميعهم استمعوا إليّ. وأصبحت على ما يرام بعد خمسة دقائق. واتصلت بي مرة أخرى بعد أسبوع لمساعدتها للتخلص من نفس الألم. وكنت في البيت اثناء ذلك. وفي حينه، تواصلت مع ألمها عن طريق الهاتف. ومرة اخرى، كنت قادراً على اقناع الألم على مغادرة جسدها. وبعد عدة شهور، حضرت الي في مكان عملي في ويمار، وفي حينه، اشتكت من شيء مختلف. أخبرتني بأنها تركت شرب الكحول

weeks ago, but since then, she was suffering continuously from bad headaches. Again, I communicated with that pain in her head, and thanks to God, that communication was successful. She was feeling better after a few minutes.

I have also learned that normal people do not feel any pain if they are having problems in their kidneys or livers or blood vessels until the diseases have damaged those organs significantly. My body is more sensitive compared to a normal person's, so whenever I receive any pains or diseases or demons, I am able to feel them immediately. Similarly, if you saw a mosquito or a spider or a fire ant or any other insect sitting on any part of your body, what would be your immediate reaction? You would definitely kill it or at least shoo it away. The point is that even though the spider was not biting you, you jump immediately and either kill that spider or throw it away from your body. If a harmless lizard or a cockroach is sitting on any part of your body, can you just leave it there and go to sleep with peace of mind? Do you know why you act like this? Because you are able to see those insects or at least you can feel them or sense them on your skin. The basic difference between me and a normal person is that you can sense or see a spider anywhere on your body but I can sense and feel these invisible insects/diseases when they come close to me or penetrate my body. I do not feel comfortable at all when these invisible insects come close to my body or go inside my body. Normal people are mostly only worried about visible insects and animals.

Demons are the ones that can possess our whole bodies, but they do not eat our organs or bodies. That's why they do not cause so much pain. Invisible insects and diseases are relatively smaller and can penetrate and cover a small area. They are damaging parasites. These diseases eat body parts and organs. Because of their small size and self-repairing system within the body, we may not feel any pains in the kidneys, liver, heart, and/or other parts of the body until the damages are too extensive and these diseases create infections.

قبل عدة أسابيع، ولكن منذ ذلك الوقت، كانت تعاني من صداع شديد بشكل مستمر. وتواصلت مع ألمها في الرأس والشكر لله، كان التواصل ناجحا. وكانت شعرت بتحسن بعد عدة دقائق.

وعلمت أن الأشخاص العاديون لا يشعرون بأي ألم في حال معاناتهم من مشاكل في الكلى أو الكبد أو صمامات الدم حتى تدمر الأمراض تلك الأعضاء بشكل كامل. وجسدي أكثر حساسية مقارنةً بجسد الشخص العادي. لذلك عندما أتلقى أي آلام أو أمراض أو شياطين، أكون قادراً على الشعور بهم مباشرة. وبشكل مشابه، في حال رؤيتك لبعوض أو عنكبوت أو نملة النار أو أي نوع من الحشرات جالسة على جزء من جسدك، ماذا سيكون رد فعلك؟ ستقوم بكل تأكيد بقتلها أو على الأقل طردها عن كتفك. ما أود قوله هو أنه على الرغم من أن العنكبوت لم يكن يريد عضك، قمت بقتله أو ابعاده عن جسدك. وحتى في حال جلوس سحلية او صرصور على أي جزء من جسدك، هل يمكنك تركه مكانه والذهاب الى النوم مرتاح البال؟ هل تعلم لماذا تتصرف كذلك؟ لأنك قادر على رؤية تلك الحشرات أو على الأقل تشعر أو تحس بهم على جسدك. إن الفرق الوحيد بيني وبين الشخص العادي هو أنه يمكنك رؤية والشعور بالعنكبوت في أي مكان على جسدك ولكن يمكنني أن أشعر بالأمراض/الحشرات الغير مرئية عندما يقتربون مني أو يتغلغلون الى جسدي. ولا أشعر بالراحة مطلقاً عندما تقترب مني أو تتغلغل في جسدي. بينما يشعر الأشخاص الطبيعيون بالقلق حيال الحشرات والحيوانات المرئية.

إن الشياطين هي التي تسيطر على أجسامنا، ولا يقومون بأكلها. لذلك السبب لا يسببون الكثير من الألم. تعد الحشرات والأمراض الغير مرئية صغيرة نسبياً ويمكنها التغلغل وتغطية مساحة صغيرة. فهي عبارة عن طفيليات مدمرة. ويأكلون الجسم. وبسبب صغير حجمهم ونظام اعادة الإصلاح في جسمهم، من المرجح أن لا نشعر بأي ألم في الكلى أو الكبد أو القلب أو أجزاء آخر من الجسم حتى تكون الأضرار فادحة وخطيرة وتسبب العدوى.

Mr. Arthur used to work with a company in EL-Campo. He worked on my air-conditioning system sometimes. One time when I asked him to fix an air-conditioning system at Mr. B's store, he showed up there, but he was limping because of some serious damages in his knee joint. When I asked him about his limping, he told that he had had some joint problems in his knee for several weeks and that he was going to have surgery in few days. I do not need to ask anyone to remove any kind of pain, but I always like permission from people. It helps me learn about their situation as well. Anyway, I asked him if he wanted me to fix his knee pain. At that time, he was not even able to keep his feet on ground because of the pain. He was not putting any pressure at all on his leg. Almost all people usually think that I am playing with them. He was thinking the same thing. First, he asked me, "How will you do it?" In answer, I just told him that I needed to see the place where he had pain. Guess what he did. He took his pants off in one second. Now he was standing in front of me in his underwear only. This was all happening at Mr. B's store in Columbus. Anyway, it took me few minutes to control my laughter. I strongly felt he was a very good person, and I have always believed that God always helps good people. Maybe I was a medium to help him, but I still communicated with his knee pains. It took less than a minute before he was okay and the pain was gone. But because he had had the pain for several weeks, he was extremely scared to put his feet on the ground. It took a few more minutes before he finally felt confident enough to start putting pressure on his feet. After one week, I meet with him at the same place. I asked him about his knee, and he said he was okay. During the time when I was talking to him, a disease came out from his body. That disease was in my body for just thirty seconds. That disease, however, was so powerful that I had no feelings at all from my right kidney all the way to a little below my knee for at least thirty seconds to one minute. I even tried to touch that part of my body, but I had no feelings and no sensation there. Anyway, that disease of paralysis just came out of his body and visited my body. After I became normal again, I tried to ask him if he had any other kinds of similar problems. He said that he didn't. In all likelihood, when I removed his knee pain, I removed that paralysis disease from

وكان السيد آرثر يعمل في شركة في الكامبو. وكان يصلح نظام التبريد الهوائي الخاص بي أحياناً. وعندما سألته ذات مرة لإصلاح نظام التبريد الهوائي في متجر السيد بي، جاء الى هناك، ولكنه كان يترنح بسبب بعض الأضرار الخطيرة في مفصل ركبته. وعندما سألته بشأن ذلك، قال لي بأنه يعاني من بعض المشاكل في المفصل الخاص بركبته منذ عدة أسابيع وكان ينوي الخضوع لعملية جراحية خلال أيام قليلة. ولا أحتاج الى أسأل أي شخص لإزالة الألم، ولكن دائماً أحبذ طلب الاستئذان منهم. حيث يساعدني على التعرف على وضعهم أكثر. على أي حال، سألته إذا ما كان يريدني ان ازيل الألم من ركبته. وفي ذلك الوقت، لم يكن حتى قادراً على وضع رجله على الأرض بسبب الألم. ولم يكن يضعها تحت الضغط مطلقاً. وعادة من يعتقد معظم الناس بأنني أعبث معه. وكان يفكر بنفس الطريقة. أولاً سألني، "كيف ستقوم بذلك؟" وكان جوابي هو أنني أريد رؤية مكان الألم. احزر ماذا فعل. قام بخلع بنطاله خلال ثوان. وكان يقف أمام بالملابس الداخلية فقط. كان كل هذا يحدث في متجر السيد بي في مدينة كولومبس. على أي حال، استغرق الوقت بضع دقائق حتى سيطرت على ضحكتي. وشعرت بقوة بانه كان شخصاً جيداً، وكنت دائماً ما أعتقد بأن الله دائماً يساعد الأشخاص الجيدون. وربما أكون أنا الوسط لمساعدته، ولكن كنت أتواصل مع ألم ركبته. واستغرق مني أقل من دقيقة قبل أن يكون على ما يرام واختفى الألم. ولكن بسبب معاناته من الألم لعدة أسابيع، لم يجرأ على وضع رجله على الأرض. واستغرق بضعة دقائق حتى شعر بالثقة ووضع قدمه على الأرض وبدأ بالضغط عليها. وبعد أسبوع قابلته في نفس التجر. وسألته عن ألم ركبته، وقال بأنه بخير. واثناء تحدثي إليه، خرج مرض من جسمه. وكان ذلك المرض داخل جسدي لبضع ثوان فقط. وكان ذلك المرض، علاوة على ذلك قوي جداً حتى أنني لم أشعر بشيء بدأ من كليتي اليمنى الى ركبتي لمدة لا تقل عن ثلاثين ثانية، ولكن لم أكن أشعر بشيء هناك. على أي حال، خرج مرض الشلل من جسده ودخلي الى جسدي. وبعد أن أصبحت شخصاً طبيعياً مرة اخرى، حاولت سؤاله في حال كان يعاني من أي آلام أخرى. وأجابني بأنه لا يعاني. ومن الممكن بأنه عندما أزلت ألم ركبته، قمت بإزالة مرض الشلل من

his body as well. That paralysis disease never visited me again after that.

I once had the option to become a doctor, but I was extremely cowardly. I am scared of lizards and all other kinds of reptiles. It is very hard for me to watch a horror movie. I can watch a little bit, if there are no scary characters in the movie, but there is no way someone can convince me to watch a horror movie easily. In the same way, I cannot watch any kind of surgery or operation, so obviously, it is not easy for me to watch doctors or nurses when they are cleaning, washing, and bandaging someone's injury or wound. I used to be extremely scared of trees at night as well. I am always surprised by the fact that I was chosen to study the mysterious world of demons and diseases. For a long time in the beginning, when I was only able to feel or sense them, I was incredibly scared for a long time. I had always imagined them as terrifying creatures. And I am such a normal person in the modern world. Plus, I had never worked with demon doctors. Until few years ago, I had no knowledge of demons or the invisible world. Suddenly, I was chosen for this job. I am always surprised by this change in my life. I am still surprised about it.

Regardless of humans or demons, both are intelligent. It is really difficult to convince both of them about my capabilities. But God helped me with that. Now in the case of demons, it is very easy to convince them that I can see them. I just point my finger toward them and move my finger with their movements. I can also tell them when they clearly touch my body. I can easily tell them how much of my body is under their control or how much of my body they have penetrated. In the case of humans, convincing them is easy too. Other than helping with injuries or major accidents, I can remove their pains from their bodies. Sometime this takes seconds, sometimes minutes, and sometimes longer, but eventually, the pains listen to me. In this way, I can easily prove myself and my abilities.

Even when I am communicating with demons and diseases, I am still the same coward and scared person. As a result, I sometimes have

جسده أيضاً. ولم يقم مرض الشلل ذلك بزيارة مجدداً.

كان الخيار متاحاً لي لأصبح طبيباً، ولكن كنت جباناً للغاية. وكنت خائفاً من السحالي وجميع أنواع الزواحف. فإنه من الصعب علي مشاهدة فلم رعب. ويمكن مشاهدة القليل منه، في حال عمد وجود شخصيات مخيفة في الفلم ولكن لا يوجد هناك أي شخص يمكنه إقناعي بمشاهدة فليم رعب بتلك السهولة. وبنفس الطريقة، لا يمكنني مشاهدة أي نوع من أنواع العمليات الجراحية، ولذلك وبكل وضوح، ليس من السهل علي مشاهدة الأطباء أو الممرضين عندما يقومون بتنظيف أو غسيل أو تعصيب حرج شخص ما. وتعودت على أن أكون خائفاً للغاية من الأشجار في الليل كذلك. ودائماً ما أكون مندهشاً بحقيقة أنني أخترت لدراسة العالم الغامض للشياطيين والأمراض. وعندما كنت قادراً على الإحساس بهم في البداية، كنت خائفاً جداً لفترة طويلة. ودائماً ما كنت أتخيل الشياطيين على أنها مخلوقات مخيفة. وأنا شخص طبيعي في العالم الحديث. بالإضافة الى ذلك، لم أعمل قط مع أي عراف. حتى قبل سنين قليلة ماضية، لم يكن لدي أي علم بالشياطيين أو العالم الخفي. وفجأة، تم اختياري لهذه المهمة. ودائماً ما كنت متفاجأ من هذا التغيير الذي حدث في حياتي. وما زلت كذلك.

وبغض النظر عن الإنسان والشياطيين، فكلاهما ذكيان. فمن الصعب حقاً اقناعهما بقدراتي. ولكن الله ساعدني في ذلك. والآن في حالة الشياطيين، من السهل إقناعهم بأنني يمكنني أن أراهم. فقط أقوم بتوجيه أصبعي باتجاه تواجد الشيطان وأقوم بتحريكه مع تحركاته. ويمكنني أن أقول له عندما يقوم بلمس جسدي. ويمكنني بكل سهولة إخبارهم كم من المكان في جسدي مسيطر عليه من قبلهم أو تغلغلوا فيه. وفي حالة الإنسان، فإقناعهم سهل أيضاً. ليس فقط المساعدة في علاج الجروح والحوادث الرئيسية، يمكنني أن أزيل آلامهم من أجسادهم. وأحياناً أفعل ذلك خلال ثوان] أو دقائق أو قد يستغرق وقتاً أكثر، ولكن في النهاية يستمع الألم إلي. وبهذه الطريقة، يمكنني بكل سهولة اثبات نفسي وإثبات قدرتي.

وحتى عندما أتواصل مع الشياطيين والأمراض، ما أزال جباناً وخائفاً. ونتيجةً لذلك، أحياناً ما أعاني من

problems when I am dealing with extremely sick people. I have tried to fix this problem, but I have not been too successful. It is easy for doctors to deal with patients because they just write prescriptions and then they're done. But my case is different. I have to keep that person in my mind. To communicate with someone's sicknesses and diseases, I first need to bring that person completely into my mind. Then I can control and negotiate with demons and diseases around him or her. This is not always an easy task.

Hopefully, no one will get upset about this next thing I can tell you. I am just a man. This is another problem with me. Sometimes I have to work on someone more frequently when he or she is not in front of me. I have to bring people into my mind to communicate with their demons and diseases or pains. Sometimes this is very hard.

I always think that I can help only those I have seen already, or I may be able to help if I have seen their photos or pictures. But there was an incident in Columbus when my daughter went to a Scrap School store. She called me from there and asked me if I would be able to help the lady who worked there. I told her that I might not be able to because I had never seen that lady, and I thought it would be difficult to help someone I had never seen. My daughter eventually called me back after few minutes and told me that that lady was sixty-five years old and she had arthritis pain all over her shoulders, arms, backbone, and legs. That lady was taking pills continuously every day. She had changed almost six doctors in last few months, but her pain was not reducing. After my daughter told me all those details, she insisted that I tried to help that lady. She mentioned that the lady was crying because of the pain. I still was not willing to do anything without at least seeing her picture, but my daughter was insisting so much that I decided to try without seeing pictures of her. My daughter put her on phone. That lady was a little confused. That's why she started asking me different questions, but instead of answering her, I asked her about the exact location of her pain. First, she said that shoulder area hurt. I communicated with the pain, and thanks to God, her pain listened to me immediately. Next, I communicated with the other pains in

مشاكل عندما أتعامل مع أشخاص مريضين للغاية. وحاولت علاج هذه المشكلة، ولكن لم أكن ناجحاً كثيراً. ومن السهل بالنسبة للأطباء التعامل مع المرضى لأنهم فقط يقومون بكتابة الوصفات الطبية. ولكن في حالتي، علي أن أبقي ذلك الشخص في عقلي. وللتواصل مع مرض شخص ما، علي أولاً وضع ذلك الشخص في عقلي. ومن ثم يمكنني السيطرة والتفاوض مع الشياطين. وليس يكون سهلاً في الغالب.

آمل أن لا يغضب احد مني بشأن الشيء التالي الذي سأقوم بإخبارهم إياه. فأنا عبارة عن رجل فقط. فهذه مشكلة أخرى أعاني منها. أحياناً علي العمل على علاج شخص أكثر من مرة عندما لا يكون أمامي. وعلي أن أضع الأشخاص في عقلي للتواصل مع شياطينهم وأمراضهم. وأحياناً يكون ذلك صعباً.

ودائماً ما أفكر في مساعدة هؤلاء الذين قد رؤيتهم من قبل، أو ربما أكون قادراً على مساعدة من رأيت صورهم. ولكن كان هناك حداثة في مدينة كولومبس عندما ذهبت ابنتي الى متجر سكراب سكول. واتصلت بي وطلبت مني حول قدرتي على مساعدة امرأة كانت تعمل هناك. وقلت لها بأنني من المرجح أن لا أكون قادراً على فعل ذلك لأنني لم أرى تلك السيدة ابداً واعتقدت أنه من الصعب مساعدة شخص ما لم أره قط. وعاودت الاتصال بي بعد عدة دقائق وأخبرتني بأن عمر السيدة خمسة وستون عاماً وتعاني من ألم التهاب المفاصل في كتفيها وذراعيها وعظم الظهر والأرجل. وكانت تتناول تلك السيدة الحبوب كل يوم وبشكل مستمر. وقامت بزيادة ستة أطباء مختلفين خلال عدة أشهر، ولكن لم يخف الألم. وبعد أن أخبرتني ابنتي عن جميع تلك التفاصيل، أصررت على أن أحاول تلك السيدة. وذكرت بأن تلك السيدة كانت تبكي بسبب شدة الألم. وكنت لا أزال لا أريد فعل أي شيء دون رؤيتها على الأقل أو رؤية صورة لها، ولكن كانت ابنتي تصر كثيراً حتى قررت المحاولة دون أن أراها. وقامت ابنتي بجلب السيدة لتتكلم معي على الهاتف. وكانت مرتبكة قليلاً. لذلك السبب بدأت بسؤال أسئلة مختلفة ولكن بدلاً من إجابتها سألتها عن موضع الألم بالضبط. أولاً، أخبرتني بأن منطقة الكتف تؤلمها. فتواصلت مع الألم والحمد لله، استمع ألمها إلي فوراً. وفي المرة الثانية، تواصلت مع آلام أخرى في

her body, and again thanks to God, all of her pains listened to me. Within four minutes, that lady was free of pain. After that, she said, "I am impressed." Anyway, I told her to give a photo of herself to my daughter, so the next time, I could feel more confident about fixing the problem if she needed me again.

Most of the time, I do not need anyone to be in front of me to help. I do not even need anyone to talk on the phone to help them. My mind can fly anywhere to anyone and try to help them. But if I have never seen someone, then it will be difficult to help him or her from a remote area.

I have a long list of these incidents, but I am mentioning these few to verify my abilities.

Mr. Alton did carpenter work. He had a backbone injury several years ago when he fell from a ladder. I had seen him suffering from that back pain and going to different doctors for sixty days. He was losing weight every day. He was wearing a support belt for his backbone all the time. But he strongly believed that that medication was the only solution for his pain. One day during work, he mentioned to me that he had a problem standing these days because his back pain had spread to his hips. Finally, I asked him if he wanted me to take his pain away I told him that once I fixed his pain, we could keep using the medications to correct the damage. Anyway, the process took two minutes, and then his back pain was gone.

Another time, the same person had a different problem. The tube between his ear and throat had an infection with some inflammation. Doctors tried antibiotics first. When those didn't work, the doctors suggested surgery. When he came to me, he was in really bad condition, and he was suffering from excruciating pain. Anyway, I communicated with his inflammation, and in two steps, his pain was gone. The process took maybe three minutes. But before he left me, I made him promise to complete his course of antibiotics. He was fine without any surgery.

جسمها. والحمد لله استمعت جميع آلامها إلي. وخلال أربعة دقائق، كان المرأة خالية من الألم. وبعد لك، قالت: " إنني متعجبة". على أي حال، أخبرتها بأن تعطي ابنتي صورة لها. حت أشعر بالمزيد من الثقة في المرات القادمة بشأن علاج أي مشكلة في حال اقتضت الضرورة.

وفي أغلب الأحيان، لا أحتاج الى أن يكون الشخص أمامي لمساعدته. ولا حتى أحتاج الى اي شخص للتحدث معي على الهاتف. يمكن لعقلي الطيران الى أي مكان لمحاولة مساعدة أي شخص. ولكن في حال لم أرى الشخص من قبل، سيكون من الصعب مساعدته من مسافة بعيدة.

ولدى قائمة طويلة من تلك الحوادث، ولكن أذكر منها القليل لإثبات قدراتي.

وكان يعمل السيد ألتون في النجارة. وكان يعاني من آلام في عظام الظهر منذ سنين عديدة عندما سقط عن السلم. ورأيته يعاني من ألم الظهر وذهب الى العديد من الأطباء لأكثر من ستين يوماً. وكان يفقد وزنه كل يوم. وكان يرتدي حزام مساعد لعظام الظهر طوال الوقت. واعتقد بأن الدواء الذي يتناوله كان حلاً للألم فقط ومسكناً له. وفي ذات مرة أثناء العمل، ذكر لي بأنه يعاني من مشكلة في الوقوف في هذه الأيام بسبب ألم ظهره قد انتشر الى عظام الورك. وفي النهاية، سألته إذا ما كان يريدني أن أخرج الألم من ظهره وأنه عندما أخرج الألم، عليه أن يستمر في تناول الأدوية لإصلاح الأضرار. على أي حال، استغرقت العملية دقيقتان، ومن ثم اختفى ألم ظهره.

وفي وقت آخر، كان يعاني شخصاً آخر من مشكلة أخرى مختلفة. حيث أن الأنبوب بين اذنه وحلقه يعاني من اصابة الالتهاب. وحاول الأطباء اعطاءه المضادات الحيوية في الأول. ولكن لم تنجح هذه المحاولة. واقترحوا اجراء عملية جراحية. وعندما جاء إلي، كان في حالة سيئة جداً، وكان يعاني من ألم مبرح. على أي حال، توالت مع ألم الإلتهاب وفي خطوتين اختفى ألمه. واستغرقت العملية ثلاثة دقائق. وقبل أن يغادرني، قطعت له وعداً بان يكمل تناول المضادات الحيوية. وكان على ما يرام بدون الخضوع للعملية الجراحية.

I strongly feel that if medical science starts believing my assertions that all these diseases and sicknesses are physical, that communication with them will become possible for everyone. Sometimes I forget that not everyone can communicate with these demons, diseases, and pains like I can. But I am ready to demonstrate this ability in front of anyone to prove to medical scientists that any pain or disease is fixable without medication. My responsibility is just to prove this point to them. After that, I am sure that all scientists will work in this alternative direction within medical science. The simple formula for curing a pain or sickness rests on the principle of like and dislike. This is common sense. Every living creature likes at least one thing and dislikes others. Consequently, medical science only needs to find out what demons, pains, and/or diseases do not like.

I have uncountable demons, diseases, and pains around me all the time, but they are not affecting me that badly. Medical scientists may want to investigate how and why I am able to keep them away from my body most of the time. I am sure that Newton's fourth law is true in my case. Everything around us is about give and take. To take something, we should be ready to give something. And I mostly agree with this because just taking something from someone or giving something to someone all the time is like one-way traffic. And oneway traffic or movement in only one direction totally goes against the universal system.

In my case, demons, diseases, and pains are getting something out of me. I am definitely a surprise to all of them, mostly because they believe that they are completely invisible and that no one can sense them, but I can. And I am doing so all the time. Secondly, I am able to communicate with them, so I can convince them to leave someone's body. Sometimes I am even capable of arguing with them or insisting that they leave a person. I am sure that they get extremely upset with me when I insist that they not do something, and I am sure I am facing many problems and obstacles as a result of their reactions.

وأشعر بأنه في حال بدا علم الطب بتصديق نظرياتي التي تقول بأن الأمراض هي أجسام فيزيائية، سيكون التواصل معهم ممكناً لأي شخص. وأحياناً أنسى بأنه لا يمكن التواصل مع تلك الأمراض والآلام والآلام من قبل أي شخص كما أفعل أنا. ولكنني مستعد لإظهار هذه القدرة أمام كل شخص لإثبات ذلك لعلماء الطب بأن أي ألم يمكن علاجه دون تناول الأدوية. حيث تقع مسؤوليتي في اثبات هذه النقطة. وبعد ذلك، أنا متأكد بأن جميع العلماء سيعملون في هذا الاتجاه البديل من علم الطب. وإن الصيغة البسيطة لعلاج ألم أو مرض ما يعتمد على مبدا الرغبة أو عدم الرغبة. فهذا شائع. حيث يرغب كل مخلوق بشيء واحد على الأقل أو لا يرغب بشيء واحد على الأقل. وبالتالي، فقط يحتاج علم الطب اكتشاف ما لا ترغبه الشياطيين والآلام والأمراض.

ولدي شياطيين وأمراض وآلام لا تعد ولا تحصى من حولي طوال الوقت. ولكن لا يأثرون علي بشكل سيء. ويمكن لعلماء الطب أن يجرون تحقيق حول مكيفية ولماذا أنا قادراً على ابقائهم بعيديين عني جسدي معظم الأوقات. وأنا متأكد من أن قانون نيوتن الرابع صحيح في حالتي. حيث أن كل شيء من حولنا هو عبارة عن تنازلات متبادلة. لأخذ شيء ما، ينبغي عليك أن تكون مستعداً للتضحية بشيء ما. وأنا غالباً ما أوافق ذلك لأن أخذ شيء ما من شخص ما أو اعطاء شيء ما لشخص ما طوال الوقت هو خط سير طريق واحد. وتلك الحركة هي فقط اتجاه واحد عكس اتجاه النظام العالمي.

وفي حالتي، تقوم الشياطيين والأمراض والآلام بإخراج شيء مني. وأنا مندهش جداً لأنهم يؤمنون بأنهم غير مرئيين بشكل كامل ولا يمكن لأحد الشعور بهم. ولكن يمكنني فعل ذلك. وأنا أفعل ذلك طوال الوقت. ثانياً، لدي القدرة على التواصل معهم، لذلك يمكنني أقناعهم بمغادرة جسم أي شخص أو اجبارهم على فعل ذلك. وأنا متأكد بأنهم يغضبون جداً عندما أجبرهم على عدم فعل شيء، وأنا متأكد من أنني اواجه مشاكل عديدة وعوائق كنتيجة لردود افعالهم.

But it is really hard for me to just sit back and not help someone if I feel that I can indeed help, especially when someone asks for help. As I have said several times, demons are master of hypnotism. No one—not human or animal—can perform at this powerful level of hypnotism.

We humans—actually, I should say *normal* humans—think and act almost in a same way. Exactly like this, most demons' actions and reactions are the same, regardless of kind or race.

There are two major things I have always noticed about demons: they protect their victims, and they work together in groups. *Victim* here is meant to reference any "body," but I will talk about only humans here because I deal with humans only and I am only capable of dealing with humans. But how do demons protect their human victims? They will block my mind and sight so that my mind will not be able to trace that person. I will not be able to recognize or store that person in my memory. If that person is already in my memory, I will not be able to find that person in my memory. I will keep looking for the person in the air or in my memory, but the demons will block me by hypnosis. This has often happened to me, but usually, I am able to break their spells of hypnotism in a few days or less. But this indeed happened years ago. I don't seem to have this problem these days. But this is definitely their first step in protecting their human victims. The second thing that demons do to protect a victim is misguide me by hypnotizing me, especially if I am trying to pull someone from my memory. If I am trying to reach XYZ, they will send my mind to ABC. And usually, ABC is always that person I never liked. By hypnotizing me, demons will keep changing the picture of the actual person I'm trying to help and bring an undesired person to disrupt my concentration.

Once scientists pay attention to my theories, I am sure they will be able to invent machines that reduce the influence of demons, diseases, and pains in our bodies, but until then, I suggest everyone use a few tricks to reduce the problems caused by demons. However, these can

ولكن هذا حقاً صعباً الجلوس وعدم مساعدة أحد في حال كان لدي القدرة على مساعدته فعلا، وخاصة عندما يطلب ذلك الشخص منك المساعدة. وكما ذكرت عدة مرات، فإن الشياطيين أسياد التنويم المغناطيسي. ولا يمكن لأحد-سواءً كان إنسان أو حيوان- انجاز هذا المستوى القوى من التنويم المغناطيسي.

فنحن البشر-في الحقيقة- ينبغي أن أقول الأشخاص العاديين- التفكير والتصرف بنفس الطريقة تقريباً. وبالضبط مثل ذلك، تعد أفعال وردود الأفعال الشياطيين هي نفسها بغض النظر عن نوع الشياطيين أو عرقها.

وهناك شيئيان لاحظتهما بشكل دائم بشأن الشياطيين: فهم يقومون بحماية ضحاياهم، ويعملون في مجموعات. والضحية هنا هي "الجسم"، ولكن سأتحدث عن الإنسان فقط هنا بسبب قدرتي على التعامل مع الشياطيين وقادراً على التعامل مع البشر أيضاً. ولكن كيف يمكن للشياطيين حماية ضحاياهم من البشر؟ سيقومون بإغلاق عقلي ونظري (بصيرتي) ولن أكون قادراً على تعقب أثر الشخص. ولن أكون قادراً على التعرف أو تخزين ذلك الشخص في ذاكرتي. وفي حال كان ذلك الشخص في ذاكرتي مسبقاً، فلن أكون قادراً على ايجاد ذلك الشخص فيها. وسأبقى ابحث عن الخص في الهواء أو في ذاكرتي، ولكن يقوم الجن بإغلاق عقلي باستخدام التنويم المغناطيسي. وهذا عادة يحدث لي، ولكن في العادة، أنا قادر على كسر نوبات التنويم المغناطيسي خلال عدة أيام أو أقل. ولكن حدث هذا فعلاً قبل سنين ماضية. ولا أبدو أنني اعاني من هذه المشكلة في هذه الأيام، ولكن هذه كانت الخطوة الأولى في حماية ضحاياهم من البشر. وإن الشيء الثاني الذي تفعله الشياطيين لحماية ضحاياهم هو تضليلي عن طريق تنويمي مغناطيسياً، وخاصة في حال محاولتي اخراج شخص ما من ذاكرتي. ففي حال محاولتي الوصول الى اكس واي زد، سيقومون بإرسالي الى اي بي سي. وعادة، اي بي سي ما تكون الشخص الي لا أحبه. وعن طريق التنويم المغناطيسي لي، ستبقى الشياطيين تقوم بتغيير طورة الشخص الحقيقي الذي أحاول مساعدته وارسالي الى الشخص الذي لا أحبه لتشتيت تركيزي.

وعندما يعير العلماء اهتماً لنظرياتي، أنا متأكد بأنهم سيكونون قادرين على اختراع آلات يمكن تخفيف تأثير الشياطيين والأمراض والآلام في اجسامنا، ولكن حتى حينه، أنصح كل شخص باستخدام بعض الخدع لتقليل مشاكل التي يسببها الجن. علاوة على ذلك، يمكن أن يتم

only be used to fight against demons. These will not work on diseases or pains. These tricks include the following:

1) Demons like *red* meat only. My understanding is that demons like *beef.* If you have more beef and eat more beef, that could mean you are inviting more and more demons into your house and into your body.

2) Rub at leave five small lemons or limes on different parts of your body, especially around you head, ears, eyes, neck, and chest for two minutes. Then move your hand around your body seven times. Make sure you undergo this process when you are driving. Avoid residential areas. Choose major roads. After you move your hand around your body seven times, do not waste time anymore. Keep driving. Open a window and throw all the lemons or limes toward any green tree. There is a 60 percent chance the demons around your body will leave to follow those lemons or limes. If you feel pressure, repeat this process every day or every other day or at least once a week. You can also cut a lemon or lime in half, rub those pieces on your left arm and shoulder, and then throw them out of your car toward a green tree. Do not stop your car during this process.

3) Demons do not leave human bodies easily, especially if they have been living around those bodies for a long time. To exorcise them, take at least fifteen sticks that are full of green mint leaves. Put them in a metal bowl with water. Boil the water and mint leaves for at least thirty minutes. Drink that mint water every three days. This mint water will reduce the negativity of those demons around you so that they do not create problems in your family or business affairs. They may even become a little positive and supportive because of the mint water.

4) As I have described before, you can use plain water in a spray bottle. You can spray each and every corner of your house frequently. Try to cover everywhere from the ceiling to floor. Do this frequently. Water does not kill demons, but they do

استخدام تلك الخدع لمقاومة الشياطيين. ولن تنجح تلك الخدع على الأمراض والآلام. وتشتمل تلك الخدع على الآتي:

1) تحب الشياطيين اللحم الأحمر فقط. ففهمي لهم هو انهم يرغبون بالعجول. وفي حال كان لديك عجول او تأكل الكثير من العجول يعني هذا بأنك تقوم بدعوة المزيد والمزيد من الشياطيين الى منزلك وجسدك.

2) قم بفرك خمس حبات من الليمون على الأقل أو حامض الليمون على اجزاء مختلفة من جسدك، وخاصة حول رأسك وأذنيك وعيونك ورقبتك وصدرك لمدة دقيقتين. ومن ثم قم بتحريك يديك حول جسمك سبعة مرات. وأتأكد من الخضوع لهذه العملية أثناء القيادة. وتجنب المناطق السكنية وقم باختيار الطرق الرئيسية. وبعد تحريكك ليدك حول جسمك سبع مرات، لا تضيع المزيد من الوقت. استمر بالقيادة. وقم بفتح النافذة وارم جميع حبات الليمون على أي شجر خضراء. وحيث يكون هناك حوالي 60% من الشياطيين حول جسمك فتغادره. في حال الشعور بالضغط، قم بتكرار هذه العملية كل يوم أو كل أسبوع على الأقل. ويمكنك أيضاً تقسيم الليمون إلى نصفين وتفرك تلك القطع على كتف الأيسر والذراع الأيسر ومن ثم ارم تلك القطع خارج سيارتك باتجاه أي شجرة خضراء. ولا تتوقف هذا القيام بهذه العملية.

3) ولا تغادر الشياطيين أجسام البشر بكل سهولة، وخاصة في حالة عيشهم في أنحاء تلك الأجسام لفترة طويلة من الزمن. ولطردهم، تناول على الأقل خمسة عشر عوداً مليئة بأوراق النعناع الأخضر وضعهم في وعاء معدني مليء بالمياه واغل الماء وأوراق النعناع لمدة لا تقل عن ثلاثين دقيقة. وقم بشرب مياه النعناع كل ثلاثة أيام. يقوم مياه النعناع بتخفيف سلبية تلك الشياطيين من حولك حتى لا يسببوا المشاكل لك أو في عملك. وربما يصبحوا ايجابيين قليلاً وداعمين بسبب مياه النعناع.

4) وكما أسلفت من قبل، يمكنك استخدام الماء الطبيعي في قنينة رش. ويمكنك رش كل زاوية من بيتك بشكل متكرر. وحاول تغطية كل مكان من السقف الى الأرض. وقم بذلك بشكل متكرر. حيث أن الماء لا تقتل الشياطيين، ولكن الشياطيين

not like water. Water keeps them uncomfortable. If you do this frequently, demons will not stay around you or in your house for a long time. Do the same thing in your cars as well. You will need to spray water routinely because once one group of demons leaves, your house will be vacant for another group of demons to occupy. If you keep spraying water, they will keep leaving your house.

5) You can also frequently use insect killer, but make sure you spray it in the air toward the ceiling. Do not leave any corner unattended. Spray everywhere frequently, and you will be surprised with the results.

Thank you all for your interest in my theory, and good luck to everyone.

لا تحبذ الماء. حيث تبقى الشياطين غير مرتاحة. وفي حال فعله لذلك بشكل متكرر، لن تبقى الشياطين حولك أو في منزلك لفترة طويلة. وافعل الشيء نفسه في سيارتك أيضاً. وستحتاج الى رش المياه بصورة روتينية لأنه عندما تغادر مجموعة من الشياطين، سيكون منزلك فارغ لمجموعة أخرى من الشياطين لاحتلاله. وفي حال استمرارك في رش المياه، ستغادر الشياطين منزلك.

5) ويمكنك أيضاً استخدام قاتل الحشرات بشكل متكرر، ولكن تأكد من أنك ستقوم برشه في الهواء باتجاه السقف. ولا تترك أي زاوية غير مرشوشة به. وقم برشها في كل مكان بشكل متكرر وستكون متفاجأ بالنتائج.

وشكراً لكم جميعاً على اهتمامكم في نظريتي، وأتمنى لكم حظاً موفقاً.

Translation done by:
Ala' Ashkar
Head of Al-Ashkar for Translation Services Center
Mobile: (+972)599 044 837
Email: ashqar89@hotmail.com
Palestine
تمت الترجمة من قبل:
المترجم: علاء الأشقر
مدير مركز الأشقر لخدمات الترجمة
فلسطين